LIBRARY SOURCES
Number 1

PARISH REGISTER COPIES
IN
THE LIBRARY OF
THE SOCIETY OF GENEALOGISTS

1992

Published by the
Society of Genealogists
14 Charterhouse Buildings
Goswell Road
London EC1M 7BA

First published 1937

New Edition 1963
Second Edition 1968
Third Edition 1970
Revised and updated impression 1972
Revised and updated impression 1975
Fourth Edition 1978
Fifth Edition 1980
Sixth Edition 1983
Seventh Edition 1985
Eighth Edition 1987
Ninth Edition 1991
Tenth Edition 1992

ISBN 0 946789 50 9

Printed by Parchment (Oxford) Ltd, Printworks, Crescent Road, Cowley, Oxford OX4 2PB

CONTENTS

The two letter codes shown here are those used in the card catalogue in the Library and appear as part of the Shelf Mark on bound items in the Society's collection.

ABBREVIATIONS

C	Christenings	Z	Births
M	Marriages		
B	Burials	D	Deaths
(I)	Index only	Ext	Extracts only
Mf	Microfilm	Mfc	Microfiche
ST	Saint (in a place name)	St	Saint (church dedication)

[xx] . . . Numbers in square brackets are the shelf numbers of bound material in the Society's collections within the [R]egisters section of the county concerned. The addition of a two letter prefix indicates that the material is to be found in a different county collection (County letters used appear on Page iii). Some register copies are not in the [R]egisters section of the county and this is shown by a single letter : [G]eneral, [L]ocal, [M]onumental Inscriptions or [P]eriodicals.

CRS . . . Catholic Record Society publication

HS . . . Huguenot Society publication

GCI . . . Great Card Index at the Society of Genealogists, entries are on slips which are sorted by surname in the Index.

* . . . Printed bound items available for loan. Where dates are enclosed in brackets only the period shown thus is available. Please read the introduction with regard to loans.

Bapt	Baptist	Bible Christ	Bible Christian
Calv	Calvinistic	Cong	Congregationalist
Diss	Dissenting	Episc	Episcopalian
Franc	Franciscan	Ind	Independent
Lady Hunt Conn	Lady Huntingdon's Connexion	Hug	Huguenot
Luth	Lutheran	Meth	Methodist
New Conn	New Connexion	Part Bapt	Particular Baptist
Plym Breth	Plymouth Brethren	Presb	Presbyterian
Prim Meth	Primitive Methodist	Prot	Protestant
Rom Cath	Roman Catholic	SFrs	Society of Friends (Quaker)
Unit	Unitarian	Wes	Wesleyan

INTRODUCTION

This new edition, the tenth, of a catalogue of transcripts in the Library of the Society of Genealogists has been extensively checked and revised. It includes accessions up to and including those appearing in the September 1992 edition of the Genealogists' Magazine. The layout of this edition is similar to that of the ninth edition and place names are shown in alphabetical order by **county** within separate sections for England, Ireland, Scotland and Wales. The county names are those in use before the 1974 reorganisation of local government. In the Overseas section, where appropriate, places are listed under the relevant state or province within each country. As an additional aid to the user, the county names have been added to the top of each page.

Details are kept to the minimum necessary to determine whether the Society possesses material for a particular place and the time period covered. Also note that no distinction is made as to the nature of the material which may be transcriptions of Parish Registers or Bishop's Transcripts or, in the case of microforms, the original documents.

In the case of parish names which include an additional physical description eg. Upper, Great, North, Old, etc., the name is given first so that all occurrences of the name in a county are together, such as LAVER, HIGH and LAVER, LITTLE. The dedications of parish churches are not included except where they are necessary for clarity. CMB (see list of abbreviations on page iv) is omitted from the entry where the holding includes all three, unless its omission would cause confusion. Indexes are included where there is no complete transcript and banns to extend the coverage of marriages.

Entries show the library shelf numbers for bound material wherever possible although it has not been practicable to indicate the dates covered by each volume. Some entries indicate material which is to be found in periodicals or material which is not at present on the appropriate county shelf, please refer to the library card catalogue if a shelf number is not shown.

There are also available two important consolidated indexes to entries in Parish Registers which are not included in this volume. These are Boyd's Marriage Index and the International Genealogical Index of baptisms and marriages compiled by the Genealogical Society of Utah. For further details of the coverage of these indexes consult **A List of Parishes in Boyd's Marriage Index (London 1987)** and, on microfiche, **Parish and Vital Records Listings (Salt Lake City 1988)**.

LOANS

Members of the Society resident in the United Kingdom are permitted to borrow material. The availability for loan of PRINTED items in this listing is indicated by an asterisk after the place name, but note that where dates are enclosed in brackets only the item covering the period thus shown can be borrowed. Application should be made to the Librarian stating the Parish and period required. Printed items are loaned at the discretion of the Librarian, having regard to the age and condition of the material requested. Manuscript and typed transcripts are NOT loaned.

Acknowledgement: The Society of Genealogists wishes to thank Neville Taylor for his considerable work in updating the text of this book for the tenth edition and for providing the camera-ready copy.

The Society of Genealogists is grateful to those users of the previous edition of this guide who have suggested minor amendments. Further comments are always welcomed particularly those resulting from a detailed local knowledge.

ENGLAND

BEDFORDSHIRE

AMPTHILL 1602-1812 [17]; Wes Mf CZ 1815-37
APSLEY GUISE 1563-1812 [48]
ARLESEY 1538-1812 [46]
ASTWICK 1602-1812 [25]
BARFORD, LITTLE 1602-1812 [6]
BARFORD, GREAT 1559-1812 [5]
BARTON IN THE CLAY 1558-1812 [4]
BATTLESDEN 1602-1812 [31]
BEDFORD St Cuthbert 1612-1812 [1]; St John
    1602-1812 [1]; St Mary 1539-1812 [30]; St Paul C
    1566-1812 M 1568-1812 B 1569-1812 [36]; St Peter
    1572-1812 [32]; First Ind (Bunyan Mtg) D 1681-88;
    Howard Ind (New Mtg House) Mf ZC 1769-1837;
    Old Ind, Mill Lane Mf ZC 1761-1836
BIDDENHAM 1602-1812 [27]
BIGGLESWADE 1637-1812 [27]
BILLINGTON C 1653-1812 M 1661-1736 B 1653-1736
    [29]
BLETSOE 1582-1812 [24]
BLUNHAM Bapt C 1738-1801 Z 1773-74 Deaths
    1736-1806 1860-90 B 1852-90 [37]
BLUNHAM with MOGERHANGER 1571-1812 [19];
    Cemetery Mfc B 1902-9
BOLNHURST 1602-1812 [11]
BROMHAM 1570-1812 [16]
CADDINGTON 1558-1812 [25]
CAMPTON 1568-1812 [38]; with SHEFFORD C 1568-
    1812 MB 1572-1812 [47]
CARDINGTON 1572-1812 [8]
CARLTON 1544-1812 [29]
CHALGRAVE 1539-1812 [18]
CHELLINGTON C 1567-1812 M 1572-1811 B 1575-1812
    [51]
CLAPHAM 1603-1812 [16]
CLIFTON 1539-1812 [48]
CLOPHILL 1567-1812 [21]
COCKAYNE HATLEY 1602-1812 [2]
COLMWORTH 1604-1812 [46]
COPLE 1561-1812 [10]
CRANFIELD 1600-1812 [26]
DEAN CB 1566-1812 M 1567-1812 [50]
DUNSTABLE 1558-1812 [33]; Cemetery Mfc B 1861-
    1987
DUNTON 1553-1812 [49]
EATON BRAY 1559-1812 [51] Mf 1559-1812
EATON SOCON CB 1566-1812 M 1572-1812 [39]
EDWORTH 1552-1812 [2]
ELSTOW 1602-1812 [1]
EVERSHOLT 1602-1812 [52]
EYEWORTH 1538-1812 [2]
FELMERSHAM 1602-1812 [9]
FLITTON with SILSOE 1581-1812 [18]
FLITWICK 1602-1812 [21]
GOLDINGTON 1558-1812 [32]
GRAVENHURST, LOWER 1602-1812 [13]
GRAVENHURST, UPPER 1567-1812 [1,13,40,44]
HARLINGTON 1602-1812 [20]
HARROLD 1598-1812 [29]
HAWNES see HAYNES
HAYNES 1596-1812 [45]

HENLOW 1558-1812 [25]
HIGHAM GOBION 1602-1812 [13]
HOCKLIFFE 1604-1812 [29]
HOLCOTE 1605-1812 [27]
HOUGHTON CONQUEST 1539-1812 [33]
HOUGHTON REGIS 1538-1812 [42]
HUSBOURNE CRAWLEY C 1557-1812 MB 1558-1812
    [51]
KEMPSTON 1570-1812 [32]
KENSWORTH 1604-1812 [48]
KEYSOE 1602-1812 [49]
KNOTTING 1592-1812 [7]
LANGFORD 1602-1812 [42]
LEIGHTON BUZZARD 1562-1812 [28,29] Mfc C 1813-
    1908 M 1813-1903 B 1813-1963
LIDLINGTON 1560-1812 [27]
LUTON 1602-1812 [43]
MARSTON MORTEYNE 1602-1812 [34]
MAULDEN 1558-1812 [22]
MAULDEN Ind Chapel Mf Z 1730-1837
MELCHBORNE 1602-1812 [7]
MEPPERSHALL 1602-1812 [31]
MILLBROOK 1558-1812 [20]
MILTON BRYANT 1559-1812 [31]
MILTON ERNEST 1538-1812 [11]
MOGERHANGER see BLUNHAM
NORTHILL 1562-1812 [13]
OAKLEY 1560-1812 [16]
ODELL 1602-1812 [11]
OLD WARDEN 1576-1812 [10]
PAVENHAM 1561-1812 [9]
PERTENHALL 1582-1812 [49]
PODINGTON 1602-1812 [51]
POTSGROVE 1602-1812 [31]
POTTON 1602-1812 [41]
PULLOXHILL 1553-1812 [22]
RAVENSDEN 1558-1812 [48]
RENHOLD 1602-1812 [5]
RIDGMONT 1539-1812 [50]
RISELEY 1602-1812 [26]
ROXTON 1602-1812 [5]; Ind Mf ZC 1824-37
SALFORD 1558-1812 [27]
SANDY 1538-1812 [6]
SHARNBROOK 1596-1812 [24]
SHELTON 1602-1812 [7]
SHILLINGTON C 1559-1812 M 1560-1812 B 1543-1812
    [30]
SILSOE see FLITTON
SOULDROP 1602-1812 [7]
SOUTHILL 1538-1812 [12]
STAGSDEN 1602-1812 [46]
STANBRIDGE C 1560-1812 M 1609-1812 B 1611-1812
    [29]
STAUGHTON, LITTLE 1598-1812 [50]
STEPPINGLEY C 1558-1812 M 1559-1812 B 1602-1812
    [50]
STEVINGTON 1603-1812 [9]
STONDON, UPPER 1602-1812 [25]
STOTFOLD 1559-1812 [31]
STREATLEY 1602-1812 [4]
STUDHAM 1570-1812 [50]
SUNDON 1569-1812 [4]
SUTTON 1538-1812 [2]
SWINESHEAD 1549-1812 [7]

1

TEMPSFORD 1602-1812 [19]
THURLEIGH 1562-1812 [26]
TILSWORTH 1602-1812 [29]
TINGRITH 1572-1812 [17]
TODDINGTON 1540-1812 [23]
TOTTERNHOE 1559-1812 [47]
TURVEY 1602-1812 [47]; Mf C 1629-1762
WESTONING 1560-1812 [20]
WHIPSNADE 1603-1812 [25]
WILDEN 1545-1812 [49]
WILLINGTON 1602-1812 [10]
WILSTEAD 1593-1812 [42]
WOBURN 1558-1812 [3]; Chapel St Ind Mf CZ 1791-1837
WOOTTON 1561-1812 [34]
WRESTLINGWORTH 1578-1812 [2]
WYMINGTON 1602-1812 [50]
YIELDEN 1602-1812 [7]

BERKSHIRE

ALDERMASTON CB 1558-1840 M 1558-1837 [74,112]
APPLEFORD C 1563-1835 M 1567-1837 B 1564-1835 [47,73,86]
APPLETON CM 1570-1839 B 1569-1839 [2]
ARBORFIELD C 1580-1840 M 1580-1837 B 1580-1841 [74,86]
ARDINGTON 1607-1974 [78]
ASHAMPSTEAD 1607-1685 (Ext)1757-1837 [65]
ASHBURY CMB 1612-37 1653-1989 [74,102]
ASTON TIRROLD 1607-37 1669-1705 1723/4 1726-1852 [76]; United Reform B 1734-1870 1908-09 [80]
AVINGTON 1699-1835(gaps) [79]
BARKHAM C 1538-1732 M 1542-1732 B 1539-1732 [3]
BASILDON CM 1538-1667 B 1538-1665 [3]; Mf 1540-1665 1691-1753
BAULKING 1850-1989 [90]
BEARWOOD St Catherine B 1846-1983 [79]
BEEDON C 1607-1716(Ext) 1722-1840 M 1607-1706(Ext) 1708-1836 B 1607-1703(Ext) 1707-1835 [108]
BEENHAM C 1561- 1837 M 1561-1836 B 1561-1840 [65,73]
BESSELSLEIGH C 1666-1851 M 1668-1835 B 1668-1859 [4]
BINFIELD C 1551-1840 M 1538-1837 B 1538-1841 [5,106]
BISHAM CB 1560-1840 M 1560-1837 [6,89] Mf 1560-1812
BLEWBURY* C (1588-1813)-1880 M (1588-1813)-82 B (1588-1813)-84 [7,69]
BOURTON C 1860-1985 M 1860-1983 B 1898-1986 [75]
BOXFORD C(I) 1558-1933 M(I) 1558-1748 1754-1981 B(I) 1558-1876 [96]
BRADFIELD* C 1539-1838 M (1559-1812)-1837 B 1540-1838 [52,70,G71]
BRAY 1653-1837 [8,9,10]
BRIMPTON C Ext 1607-1674 C 1709-1840 M Ext 1607-1671 M 1754-1836 B Ext 1607-1767 B 1769-1840 [3,74,82]
BUCKLAND C 1691-1974 M 1693-1974 B 1678-1974 [50]; Rom Cath C 1753-1845 M 1831-55 [56]
BUCKLEBURY C 1538-1840 M 1538-1837 B 1539-1840 [77]

BUSCOT* CB 1676-84 (M 1676-1812) [52,56]
CHARNEY BASSETT C 1617-1974 MB 1619-1974 [56]
CHIEVELY C 1813-65 M 1813-37 B 1813-74 [11]
CLEWER Cath Chapel Ext C 1824-55 [CU/R39]
COLESHILL C 1559-78 1581-1980 M 1561-1980 B 1559-1657 1668-1979 [83]
COOKHAM C 1563-1837 M 1563-1635 1655-1837 B 1566-1838 [73,82,94,95]
COOMBE see COOMBE Hampshire
COXWELL, GREAT CB 1557-1978 M 1558-1978 [12]
COXWELL, LITTLE C 1582-1770 1813-1984 M 1583-1749 1840-1949 B 1583-1771 1839-1983
CUMNOR C 1559-1682 1755-61 M 1559-1682 B 1559-1681 [13]
DENCHWORTH* 1540-1812 [14]
DENFORD C 1832-1949 [79]
DIDCOT C 1562-1840 M 1571-1840 B 1568-1840 [15,79]
DONNINGTON see SHAW CUM DONNINGTON
DRAYTON 1607-1837 [73]
EATON HASTINGS C 1574-1980 M 1574-1961 B 1575-1981 [76]
FARINGDON C 1589-1964 M 1589-1974 B 1589-1962; Anabaptists B 1678-1766; SFrs 1678-1766 [57,58,59]
FARNDISH CB 1587-1902 M 1587-1837 [53]
FERNHAM 1860-1988 [86]
FINCHAMPSTEAD 1607-35 [16]
FRILFORD with LONGWORTH Mission C 1845-1955 [56]
FRILSHAM CB 1607-1804 1813-1835 M 1607-1837 [76]
FYFIELD C 1605-1906 M 1605-1913 B 1605-1906 [90]
GARSTON, EAST C 1554-1563 1660-1812 M 1554-62 1669-1812 B 1554-62 1669-1812 [79]
GREENHAM 1612-1637 CB 1706-1840 M 1706-1837 [86]
HAMPSTEAD MARSHALL C 1605-1670(gaps) 1675-1837 M 1605-1637(gaps) 1676-1837 B 1605-1670(gaps) 1675-1836 [80]
HANNEY C 1582-1845 M 1564-1845 B 1564-1845 [17,56]
HANNEY, WEST* M 1564-1837 [52]
HARWELL* C 1558-1952 M 1558-(1559-1837)-1962 B 1558-1943 [52,121-2]
HATFORD C 1540-1884 M 1538-1845 B 1539-1846 [18]
HENDRED, EAST C 1538-1974 MB 1558-1974 [60]
HENDRED, WEST* CB 1558-1974 M (1558-1837)-1974 [52,63]
HINKSEY, NORTH C 1607-1944 M 1607-1950 B 1607-1984 [67]
HINKSEY, SOUTH C 1607-1906 M 1607-1924 B 1607-1894 [66]
HINTON WALDRIST Ext 1559-1974 [19,20]
HUNGERFORD CB 1559-1700 M 1559-1732 [49,64,84]; Ind Chapel Mf C 1803-37
HURLEY C 1560-1839 M 1563-1837 B 1563-1838 [108]
ILSLEY, EAST* M (I) 1654-1812 [P]
INKPEN C 1607-1850 M 1607-1837 B 1541-1860 [82]
KINGSTON BAGPUIZE C 1539-1880 M 1542-1884 B 1541-1880 [65]
KINGSTON LISLE* M 1560-1837 [52]
KINTBURY C 1558-1842 M 1558-1652 1666-1716 1718-1842 B 1558-1842 [68,107]
LAMBOURNE 1560-1837 [91,93]
LONGCOT with FERNHAM Ext 1612-37 1669-1989 [98]
LONGWORTH 1559-1974 [21] see also FRILFORD
LYFORD 1845-1974 [56] see also HANNEY
MAIDENHEAD Diss Ext ZC 1769-89 1791-1834 B 1786-89 1791-1834 [90]; C 1745-49 see KINGS LYNN, NFK, Broad St Ind [NO/R83]

MARCHAM C 1653-1801 M 1658-1754 B 1658-1804 [22]
MIDGHAM C 1607-1840 M 1607-1837 B 1607-1812 [110]
MOULSFORD C 1607-37 1767-1841 M 1617-35 1754-1837 B 1616-34 1770-1840 CMB(I) 1508-1710 [109]
NEW WINDSOR See WINDSOR
NEWBURY St Nicholas C 1538-1746 B 1538-1746 [53-5,104-5]; Newton Road Cemetery B 1917-79 [23,24]; Mf Lower Ind Mtg House C 1695-1837; Mf Northbrook St Wes CZ 1796-1837; Mf Upper Presb C 1763-1837; Mfc C 1828-44
OLD WINDSOR see WINDSOR
PADWORTH CB 1607-1837 M 1617-1838 [72]
PEASEMORE C 1762-70 1804-1855 M 1755-1876 B(I) 1538-1974 B 1805-79 [79,101]
PURLEY* M 1662-1840 [52]
PUSEY C 1607-1874 M 1615-1877 B 1607-1877 [18]
READING St Mary 1538-1812 [25,26]; Mf Broad St Ind CZ 1715-1837; Church St Wes CZ 1813-37; Rom Cath C 1783-1837 M 1780-1840 D 1780-1816 [CRS32]; Rom Cath, Old French Cemetery B 1797-1802 [CRS32]
RUSCOMBE M (I) 1559-1812 [48]
SANDHURST C 1579-93 1603-1840 MB 1579-93 1603-1837 [85]
SHAW CUM DONNINGTON CMB Ext 1563-1636 C 1646-1840 M 1646-1837 B 1647-1840 [114] Mfc C 1646-1965 M 1646-1960 B 1647-1932
SHEFFORD, EAST C 1603-1734 1774-1811 M 1603-1717 1779-1808 Banns 1826-29 B 1604-1733 1774-1812 [27]
SHEFFORD, GREAT see SHEFFORD, WEST
SHEFFORD, WEST CB 1571-1840 M 1571-1837 [114]
SHELLINGFORD C 1580-1899 M 1578-1899 B 1581-1899 [28]
SHOTTESBROOKE C 1585-1836 M 1566-1837 B 1567-1850 [80]
SONNING C 1592-1836 M 1592-1837 B 1592-1846 [OX/R150,151,152]
SOTWELL CB 1607-1837 M 1607-1835 [72]
SPARSHOLT* C Ext 1572-1865 M (1559-1812) B Ext 1569-1808 [2,52]
SPEEN 1614-1749 [87]
STANFORD DINGLEY M 1813-37 [79]
STANFORD IN THE VALE C 1558-1839 M 1563-1914 B 1558-1840 [29,56]; Mf M 1555-1754 1808-1834
STRATFIELD MORTIMER 1681-1753 CB 1752-1840 M 1754-1837 [74,81]
STREATLEY CB 1607-1840 M 1607-1836 [76,85]
SULHAM* M 1723-1837 [52]
SULHAMPSTEAD ABBOT CM 1602-1837 M 1602-1835 [89]
SULHAMSTEAD BANNISTER CMB 1608-38(gaps) CM 1654-1837 B 1661-1812 [68]
SUTTON COURTENAY C 1539-1840 M 1538-1840 B 1584-1840 [110]
THATCHAM CM 1561-1840 [31,125]
TILEHURST Mf M 1630-1754
UFFINGTON 1607-1637 C 1654-1988 M 1663-1737 1751-1990 B 1654-1749 1751-1946 [111]
UFTON COURT Rom Cath 1741-1828 [32]
UFTON NERVET C 1607-1837 M 1607-1836 B 1607-1834 [72]
UPTON* CB 1588-1741 M 1558-1735 [33]
WALLINGFORD Mfc St Mary M 1813-37
WALTHAM ST LAWRENCE C 1539-1844 C(I) 1844-1962 M 1539-1837 M(I) 1837-1933 B 1559-1844 B(I) 1813-

1969 [34,81]
WANTAGE* M (1538-1837) CB 1538-1653 [51,61,62]
WARFIELD CB 1568-70 1607-35 1669-1840 M 1569 1593-1635 1669-1840 B 1568-1839 [109]; Rom Cath C 1776-84 [80]
WARGRAVE 1538-1840 [123]
WASING 1607-1728 C 1730-1841 M 1730-1832 B 1763-1841 [109]
WATCHFIELD C 1858-1946 M 1858-1958 B 1861-1982 [75]
WELFORD cum WICKHAM 1559-1840 [35/6]
WHITE WALTHAM 1563-1837 [37]
WICKHAM see WELFORD
WINDSOR, NEW CM 1559-1837 B 1560-1837 Banns out of parish 1754-1837 [39-46,56]
WINDSOR* St George's Chapel C 1618-1956 M 1627-1956 B 1625-1954 [38]
WINDSOR, OLD C 1612-1634 1668-1772(gaps) [74]
WINKFIELD C 1564-1841 M 1564-1832 B 1564-1838 [74,99,100]
WINTERBOURNE B(I) 1567-1979 [90]
WITTENHAM, LITTLE C 1539-1679 B 1544-1674(gaps) [79]
WOODHAY, WEST* CMB 1612-37 C 1653-1851 M (1653-1812)-1837 B 1653-1812 [63,80]
WOODLEY LODGE Rom Cath 1802-69 [CRS32]
WOOLHAMPTON CB 1607-1840 M 1607-1837 [89]; Rom Cath see UFTON COURT
WOOLSTONE C 1849-1988 M 1849-1981 B 1849-1987 [85]
WYTHAM C 1558-1984 M 1558-1979 B 1558-1981 [53]
YATTENDON* M (I) 1559-1812 [P]

BUCKINGHAMSHIRE

ADDINGTON* CB 1558-1837 M 1558-1908 [1]
AKELEY M 1600-1837 [81]
AMERSHAM* (M 1561-1812) [66]; Lower Diss Meeting Z 1776-1813
ASHENDON C 1732-1840 M 1734-1840 B 1732-1813 [2]
ASTON ABBOTS* 1559-1837 [3]
ASTON CLINTON* St Leonard M 1737-54 [65]; St Michael M 1560-1812 [64]
AYLESBURY Mf C 1567-1877 M 1567-1875 B 1567-1876 Banns 1754-1784 1817-1891
BARTON HARTSHORN* Ext 1575-1751 CB 1752-1840 M 1754-1840 [4]
BEACONSFIELD* C 1631-1837 M (1631-1812)-1837 B 1575-1837 Ext 1540-1575 [5,67]; Diss Z 1709-47 [P]
BIDDLESDEN C 1686-1809 1811-37 M 1695-1807 1813-37 B 1695-1809 1813-37 [6]
BLEDLOW C Ext 1590-1628 C 1629-1706 M 1590-1812 1835 1838 B Ext 1590-1631 [7,83]
BOW BRICKHILL C 1600-1969 M 1600-1837 Banns 1824-1904 B 1600-1885 [72]
BRADENHAM* M 1627-1812 [68]
BRADWELL Ext C 1577-1878 M 1582-1837 B 1578-1914 [8]
BRICKHILL, GREAT C 1558-1917 M 1558-1982 B 1558-1883 [72]
BRICKHILL, LITTLE 1559-1988 [84]
BROUGHTON* M 1720-1837 [71]
BURNHAM* M 1561-1812 [67]

CHALFONT SAINT GILES* C(M)B 1584-1812 [9,66]
CHALFONT SAINT PETER* CB 1539-1674 (M 1538-1812) [10,66]; Bapt Gold Hill Z 1779-1836 [P]
CHEARSLEY C 1715/6-74 M 1718-31 1746-53 B 1678-1768 [77]; Mf C 1570-1812
CHEDDINGTON* M 1552-1812 [63]
CHENIES* C 1592-1812 (M 1593-1837) [66,77]
CHESHAM* CB (1538-1636)-1730 (M 1538-1837) [62,70,74,85/6]
CHETWODE 1583-1840 [4]
CHICHELEY* M 1539-1812 [65]
CHILTON CB 1600-1732 M 1600-1812 [18]
CHOLESBURY* CB 1583-1840 M (1576-1812)-40 [11,63]
CRENDON, LONG 1559-1684 [14]
CUBLINGTON C 1566-1812 M 1570-1812 B 1757-1812 [12]
DATCHET CM 1559-1900 B 1559-1861 [15,77]
DENHAM* M 1569-1812 [69]
DORNEY* C 1726-1850 (M 1538-1812) B 1726-1900 [67,77]
DORTON CB 1590-1700 M 1590-1842 [13]
DRAYTON PARSLOW* 1559-1837 [16,65]
EDGCOTT* 1538-1837 [3]
EDLESBOROUGH* M 1568-1812 [63]
ETON C 1594-1849 MB 1603-1849 [17,18]
FARNHAM ROYAL C 1634-1786 M 1653-1754 B 1635-1786 [19,20]
FENNY STRATFORD* (1730-1812) [21]
FINGEST* CB Ext 1608-1689 CB 1690-1841 M (1607-1810)-1836 [68,72]
FLEET MARSTON M 1677-91 [P]
FULMER* M 1688-1812 [67]
GROVE* M 1711-1812 [65]
HAMBLEDEN 1566-1837 [22]
HAMPDEN, GREAT 1557-1812 [23]
HARDMEAD* M 1575-1813 [64]
HARTWELL* M 1553-1812 [65]
HAWRIDGE* CB 1786-1840 M (1600-1812)-40 [11,63]
HEDGERLEY* M 1539-1812 [66]
HEDSOR* M 1678-1837 [67]
HITCHAM* M 1559-1812 [67]
HITCHENDEN see HUGHENDEN
HORMEAD* see HARDMEAD
HORSENDEN C 1632-40 1663-1842 M 1631-33 1707-1837 B 1632-39 1695-1837 [72]
HORTON C 1571-1874 M 1571-1855 Banns 1754-1871 B 1571-1858 [24]
HUGHENDEN/HITCHENDEN* (M 1559-1812) [69]
IBSTONE* M 1665-1812 [68]
ILMER CMB Ext 1600-1662 C 1660-1839 M 1679-1839 B 1687-1837 [72]
IVER* CB 1605-1840 M (1605-1812)-40 [25,26,70]
IVINGHOE* C 1916-1950 M (1559-1812) [64,81]
LANGLEY MARISH C 1637-1841 MB 1663-1841 [27]
LATHBURY* M 1690-1837 [71]
LECKHAMSTEAD* 1558-1812 [28]
LILLINGSTONE DAYRELL 1584-1840 [26]
LILLINGSTONE LOVELL 1558-1840 [26]
LINSLADE* M 1575-1812 [65]
LUDGERSHALL C 1573-1837 M 1570-1837 B 1566-1837 [29,69]
MARLOW, GREAT* CB (1592-1611)-1716 C 1800-1875 M (1592-1711)-1925 [30,31,32,73,75]
MARLOW, LITTLE C 1562-1812 M 1559-1754 B 1559-1812 [73,76]
MASWORTH M 1591-1812 [63]
MEDMENHAM* 1575-1930 [33]

MENTMORE* (CB 1685-1829 M 1575-1829)-37 [34,63,73]
MISSENDEN, GREAT CB 1601-1682 M 1575-1725 [35,77]
MISSENDEN, LITTLE* CB Ext 1559-1775 (M 1559-1812) C(I) 1599-1812 [36,37,69]
MONKS RISBOROUGH 1587-1841 [38]
MOULSOE* M 1559-1837 [71]
NETTLEDEN CB 1813-40 [77]
NEWPORT PAGNELL* M 1558-1837 [71]
NEWTON LONGVILLE* 1560-1840 [39,40]
OLNEY* 1665-1812 [41]
PENN 1559-1837 [86-7]
PITSTONE* M 1576-1812 [63]
PRESTON BISSETT 1576-1840 [4]
PRINCES RISBOROUGH CB 1561-1844 M 1561-1837 [42]; Bapt Z 1796-1837 [82]
QUAINTON C 1733 1737-57 1791 M 1791 B 1791-2 [77]
RADNAGE CB 1574-1769 M 1574-1755 [13]
RAVENSTONE* 1568-1812 [43]
ST LEONARDS C 1738-1850 M 1739-54 B 1739-1859 [44]
SEER GREEN 1846-1986 [78]
SHALSTONE 1538-1836 [45]
SHERINGTON* M 1698-1812 [65]
SLAPTON* (M 1653-1812) CMB Ext 1575-1647 [63,77]
SOULBURY* M 1575-1812 [63]; Wes ZC Mf 1816-37
SPEEN (near Aylesbury) Bapt B 1813-37 [82]
STEWKLEY 1545-1653 [46,47]
STOKE MANDEVILLE CMB Ext 1605-1696 CMB 1699-1840 [12,77]
STOKE POGES* CB 1563-1753 M 1563-1812 [48,66]
STONE* M 1538-1812 [65]
STOWE 1569-1836 [49]
SWANBOURNE* 1565-1836 [50]
TAPLOW* M 1710-1812 [67]
TATTENHOE M 1813-37 [73]
THORNBOROUGH Ext 1602-1812
THORNTON 1562-1812 [51]
TURVILLE* M 1582-1812 [68,GCI]
TURWESTON CB 1695-1850 M 1699-1812 [10]
TWYFORD B 1813-40 [73]
WALTON* 1598-1812 [52]
WENDOVER* M (1576-1812)-1837 [64,82]
WESTBURY* 1558-1812 [GCI] M 1558-1837 [65]
WESTON UNDERWOOD* Rom Cath C 1710-21 1740-85 1791-1828 M 1710-1723 1727-1740 1774-1839 B 1711-1723 D 1778-1818 1827-29 [53,73,82]
WING* 1546-1812 [54,55,65]
WOLVERTON CB 1536-1727 M 1536-1728 [56]
WOOBURN* C 1653-1888 M (1653-1812)-1848 B 1653-1897 [67,79,80]
WOOLSTONE, GREAT* CB 1538-1811 M 1538-1750 [21]
WOOLSTONE, LITTLE* CB 1596-1813 M 1596-1810 [21]
WOUGHTON ON THE GREEN* 1558-1812 [59]
WYCOMBE, HIGH* C 1813-37 (M 1600-1812) B 1674-1732 [60,68]
WYCOMBE, WEST 1602-1640 [61]

CAMBRIDGESHIRE

ABINGTON, GREAT Ext 1599-1844 [1]
ABINGTON JUXTA SHINGAY see ABINGTON PIGOTTS
ABINGTON, LITTLE 1599-1844 [1]
ABINGTON PIGOTTS* 1559-1641 (1653-1812)-37 [2,83,172]
ARRINGTON CB 1538-1812 M 1538-1837 [3,172]
ASHLEY with SILVERLEY 1630-1840 [4,172]
BABRAHAM C 1561-1923 M 1561-1925 B 1561-1812 [5,83]
BALSHAM 1558-1851 [6,83]
BARNWELL 1599-1729 [7]
BARRINGTON 1570-1890 [83,143]
BARTLOW CB 1573-1862 M 1573-1862 [8,9]
BARTON 1600-1851 [10,83]
BASSINGBOURNE 1558-1851 [11]
BOTTISHAM C Ext 1564-1714 M 1563-1837 B Ext 1572-1716 [84,139]
BOURN C 1563-69 1592-1851 M 1599-1641 1662-1851 B 1602-1861 [12,84]
BOXWORTH* CB 1588-1812 M (1588-1812)-36 [13,14,84,130]
BRINKLEY CB 1599-1851 M 1599-1838 [9]
BURROUGH GREEN CB 1571-1840 M 1586-1836 [1]
BURWELL 1561-1890 [85,146]
CALDECOTE* C 1662-1917 M (1599-1812)-1915 B 1671-1918 [15,130]
CAMBRIDGE* All Saints C 1538-1836 (M 1539-1837) [16,131]; Holy Sepulchre M (1569-1812)-37 [88,129]; Holy Trinity M 1564-1837 [89]; St Andrew the Great C 1635-1860 M (1600-1837)-1860 B 1635-1860 [132,161,162]; St Andrew the Less C 1753-1851 M (1599-1837)-1851 B 1754-1851 [134,155,156]; St Benedict 1539-1851 [17,134]; St Botolph C 1564-1853 M (1564-1812)-1851 B 1564-1863 [18,88,130]; St Clement (M 1560-1837) [135] Mf C 1567-1876 M 1560-1837 Banns 1754-1877 B 1560-1847; St Edward C 1558-1840 (M 1558-1840) B 1558-1837 [19,88,128,134]; St Giles C 1585-1860 M (1599-1837)-1860 B 1609-1860 [133,196/7]; St Mary the Great M (1559-1837) [135]; St Mary the Less M (1558-1837) [135]; St Michael 1538-1837 [20]; St Peter M (1586-1758) [132]; Rom Cath Our Lady & English Martyrs C 1856-1900 M 1849-1918 DB 1881-1908 [198]
CARLTON/CARLTON CUM WILLINGHAM C 1588-1851 M 1599-1837 B 1599-1812 [9]
CASTLE CAMPS C 1563-1845 MB 1567-1845 [21,88]
CAXTON 1599-1851 [10,88,154]
CHATTERIS C 1614-1767 M 1600-1837 B 1613-1775 [87,175]
CHERRY HINTON C 1538-1908 M 1538-1912 B 1538-1876 [22,88]
CHESTERTON* CB 1564-1940 M (1564-1837)-1940 [134,169/70,178/9,189]
CHETTISHAM C 1700-1812 M 1600-1809 B 1702-63 [23,86]
CHEVELEY C 1560-1902 M 1559-1885 B 1559-1886 [86,126]
CHIPPENHAM 1567-1837 [86,159]
COATES (Whittlesey) CB 1850-1921 M 1850-1920 [201]
COMBERTON C 1564-1924 M 1560-1924 B 1754-1924 [86,152]

CONINGTON* CB 1538-1812 M (1538-1812)-37 [24,86,129]
COTON M(I) 1538-1837 [86]
COTTENHAM C Ext 1573-1812 M 1573-1837 B Ext 1583-1648 [90]
COVENEY M 1703-1809 [86]
CROXTON* CB 1538-1890 M (1538-1837)-92 [131,154]
CROYDON CUM CLAPTON CB 1599-1845 M 1599-1837 [25,91]
DITTON FEN see FEN DITTON
DITTON WOOD see WOOD DITTON
DODDINGTON M 1681-1837 C Ext 1681-1786 B Ext 1681-1784 [93]
DOWNHAM M 1558-1754 [92,122]
DRY DRAYTON* C 1564-1851 M (1565-1812)-29 B 1564-1851 [91,130,190]
DULLINGHAM C 1558-1873 MB 1558-1869 [26]
DUXFORD ST PETER CB 1684-1851 M 1599-18 [27,91,172]
DUXFORD ST JOHN CB 1599-1851 M 1599-1851 [27,91,172]
ELM M 1539-1754 [95]
ELSWORTH C 1538-1848 M (1538-1837) B 1538-1867 [28,131]
ELTISLEY* CB 1599-1655 M (1599-1837) [131,176]
ELY Cathedral C 1693-1900 M 1691-1752 1861 B 1690-1974 [151]; Holy Trinity CB 1559-1812 M 1559-1753 1775-1792 [29,30,31,95,169]; St Mary 1599-1754 M 1703-1754 [32,33,91]
EVERSDEN, GREAT M 1541-1837 [97]
EVERSDEN, LITTLE CB Ext 1599-1672 M 1599-1837 [97,177]
FEN DITTON M 1538-1837 [91]
FEN DRAYTON* C 1576-1916 M (1580-1812)-1916 B 1573-1916 [91,128,189]
FORDHAM CB 1567-1852 M 1568-1850 [97,144]
FOWLMERE 1561-1991 [15,36,37]
FOXTON CMB Ext 1599-1679 C 1695-1891 M 1693-1892 B 1678-1891 [173]
FULBOURN All Saints 1558-1851; St Vigor C 1538-1851 MB 1556-1851 [38,39,97]
GAMLINGAY 1602-1851 [40,98]
GIRTON* M (1599-1812)-1837 [98,130]
GRANSDEN, LITTLE 1600-1837 [10,98]
GRANTCHESTER C 1555-1851 MB 1539-1851 [5,98]
GRAVELEY* C 1599-1907 M (1599-1837)-1939 B 1599-1875 [41,131]
GUILDEN MORDEN 1599-1845 [25,98]
HADDENHAM 1570-1851 [42,43,99,122]
HARDWICK M 1578-1837 [100]
HARLTON M 1574-1837 [100]
HARSTON 1599-1840 [44,100]
HASLINGFIELD C 1599-1909 M 1599-1909 B 1599-1873 1876-1929 [10,26,45,100]
HATLEY, EAST C 1585-1812 M 1585-1837 B 1595-1812 [46,100]
HATLEY ST GEORGE CB 1591-1812 M 1591-1837 [47,100]
HAUXTON C 1560-1842 M 1560-1836 B 1560-1812 [48,101]
HILDERSHAM C 1559-1938 M 1561-1937 B 1560-1938 [48]
HINXTON C 1538-41 1560-1902 M 1539-40 1560-1836 B 1538-1540 1560-1938 [101,125]
HISTON* CB 1728-1812 M (1599-1837) [23,46,49,132]
HORNINGSEA C 1628-1878 M 1599-1837 B 1628-56 1661-1878 [101,160]

HORSEHEATH C 1558-1927 M 1558-1836 B 1558-1924 [50]
ICKLETON CB 1558-1800 M 1558-1769 [52]
IMPINGTON* M 1562-1837 [132]
ISLEHAM 1566-1851 [51,102]
KENNETT M 1558-1837 [101]
KINGSTON M 1589-1837 [101]
KIRTLING C 1585-1851 M 1592-1837 B 1592-1851 [4,147,182]
KNAPWELL* CB 1598-1812 M (1598-1812)-37 [53,101,128]
LANDBEACH CB 1538-1851 M 1539-1837 [101,171]
LANDWADE 1693-1736; Chapel M 1695-1802 [103,160]
LEVERINGTON M 1565-1812 [104,122]
LINTON CM 1559-1844 B 1566-1844 [54,55]
LITLINGTON 1599-1845 [25,103]
LITTLEPORT C 1753-1812 M 1599-1812 B 1756-1812 [103,122,190]
LOLWORTH* C 1572-1920 M (1567-1812)-1920 B 1565-1920 [103,127,130,147]
LONG STANTON see STANTON, LONG
LONGSTOWE CB 1568-77 1584-1861 M 1569-1837 [103,173]
MADINGLEY* M (1539-1812)-37 [103,130,175]
MANEA 1646-1707 CMB 1708-1900 [103,195]
MARCH M 1548-1837 Ext C 1570-1798 B 1574-1797 [121]
MELBOURN 1558-1851 [56,105]
MELDRETH CB 1599-1851 M 1599-1683 1698-1851 [7,46]
MEPAL M 1600-1837 [106]
MILTON* CMB Ext 1599-1705 C 1705-1870 M (1599-1837)-1870 B 1710-60 1768-1870 [8,133,201]
NEWTON (Cambridge) CB 1560-1829 M 1557-1837 [1,106]
NEWTON (Ely) C 1600-39 1646-48 1654-1852 MB 1600-39 1654-1851 [106,201]
OAKINGTON* CB 1561-1858 M (1561-1812)-1858 [106,130,145]
ORWELL* CB (1560-1653)-1895 M 1560-1901 [15,57]
OVER* C 1577-1850 M (1577-1587 1596-1812)-1852 B 1577-1851 [106,129,148]
PAMPISFORD C 1560-1889 M 1584-1837 B 1561-1812 [53]
PAPWORTH EVERARD* C 1565-1901 M (1565-1837)-1900 B 1565-1905 [131,173]
PAPWORTH SAINT AGNES* M 1558-1837 [131]
PARSON DROVE M 1603-1754 [106]
PAXTON, LITTLE see Huntingdonshire
QUY see STOW CUM QUY
RAMPTON CB 1674-1812 M 1599-1809 CMB(I) 1599-1812 [106,160]
SAWSTON C 1599-1940 M 1599-1899 B 1599-1940 [58-60,151]
SHELFORD, GREAT 1557-1844 [61,108]
SHELFORD, LITTLE CB 1600-1842 M 1600-1837 [7,108]
SHEPRETH 1559-1837 [62]
SHUDY CAMPS 1558-1841 [44]
SILVERLEY see ASHLEY cum SILVERLEY
SNAILWELL CM 1629-1901 B 1629-1903 [108,124]
SOHAM C 1558-1876 M 1559-1876 B 1558-1883 [109,185-188]; Diss CB 1695-1725
STANTON, LONG* All Saints C 1599-1974 M (1559-1812)-1961 B 1599-1961 [108,127,130]; St Michael C 1559-1783 1792-1968 M (1559-1812)-1959 B 1559-1783 1794-1965 [108,160,142]
STAPLEFORD C 1557-1935 M 1557-1941 B 1557-1921 [63,108]
STEEPLE MORDEN CB 1599-1851 M 1599-1840 [64]
STETCHWORTH CB 1599-1840 M 1599-1837 [47]
STOW CUM QUY CMB Ext 1539-1597 CM 1599-1900 B 1599-1902 [108,174]
STRETHAM C 1558-1861 M 1558-1917 B 1558-1945 [65,107]
STUNTNEY C 1545-1764 M 1545-1837 B 1545-1750 [23,111]
SUTTON C Ext 1558-1743 M 1558-1837 B Ext 1558-1732 [110]
SWAFFHAM BULBECK C 1558-1945 M 1558-1953 B 1599-1982 [111,158]
SWAFFHAM PRIOR C 1559-1851 M 1559-1851 B 1559-1848 [112,149,151]
SWAVESEY* M (1599-1812)-37 [111,129]
TADLOW CB 1599-1812 M 1599-1837 [25,111]
TEVERSHAM CB 1592-1840 M 1595-1838 [66,111]
THETFORD C 1599-1894 M 1599-1963 B 1599-1812 [45,96]
THORNEY ABBEY 1653-1837 [111,140/1,180]; French Colony C 1654-1727 [67]
THRIPLOW C 1538-1840 M 1599-1840 B 1600-1840 [37]
TOFT* CB 1539-1916 M (1539-1780)-1916 [69,130]
TRUMPINGTON CB Ext 1600-1740 C 1741-1875 M 1599-1875 B 1741-1875 [70/1,113,174,198]
TYDD SAINT GILES M 1559-1837 [113]
WATERBEACH M 1599-1837 [113,122]
WELNEY M 1653-1753 [15,72]
WENDY cum SHINGAY CB 1550-1837 M 1550-1845 [73,116]
WENTWORTH CM 1600-1812 B 1606-1812 [116,160,174]
WESTLEY WATERLESS 1557-1901 [74/5]
WESTON COLVILLE CB 1599-1851 M 1602-1849 [76]
WHADDON CM 1599-1851 B 1599-1812 [53,116]
WHITTLESEY ST ANDREW C 1602-1851 M 1602-1812 1815-1851 B 1602-43 1653-87 1695-1851 [114,163-5,183/4]
WHITTLESEY ST MARY C 1600-1851 MB 1599-1851 [77,115,163-6]
WHITTLESFORD M 1559-1837 [116]
WICKEN CB 1564-1866 M 1566-1866 [116,150]
WICKHAM, WEST C 1599-1858 M 1599-1841 B 1599-1922 [79,151]
WILBRAHAM, GREAT CB 1561-1851 M 1561-1837 [78]
WILBRAHAM, LITTLE C 1538-1852 M 1538-1837 B 1561-1852 [78]
WILBURTON 1599-1851 [78,117]
WILLINGHAM* amend to CB 1559-1891 M (1559-1837)-1891 [133,200]; Bapt 1754-1840 [80]
WIMPOLE 1560-1863 [117,122,123]
WISBECH St Mary M 1560-1812 [120]; St Peter M 1558-1754 [118/9,122]; Bapt ZMB 1700-1838 [117,160]
WITCHAM 1599-1900 [117,153]
WITCHFORD 1599-1753 [117]
WOOD DITTON 1567-1812 [73,81]
WRATTING, WEST C 1579-1889 M 1579-1837 B 1579-1869 [82]

CHESHIRE

ACTON C 1653-1812 M 1653-1754 B 1653-1750 [2]
ALDERLEY* M 1629-1837 [39]
BARROW, GREAT 1571-1880 [3,4]
BARTHOMLEY M 1562-1839 [33]
BEBINGTON 1558-1701 [5]
BIRKENHEAD Abbey 1719-88 [6]; Chapel of St Mary
1719-1812 [7]
BOSLEY* M 1729-50 [39]
BRAMHALL Bapt Z 1866-76 1883-92 B 1860-1911
BRERETON M 1754-1837 [33]
BROMBOROUGH* 1600-1726 [8]
BRUERA 1662-1812 [9]
CAPESTHORNE* M 1722-47 [39]
CHELFORD* M 1674-1752 [39]
CHESTER* Cathedral (1687-1812) [12]; Holy Trinity (CM
1598-1837 B 1532-1837) [10]; St Bridget 1560-1642
C(l) 1813-32 [13,P]; St John C 1790-91 M 1735-40
[13]: St Mary on the Hill Ext 1547-72 [L/6]; St Mary
within the Walls C(l) 1820-24 B(l) 1837-42 [P]; St
Oswald 1581-1628 M 1634-1700 [33]
CHRISTLETON* M 1600-1812 [33,35]
CHURCH LAWTON M 1596-1830 [33]
DISLEY* M 1591-1739 [35]
DODLESTON 1662-1724
DUKINFIELD Chapel M 1677-1708 [33]; Non Conf Ext
1677-1713
EASTHAM 1598-1700 [14]
FRODSHAM* 1558-1812 [15,16,17]
GATLEY Cong B 1777-1967 [13]
GAWSWORTH* 1557-1837 [18,35]
HARTHILL Malpas M 1599-1837 [33]
HESWALL* 1559-1729 [19]
INCE M 1600-1812 [33]
KIRBY, WEST 1561-1619 [21]
LYMM* M (1568-1812) [35]; Prim Meth CZ 1837-62 [13];
MACCLESFIELD C 1575-1665 M 1574-1680 1699-1754 B
1574-1667 [22,33]
MARPLE* M 1656-1754 [35]
MARTON* M 1563-1769 [39]
POTT SHRIGLEY* M 1685-1751 [39]
POYNTON WITH WORTH* M 1723-53 [39]
PRESTBURY CB 1560-1685 M 1560-1812 [33/4,36-
38,41]
PULFORD Ext C 1606-1753 M 1594-1753 B 1582-1771
[13]
ROSTHERNE C 1595-1735 MB 1594-1735 [13,23-25]
SIDDINGTON* M 1722-83 [39]
STOCKPORT St Mary 1584-1620 [26,27] Mfc M 1799-
1837
SWETTENHAM C 1561-1812 M 1570-1835 B 1570-1812
[28,33,42]
TARPORLEY Ext C 1559-1754 M 1589-1754 B 1559-1755
[G/13]
TATTENHALL C(l) 1812-35 [P]
TAXAL* CB 1610-1837 [29] M (1611-1837) [35,39]
THURSTASTON 1706-47 [13,30]
UPTON IN OVERCHURCH* 1600-1812 [9]
WALLASEY 1574-1812 [40]
WARFORD, GREAT Bapt Z 1757-1854 B 1800-1859
1880-1929 [31]
WITTON M Ext (l) 1754-1792 [33] 1792-1851
WOODCHURCH CM 1571-1840 B 1580-1840 [32]
WORTH see POYNTON WITH WORTH
WRENBURY Ext 1593-1812 [13]

CORNWALL

NB Names of places in Cornwall should be checked
under both "NAME" and "ST NAME".

Marriages 1597-1673 [R18-21] are from Bishops'
Transcripts

ADVENT* M 1616-65 1676-1801 [18,GCI]
ALTARNON M 1611-73 [18]
ANTHONY ST JACOB see TORPOINT
BLISLAND* C 1563-1837 M (1539-1812)-37 B 1539-1837
[6,81]
BOCONNOC M 1608-36 1712-1837 [18,105]
BODMIN* C(M)B 1558-1812 [7,8,88,GCI]; Lady Hunt
Conn CZ 1826-37 [22]; Wes CZ 1804-36 [22]
BOTUS FLEMING* M 1550-1812 [97]
BOYTON* M (1568-1812)-37 [18,94,96,106]
BRADOC M 1600-1837 [105]
BREAGE* C 1597-1700 (M 1559-1812) B 1559-1694
[82,111]; Bible Christian CZ 1821-37 [22]
BRIDGERULE see BRIDGERULE, Devonshire
BROADOAK see BRADOC
BRYHER see SCILLY ISLES
BUDE HAVEN C 1837-60 M 1849-60 B 1848-60 [76] see
also STRATTON
BUDOCK* 1610-(1653-1812) [90]
CALLINGTON with SOUTHILL M 1598-1673 [18]
CALSTOCK M 1602-74 [18]
CAMBORNE* (C 1558-1837 MB 1538-1837)
[29,30,67,96]; Mf M 1538-1837; Wes CZ 1828-37
[22]
CAMELFORD see LANTEGLOS
CANWORTHY WATER Bible Christian CZ 1821-24 [22]
CARDYNHAM* CB 1701-1812 M 1613-(1675-1812)
[1,18,81,GCI]
CARHARRACK Wes CZ 1820-42 [22] see also
GWENNAP
CAWSAND Rame Ind C 1810-37 [22]
COLAN* M 1600-(1665-1812) [18,90]
CONSTANTINE* M 1571-1812 [92]; Mf M 1571-1875
CORNELLY* M 1612-23,(1679-1812) [18,100]
CRANTOCK* C 1597-1721 (M 1559-1812) B 1559-1721
[17,93]
CREED* with GRAMPOUND M 1602-(1611-1837)
[18,103]
CROWAN* M 1614-(1674-1812) [18,95]
CUBERT* C 1678-1812 (M 1608-1812) B 1653-1812
[31,93]
CUBY* see TREGONY
CURY M 1608-74 [18]
DAVIDSTOW* M 1614-(1676-1812) [78]
DULOE C 1607-35 1664-1837 M 1607-1837 B 1608-1837
[32]
EGLOSHAYLE M 1600-1812 [83]
EGLOSKERRY* M 1574-1812 [79]
ENDELLION see ST ENDILLION
FALMOUTH* (1664-1812) [34/5]; Ind CZ 1783-1833 B
1808-37 [23,27]; Bible Christ CZ 1822-37 [23]; Wes
CZ 1813-37 [23] Mf CZ 1813-37
FEOCK 1671-1812 [36]
FILLEIGH see PHILLEIGH
FLUSHING Wes C 1817-37 [23] Mf CZ 1816-1837
FORRABURY* M 1601-(1676-1812) [19,78]
FOWEY CB 1750-1836 M (1568-1812)-36 [19,37,85]; Ind
CZ 1798-1836 [23]

GERMOE* CB 1813-37 M 1610-(1674-1812)-37 [38,82,111]

GERRANS* C 1813-37 M (1538-1837) [17,103,113]; Port Scatha Ind CZ 1826-36 [23]

GRADE* M 1597-1673 (1708-1812)-37 [19,102,105]

GRAMPOUND* see CREED

GULVAL* (1598-1812)-37 [68,104]

GUNWALLOE M 1608-65 [18]

GWENNAP* M 1610-(1660-1812)-19 [19,102,105]; Wes C 1843-51 [22] see also STITHIANS

GWINEAR* M 1560-1812 [89]

GWITHIAN* M 1560-1812 [80]

HAYLE Wes CZ 1819-37 [23]

HELLAND* CB 1722-1812 M 1608-(1677-1812) [2,19,81,GCI]

HELSTON* (M 1599-1812) [98]; Bapt Z 1805-37 [23]; Wes CZ 1804-37 [23]

HILL, NORTH C 1621-1865 M 1555-1840 B 1630-1840 [74]

ILLOGAN M 1613-74 [19]

JACOBSTOW* CB Ext 1612-73 M 1612-(1656-1812)-37 [19,102,106]

KEA* M 1607-(1653-1812) [19,99]

KENWYN* M 1559-1812 [99]

KILKHAMPTON* M (1539-1812)-1839 [97,106]; Bible Christian CZ 1816-37 [23]

LADOCK* C 1669-1837 M 1609-(1686-1812)-37 B 1675-1837 [15,100]

LAMORRAN M 1621-24 [19]; Mf C 1699-1805

LANDEWEDNACK* M 1598-(1654-1812) [19,102]

LANDRAKE* M 1583-1812 [98]

LANDULPH* C 1540-1747 (M 1541-1812) B 1540-1744 [98,112]

LANEAST* M 1597-(1680-1812) [19,79]

LANHERNE* Convent M 1710-1834 [93]

LANHYDROCK CB 1558-1812 (M 1559-1812) [3,81,GCI]

LANISLEY see GULVAL

LANIVET* M 1608-1812 [79]; Mf C 1608-1727

LANLIVERY* C 1583-1812 (M 1600-1812) B 1600-1812 [5,87,GCI]

LANREATH CB 1813-37 M 1597-1668 1813-37 [19,39,107] Mf C 1555-1674; Ind CZ 1816-24 [24]

LANSALLOS M 1600-1837 [105]

LANTEGLOS BY CAMELFORD* 1558-1812 [78]; Wes CZ 1800-1837 [22] Mf CZ 1800-37

LANTEGLOS BY FOWEY M 1610-74 [19]

LAUNCELLS* CB 1618-1708 M (1642-1812) [69,100]

LAUNCESTON* St Mary Magdalene (M 1559-1812) [101]; Ind CZ 1777-1837 [24]; Wes CZ 1794-1837 B 1823-37 [24,27]; see also ST STEPHENS by LAUNCESTON

LAWHITTON M 1608-76 [20]

LELANT* M 1611-(1679-1812) [20,86]

LESNEWTH* M 1559-1812 [20,78]

LEWANNICK* C 1660-1812 M 1597-(1675-1812) B 1738-1812 [10,20,91,GCI]

LEZANT* C(M)B 1539-1812 [16,70,88,GCI]

LINKINHORNE* C(M) 1576-1812 B 1641-1812 [9,94,GCI]

LISKEARD M 1597-1638 1813-37 [20,105]; Wes CZ 1806-37 [24]

LOOE, EAST C 1709-1807; Wes CZ 1815-36 [22]

LOOE, WEST Ind CZ 1788-1836 B 1819-36 [27]

LOSTWITHIEL* M 1609-1812 [85]; Ind CZ 1811-37 [24]

LUDGVAN* CB 1813-37 (M 1563-1812)-37 [39,82,111]

LUXULYAN* C(M)B 1594-1812 [6,85] Mf C 1594-1711; Bible Christian CZ 1819-37 [24]

MABE* M 1611-1812 [20,61]

MADRON* C 1592-1687 1700-1810 M 1577-(1674-1812)-1837 B 1577-1681 1700-1810 [40,71-73,89] Mf M 1577-1678 1700-1876

MAKER C 1630-1843 M 1607-1837 B 1630-1849 [41-45,113]

MANACCAN* M 1597-(1633-1812) [20,84]

MARAZION C 1754-1812 [58/9] see also ST HILARY

MARHAMCHURCH* M 1558-1812 [100]

MAWGAN IN MENEAGE M 1563-1812 [91]

MAWGAN IN PYDAR (M 1608-1812) [93] CB Ext 1608-73

MAWNAN* M 1553-1812 [84]

MENHENIOT* M 1554-1812 [87]

MERTHER 1613-66 [20]

MEVAGISSEY C 1590-1841 MB 1598-1838 [14]; Ind C 1786-1837 [24]

MICHAELSTOW* C 1680-1812 (M 1548-1812) B 1544-1812 [78,GCI]; Bible Christian CZ 1822-37 [3,24] Mf CZ 1822-37

MINSTER* M 1611-(1676-1812) [78,19]

MORVAH* C 1650-1837 M (1617-1772) 1813-37 B 1655-1837 [46,89] see also MADRON

MORVAL M 1610-71 [20]

MORWENSTOW* C(M)B 1558-1837 [94,113,GCI] Mf C 1813-77

MULLION M 1610-73 CMB 1813-37 [20,107]

MYLOR BRIDGE Wes CZ 1823-37 [24]

MYLOR* M 1607-(1673-1812) [20,84] see also FLUSHING

NEWLYN, EAST M 1559-1812 [93] Mf C 1560-1720

NEWLYN IN PYDAR see NEWLYN, EAST

NORTHILL see HILL, NORTH

OTTERHAM* M 1614-(1680-1812) [20,78] Mf CZ 1681-1772, 1804

PADSTOW* (M 1599-1812) CB(I) 1611-1812 [83,GCI]; Bapt CZ 1836 [25]; Wes CZ 1819-37 [25]

PAUL* C(M)B 1595-1812 [47-49,86]

PELYNT C 1693-1837 [105]

PENRYN Ind CZ 1806-37 B 1808-34 [25,27]; Wes CZ 1813-37 [25]

PENZANCE Bible Christ CZ 1821-37 [25] Mf CZ 1821-37; Ind CZ 1791-1837 B 1806-37 [25,27]; Wes CZ 1804-37 [25]; see also MADRON

PERRANARWORTHAL* M 1601-(1684-1812) [20,84]

PERRANUTHNOE* CB 1562-1812 (M 1589-1812) [62,92]

PERRANZABULO* M 1619-1812 [93]

PETHERICK, LITTLE* CB 1708-1812 (M 1636-1812) [2,93]

PETHERWYN, SOUTH* M 1608-(1656-1812) [94]

PHILLACK* M 1572-1812 [79 Mf C 1614-1717 see also HAYLE

PHILLEIGH* M 1613-1837 [103]

PILLATON* C(M) 1557-1812 B 1721-1812 [94,GCI]

POLPERRO Wes CZ 1818-37 [25]

PONSONOOTH Wes CZB 1813-36 [25,27]

POUGHILL* M 1537-1812 [97]

POUNDSTOCK* CB Ext 1597-1673 M 1597-(1615-1812)-37 [102,106] Mf M 1838-75

PROBUS* M 1597-(1641-1812) [21,100]; Wes CZ 1815-37 [25] Mf CZ 1815-37

QUETHIOCK M 1611-73 [21] Mf C 1573-1766

RAME CB 1813-40 M 1619-1837 [21,50,113] see also CAWSAND

REDRUTH* CB 1560-1716 M 1560-(1717-1812) [21,51,96]; Wes CZ 1817-37 [25]; Prim Meth CZ 1832-37 [25]

ROCHE* M 1578-1812 [94]

RUAN LANIHORNE* M 1608-1837 [103]
RUAN MAJOR* M 1611-(1683-1812) [21,102]
RUAN MINOR* M 1625-(1667-1812)-37 [21,102,105]
SALTASH (Chapelry) M 1599 1608 1617 [21]; Wes ZC 1820-1837 [25]
SANCREED* C 1566-1812 (M 1559-1812) B 1579-1812 [62,82]
SCILLY, ISLES OF C 1726-1889 M 1726-1940 B 1726-1886 [109,110]; Bible Christian CZ 1823-37 [26]
SENNEN* CB 1700-1812 (M 1699-1812) [46,80,107]
SHEVIOCKE* M 1570-1812 [81] Mf M 1670-1709
SITHNEY* M (1608-54)-1812 [21,84]
SOUTHILL see CALLINGTON
ST AGNES, Scilly see SCILLY ISLES
ST AGNES* M (1596-1812)-37 [95,105]; Ind CZ 1807-37 [25]; Wes CZ 1799-1838 [25]
ST ALLEN* M (1611-1812)-40 [95,111]
ST ANTHONY BY SALTASH M 1608-39 [18]
ST ANTHONY IN MENEAGE* M 1597-1673 (1726-1812) [18,97]
ST ANTHONY IN ROSELAND M 1623-99 1813-37 [18,107]
ST AUSTELL C 1564-1713 M 1565-1840 B 1564-1695 [13]; Ind CZ 1789-1835 [25]; Wes CZ 1803-37 [25]
ST BLAZEY M 1608-74 [18]
ST BREOCK M 1561-1812 [95]
ST BREWARD C 1558-1899 M 1558-1897 B 1558-1900 [75]
ST BURYAN* C(M)B 1653-1812 [52-4,80]
ST CLEER* C 1678-1812 M 1597-(1678-1812) B 1675-1812 [18,85,114]
ST CLEMENT* M 1538-1837 [103]
ST CLETHER* M 1610-(1640-1812) [18,78]
ST COLUMB MAJOR* CB 1539-1780 M 1539-(1781-1812) [55,93,GCI]
ST COLUMB MINOR* C 1560-1689,1715-27 (M 1560-1812) B 1718-19 [17,91,112]
ST COLUMB Cong CZ 1795-1837 [26]
ST DENNIS* CB 1687-1812 M (1610-1812)-1815 [56,98]
ST DENYS see ST DENNIS
ST DOMINIC M 1607-73 [18]
ST ENDELLION C 1732-1812 M 1684-1812 B 1738-1811 [2,81,GCI]
ST ENODER* M 1571-1812 [19,97]
ST ERME* CB 1671-1837 M (1614-1812)-40 [15,97]
ST ERNEY* M 1555-1812 [98]
ST ERTH* M 1563-1812 [97]
ST ERVAN* CB 1602-99 (M 1602-1812) [93,111]; Bible Christian CZ 1820-37 [26]
ST EVAL* M 1631-1812 [93]
ST EWE* M 1560-1812 [87]
ST GENNYS M 1612-74 [19]
ST GERMANS C 1590-1694 M 1608-75 1786-1837 B 1590-1695 [19,108]
ST GLUVIAS* M 1599-1812 [90]
ST GORAN* C 1661-1839 M 1607-(1668-1812)-39 B 1661-1840 [12,19,88]
ST HILARY* C 1671-1812 M 1609-(1676-1812) B 1677-1812 [58,59,86]
ST ISSEY* C(M)B 1596-1812 [10,115,GCI]
ST IVES* M (1653-1812) [91]; Lady Hunt Conn CZ 1800-37 [26]; Prim Meth CZ 1832-37 [26]; Wes CZ 1818-37 [26]
ST JOHN M 1611-74 [19]
ST JULIOT* M 1623-(1656-1812) [19,78]
ST JUST IN PENWITH* C 1612-1809 (M 1599-1812) B 1599-1711 [60,80] Mf C 1612-1812 B 1599-1711;

Wes CZ 1826-37 [26]
ST JUST IN ROSELAND* with ST MAWES M 1538-1837 [103]
ST KEVERNE* M 1597-(1608-1812) [101,112]
ST KEW* M 1564-1812 [83]
ST KEYNE M 1601-74 1722-1837 [19,105] Ext C 1533-1609 B 1555-1790 [70]
ST LEVAN* C(M) 1694-1812 B 1700-1812 [61,80]
ST MABYN* C(M)B 1562-1812 [11,20,79]
ST MARTIN, Scilly see SCILLY ISLES
ST MARTIN BY LOOE M 1597-1673 [20] see also LOOE, EAST
ST MARTIN IN MENEAGE* M 1571-1812 [92] Mf C 1694-1730
ST MARY, Scilly see SCILLY ISLES
ST MAWES Ind CZ 1798-1837 [26] see also ST JUST IN ROSELAND
ST MELLION* C(M)B 1558-1812 [1,94]
ST MERRYN* CB 1688-1812 M 1616-(1689-1812) [3,20,81,GCI] Mf C 1813-77
ST MEWAN M 1607-74 [20]
ST MICHAEL CARHAY M 1608-73 [20]
ST MICHAEL PENKEVIL* M 1577-1836 [103]
ST MICHAEL'S MOUNT B 1754-1812 [59] see also ST HILARY
ST MINVER* CB 1558-1812 (M 1559-1812) [20,81,GCI] Mf C 1813-77
ST NEOT M 1610-75 [20]; Bible Christian CZ 1820-37 [26]
ST PETROCK MINOR* see PETHERICK, LITTLE
ST PINNOCK M 1539-1837 [105]
ST RUAN see RUAN MINOR
ST SAMPSON* (alias GOLANT) C(M)B 1568-1812 [83,GCI]
ST STEPHEN BY LAUNCESTON C(M)B 1566-1812 [4,100,107,GCI]
ST STEPHEN IN BRANNEL* C 1694-1839 M 1608-(1681-1812)-50 B 1695-1840 [15,21,87,GCI]
ST STEPHENS BY SALTASH Ext 1608-73 [21]
ST TEATH* M 1558-1812 [78]
ST THOMAS BY LAUNCESTON M 1623-72 [21]
ST TUDY* CB 1559-1812 (M 1560-1812) [79,GCI]
ST UNY see LELANT
ST VEEP M 1611-73 [21]
ST WENN* M 1609-(1678-1812) [21,88]
ST WINNOW* CB 1622-1812 M 1612-(1622-1812) [2,87] Mf C 1753-1812; Wes Meth C 1844-57 [22]
STITHIANS* M 1598-(1654-1812) [21,84] Mf C 1753-1812; Wes Meth C 1844-57 [22]
STOKE CLIMSLAND M 1597-1674 [21]
STRATTON* CB 1611-1860 M 1611-(1674-1812)-60 [76,98]
TALLAND M 1617-74 [21] Mf CMB Ext 1617-36 CMB 1653-1837; see also POLPERRO
TAMERTON, NORTH M 1599-1674 [21]
TINTAGEL* M 1588-1812 [79]
TORPOINT Ind CZ 1815-37 [26]
TOWEDNACK* C 1671-1812 M (1676-1812) B 1683-1812 [80,63]
TREGONY* with CUBY M (1661-1812) [99] Mf CB 1611-1837
TREMAINE* M 1612-(1674-1812) [21,79] Mf C Ext 1674-1729
TRENEGLOS* M 1614-(1694-1812) [21,102]
TRESCO, Scilly see SCILLY ISLES
TRESMERE M 1613-65 [21]
TREVALGA* M 1539-1812 [78]

TREWEN M 1610-74 [21]

TRURO* (1597-1837) [64]; Bapt Z 1760-1837 [27]; Bible Christian CZ 1822-37 [27]; Ind CZ 1769-1837 [26]; New Conn Meth CZ 1834-37 [27]; Wes CZ 1805-37 [26]

TYWARDREATH* M 1608-(1642-1812) [21,85]

VERYAN* C 1681-1742 M 1602-73 (1676-1812) [21,100,113]

WARBSTOW* M 1612-(1695-1812) [21,102]

WARLEGGAN* CB 1547-1719 (M 1547-1812) [81,83,113,GCI]

WEEK ST MARY* M 1602-1812 [102]

WENDRON* M 1560-1812 [92]

WHITSTONE M 1598-1674 [21]

WITHIEL* CB 1567-1812 (M 1568-1812) [1,83]

ZENNOR* C 1599-1600 1713-1837 (M 1611-1837) B 1813-1837 [21,65,86]

CUMBERLAND

ADDINGHAM Mf C 1814-1866

AINSTABLE Mf C 1813-1875

ALSTON C 1700-1812 M 1700-1837 [1,2,40]

ARLECDON M 1720-1811 [40] Mf C 1814-1877

ARTHURET C 1790-1812 M Ext 1751-1808 [SC/L169]

BEAUMONT Mf C 1814-1877

BECKERMET St Bridget M 1687-1824 [40]; St John M 1689-1826 [40]

BEWCASTLE Z Ext 1793-1848 [SC/L169] Mf C 1813-1877

BRIDEKIRK* C 1585-1812 MB 1584-1812 [34

CAMERTON Mf C 1813-1870

CARLISLE St Cuthbert M Ext 1718-1815 [SC/L169]; St Mary (Rom Cath) C 1798-1840 M 1799-1840 D 1799-1827 [39]

CLEATOR M 1690-1812 [40]

CLIFTON, GREAT and LITTLE Mf C 1822-1877

COCKERMOUTH 1632-1701 1854/5 [4,5,42,L9]; Cong C 1651-1700 [L9]

CROSBY ON EDEN* M 1665-1837 [36]

CROSTHWAITE* 1562-1812 M 1883-85 [6,7,P] Mf M 1562-1858

CUMWHITTON M 1665-1672 [40]

DACRE* 1559-1716 [8]

DEAN M 1689-1704 [P]

DRIGG M 1632-53 [40]

EGREMONT M 1726-1834 [40,P] Mf C 1856-1875

ENNERDALE M 1645-1664 1676-1758 [40,P]

ESKDALE M 1676 1689-1758 [40]

GARRIGILL C 1708-1812 M 1699-1812 B 1694-1811 [9,40]; Non-conf Z 1705-1728 [40]

GOSFORTH* C 1572-1740 (M 1571-1837) B 1571-1746 [36,GCI] CB 1571-1728 [3]

GREYSTOKE* 1559-1757 [10]

HAILE M 1676-1845 [40,P]

HARRINGTON M 1652-1837 [36]

HAYTON 1775-77 [P]

HOLME LAW Mf C 1850-1871

HOLME CULTRAM* CB 1580-97 M 1582-97 [11]

HUTTON in the FOREST M 1662-1701 [40]

IRTON 1676-1800 M 1813-1842 [40,GCI]

KESWICK see CROSTHWAITE and ST JOHNS-in-the-VALE

KIRKANDREWS upon ESK Ext M 1665-1853 D 1727-1771 [SC/L169]

KIRKBRIDE Mfc 1762-1875

KIRKLINGTON M Ext 1753-1846 [SC/L169,P]

KIRKOSWALD* 1577-1812 [12]

KNOWEL see BEWCASTLE

LAMPLUGH* CB 1581-1812 M 1583-1812 [13]

LANERCOST* 1731-1837 [14]

LONGTOWN see ARTHURET

MATTERDALE* CB 1634-1720 M 1634-1719 [15]

MELMERBY M 1660-1702 [40]

MILLOM* 1591-1839 [16,42]

MORESBY* M 1676-1837 [35]

MUNCASTER M 1813-42 [40] Mf 1735-1812

NETHER WASDALE Mf C 1813-1854

NEWTON REIGNY* 1571-1837 [17,40]

NEWTON ARLOSH Mf C 1850-1877

NICHOL FOREST Ext M 1761-1830 Z 1764-1855 [SC/L169]

ORTON, GREAT* 1568-1812 [18]

PENRITH* (I) 1556-1601 CMB 1605-1812 [19-23]

PONSONBY 1702-1770 [GCI] M 1723-1850 [40]

SKELTON* 1580-1812 [27] Mf 1580-1812

ST BEES* 1538-1837 [24-6]

ST JOHNS-in-the-VALE Mf C 1776-1877

STANWIX* M 1662-1837 [36]

THRELKELD Mf C 1761-1875

THWAITES C 1724-1837 MB 1725-1837 [42] see also MILLOM

WABERTHWAITE C 1656-1812 MB 1657-1812 [28]

WARWICK BRIDGE Rom Cath C 1766-1856 M 1747-63 1769-1842 D 1765-1841 [39,40]

WASDALE HEAD 1721-1800 [GCI]

WATERMILLOCK* CB 1579-1812 M 1580-1812 [15]

WETHERAL see WARWICK BRIDGE

WHICHAM* 1569-1812 C 1813-1862 M 1813-1841 1848 B 1813-1862 [29,40]

WHITBECK Mf C 1813-1875

WHITEHAVEN* St James (C 1753-1837) [30]; St Nicholas M 1694-1837 [37]; St Nicholas Old Chapel M 1705-09 [40]

WIGTON* C 1604-1797 M 1604-1781 B 1604-1779 [31,32,]; Ch Scot C 1809-1812 [40]

WORKINGTON* M 1670-1837 [35]

DERBYSHIRE

ALFRETON* M 1706-1837 [44]; Christ the King Rom Cath Mfc C 1862-87

ALLESTREE* M 1596-1812 [30]

ALSOP EN LE DALE* M 1702-1837 [37]

ALVASTON* M 1614-1811 [35]

ASHBOURNE 1538-53 1564-76 [47]; All Ss Rom Cath Mfc C 1876-1908

ASHOVER* (M 1642-1780 B 1653-1679)-1730 1761-1828 1883-88 [1-3]

ASTON UPON TRENT* M 1670-1812 [37]

BAKEWELL Ind C 1799-1837; Wes C 1807-36 [46]

BARROW ON TRENT* with TWYFORD M 1663-1812 [37]; Indep ZC 1814-1837 [46] see also REPTON and BARROW

BEAUCHIEF* M 1696-1837 [40]

BEIGHTON* M 1653-1837 [40]
BLACKWELL by ALFRETON Mf C 1813-1864
BOLSOVER Mf C 1813-1865
BOULTON* M 1756-1812 [30]
BRADWELL Wes Mf ZC 1811-1837
BRAILSFORD* (M 1653-1810) [31] Mf 1662-1812
BRAMPTON M 1658-1752 [P]
BREADSALL* M 1573-1837 [42]
BREASTON* C 1719-1892 (M 1719-1810) 1814-1908 B 1824-1936 [30,49]
BRIMINGTON Mf C 1813-1871
BUXTON* CB 1718-1840 M (1718-1837)-40 [4,41]; Meth C 1797-1855 [46]; St Anne Rom Cath Mfc C 1863-93 M 1863-1908
CALKE C 1813-1981 M 1837-1949 B 1816-1981 [48]
CASTLETON C 1646-51 1662-1730 M 1662-85 1722-54 B 1648-50 [5]
CHADDESDEN* M 1718-1812 [34]
CHAPEL EN LE FRITH* C(M)B 1620-1837 [6,7,41]
CHELLASTON* M 1570-1812 [35]
CHESTERFIELD 1558-1600 1601-1635 [45,50]
CHINLEY Wes Mf ZC 1808-1829
CHURCH BROUGHTON* (M 1538-1812) [30] Mf 1662-1810
CHURCH GRESLEY Mf C 1664-1812 (gaps)
COTMANHAY C 1848-85 M 1848-95 B 1848-90
CROXALL CB 1586-1812 M 1586-1752 [8]
DALBURY 1722-1732 [47]
DALE ABBEY* M 1667-1813 [30]
DENBY* M 1577-1837 [43]
DERBY* All Saints M 1558-1837 [38]; St Alkmund (M 1538-1812) DB Ext 1720-78 [33]; St Michael (M 1559-1812) [34]; St Peter M (1558-1812) [35]; St Werburgh (M 1558-1837) [39]; Meth Lynton Street C 1880-1900 [46]; Rom Cath Old Chapel 1813-42 [46] Mfc C 1777-1842; St Mary Rom Cath Mfc C 1843-99 D 1855-92
DERWENT Mf C 1813-1843
DRONFIELD* M 1560-1837 [40]
DUFFIELD M 1598-1812 [31/2] Mf CB 1598-1742
EATON, LONG Wes Meth B 1831-1837 [46]
ECKINGTON Rom Cath see SPINKHALL
EDENSOR CM 1539-1602 B 1540-97 [9]
ELVASTON* M 1651-1837 [42]
ETWALL* (M 1557-1837) [43] Mf 1674-1810
FAIRFIELD* CB 1738-1840 (M 1756-1837) [10,41]
FOREMARK* M 1663-1836 [33]
GLOSSOP C 1620-1733 M 1620-1732 B 1620-1727 [5]
HALLAM, WEST* M 1638-1812 [34] Mf C 1662-1773
HARTSHORNE Mf C 1813-1849 1868-9
HASSOP All Ss Rom Cath Mfc C 1816-43 M 1817-61
HATHERSAGE* CB (1627-1700)-1837 M (1627-1700)-1980 [12-15]
HAULT HUCKNALL* M 1660-1812 [30]
HEANOR* M 1558-1837 [44]
HEATH* alias LOWND M 1682-1812 [30]
HOLBROOK CB 1833-37 [47]
HOLMESFIELD Mf C 1813-1876
HOPE C 1599-1645 1661-1837 M 1598-1640 1661-1745 1748-65 1767-1839 B 1598-1641 1661-1858 [16-22]
HORSLEY* M 1558-1812 [36]
ILKESTON* M 1588-1812 [36/7]; Our Lady & St Thomas Rom Cath Mfc C 1858-89 D 1876-1905
KEDLESTON* M 1600-1837 [42]
KIRK HALLAM* M 1700-1837 [36]
KIRK IRETON* M 1576-1812 [32]
KIRK LANGLEY* M 1654-1837 [35,47]

LITTLEOVER* 1680-1812 [23]
LONGFORD* (M 1537-1837) [43] Mf 1661-1809
LOWND* see HEATH
MACKWORTH* M (1603-1812)-37 [30,47]
MARSTON MONTGOMERY Mf 1662-1810
MARSTON upon DOVE Mf 1662-1809
MATLOCK* M 1637-1812 [36]
MELBOURNE* M 1653-1812 [37]; New Jerusalemite Mf ZC 1831-1837
MELLOR* M 1678-1775 [32]
MICKLEOVER* CB 1607-1805 M 1607-1814 [23]
MORLEY* CB 1540-1812 (M 1540-1837) [24,42]
MORTON* M 1575-1812 [34] Mf C 1813-1863
NEVERGREEN see YEAVELEY
NEWTON SOLNEY C 1664-1841 M 1664-1839 B 1663-1841 [47]
NORBURY and ROSTON Mf M 1673-1812
NORMANTON* M 1769-1812 [35]
NORMANTON, SOUTH 1540-1634 1664-1812 [53] Mf C 1810-1868
NORTON* 1559-1812 [34]
OCKBROOK* M 1631-1812 [30]
OSMASTON* M 1743-1812 [35]
PARWICH* M 1639-1837 [37]
PEAK FOREST Chapel M 1727-1815 [27]
PENTRICH* (M 1640-1837) [43] CB Ext 1713-78
PINXTON C 1561-1640 M 1561-1627 [GCI]
QUARNDON* M (1755-1812)-37 [33,47]
REPTON* CB 1578-1670 M 1578-1837 [28,41]; REPTON and BARROW Ind Mf ZC 1814-1837
RIDDINGS Mf Ind C 1823-1837
RIDGWAY Mf Wes C 1810-1837 B 1830-1837
RIPLEY & PENTRICH Non-Conf C 1753-1805
RISLEY* M 1720-1812 [30]
ROSTON see NORBURY and ROSTON
SANDIACRE* M 1581-1812 [30]
SAWLEY* M 1656-1837 [42]; see also EATON, LONG Wes
SHELDON C 1672-75 1745-1812 M 1745-1812 Ext 1669-1807 [29]
SHIPLEY WOOD Prim Meth Mf C 1827-37
SHIRLAND* 1661-1698 M 1695-1837 [43,47]
SMALLEY* C 1655-1862 (M 1624-1837) B 1655-1812 [24,42,52]
SMISBY* M 1720-1812 [37]
SPINKHILL Rom Cath 1757-1860 [46]
SPONDON* M 1654-1812 [32]
STANLEY* M 1754-1837 [30,43]
STANTON BY BRIDGE* 1662-1810 (M 1664-1835) [37,47]
STANTON BY DALE* M 1605-1812 [30]
STAVELEY C 1558-1618 [47]
SUDBURY Mf 1634-1810
SWADLINCOTE Mf Wes C 1807-1837
SWARKESTON* M 1604-1837 [37] Mf C 1723-1868(gaps)
TICKENHALL* M 1628-1812 [33] Mf C 1662-1805(gaps); Mf Wes C 1817-1837
TICKNELL see TICKENHALL
TWYFORD see BARROW ON TRENT
WESTON UPON TRENT* CB 1565-1837 M (1565-1812)-37 [24,37]
WHITFIELD Mf Wes Chap ZC 1813-1837
WILLINGTON* M 1608-1812 [35]
WILNE* C 1724-1880 M (1540-1837) [42,47]
WINGFIELD, SOUTH* M 1585-1837 [43]
WINSTER Mf Prim Meth C 1825-1837

11

WIRKSWORTH Mf Bapt Chap Z 1821-1837; Old Ind
Chap ZC 1813-1836
YEAVELEY Mf Nethergreen Ind Chap ZC 1816-1824

DEVON

ABBOTS BICKINGTON 1609-1837 [41,90]
ABBOTSHAM Ext 1597-1637 [90]
ALVERDISCOTT 1617-18 1624 [90] Mfc C 1602-1896 M
1602-1837 B 1602-1812
ALVINGTON, WEST 1628 [90] Mfc C 1558-1853 M
1558-1947 B 1558-1943
ALWINGTON 1596-1644 [GCI] Ext C 1578-1799 M
1586-1753 B 1551-1796 [88,90]
ANSTEY, EAST 1610 [90]
ANSTEY, WEST Ext 1608-36 [90]
APPLEDORE M(I) 1844-1894 [102]; Bapt ZC 1834-37
[94,Mf]
ARLINGTON 1596-1644 [90,GCI]
ASHBURTON Ind ZC 1817-37; Wes ZC 1801-36 [94,Mf]
ASHBURY 1596-1644 [90,GCI]
ASHCOMBE 1581-1837 [23,90]
ASHFORD Ext 1596-1640 [GCI] C 1596-1640/1 1813-
1964 M 1597-1640 1774-1964 B 1597-1640/1 1813-
1966 [107]
ASHPRINGTON 1596-1644 [90,GCI] Mfc C 1607-1940 M
1607-1856 Banns 1824-1925 B 1607-1908
ASHREIGNEY 1596-1644 C 1607-1981 M 1607-1978
Banns 1754-1981 B 1607-1982 [48,90,GCI]
ATHERINGTON 1596-1644 [90,GCI]
AVETON GIFFORD 1596-1644 [90,GCI]
AWLISCOMBE Mfc C 1559-1657 1690-1855 M 1559-
1640 1690-1837 B 1559-1645 1690-1812
AXMINSTER 1596-1644 [90,GCI]; Ind ZC 1786-1837;
Wes ZC 1809-37 [94,Mf]
AYLESBEARE Mfc C 1580-1867 M 1580-1837 Banns
1754-1974 B 1580-1883
BAMPTON 1609-17 [90,GCI]; Bapt ZC 1807-37 [95,Mf]
BARNSTAPLE* 1538-1812 [24,(I)106,GCI]; Bapt ZC
1821-37; Ind ZC 1701/2-68 1777-1837; Wes ZC
1807-37 [94,Mf] see also CHARLES
BEAFORD 1598-1602 1607 1615 [90]
BEAWORTHY Ext 1602-36 [90]
BEER Ind ZC 1788-1835 [94,Mf]
BEERALSTON Ind ZC 1813-37 [94,Mf]
BELSTONE M 1553-1809 B 1635-41 [25,88,90]
BERE FERRERS 1605-06 [90]
BERRY NARBOR M 1540-1783 B Ext 1599-1642 [42,90]
BERRY POMEROY 1596-1602 [90]
BICKINGTON 1620-22 1636 [90]
BICKLEIGH Plymouth Ext 1609-42 [90]
BICTON Ext 1620-39 [90] Mfc C 1642-1812 M 1557-1926
Banns 1770-1974 B 1557-1812
BIDEFORD Mfc C 1561-1951 M 1561-1968 B 1561-1968;
Ind C 1753-1837; Wes CZ 1819-37 [95,Mf]
BIGBURY Ext 1613-27 [90]
BISHOPS NYMPTON 1607-1614 1633 M 1558-1600 [88-
90]
BISHOPS TEIGHTON Mfc C 1558-1812 M 1558-1949 B
1558-1863
BLACK TORRINGTON 1545-1837 C(I) 1837-1848 B(I)
1837-1879 [26,90]

BLACKAWTON B Ext 1609-18 [90] Mfc C 1538-1856 M
1538-1837 B 1538-1812
BLACKBOROUGH Mfc M 1840-1973
BOLTON, SOUTH M 1601-42 B 1678-1704 [107]
BONDLEIGH Ext 1607-37 [90] Mfc M 1754-1837
BOVEY, NORTH 1572-1840 [65,90]
BOVEY TRACEY Ext 1613-39 [90] Mfc C 1538-1965 M
1538-1960 B 1539-1973; Bapt CB 1778-1837 [95]
Mf Bapt Z 1778-1837 B 1784-1837
BOW Ext 1598-1639 [90]; Ind ZC 1825-36 [95,Mf]
BRADFORD 1558-1837 C(I) 1837-1927 [27,90]
BRADNINCH CB 1559-1840 M 1557-1840 [28-31]
BRADSTONE Ext 1611-27 [90]
BRADWORTHY 1548-1860 [32] Mf 1592-1860;
Nonparochial C 1815-1909 [33]
BRAMPFORD SPEKE Ext 1608-45 [90]
BRANSCOMBE* C 1539-1812 M 1745-1812 B 1578-1812
[1,90]
BRATTON FLEMING 1560-1629 1641-1656 [90]
BRAUNTON 1538-1837 [40]; Ind ZC 1818-37 [95] Mf Ind
ZC 1818-37 B 1833-37
BRAYFORD Bapt ZC 1831-37 [95,Mf]
BRENT, SOUTH Mfc C 1677-1918 M 1677-1921 B 1677-
1883
BRIDGERULE C 1692 CB 1702-1812 M 1702-1812
[34,42,44,107]
BRIXHAM Wes ZC 1811-37 [95,Mf]
BUCKFASTLEIGH Ind ZC 1787-1837 B 1807-1810 ; Bible
Christ ZC 1820-37 [95,Mf]
BUCKLAND, EAST MfC 1684-1812 M 1684-1836
Banns 1755-1872 B 1684-1794
BUCKLAND FILLEIGH 1603-12 1626-1837 [35]
BUCKLAND MONACHORUM MfC 1552-1853 M 1540-
1837 B 1538-1892
BUCKLAND TOUT SAINTS Mfc M 1818-1822
BUCKLAND, WEST 1598-1793 [44] Mfc C 1654-1904 M
1625-1837 B 1686-1812
BUDLEIGH, EAST Mfc C 1555-1845 M 1556-1837 B
1562-1863; Ind C 1762-1837 B 1832-37 [95,Mf]
BUDLEIGH SALTERTON Wes ZC 1820-37 [95,Mf]
BULKWORTHY 1605-1641 1674-1837 [36]
CHALLACOMBE M 1673-1834 [42] Mfc C 1673-1955 M
1673-1837 Banns 1754-1858 B 1673-1812
CHAGFORD Mf Bible Christ C 1822-37
CHARLES Barnstaple C 1579-1837 M 1539-1837 B
1531-1837 [37]
CHARLETON Mfc C 1560/1-1861 M 1562/3-1837 B
1561/2-1812
CHIVELSTOKE see STOKENHAM & CHIVELSTOKE
CHIVELSTONE Mfc C 1630-1873 M 1630-1836 B 1630-
1920
CHRISTOW Mfc C 1557-1858 M 1557-1812 B 1557-1800
CHUDLEIGH Mfc C 1558-1858 M 1538-1837 B 1558-
1853; Ind Presb C 1711-1837; Ind C 1749-1777 [95]
Mf Ind C 1711-1837 Z 1749-1777; Rom Cath
(Ugbrook Hall Chapel) C 1736-55 [CRS 25]
CHUMLEIGH Ext CB 1655-1726 M 1655-1747 [89] M
1610-1812 [GCI]; Ind ZC 1812-1837 [95,Mf]
CHURCHSTOW Mfc C 1542-1652 1695-1876 M 1539-
1653 1695-1837 B 1539-1641 1695-1812
CLOVELLY Mfc C 1686-1838 M 1695-1837 Banns 1858-
1946 B 1686-1863
CLYST ST GEORGE* (CB 1565-1812 M 1565-1812)-37
[2,89]
CLYST ST MARY Mfc C 1662-1901 M 1676-1836 B 1662-
1958
COFFINSWELL M 1601-25 [89]

COLATON RALEIGH Mfc C 1673-1842 M 1673-1837 B 1673-1871

COLEBROOKE Mfc C 1558-1845 M 1558-1838 B 1558-1865

COLYTON* 1538-1837 [3,4,102]; Ind ZC 1815-57; Presb C 1773-1826 ZC 1823-36 DB 1832-36 [95,Mf]; Mf Unit ZC 1823-1862 B 1832-1862

COMBE MARTIN Ind ZC 1828-37 [95,Mf]

COMBE RALEIGH Mfc C 1653-1914 M 1654-1837 B 1653-1812

COOKBURY 1609-1634 1663-1837 [38]

COOMBE in TEIGNHEAD 1669-1913 M 1653-1837 1880-1913 B 1653-1913 [39]

CORNWOOD Ext 1685-1834 [P]

CORNWORTHY Mfc Ext C 1565-1859 M 1568-1837 B 1562-1889

COUNTISBURY* M 1676-1837 [91,GCI]

CREDITON Presb ZC 1735-1837 B 1785-1837; Ind ZC 1805-37 [96,Mf]

CROYDE Bapt ZC 1821-35 [96]

CULLOMPTON Mfc C 1601-1844 M 1601-1643 1678-1837 B 1601-1645 1678-1837; Presb ZC 1694-1823 CB 1823-37; Ind ZC 1831-36; Wes ZC 1805-31 [95,Mf]

CULMSTOCK Bapt ZB 1786-1836 [96,Mf]

DALWOOD Mfc Ext C 1568-1644 1713-1855 M 1568-1650 1716-1837 B 1585-1655 1714-1915

DARTMOUTH Presb ZC 1726-1837 [96,Mf]

DAWLISH Ind C 1814-37 [96,Mf]

DENBURY C 1559-1746 M 1559-1743 B 1559-1681 [88/9] Mfc C 1559-1874 M 1559-1837 B 1559-1691 1739-1924

DEVONPORT Bapt Liberty-Pembroke Street Z 1779-1810 [97,Mf]; Bible Christ Arminian Dock ZC 1820-37 [97,Mf]; Ind Granby Street ZC 1838-1818 [Mf]; Ind Mount Street ZC 1808-37 [97,Mf]; Ind Mount Zion C 1824-37 [96,Mf]; Ind Princes Street C 1763-1837 [96,Mf]; Ind Salem C 1826-37 [96,Mf]; Moravian James Street ZC 1785-1836 [97,Mf]; Unit Granby St C 1828-35 [95,Mf]; Wes & Meth Circuit C(I) 1839-1944 [108]; Wes Morice Street ZC 1787-1837 [97,Mf]; Bapt Morice Sq Z 1785-1837 [96,Mf]; Navy Row (Morice Town) Ind ZC 1826-37 [Mf]

DITTISHAM Mfc C 1651-1884 M 1654-1837 M 1650-1711

DODBROOKE Mfc C 1725-1881 M 1727-1837 B 1727-1881; Mf Refuge Bapt Z 1819-1837

DOLTON M 1610-1812 [GCI]

DOWN, EAST M 1539-1837 [88/9]

DREWSTEIGNTON M 1599-1812 [45]

DUNCHIDEOCK 1538-1837 [46]

DUNKESWELL Mfc C 1750-1876 M 1743-1838 B 1740-1812

EGGESFORD Ext C 1596-1702 M 1580-1696 B 1596-1671 [89]

EXETER* Cathedral (1594-1812)-1837 [5,49]; St Thomas CB 1541-1837 M 1576-1837; All Hallows Goldsmith Street C 1566-1837 M 1561-1753 1813-1837 B 1561-1837 [6]; St Pancras CB 1664-1837 M 1664-1774 1784-1796 1813-1837 [6]; St Paul 1562-1837 [6];Mf: Bapt Bartholomew Street Z 1817-1837; Bow Presb C 1687-1823 B 1748-1824; Ind Castle Street ZC 1798-1816 C 1817-1836 B 1824-1836; Ind Coombe Street C 1776-1836; Presb George's CB 1818-1837; Ind High Street C 1820-1836; Presb Mint C 1719-1810 B 1773-1810; Wes Mint ZC 1802-1837 B 1818-1828; Bapt South Street Z 1786-1837 B 1785-1837

EXMINSTER 1562-1837 [50,51]

EXMOUTH Mf Ebenezer Ind ZC 1809-1837; Glenorchy Ind C 1779-1837 B 1784-1818; see also WITHYCOMBE RALEIGH

FARRINGDON M 1620-1788 [42]

FREMINGTON Mfc C 1602-1896 M 1602-1927 B 1602-1948

GITTISHAM Mfc C Ext 1559-1888 M 1571-1838 B Ext 1559-1952

HALBERTON C 1612-18 1619-1837 M 1612-1837 B 1605-1837 [52-4]

HARTLAND* (1558-1837) [7,105]; Indep Chapel ZC 1821-1837 [44,Mf]

HATHERLEIGH 1558-1837 [55]; Mf Presb C 1729-1789

HEMYOCK* 1635-1837 [8]

HENNOCK Mfc C 1552-1600 1756-1850 M 1552-1600 1754-1837 B 1552-1600 1756-1812

HIGHAMPTON 1653-1703 1734-1837 [56]

HIGH BRAY Mfc Ext CB 1605-1792 M 1605-1837

HOLLACOMBE 1638-1738 1813-1837 [57/8]

HOLSWORTHY 1563-1837 [59]; Mf Ind ZC 1828-1830; Wes ZC 1818-1837

HONEYCHURCH Mfc C 1728-1812 M 1757-1837 B 1730-1813

HONITON Mfc Ext C 1598-1850 MB 1598-1837; Mf Ind C 1689-1752 1772-1780 1820-1837 B 1774-1836; Part Bapt C 1829-1837

HORWOOD C 1653-1837 MB 1654-1837 [43] Mfc C 1653-1812 M 1654-1837 B 1654-1812

HUISH Mfc C 1595-1812 M 1600-1981 B 1595-1812 (gaps)

HUNTSHAM 1559-1900 [43]

IDDESLEIGH Ext 1542-1801

INWARDLEIGH CM 1608-18 1663-1838 B 1608-18 1663-1842 [60]

IPPLEPEN* M 1612-1837 [91,GCI]

KENN 1538-1837 [61,62]

KENTISBEARE Mfc C 1695-1865 M 1695-1839 B 1695-1825; Mf Bapt C 1806-1836

KENTON 1694-1837 [63]

KERSWELL Mf Ind ZC 1813-1832

KILMINGTON Mfc C 1577-1600 1723-1875 M 1577-1589 1727-1837 B 1577-1598 1723-1891 (gaps)

KING ASH Bible Christ Mf ZC 1820-1837

KINGSBRIDE Mf Bapt Z 1785-1813 B 1785-1857; Ebenezer Ind C 1830-1837; Wes ZC 1813-1837; Ind ZC 1787-1837 B 1793-1837

KINGSKERSWELL* M 1752-1837 [91,GCI]

KINGS NYMPTON Mfc C 1538-1860 M 1539-1837 B 1538-1812 (gaps)

KINGSTEIGNTON Mf Ind C 1818-35

KINGSWEAR Mfc C 1601-1882 M 1601-1837 B 1601-1925 (gaps)

LAMERTON Mfc C 1545-1841 M Ext 1538-1844 B 1549-1854

LANDKEY Mf Wes ZC 1816-37

LAPFORD* 1567-1850 [9,102]

LUPPITT MfC C 1711-1852 M Ext 1711-1838 B 1711-1884

LUSTLEIGH* 1608-1837 [10]

LYDFORD 1716-1869 [88]

LYNTON M 1568-1837 [42]

MAMHEAD 1556-1837 [64]

MANATON 1653-1840 B Ext 1840-1861 [65] Mfc C 1653-1898 M 1654-1837 B 1653-1813

MARTINHOE* M 1500-(1597-1812) [91,GCI]

MARY TAVY Ext C 1562-1798 M 1581-1760 B 1563-1809 [89]
MEETH Mfc C 1653-1812 M 1653-1981 B 1653-1812
MEMBURY CB 1637-1686 M 1638-1676 [44] Mfc C 1637-1846 M Ext 1638-1837 B 1637-1868; SFrs 1660-1788 [89]
MERTON Mfc C 1687-1846 M Ext 1688-1981 B Ext 1687-1875
MILTON DAMEREL CM 1606-1682 1683-1837 B 1606-1837 [67]
MILTON, SOUTH Mfc C 1686-1879 B 1735-1836 B 1686-1963
MOLTON, SOUTH M 1601-42 B 1678-1704 [11,104]; Mf Ind ZC 1758-1837
MONKTON Mfc C 1737-1812 M 1742-1837 B 1741-1812
MORCHARD BISHOP 1606-44 1660-1850 [68/9,101]
MORETONHAMPSTEAD 1603-1710 [70] Mfc C 1711-1849 M 1711-1837 B 1711-1864; Presb C 1672-1836 B 1802-21 [108] Mf Presb C 1672-1836 see also OKEHAMPTON; Wes ZC 1815-37 [108]
NEWTON ABBOT Mf Salem Ind C 1726-1837
NEWTON ST CYRES Ext C 1555-1789 M 1557-1735 B 1556-1887 [89]
NEWTON ST PETROCK CM 1578-1837 B 1607-1837 [71]
NEWTON TRACEY C 1569-1837 M 1570-1837 B 1562-1837 [43]
NYMET ROWLAND C 1719-1812 M 1734-55 B 1734-1812 [72]
OFFWELL Mfc B 1943-1964
OGWELL, EAST Mfc C 1674-1909 M 1675-1837 B 1674-1812
OGWELL, WEST Mfc C 1684-1811 M 1695-1843 B 1696-1812
OAKFORD 1568-1812 [41]
OKEHAMPTON Mf Wes C 1815-1837; Ebenezer Ind ZC 1799-1810 1821-1836 B 1829-1837
OTTERTON 1558-1837 [GCI]
OTTERY ST MARY* 1601-1837 [12,13,43]; Mf Ind C 1746-1837 B Ext 1746-1837
PAIGNTON Mf Ind C 1818-1837 B 1826-1836
PARKHAM* CB 1537-1812 M (1537-1604 1628-1812)-37 [14/5,89]
PARRACOMBE* 1597-1635 1668-1836 [16]
PENNYCROSS CB 1634-1812 M 1636-1752 [44]
PETERS MARLAND Mfc C 1696-1913 M 1697-1980(gaps) B 1696-1812
PETHERWIN, NORTH M Ext 1611-73 [89]
PETROCKSTOW Mfc C 1597-1860 M 1597-1979 B 1597-1908
PINHOE M 1687-1837 [42] Mfc C 1813-1860 M 1754-1837 B 1813-1901
PLYMOUTH* St Andrew C 1581-1633 (I) 1781-1805 [107] M 1581-1654 B 1581-1618 [17,41,92] Mfc 1581-1674 C 1813-1842 M 1754-1837 B 1813-1843; Charles the Martyr Mfc C 1645-1840 M 1644-1837 B 1646-1841; French 1733-1807 [HS20]; Mf Batter Street Presb C 1704-1837 M 1760-1794 B 1768-1837; Mf Buckwell Lane Ind ZC 1833-1837; Salem St Ind ZC 1831-1878; Monice Sq Ind C 1785-1806; Ebenezer Wes CB 1813-1863; How St Bapt Z 1786-1837 B 1787-1837; Norley Ind C 1798-1837; Norley St Presb C 1672-1835 B 1721-1749
PLYMPTON ST MARY Mfc CM 1684-1837 B 1684-1849; Mf Lee Mill Bridge Ind ZC 1836-7
PLYMSTOCK M 1591-1812 [42] Mfc C 1592-1852 M 1592-1836 B 1592-1843

PLYMTREE* 1538-1837 [18]
POOL, SOUTH Mfc C 1664-1874 M 1665-1837 B 1664-1941
PORTLEMOUTH, EAST Mfc C 1563-1669 1692-1878 M 1594-1666 1693-1836 B 1562-1670 1692-1978
POWDERHAM C 1575-1837 M 1559-1835 B 1558-1837 [73]
PUDDINGTON Mfc CB 1555-1812 M Ext 1555-1848 Banns 1759-1834
PYWORTHY Mfc C 1653-1857 M 1681-1837 B 1682-1891
REWE M 1686-1837 [42]
RINGSASH Mf Bible Christ C 1820-1836
ROMANSLEIGH Mfc C 1697-1812 M Ext 1698-1836 B 1539-1804
ST BUDEAUX M 1539-1837 [44]
ST GILES IN THE HEATH M Ext 1601-73 [89]
ST MARY CHURCH Mfc 1641-1812
ST MARY TAVEY See MARY TAVEY
SAMPFORD PEVERELL Mf Wes C 1825-1833
SATTERLEIGH Mfc C Ext 1574-1812 M Ext 1574-1935 B 1574-1812
SHALDON Mf Ebenezer Ind ZC 1824-1836
SHEBBEAR 1576-1837 [78]; Mf Bible Christ C 1818-1837
SHEEPWASH 1602-1668(Ext) 1674-1838 [79]
SHELDON Mfc C 1715-1812 M 1715-1836 B 1715-1836
SHERFORD Mfc C 1713-1878 M 1713-1837 B 1713-1946
SHILLINGFORD C 1577-1837 M 1569-1837 B 1565-1837 [80]
SHIRWELL M 1540-1599 [89]
SHUTE Mfc C 1568-1855 M 1561-1837 B 1563-1883
SIDBURY Mf Ind C 1771-1826 B 1820-1836
SIDMOUTH Mf Marsh Ind C 1815-1836; Presb C 1753-1836 B 1834-1834
STARCROSS 1828-37 [81]
STOCKLAND M(I) 1746-1812 [42] Mfc C 1640-1976 M 1640-1837 B 1640-1858
STOKE DAMEREL Mfc C 1596-1719 1746-1758 1813-1840 M 1596-1734 1746-1754 B 1596-1722 1746-1758 1813-1837; see also DEVONPORT Ind Mt Zion
STOKE FLEMING Mfc C 1538-1602 1639-42 1670-1853 M 1538-1603 1671-1836 B 1539-1627 1670-1863
STOKENHAM C 1578-1591 M 1574-1582 B 1570-1580 [41] Mfc C 1578-1867 M 1574-1837 B 1570-1883 ; with CHIVELSTOKE Mf Ford Ind ZCB 1772-1837
STOKE RIVERS Mfc CB 1553-1812 M 1556-1837
STONEHOUSE French 1692-1791 [HS20]; Mf Emma Place Ind ZC 1794-1836 B 1796-1836; Corpus Christi Ind Z 1833-36; Ebenezer Bapt Z 1833-36
STONEHOUSE, EAST M 1697-1812 [42]
SYDENHAM DAMEREL Mfc C 1540-1870 M 1539-1837 B 1540-1812 (gaps)
TAMERTON FOLIOTT Mfc C 1794-1897 M 1794-1837 B 1794-1850 (gaps)
TAVISTOCK Mfc C 1761-1840 M 1745-1837 B 1761-1856; Mf Abbey Presb ZC 1692-1837; Brook St Cong ZC 1796-1836; Wes ZC 1809-1837 B 1832-1836
TAWSTOCK Mfc C 1805-1893 M 1754-1966 B 1795-1847
TAWTON, NORTH Mfc C Ext 1538-1843 M Ext 1538-1837 B 1538-1868; Mf Ind C 1812-1836
TAWTON, SOUTH Mfc C 1541-1837 M 1558-1837 B 1558-1866
TEIGNMOUTH Mf Ind ZC 1804-1836 B 1809-1830; Wes ZC 1813-1837
THORNBURY 1652-1837 [82]

THURLSTONE Mfc C 1558-1878 M 1558-1837 B 1558-1812
TIVERTON Mf Ind ZC 1766-1837; Newport St Bapt Z 1767-1837 B 1816-1837; Wes C 1812-1837
TOPSHAM* (1600-1837) [20]; Ind C 1808-37; Presb Prot Diss C 1744-1837 B 1771-1837 [20,Mf]; Sfrs Z 1642-1794 M 1665-1719 B 1658-1833 [20]
TORBRYAN Mfc Z 1653-64 C 1715-1812 M 1653-64 1715-1838 M 1653-4 1715-1811
TORMOHAM C 1637-1739 MB 1637-1743 [83] Mfc C 1637-1849 M 1637-1837 B 1637-1842
TORQUAY see also ST MARY CHURCH; Mf Ind C 1809-1836; Presb C 1744-1837 B 1771-1837
TORRE ABBEY Rom Cath Chapel C 1788-1852 D 1788-1848 [107]
TOTNES C 1565-1740 M 1556-1751 B 1556-1735 [88/9]; Mf Fore St Ind ZC 1794-1837
TRENTISHOE* M 1697-1812 [91,GCl]
UFFCULME* M 1538-1837 [91,GCl]; Mf Ind C 1806-1837
UPLYME Mfc C 1710-1841 M 1710-1838 B 1710-1857
UPOTTERY Mfc C 1559-1843 M 1576-1831 B 1559-1862
WARKLEIGH Mfc C 1538-1932 MB 1538-1812
WELCOMBE Mfc C 1777-1812 M 1757-1786 1813-1836 B 1778-1812
WEMBWORTHY Ext 1674-1750 [89]
WERRINGTON* M 1608-(1654-1812) [89,91,GCl]
WESTLEIGH C 1820-1829 M 1812-1837 [44]
WHITCHURCH Mfc C 1560-1860 M 1559-1838 B 1562-1881
WIDECOMBE IN THE MOOR* 1573-1837 [21]
WITHERIDGE 1585-1837 [42,84-86]
WITHYCOMBE RALEIGH M 1562-1600 [88/9]; Plym Breth B 1843-1953 [41]
WOLBOROUGH Mf Providence Ind C 1817-1837
WOODBURY Mf Gulliford Presb C 1773-1828 B 1786-1837
WORLINGTON, EAST C 1725-1884 MB 1725-1850 [47]
WORLINGTON, WEST CM 1693-1850 B 1681-1850 [87]
WOOLFARDISWORTHY, WEST Mfc C 1723-1846 M 1723-1837 B 1723-1885
WYTHYCOMBE RAWLEIGH Mf Ind C 1829-1837
YARNSCOMBE Mfc C 1653-1888 M 1653-1837 B 1653-1812
YEALMPTON 1600-50 [87]

DORSET

ABBOTSBURY C 1574-1704 [19]
AFFPUDDLE M 1731-1837 [83]
ALLINGTON* C 1570-1751 (M 1570-1812) B 1672-1757 [22,28,74]
ALMER* 1538-1812 [81]
ALTON PANCRAS* M 1674-1812 [78]
ARNE M 1763-1840 [83]
ASHMORE CB 1651-1900 M 1651-1838 [59,83,90]
ASKERSWELL* CB 1559-1722 (M 1560-1812) [10,78]
ATHELHAMPTON M 1755-1851 [83,91]
BATCOMBE Ext 1767-1808 [25]
BEAMINSTER* CB 1585-1736 M 1558-(1585-1812)-1837 [12,73,75,85]; Indep ZC 1796-1836
BELCHALWELL see FIFEHEAD NEVILLE
BERE REGIS 1585-1713 [1]
BETTISCOMBE M 1746-1836 [91]

BINCOMBE C 1658-1812 M 1658-1837 B 1658-1813 [24,92]
BISHOPS CAUNDLE 1570-1814 [37] Mf M 1570-1812
BLANDFORD FORUM CB 1732-1883 M 1731-1883 [30/1]; Indep ZC 1760-1836 B 1803-1837 [88]
BLANDFORD ST MARY 1581-1812 [32-34]
BLOXWORTH C 1579-1870 M 1581-1869 B 1579-1869 [35]
BOTHENHAMPTON* M 1636-41 1734-1837 [73]
BRADFORD ABBAS* C 1572-81 [84]
BRADFORD PEVERELL CB 1572-1800 M 1572-1838 [13,83/4]
BRADPOLE* M 1695-1812 [73]
BREDY, LITTLE M 1717-1836 [88]
BREDY, LONG M 1680-1837 [91]
BRIDPORT CB 1600-38 M 1600-80 [8]; Ind New Meeting, Barrack Street C 1751-1837 D 1750-1786 [90]
BROADMAYNE M 1667-1837 [92]
BROADWAY CB 1808-13 M 1673-1837 [24,85]
BROADWINSOR* M 1563-1812 [75]
BRYANSTON C 1598-1899 M 1599-1899 B 1598-1888 [9,29]
BUCKLAND RIPERS CB 1695-1812 M 1695-1840 [16,92]
BURSTOCK* M 1563-1811 [76]
BURTON BRADSTOCK* with SHIPTON GORGE CB 1614-1639 1660-1668 (M 1614-1812) [17,77]
BURTON, LONG 1580-1812 [55]
CANFORD Rom Cath C 1799-1826 [CRS43] see also STAPLE HILL
CANN Ext C 1582-1824 M 1661-1827 B 1582-1775 [22]
CATTISTOCK* CB 1558-1838 M (1558-1812)-1838 [2,36,73]
CAUNDLE MARSH M 1704-1831 [85]
CERNE ABBAS* M (1654-1812)-1841 [75,85]
CERNE, NETHER* M 1716-1744 [78] see also GODMANSTONE
CHALBURY 1629-1700 [13,38]
CHARDSTOCK 1597-1850 [13,39]
CHARLTON MARSHALL 1575-1900 [26]
CHARMINSTER* M 1561-1812 [74]
CHARMOUTH* M 1654-1812 [76]
CHEDINGTON* M 1756-1812 [77,90]
CHELBOROUGH, EAST* M (1690-1812)-1837 [77,91]
CHELBOROUGH, WEST* M 1673-1811 [76]
CHESELBOURNE C 1633-1783 M 1664-1838 B 1653-1784 [3,92]
CHETTLE 1538-1814 [40,80]
CHICKERELL* M 1723-1812 [79]
CHIDEOCK* CB 1652-1700 (M 1654-1812) [20,74]; Rom Cath C 1788-1838 D 1810-1839 [90]
CHILCOMBE M 1748-1828 [90]
CHILFROME* C 1695-1750 M (1709-1811)-1834 B 1678-1750 [3,73,83]
COMBE KEYNES and WOOL C 1585-1811 M 1583-1750 1811 B 1586-1793 1810 [88]
COMPTON ABBAS CB Ext 1538-1798 M Ext 1538-1811 M 1754-1837 [1,83]
COMPTON, NETHER M 1696-1837 [88]
COMPTON, OVER M 1723-1837 [88]
COMPTON VALENCE 1655-1812 [18,92]
COMPTON, WEST C 1538-1798 M 1539-1812 B 1539-1794 [1,88] see also COMPTON ABBAS
CORFE CASTLE C 1653-1889 M 1695-1943 B 1695-1947 [41,91]
CORFE MULLEN C 1651-1840 MB 1652-1840 [42/3,80] see also STURMINSTER MARSHALL
CORSCOMBE* CB 1595-1742 (M 1595-1837) [16,78,83]

CRANBORNE 1602-1837 [6,38,82]

DEWLISH 1610-1647 1652-1812 [21]

DORCHESTER* All Saints CB 1653-1812 M 1654-1836 [14]; Holy Trinity C 1559-1805 (M 1560-1812) B 1559-1799 [15,79]; St Peter CB 1653-1802 M 1653-1812 [4,5]

DURWESTON 1731-1899 [29]

EDMUNDSHAM C 1573-88 M 1573-1645 [7,20]

FIFEHEAD NEVILLE 1573-1711 [80] Ext CB 1703-1800 [88]

FLEET* C 1664-1812 M (1663-1753)-1835 B 1664-1809 [18,78,80,92]

FOLKE M 1538-1837 [90]

FORDINGTON* C 1577-1812 M 1575-(1577-1812) B 1564-1812 [11,76]

FORTUNESWELL see PORTLAND

FRAMPTON 1627-1812 [7]

FROME BILLETT see STAFFORD, WEST

FROME VAUCHURCH* CB Ext 1643-1812 M 1643-(1667-1810) [25,75]

GOATHILL M 1813-37 [80]

GODMANSTONE* M (1654-1812)-1836 [78,92]

GRIMSTONE see STRATTON

GUSSAGE ALL SAINTS 1560-1840 [45]

HALSTOCK* C 1698-1751 1760-1806 1810-12 M (1701-1814)-1837 B 1698-1812 [11,75,91]

HAMMOON Ext C 1662-1764 M 1687-1765 B 1657-1713 [22]

HAMPRESTON CB 1617-53 M 1617-62 [28]

HANFORD C 1669-1812 M 1672-1836B 1671-1864 [88]

HAWKCHURCH* CB 1663-1851 M (1664-1812)-64 [46,74,83]

HAYDON 1711-1812 [13]

HAZELBURY BRYAN 1562-87 Ext 1593-1657 [47]

HERMITAGE Ext CB 1712-1820 M 1712-1849 [25]

HILLFIELD see SYDLING ST NICHOLAS

HOLNEST 1589-1812 [50]

HOLT 1660-653 1836 see also WIMBOURNE MINSTER

HOOK* M 1734-(1771-1812) [74,80]

HORTON 1563-1870 [48/9]

IWERNE COURTNEY C 1562-1900 M 1563-1900 B 1562-1900 [1,51]

KIMMERIDGE M 1702-1837 [83]

KNIGHTON, WEST M 1693-1837 [83]

LANGTON HERRING* CB 1682-1801 (M 1681-1812) [24,78]

LANGTON LONG BLANDFORD 1591-1728 [53]

LANGTON MATRAVERS 1670-1837 [36,54,88]

LEWCOMBE see CHELBOROUGH, EAST

LITTON CHENEY* CB 1614-1770 (M 1614-1812) [17,76]

LODERS* M 1636-1812 [76]

LULWORTH CASTLE* Rom Cath C 1755-1840 [CRS6]

LYDLINCH* 1559-1812 [56] Mf 1559-1812

LYME REGIS* M 1654-1812 [75]

LYTCHETT MATRAVERS CB 1656-1808 M 1657-1753 [10]

MAIDEN NEWTON* CB 1553-1812 (M 1556-1812) [8,76]

MAIDENWELL see PORTLAND

MANSTON 1620-1837 [90]

MAPPERTON* M (1669-1812)-1837 [73,90]

MARGARET MARSH M 1694-1837 [90]

MARNHULL Ext C 1560-1717 M 1561-1726 B 1560-1742; Rom Cath C 1772-1826 [22,CRS56]

MARSHWOOD* CB 1614-1728 M (1614-1673)-1696 [16,77,79,90]

MELCOMBE HORSEY C 1690-1812 M 1696-1815 B 1735-1838 [24]

MILBORNE ST ANDREW 1570-1812 [6]

MILTON ABBEY* M Ext 1569-1812 [73]

MILTON, WEST see POWERSTOCK

MORDEN CM 1575-1691 B 1575-1688 [22]

MORE CRICHELL M 1664-1836 [83]

MOSTERTON see PERROTT SOUTH

MOTCOMBE Ext CB 1676-1787 M 1677-1743 [22]

NETHERBURY* C 1592-1709 (M 1592-1839) B 1592-1692 1813-21 1850-1 [21,28,79,83,88]

OBORNE M 1814-40 [80]

ORCHARD, EAST M 1783-1836 [92]

ORCHARD, WEST M 1754-1839 [83]

OWERMOIGNE 1569-1812 [9]

PENTRIDGE C 1718-1810 M 1713-1835 B 1714-1810 [57,83]

PERROTT, SOUTH* with MOSTERTON M 1539-1812 [76]

PIDDLEHINTON CB 1539-1652 M 1540-1837 [2,85]

PIDDLETOWN* see PUDDLETOWN

PILSDON* M 1754-1809 [77]

PIMPERNE 1559-1900 [22,38]

POOLE Wes C 1809-1840 [87/8]

POORTON, NORTH* M 1698-1812 [73/4]

PORTISHAM C 1568-1733 M 1568-1645 1664-78 1696-1837 B 1568-1730 [9,19,92]

PORTLAND 1591-1803 Prim Meth Fortuneswell C 1858-1971; Wes Meth C 1796-1971 [44,58,89]; Bible Christ/Wes Meth WAKEHAM C 1858-1933; MAIDENWELL C 1920-71 [80]

POWERSTOCK* with MILTON, WEST C 1568-1716 (M 1568-1812) B 1568-1661 Ext C 1719-56 M 1717-50 B 1722-84 [14,73]

PRESTON* cum SUTTON POYNTZ CB 1693-1798 (M 1695-1837) [18,78]

PUDDLETOWN* C 1546-1812 M (1538-1812) B 1538-1812 [23,79,80]

PULHAM C 1734-1837 MB 1734-1902 [60]

PUNCKNOWLE M 1632-1753 [3]

RAMPISHAM* CB 1574-1812 M (1574-1741)-1812 [10,78,80]

SANDFORD ORCAS CB 1538-86 M 1540-86 [80]

SHAFTESBURY Holy Trinity M 1560-1842 [83,92]

SHAPWICK Ext C 1655-1722 M 1656-1732 B 1654-1732 [22]

SHERBORNE Ext CB 1538-1812 M 1538-1754 [18]

SHILLING OCKFORD see SHILLINGSTONE

SHILLINGSTONE 1654-1812 [25,62]

SHIPTON GORGE see BURTON BRADSTOCK

SHROTON see IWERNE COURTNEY

SPETTISBURY 1705-1899 [27]

STAFFORD, WEST with FROME BILLET C 1573-1778 M 1558-1815 B 1558-1766 [38]

STALBRIDGE* M 1691-1812 [76]

STAPLEHILL Rom Cath CB 1770-1859 [CRS43] see also CANFORD

STEEPLETON IWERNE 1755-1945 [29]

STINSFORD C 1631-1812 M 1579-1812 B 1577-1812 [7,20]

STOCK GAYLARD C 1582-1811 M 1567-1838 B 1568-1812 [63,89]

STOCKWOOD C 1586-1849 M 1586-1838 B 1586-1851 [89]

STOKE ABBOTT* M 1560-1837 [78]

STOURPAINE* CB 1631-1799 M 1631-1752 [56]

STOURTON CAUNDLE Ext C 1670-1721 M 1670-1763 [1]

STOWER, EAST* M 1584-1812 [78]

STRATTON and GRIMSTONE 1561-1812 [13]
STURMINSTER MARSHALL* 1563-1812 [64,80]
SUTTON POYNTZ* see PRESTON cum SUTTON
POYNTZ
SUTTON WALDRON M 1754-1779 Banns 1759-1781
[91]
SWANAGE* 1563-1812 [65]
SWYRE* C 1587-1794 (M 1588-1837) B 1588-1803
[1,78]
SYDLING ST NICHOLAS and HILLFIELD 1565-1812 [24]
SYMONDSBURY* C 1558-1739 (M 1558-1812) B 1558-
1626 [10,74]
TARRANT CRAWFORD C 1597-1936 M 1599-1935 B
1597-1940 [29]
TARRANT GUNVILLE 1719-1919 [27,67]
TARRANT HINTON* 1545-1812 [66,56]
TARRANT KEYNSTON 1737-1939 [29]
TARRANT RAWSTON C 1814-1931 M 1760-1921 B
1815-94 [61]
TARRANT RUSHTON C 1696-1919 M 1698-1919 N
1697-1919 [61]
THORNCOMBE* C 1551-1840 M (1552-1812)-50 B 1551-
1840 [69,74]
THORNFORD* CB 1677-1812 M 1677-1754 [68]
TINCLETON 1576-1812 [17]
TOLLER, GREAT* M 1615-1812 [75] see also TOLLER
PORCORUM
TOLLER PORCORUM 1615-80 [13,28] see TOLLER,
GREAT
TURNERS PUDDLE M 1745-1837 [83]
TURNWORTH 1577-1684 [6]
UPCERNE* M 1682-1811 [75]
UP-WIMBORNE 1589-1689 (united with Wimborne St
Giles 1732)
WAKEHAM see PORTLAND
WALDITCH* M 1738-1812 [73]
WAMBROOK M 1655-1837 [89]
WARMWELL 1641-1754 [24]
WHITCHURCH CANONICORUM* CB 1558-1728 (M
1583-1812) [16,77]
WIMBORNE All Saints see UP-WIMBORNE
WIMBORNE ST GILES 1594-1685 M 1800-1837 [83,89]
WIMBORNE MINSTER 1635-72 1721-1812 [70/1]
WINFRITH NEWBURGH C 1585-1750 MB 1585-1742
[7,89]
WINTERBOURNE ABBAS C 1792-1812 M 1754-1837
[19]
WINTERBOURNE ANDERSON M 1813-37 [80]
WINTERBOURNE CAME 1696-1837 [19]
WINTERBOURNE STEEPLETON 1558-1812 [20]
WINTERBOURNE STICKLAND CM 1615-1750 B 1615-78
[1]
WINTERBOURNE TOMSON C 1770-1893 M 1767-1890
B 1769-1797 [35]
WINTERBOURNE ZELSTONE Ext C 1548-1692 M 1565-
1697 B 1551-1740 [22]
WOODSFORD C 1678-1812 M 1681-1826 B 1678-1811
[25]
WOOL see COOMBE KEYNES
WOOTTON FITZPAINE* M 1677-1812 [78]
WOOTTON GLANVILLE 1546-1731 [7]
WOOTTON, NORTH 1539-1786 M 1813-37 [72]
WORTH MATRAVERS 1584-1696 [17]
WRAXALL* CB 1648-1709 M 1648-(1710-1807)-1811
[13,75]
WYKE REGIS* (M 1676-1812); SFrs B 1703-12 [77,M14]
YETMINSTER Ext 1579-1621 [89]

DURHAM

Stray marriages : Northumberland and Durham [NU/R
56]

AUCKLAND ST ANDREW Mf C 1558-1801 M 1558-1754
1892-1907 B 1558-1864
AUCKLAND ST HELEN M 1593-1837 [76]
AYCLIFFE CB 1560-1812 M 1560-1837 [1-4,72] Mf C
1560-1885 MB 1560-1812 BARNARD CASTLE C
1813-37 M 1619-1837 B 1813-1837 [5,6,81]
BARNARD CASTLE Mf C 1609-1829 M 1619-1753 B
1617-1812
BEAMISHC 1876-1897 [89]
BILLINGHAM Mf C 1911-29 M 1754-1946
BIRTLEY M(I) 1850-1910 [92]
BISHOP MIDDLEHAM* C(M)B 1559-1812 M 1813-1837
[7,8,72]
BISHOP WEARMOUTH M 1568-1837 [9]; Rom Cath
Mission C 1794-1834 M 1825-1852 [28,88]
BISHOPTON M 1653-80 1763-1837 [87] Mf C 1653-1965
M 1653-1753 1784-1945 B 1654-1908
BOLDON M 1579-1837 [71] M(I) 1837-1814 [71,92]
BRANCEPETH M 1599-1837 [72]
CASTLE EDEN* (C 1661-1812) M (1698-1794)-1837 (B
1696-1812) [10,72] Mf C 1813-1871
CHESTER LE STREET M 1582-1663 1673-78 1708-1837
[11]
COCKFIELD C 1813-40 M 1579-1837 B 1807-40 [12,72]
CONISCLIFFE* (CB 1590-1812 M 1590-1812)-37 [13,72]
CROXDALE M 1732-1837 [73]
DALTON LE DALE* (1653-1812)-37 [14,71,GCI]
DARLINGTON St Cuthbert Mf C 1590-1953 M 1590-1912
B 1590-1856
DENTON M 1579-1837 [73]
DINSDALE* (1556-1813) M 1814-1837 [15,73]
DUMLEY M(I) 1862-1912 [89]
DURHAM* Cathedral 1609-1896 [16,73]; St Giles M
1584-1837 [17]; St Margaret M (1558-1812)-37
[17,18,19]; St Mary le Bow (1571-1812) M 1813-
1837 [17,20,21]; St Mary, South Bailey (1559-1812)
M 1813-1842 [17,22]; St Nicholas CB 1540-1812 M
(1540-1812)-1837 [17,23-27]; St Oswald 1538-1837
[17,29] with SHINCLIFFE M 1827-1837 [17]; St
Cuthbert Rom Cath C 1739-1841 M 1739-1840
[85,88,90]; St Mary Jesuit Chapel C 1768-1824 [88];
Rom Cath Missions: see SHERBURN HOSPITAL
EAGLESCLIFFE M 1540-1837 [73]
EASINGTON M 1570-1837 [71]
EBCHESTER* (CB 1619-1812) M (1619-1812)-37
[30,69,73]
EDMUNDBYERS M 1764-1840 [69,73]
EGGLESTON CB 1795-1840 [78,89]
EIGHTON BANKS M(I) 1863-1922 [89]
ELTON M 1534-1837 [73]
ELWICK HALL 1592-1900 [31,32,73]
EMBLETON M 1650-1760 [73]
ESCOMB M 1543-1837 [73]
ESH 1567-1812 M(I) 1813-1837 [33,69] Mf C 1813-1877
ETHERLEY see also DINSDALE and AUCKLAND ST
HELEN
GAINFORD C 1560-1784 M 1569-1837 B 1569-1784
[34,35,73]

GATESHEAD M 1559-1837 [36] Mf St Mary 1559-1587
CM 1608-1960 B 1608-1889
GATESHEAD FELL M 1825-37 M(I) 1837-1917 [74,89]
GREATHAM M 1564-1837 [74]
GRINDON M 1565-1837 [74]
HAGGERSTON CASTLE Rom Cath Mf C 1786-1840
HAMSTERLEY M 1580-1837 [74]; Bapt C 1729-1848
Deaths 1771-1848 [NU/R32]
HARDWICK Rom Cath C 1743-47 [85,90]
HART Mf C 1577-1856 M 1577-1934 B 1577-1884
HARTLEPOOL St Hilda 1566-1837 [37-9]; St Paul Mf C
1883-1909; Prim Meth Brougham Street C 1834-97
[79]
HARTON (South Shields) M(I) 1867-1920 [92]
HARTON COLLIERY (All Ss Boldon Lane) M(I) 1890-
1907 [92]
HEATHERY CLEUGH M 1828-37 [74] see also
STANHOPE
HEDWORTH M(I) 1882-1910 [87]
HEIGHINGTON M 1570-1837 [74] Mf C 1585-1894 M
1571-1837 B 1559-1847
HETTON LE HOLE M 1832-37 [71]
HEWORTH M 1696-1837 [41]
HOUGHTON LE SPRING* (Ext 1563-1812) [40,41] M
1653-1837 [41]
HUNSTANWORTH C 1659-1851 M 1693-1851 B 1672-
1851 [69,90]
HURWORTH ON TEES 1559-1799 M 1800-1837 [42-
4,74]
IRESHOPEBURN Presb C 1766-1822 [85,90]
JARROW CB 1813-37 M 1568-1837 [45]; St Paul M(I)
1837-1900 [92]; St Peter M(I) 1881-1923 [87]; St
Mark M(I) 1896-1948 [87] see also HEWORTH
JARROW GRANGE Christ Church M(I) 1869-1900 [87];
Good Shepherd M(I) 1893-1949 [87]
KELLOE CM 1693-1837 [71,84]
KIRK MERRINGTON see MERRINGTON
LAMESLEY M 1603-1837 [75]
LANCHESTER* (1560-1603) M 1604-1837 [46,69,70] see
also SATLEY
MEDOMSLEY M 1608-1837 [69,75]
MERRINGTON M 1579-1837 [75] Mf C 1813-1944 M
1787-1812 B 1787-1814
MIDDLETON in TEESDALE C 1753-1837 M 1621-1837 B
1753-1840 [47,75]
MIDDLETON ST GEORGE* (C 1652-1812 MB 1616-
1812) [48,75,GCI] Mf Banns 1824-29 1939-72 B
1813-1903
MONK HESLEDON M 1592-1837 [76]; Rom Cath
(Hardwick & Hutton Homes) Mf B 1808-1839
MONKWEARMOUTH M Ext 1683-1790 M(I) 1790-1837
[55]
MUGGLESWICK* CB (1784-1812) M (1784-1812)-46
[49,69,75,85,90]
NEWTON, LONG M 1564-1837 [75] Mf C 1564-1952 M
1564-1837 B 1564-1812
PENSHAW M 1754-1837 [71]
PITTINGTON M 1575-1837 [71]
RAINTON, WEST M 1827-37 [71]
REDMARSHALL M 1560-1837 [76]
RYTON* M (1581-1812) (I) 1813-37 [50,66,69] see also
WINLATON
SADBERGE Mf C 1662-1907 M 1663-1959 B 1662-1910
SAINT HELEN'S AUCKLAND see AUCKLAND ST HELEN
SATLEY* (CB 1560-1812 M 1560-1812)-37 [51,69,76]
see also LANCHESTER
SEAHAM* (C 1646-1812 M 1652-1812)-37 (B 1653-1812)

[52,71]
SEDGEFIELD M 1581-1837 [76]
SHERBURN HOSPITAL* (C 1692-1812 M 1695-1763 B
1678-1812) [53,77]; Rom Cath Secular Mission C
1739-1839 M 1739-69 1800-41 [28,88]; Rom Cath
Jesuit Mission C 1768-1807 [28,88]
SHIELDS, SOUTH Holy Trinity B(I) 1835-1917 [90]; St
Aidan M(I) 1888-1910 [80]; St Hilda M(I) 1653-1901
[54/5,78,80] Mf B 1746-1812; St Jude M(I) 1887-
1914 [80]; St Mark M(I) 1875-1902 [91]; St Mary
(Jarrow Dock) M(I) 1864-1904 [91]; St Michael M(I)
1883-1908 [80]; St Simon M(I) 1880-1910 [91]; St
Stephen M(I) 1848-1903 [91]; St Thomas M(I) 1864-
1962 [87]; Presb Mf C 1786-1857
SHILDON M 1834-37 [77]
SHINCLIFFE see DURHAM (St Oswald)
SOCKBURN M 1580-1837 [77]
STAINDROP C 1813-1840 M 1635-1837 B 1807-1840
[56,77]
STAINTON, GREAT M 1561-1837 [77] Mf C 1562-1958
M 1561-1944 B 1561-1975
STANHOPE* M (1613-1812)-37 [46,57] Mf C 1609-1786
M 1614-1772 B 1607-1780
STELLA St Thomas Aquinas Rom Cath C 1768-1825 M
1776-1797 D 1775-1783 [28,88]
STOCKTON St Mark Mf M 1966-78; St Peter Mf C 1943-
62 M 1940-46; St Thomas Mf C 1637-1942 M 1637-
1943 Banns 1937-58 B 1637-1935; St James Mf C
1899-1957 M 18798-1902 Banns 1929-53
STRANTON 1580-1837 [58]
SUNDERLAND Holy Trinity M(I) 1719-1837 [59]; Old
Meeting or Corn Market Chap Mf C 1765-1837
SWALWELL Presb Mf C 1733-1836
TANFIELD M 1719-1837 [46,69]
TRIMDON M 1721-1837 [77]
UNSWORTH see WASHINGTON
WASHINGTON M(I) 1603-1900 [87,89]; with
UNSWORTH 1835-41 [87]
WEARDALE SAINT JOHN M 1828-37 [77] see also
STANHOPE
WHICKHAM* C 1576-1754 M (1579-1812)-1837 [60-
63,69]
WHITBURN* (C 1611-1812) M (1579-1812)-1904 B 1579-
1812 [63/4,83,87]
WHITWORTH M 1569-1837 [77] Mf C 1569-1860 M
1569-1954 B 1569-1958
WHORLTON* C (1626-1812)-1982 M (1669-1812)-1968 B
(1669-1812)-1982 [28,65,77,88/9]
WINLATON M(I) 1833-37 [66,69] see also RYTON
WINSTON* CB (1572-1812)-1840 M (1572-1812)-37
[28,67,77,88]
WITTON GILBERT M 1568-1837 [63]; Mf C 1571-1714 M
1570-1714 1754-1812 B 1570-1715; Rom Cath with
Bishop Auckland C 1768-1794 [28,88]
WITTON LE WEAR C1558-1734 M 1558-1837 B 1558-
1732 [63,68]
WOLSINGHAM M 1655-1837 [46]
WOLVISTON Mf C 1759-1953 M 1763-1780 1860-1965 B
1869-1936 see also BILLINGHAM

18

ESSEX

ABBERTON M 1754-1851 [92,94]
ABBESS RODING/ROOTHING M 1756-1812 [99]
ALDHAM M 1755-1851 [92,94]
ALPHAMSTONE CB 1705-1812 M 1707-1837 [141]
ALRESFORD M 1743-1851 [98,104]
ALTHORNE CB 1813-99 M 1800-99 [3,101] Mf CB
1813-1929 M 1800-1929
ARDLEIGH M 1754-1851 [92]
ARKESDEN C 1690-1812 M 1690-1837 [165]
ASHDON* CB 1558-1755 (M 1557-1812)-1837
[1,93,112,141,164] Mf C 1557-1755 M 1557-1837 B
1553-1755
ASHELDHAM CM 1721-1937 B 1722-1935 [2]
ASHEN M 1754-1851 [93,100,156]
ASHINGDON M 1804-35 [104]
AVELEY M 1813-36 [92]
AYTHORPE RODING/ROOTHING M 1560-1837
[102,156] Mf C 1559-1644 M 1560-1642 B
1560-1644
BADDOW, GREAT M 1754-1851 [93]
BADDOW, LITTLE CB 1559-1788 M 1559-1783
1812-1851 [4,104,106] Mf CB 1559-1789 M
1559-1783
BARDFIELD, GREAT C 1662-1876 M 1662-1837 B
1662-1859 [5,92]
BARDFIELD, LITTLE C 1539-1876 M 1538-1837 B
1538-1958 [6]
BARDFIELD SALING C 1561-1812 M 1561-1839
[102,162]
BARKING M 1754-1837 [102]; SoF B 1826-1878 [170]
BARNSTON M 1539-1837 [103,156]
BASILDON M 1813-51 [104]
BEAUMONT CUM MOZE* (C 1564-1678 M 1567-1677)
M 1754-1837 (B 1564-1678) [7,97]
BEAUCHAMP ROOTHING M 1754-1811 [99]
BELCHAMP WALTER C 1559-1757 M 1560-1837 B
1560-1757 [103,142] Mf C 1559-1812 M 1560-1753
B 1560-1812
BELCHAMP OTTEN CB 1578-1812 M 1578-1837 [142]
BELCHAMP ST PAUL C 1538-1778 M 1538-1837 B
1538-1800 [138]
BENFLEET, NORTH M 1814-1851 [105]
BENFLEET, SOUTH M 1754-1837 [93]
BENTLEY, GREAT M 1678-1854 [93,102]
BENTLEY, LITTLE M 1754-1851 [92,104]
BERDEN M 1754-1838 [93]
BERECHURCH CB 1664-1812 M 1664-1837 [8] Mf C
1664-1741 1767-1812 M 1664-1740 1769-1837 B
1664-1740 1767-1812
BERGHOLT, WEST M 1754-1851 [99]
BERNERS RODING/ROOTHING C 1590-1812 M
1589-1837 [99,104,156]
BIRCH M 1754-1837 [95]
BIRCHANGER CM 1688-1837 [156]
BIRDBROOK CB 1635-1783 M 1633-1836 [143]
BLACKMORE M 1755-1851 [100] Mf C 1602-1812
BOBBINGWORTH CB 1559-1785 M 1559-1851 [9,94]
BOCKING M 1655-1851 [103,118]
BOREHAM M 1767-1837 [100]
BORLEY CB 1652-1806 M 1709-1836 B 1656-1806 [10]
Mf C 1652-1806 M 1709-54 B 1656-1806
BOWERS GIFFORD M 1814-1851 [105]
BOXTED* M (1559-1837)-51 [101,112]

BRADFIELD M 1837-51 [104]
BRADWELL ON SEA M 1558-1879 [11] Mf 1558-1879
BRADWELL Coggeshall M 1755-1837 [96]
BRAINTREE C 1660-1812 M 1664-1852 [102,119,120]
BRAXTED, GREAT M 1754-1811 [98]
BRAXTED, LITTLE M 1730-1851 [98,104]
BRENTWOOD M 1838-1851 [105]
BRIGHTLINGSEA M 1754-1851 [95,101]
BROMLEY, LITTLE Mf C 1538-44 M 1539-92
BROMLEY, GREAT M 1754-1839 [101] Mf C 1559-1735
M 1559-1729 B 1725-30
BROOMFIELD M 1754-1842 [106]
BROXTED M 1801-51 [103]
BULMER M 1754-1837 [92] Mf CB 1559-1803 M
1558-1701 1735-53
BULPHAN M 1755-1811 [96]
BURNHAM ON CROUCH 1559-1870 [13,14,15] M(I)
1559-1837 [140] Mf C 1559-1870 M 1559-98
1621-1753 1775-1870 B 1559-99 1620-1871
BURSTEAD, LITTLE C 1681-1837 M 1679-1837 B
1678-1837 [96,153]
BURSTEAD, GREAT CB 1559-1654 M 1559-1837
[19,100]
BUTTSBURY M 1725-1837 Mf C 1657-1803 M 1669-1762
B 1668-1802
CANEWDON 1636-1899 [12]
CANFIELD, LITTLE C 1565-1603 1615-1634 1649-1725
1729-1812 M 1561-1642 1662-1837 [156]
CANFIELD, GREAT C 1565-1812 M 1561-1837
[92,106,156] Mf C 1538-1778 M 1539-1778 B 1539-
1731
CHAPEL M 1754-1838 [93]
CHELMSFORD* (M 1538-1837)-1851 CB 1813-38
[16,106,113,114] Mf St Mary CB 1538-1812 M 1539-
1753
CHESTERFORD, GREAT C 1586-1775 M 1586-1837
[100,104,156] Mf CB 1586-1812 M 1586-1754
CHESTERFORD, LITTLE C 1559-1812 M 1559-1866
[100,104,156] Mf CB 1559-1812 M 1559-1754
CHICKNEY C 1554-1812 M 1556-1943 [101,155] Mf C
1557-1810 M 1556-1811 B 1556-1808
CHIGNALL SMEALEY M 1755-1851 [99] Mf Ext CB
1600-1812 M 1650-1748
CHIGNALL ST JAMES M 1813-36 1838-51 [92,98] Mf C
1723-1810 M 1725-83 B 1776-1812 see also
MASHBURY
CHIGWELL C 1555-1850 M 1555-1853 [17/8] Mf C
1555-1850 M 1555-1853 B 1555-1864
CHILDERDITCH* M 1754-1851 [97] Mf C 1538-1710 M
1538-1668 B 1538-1710
CHINGFORD 1639-40 1790-1812 M 1813-51 [103,153]
CHIPPING ONGAR CB 1558-1750 M 1558-1750 1754-
1851 [20,94]
CHISHALL, GREAT M 1801-37 [101]
CHISHALL, LITTLE M 1577-1813 1658-1837 1721-1835
[106,155,168]
CHRISHALL C 1687-1709 M 1801-37 B 1687-1714
[103,155]
CLACTON, LITTLE M 1754-1851 [101]
CLACTON, GREAT (with LITTLE HOLLAND) 1542-1552
CB 1560-1837 M 1560-1851 [21,99]
CLAVERING C 1554-1755 M 1554-1754 1801-51
[106,157,170] Mf M 1554-1754
COGGESHALL M 1754-1851 [103]

19

COLCHESTER All Saints M 1754-1812 [105]; Holy
Trinity CB 1696-1812 M 1696-1851 [22,98]; St
Botolph M 1849-51 [95]; St Giles M 1749-1851 [98];
St James M 1754-1812 [106]; St Leonard 1754-1851
[101]; St Martin M 1750-1851 [98]; St Mary Magd M
1750-1851 [97,106]; St Mary at Walls M 1754-1851
[95]; St Nicholas M 1754-1812 [105]; St Peter 1754-
1851 [96]; St Runwald M 1762-1811 [106]; Dutch C
1654-1728
COLD NORTON 1539-1869 [23]; Mf CB 1539-1810 M
1539-1838
COLNE ENGAINE M 1754-1840 [97]
COPFORD M 1754-1851 [96]
CORRINGHAM M 1760-1837 [95,101]
CRANHAM M 1559-1851 [102,151]
CREEKSEA 1753-1899 [24,102]
CRESSING Mf M 1754-82
CRONDON PARK Rom Cath C 1770-1831 B 1654-1831
[CRS6]
DAGENHAM M 1754-1851 [106]
DANBURY CB 1673-1837 M 1705-1837 [98,167]
DEBDEN C 1556-1795 M 1556-1837
DEDHAM M 1813-51 [103] Mf C 1560-1905 M 1560-1890
B 1560-1894
DENGIE 1550-1930 [26,35,102]
DODDINGHURST M 1754-1851 [93] Mf CB 1560-1812 M
1560-1752
DONYLAND, WEST see BERECHURCH
DOVERCOURT M 1755-1851 [101]
DOWNHAM M 1754-1851 [92,98]
DUNMOW, LITTLE CB 1549-1770 M 1551-1851 [1,106]
Mf C 1549-1897 M 1550-1682 1696-1943 B 1549-
1684 1696-1812
DUNMOW, GREAT C 1538-1751 M 1558-1851 B 1558-
1751 [98,121-3,150]; Ind Mf C 1733-1769 1800-1837
EARLS COLNE M 1754-1851 [94]
EASTER, HIGH C 1657-1812 M 1654-1837 B 1654-78
[102,158,170]
EASTHORPE M 1838-1851 [104]
EASTON, LITTLE C 1559-1812 [102,157] Mf 1559-1812 Ext
1813-1931
EASTON, GREAT C 1561-1812 M 1561-1851 [92,124]
EASTWOOD M 1755-1851 [93]
ELMDON C 1618-1802 M 1618-42 1670-1837 [175]
ELMSTEAD M 1754-1851 [92,94]
ELSENHAM C 1732-1812 M 1731-1836 [157] Mf C 1731-
1812 M 1731-1836 B 1731-1804
EPPING M 1754-1851 [104,105] Mf 1538-1812
FAIRSTEAD C 1538-1840 MB 1539-1840 [70]
FAMBRIDGE, NORTH 1556-1900 [28,93]
FAMBRIDGE, SOUTH M 1754-1837 [92]
FAULKBOURN(E) CB 1574-1704 M 1576-1660 1755-
1812 [29,98] Mf C 1574-1703 M 1576-1660 B 1575-
1704
FEERING M 1754-1851 [98]
FELSTEAD M 1754-1837 [101,106]
FINCHINGFIELD 1617-1837 M 1837-1851 [100,116/7]
FORDHAM M 1754-1839 [95]
FOULNESS M 1754-1836 [92,95] Mf 1695-1812
FOXEARTH M 1754-1812 [93]
FRATING M 1754-1851 [93] Mf C 1560-1694 1708-1812
M 1560-1753 B 1560-1684 1708-1812
FRINTON M 1762-1829 [104]
FRYERNING M 1754-1851 [95]
FYFIELD CB 1538-1700 M 1538-1700 1754-1837 [30,94]
GOLDHANGER M 1754-1836 [97]
GOOD EASTER C 1539-1803 M 1539-1837 [102,155]
GOSFIELD CB 1538-1812 M 1538-1851 [1,96,139]

GRAYS THURROCK M 1755-1851 [103]
GREENSTEAD Colchester M 1754-1851 [103]
GREENSTEAD Ongar CB 1562-1812 M 1562-1835
[31,93]
HADLEIGH C 1653-1840 MB 1568-1840 [32,93]
HADSTOCK C 1559-1786 M 1558-1837 [102,157]
HALLINGBURY, GREAT M 1801-37 [102]
HALLINGBURY, LITTLE M 1754-1837 [105] Mf M 1710-
53
HALSTEAD M 1564-1851 [94,125] Mf C 1564-1859 M
1564-1837 B 1564-1678 1713-1840
HAM, EAST M 1803-51 [92]
HAM, WEST M(I) 1653-1847 [87]
HANNINGFIELD, SOUTH M 1654-1837 [101]
HANNINGFIELD, WEST M 1787-1837 [101] Mf CB 1558-
1812 M 1558-1787
HANNINGFIELD, EAST M 1754-1837 [105,154] Mf C
1540-1812 M 1539-1753 B 1538-1812
HARLOW 1629-31 1639-40 1706-7 M 1754-1851
[19,104,110]
HARWICH M 1754-1851 [102,105]; Wes C 1837-1968
[33]
HATFIELD PEVERELL C 1614-1721 M 1673-1721 B
1626-1721 [10]
HATFIELD BROAD OAK Mf M 1662-1753
HAWKWELL M 1752-1851 [93]
HAZELEIGH C 1590-1952 M 1734-1921 B 1590-1986
[103,153,170] Mf C 1575-1812 M 1589-1812
HELIONS BUMPSTEAD CB 1558-1812 M 1559-1851
[40,97,144]
HEMPSTEAD M 1664-1748 1754-1812 [93/4,102]
HENHAM C 1539-1812 M 1539-1837 [158]
HENNY, GREAT C 1688-1945 M 1695-1945 B 1678-1945
[23,143] Mf C 1688-1945 M 1695-1945 B 1678-1945
HEYBRIDGE M 1754-1851 [93]
HEYDON C 1538-1755 M 1540-1837 [103,166]
HOCKLEY C 1732-1761 1768-1814 M 1754-1812 B 1768-
1814 [12,92]
HOLLAND, GREAT M 1754-1837 [105]
HOLLAND, GREAT see CLACTON, GREAT
HORKESLEY, GREAT* M 1558-1837 [112]
HORKESLEY, LITTLE* M (1568-1835)-51 [101,112]
HORNCHURCH M 1754-1851 [99] Mf CB 1576-1812 M
1576-1753
HORNDON ON THE HILL M 1754-1851 [97]
HORNDON, WEST M 1742-1851 [101]
HORNDON, EAST M 1754-1851 [101] Mf C 1558-1804 M
1557-1686 1704-54 B 1558-1679 1704-1811
ILFORD, LITTLE M 1755-1834 [76] Mf C 1813-1875
INGATESTONE CB 1732-1803 M 1754-1851 [34,94,153]
Mf C 1558-1803 M 1558-1732 B 1558-1777
INGRAVE M 1679-1851 [101]
INWORTH M 1754-1837 [96]
KELVEDON HATCH M 1561-1836 [25]
KELVEDON M 1755-1837 [95] Mf C 1558-1880 M 1558-
1907 B 1559-1900
KIRBY LE SOKEN M 1754-1851 [105]
LAINDON M 1755-1851 [97,104]
LAMARSH C 1555-1812 M 1556-1837 B Ext 1556-1720
[145]
LAMBOURNE C 1582-1840 MB 1584-1840 [34]
LANGDON HILLS M 1754-1834 [104]
LANGENHOE M 1796-1851 [95]
LANGFORD M 1754-1836 [96]
LANGHAM M 1754-1851 [105] Mf C 1639-1950 M 1638-
1969 B 1638-1979
LANGLEY C 1678-1812 M 1690-1812 [102,158]

LATCHINGDON cum SNOREHAM M 1725-1837 [35,96]
LATTON M 1683-1851 [92,100]
LAVER, HIGH M 1754-1838 [94]
LAVER, LITTLE M 1813-38 [94]
LAWFORD M 1755-1851 [100]
LAYER BRETON M 1755-1838 [95]
LAYER DE LA HAYE M 1755-1851 [92,94,104]
LAYER MARNEY M 1754-1851 [95]
LEIGH ST CLEMENT C 1684-1812 M 1691-1851 B 1685-1812 [93,104,154]
LEIGHS, GREAT* M 1560-1837 [115]
LEIGHS, LITTLE* M 1680-1837 [115]
LEXDEN M 1754-1812 [100] Mf 1560-1656
LEYTON C 1695-1706 1783-1832 M 1574-1681 1754-1851 B 1726-1837 [36-39,97,154]
LINDSELL CB 1568-1812 M 1568-1837 [40,93,162]
LISTON CB 1599-1812 M 1602-1837 [10,104,163]
LITTLEBURY C 1545-1775 M 1545-1837 [163]
LOUGHTON C 1674-1839 M 1674-1765 1801-37 B 1831-40 [41,42,101]
MAGDALEN LAVER M 1754-1836 [94]
MALDON C males 1751-1812 M 1754-1837 [43,92] Mf All Ss & St Peter (I) C 1695-1813 M 1754-1812 B 1750-1813
MANNINGTREE M 1754-1851 [100] see also MISTLEY
MANUDEN C 1561-1812 M 1564-1837 [163]
MAPLESTEAD, PARVA C 1690-1812 M 1691-1813 B 1688-1812 [145]
MAPLESTEAD MAGNA C 1688-1812 M 1697-1812 B 1678-1812 [145,158]
MARGARET RODING/ROOTHING C 1538-1664 M 1541-1851 [97,154]
MARGARETTING M 1754-1851 [99]
MARKS TEY M 1754-1851 [99] Mf C 1560-1812 M 1562-1753 B 1560-1812
MARKSHALL M 1755-1851 [96]
MASHBURY M 1755-1851 [98,106]; with CHIGNALL ST JAMES Mf C 1539-1804 M 1540-1753 B 1546-1812
MATCHING M 1754-1851 [106]
MAYLAND M 1754-1837 [92]
MERSEA, EAST Mf M 1725-55
MESSING M 1754-1837 [95]
MIDDLETON C 1700-1851 M 1700-1808 B 1700-1807 [102,146]
MILE END Colchester M 1754-1851 [104]
MISTLEY C 1755-1812 M 1754-1851 [90,103] with MANNINGTREE Mf 1559-1812
MORETON CB 1558-1759 M 1558-1836 [45,94]
MOUNT BURES M 1754-1837 [92,94]
MOUNTNESSING M 1754-1851 [99] Mf 1653-1812
MOZE* C 1549-1678 M 1557-1674 B 1558-1678 [46] see also BEAUMONT
MUCKING M 1801-51 [104]
MUNDON 1741-1940 [12,47] Mf C 1741-1940 MB 1741-1939
NAVESTOCK* M (1538-1812)-37 [97,112] Mf CB 1538-1812 M 1538-1791
NETTESWELL M 1755-1836 [97] Mf M 1558-1753
NEVENDON M 1755-1851 [98,104]
NEWPORT CB 1558-1812 M 1559-1851 [48,102,164]
NORTON MANDEVILLE M 1779-1836 [92]
NOTLEY, BLACK M 1570-1851 [92,102,103]
NOTLEY, WHITE M 1837-51 [106] Mf 1538-1932
OAKLEY, GREAT M 1754-1851 [103]
OAKLEY, LITTLE 1558-1678 M 1754-1837 [104,154]
OCKENDEN, SOUTH M 1754-1851 [104]
ONGAR, CHIPPING see CHIPPING ONGAR

ONGAR, HIGH M 1743-1836 [94]
ORSETT M 1670-1812 [96,103]
OVINGTON M 1755-1836 [104]
PANFIELD CB 1570-1711 M 1570-1838 [106,162]
PARNDON, LITTLE M 1755-1809 [97] Mf M 1622-1744
PARNDON, GREAT CB 1547-1862 M 1548-1836 [49,97]
PATTISWICK M 1755-1837 [96]
PEBMARSH M 1654-1837 [159]
PELDON C 1724-63 M 1724-1812 B 1728-62 [19,99]
PENTLOW C 1539-1814 M 1539-1836 B 1539-1812 [103,146]
PITSEA C 1688-1840 M 1688-1851 B 1738-1840 [50,92,106]
PLESHEY C 1656-1696 1710-1812 M 1657-1851 [95,159]
PRITTLEWELL* 1645-1812 [51]
PURLEIGH C 1669-1919 M 1690-1919 B 1593-1919 [52,96]
QUENDON 1687-1860 [54,159]
RADWINTER C 1638-1642 1660-1812 [159]
RAINHAM C 1570-1630 1665-1846 M 1583-86 1666-1722 1724-49 1755-1851 B 1579-97 1623-64 1666-1859 [100,106,160,161]
RAMSDEN BELLHOUSE M 1565-1753 1755-1851 [49,103,106]
RAMSDEN GREYS M 1754-1837 [94]
RAMSEY M 1754-1837 [98]
RAWRETH M 1754-1812 [93]
RAYLEIGH M 1754-1851 [92,105]
RAYNE C 1538-1812 M 1538-1851 [106,159]
RETTENDON M 1754-1837 [95]
RICKLING C 1660-1860 M 1663-1860 B 1662-1860 [55]
RIDGEWELL M 1745-1837 [96]
RIVENHALL M 1754-1851 [104]
ROCHFORD M 1680-1851 [94]
RODING/ROOTHING, HIGH M 1538-1838 [99,163]
RODING/ROOTHING, LEADEN M 1574-1851 [104]
RODING/ROOTHING THE see also ABBESS; AYTHORPE; BEAUCHAMP; MARGARET; WHITE
ROMFORD M 1754-37 [104,106] Mf B 1746-1812
ROXWELL* M 1559-1837 [115] Mf C 1558-1812 M 1559-1753 B 1559-1812
ROYDON M 1754-1836 [101]
RUNWELL M 1755-1837 [95]
SAFFRON WALDEN C 1558-1793 M 1559-1837 B 1558-1793 [57,58,105,126-132]; Bapt 1827-37 [19]
ST LAWRENCE 1704-1899 [35,56,93]
ST MARY MALDON M 1754-1851 [99]
ST OSYTH M 1754-1837 [104]
SALING, BARDFIELD see BARDFIELD SALING
SALING, GREAT M 1715-1812 M 1715-1837 [102,162]
SALING, LITTLE see BARDFIELD SALING
SAMPFORD, LITTLE M 1754-1837 [94]
SAMPFORD, GREAT M 1559-1812 [102]
SHALFORD 1558-1837 [59,98]
SHEERING M 1754-1837 [97]
SHELLEY M 1813-36 [94]
SHELLOW BOWELLS C 1555-1812 M 1553-1837 [102,162] Mf CB 1555-1783 M 1553-1778
SHENFIELD C 1538-1812 M 1754-1851 B 1539-1812 [60,97,98]
SHOEBURY, NORTH M 1687-1837 [96]
SHOEBURY, SOUTH M 1754-1851 [93]
SHOPLAND M 1742-1836 [93]
SIBLE HEDINGHAM M 1599-1851 [103,165] Mf C 1560-1897 M 1599-1903 B 1560-1892
SOUTHCHURCH 1695-1899 [61,104]
SOUTHMINSTER 1700-1840 M 1838-51 [62,63,104]

SPRINGFIELD M 1797-1851 [104,106]
STAMBOURNE C 1559-1812 M 1569-1837 B 1569-1812 [49,103,147]
STAMBRIDGE, LITTLE M 1752-1851 [101,106]
STAMBRIDGE, GREAT M 1754-1836 [106]
STAN(E)SGATE see STEEPLE WITH STANSGATE
STANFORD RIVERS M 1837-51 [102] Mf CB 1538-1744 1775-1812 M 1538-1744 1754-1837
STANFORD LE HOPE M 1754-1837 [96]
STANSTED MOUNTFITCHET C 1558-1762 M 1558-1837 [102,168]
STANWAY M 1754-1837 [101]
STAPLEFORD TAWNEY 1558-1752 M 1756-1851 [69,94]
STEBBING M 1754-1851 [92,93]
STEEPLE BUMPSTEAD C 1676-1812 M 1689-1851 B 1689-1812 [49,104,147]
STEEPLE WITH STAN(E)SGATE 1660-1900 [64,92]
STIFFORD C 1568-1783 M 1568-1812 B 1567-1783 [65,103]
STISTED CB 1538-1764 M 1539-1851 B 1538-1764 [103,148]
STOCK M 1755-1837 [99]; Rom Cath CM 1759-1831 [CRS6]; Ind Cong C 1814-37 [68]
STOCK HARVARD 1563-1950 [66-68,153]; Cong B 1919-1941 [153]
STONDON MASSEY M 1754-1851 [94]
STOWE MARIES CM 1559-1939 B 1559-1943 [12,92]
STRETHALL C 1742-1812 M 1740-1836 [94,163]
STURMER C 1733-69 M 1733-1851 B 1733-68 [96,154]
SUTTON M 1740-1836 [93]
TAKELEY C 1663-1744 1752-1812 M 1661-1743 B 1753-1836 [165]
TENDRING M 1754-1837 [95,104]
TERLING 1538-1840 [70]; Ind ZC 1784-1837 [70]
TEY, GREAT M 1754-1837 [95]
TEY, LITTLE M 1757-1853 [95]
THAXTED C 1558-1812 M 1538-1851 B 1538-1812 [71-73,97,133-137]
THEYDON MOUNT C 1564-1800 M 1564-1810 1814-51 B 1564-1815 [74,92]
THORPE LE SOKEN M 1754-1851 [105]; French 1684-1726
THORRINGTON M 1754-1851 [93] Mf 1558-1812
THUNDERSLEY M 1754-1851 [93]
THURROCK, GRAYS see GRAYS
THURROCK, WEST M 1754-1812 [101]
TILBURY JUXTA CLARE M 1755-1837 [104]
TILBURY, EAST M 1754-1851 [95,101]
TILBURY, WEST C 1546-94 M 1567-1690 1755-1813 1813-51 B 1540-1695 (with gaps) [96,101,155]
TILLINGHAM C 1614-1910 M 1618-1910 B 1561-1900 [75,76,170]
TILTY C 1673-86 1725-1812 M 1675-86 1727-1851 [92,164]
TOLLESBURY M 1754-1913 [99]
TOLLESHUNT KNIGHTS 1696-1836 [85]
TOPPESFIELD* C (1559-1650) M (1560-1647) 1754-1851 B (1560-1641) [77,92,95]
TOTHAM, GREAT M 1754-1851 [102]
TOTHAM, LITTLE M 1754-1837 [96]
TWINSTEAD CB 1562-1812 M 1567-1837 [103,154]
UGLEY CB 1559-1840 M 1559-1837 [78,101]
VANGE M 1756-1851 [104]
WAKERING, GREAT M 1754-1837 [98]; Cong C 1849-73 M 1851-1902 [79]
WAKES COLNE C 1559-60 1604-1837 M 1605-1836 B 1605-1837 [168]

WALTHAM, GREAT M 1756-1851 [102]
WALTHAM, LITTLE CB 1539-1812 M 1539-1837 [82,84,105]
WALTHAM HOLY CROSS M 1754-1851 [106] Mf 1563-1812
WALTHAMSTOW* M 1650-1837 [83,115]
WALTON LE SOKEN M 1754-1837 [104]
WANSTEAD C 1640-1749 M 1640-1743 1754-1837 B 1640-1812 [81,99]
WARLEY, GREAT C 1539-1859 M 1539-1880 B 1539-1887 [10,96]
WARLEY, LITTLE CB 1539-1812 M 1539-1722 1726-35 1757-1835 [90,96]
WEALD BASSETT, NORTH M 1754-1851 [104]
WEALD, SOUTH C 1540-45 1559-72 M 1539-45 1559-73 1754-1851 B 1539-54 1559-61 [101,159]
WEELEY M 1754-1837 [104]
WENDEN LOFTS C 1674-1878 M 1538-1837 [164]
WENDENS AMBO C 1549-1812 M 1540-81 1604-9 1633-40 1651-1837 [166]
WENNINGTON 1654-1850 [106,152,165]
WETHERSFIELD C 1647-1837 M 1701-1851 B 1647-81 1701-1837 [86,95]
WHITE COLNE CB 1560-1812 M 1560-1835 [82,94,111]
WHITE RODING/ROOTHING M 1547-1646 1660-1840 [166] Mf C 1681-1723 M 1702-44 B 1687-1761
WHITE NOTLEY see NOTLEY, WHITE
WICKEN BONHUNT C 1597-1811 M 1590-1837 [166]
WICKFORD M 1755-1838 [93]
WICKHAM ST PAULS C 1609-1795 M 1609-1837 B 1609-1789 [103,154]
WICKHAM BISHOPS Mf C 1662-1856 M 1663-1837 B 1662-1850
WIDDINGTON C 1666-1756 M 1666-1837 [166]
WIDFORD* M 1619-1837 [114]
WIGBOROUGH, GREAT M 1754-1837 [98]
WILLINGALE DOE C 1705-1812 M 1705-1837 [103,166] Mf CB 1570-1812 M 1571-1812
WILLINGALE SPAIN C 1576-1763 M 1576-1837 [102,166]
WIMBISH C 1572-1756 M 1582-1837 [102,164]
WITHAM M 1754-1837 [96]
WIVENHOE M 1754-1851 [94]
WIX C 1696-1755 M 1710-1837 B 1697-1755 [88,98,154]
WOODFORD C 1628-1789 M 1638-1812 1837-51 B 1638-1812 [89,102]
WOODHAM FERRERS CB 1558-1919 M 1559-1919 [90,91,93]
WOODHAM MORTIMER C 1662-1950 M 1664-1928 B 1664-1981 [90,98,169]
WOODHAM WALTER M 1754-1851 [98]
WORMINGFORD* M 1559-1837 [112]
WRABNESS M 1754-1851 [96]
WRITTLE* M 1634-1837 [105,114]
YELDHAM, GREAT M 1754-1851 [93,101] Mf 1560-1812

GLOUCESTERSHIRE

Gloucestershire M(I) grooms 1800-1837 [84/5]

ABENHALL M 1800-1837 [83]
ABSON see WICK
ACTON TURVILLE* M (1671-1723) 1813-37 [8,9,75]
ALDERLEY* M (1559-1812)-37 [8,9,72]
ALDERTON M 1800-1837 [89]
ADLESTROP M 1800-1837 [89]
ALDSWORTH* M 1800-1837 [89] Mf C 1683-1880 M
  1683-1970 B 1683-1967
ALMONDSBURY M(I) 1813-37 [11]
ALVESTON M(I) 1813-37 [11]
ALVINGTON* M 1698-1836 [76] Mf C 1688-1917 M
  1688-1837 B 1688-1914
AMPNEY CRUCIS* M 1561-1837 [77] Mf C 1813-1930 M
  1810-37 B 1813-1903
AMPNEY ST MARY M 1800-1837 [83]
AMPNEY ST PETER M 1800-1837 [83]
ARLINGHAM* M 1566-1837 [3,4,17]
ASHCHURCH* M 1555-1837 [76]
ASHLEWORTH M 1800-1837 [83]
ASHTON UNDER HILL Ext CB 1606-1700 [18] M 1800-
  1837 [89]
ASTON BLANK Mf C 1580-1726 see also COLD ASTON
ASTON SOMERVILLE* M 1661-1812 1819-1835 [66,89]
ASTON SUB EDGE* M (1539-1812)-1837 [65,89] C Ext
  1539-86 [18]
AUST see HENBURY
AVENING* M (1557-1812)-37 [8,9,72]
AWRE M 1538-1837 [19]
BADGEWORTH* M 1800-1837 [89] Mf C 1559-1907 M
  1559-1784 1813-1947 B 1559-1922
BADMINTON, GREAT* M (1538-1812)-37 [8,9,75]
BADSEY (Worcs) Ext M 1538-1733 [18]
BAGENDON M 1800-1837 [89]
BARNSLEY M 1800-1837 [89]
BARNWOOD* M 1800-1837 [81] Mf C 1651-1812 M
  1754-1913 B 1670-1885
BARRINGTON, GREAT M 1800-1837 [89]
BARRINGTON, LITTLE M 1800-1837 [89]
BATSFORD C 1562-1756 M 1565-1832 B 1696-1754
  [20,68,89]
BAUNTON* M 1802-1836 [89] Mf C 1625-1950 M
  1625-1838 B 1625-1811
BECKFORD Ext 1600-97 M 1814-1836 [18,87]; Rom
  Cath C 1817-50 [98] [
BERKELEY C 1560-(1653-77)-1845 M
  1598-(1653-77)-1837 B 1597-1650 (1653-77)-1840
  [2-4,21-27] Mf C 1813-1877
BEVERSTON* M (1563-1837) [8,9,68]
BIBURY M 1800-1837 [89] Mf C 1551-1885 M 1551-1946
  B 1551-1871
BISHOPS CLEEVE* M 1563-1812 [65]
BISLEY M 1800-1837 [89] Mf C 1548-1920 M 1548-1942
  B 1548-1847
BITTON* CB (1572-1674) M (1571-1674) 1813-37 [11,28]
BLAISDON M 1800-1837 [83]
BLEDINGTON M 1800-1837 [89]
BODDINGTON M 1800-1837 [89] Mf 1695-1979 M
  1695-1978 B 1695-1966
BOURTON ON THE HILL M 1800-1837 [89]
BOURTON ON THE WATER* M 1654-1837 [79]
BOXWELL* with LEIGHTERTON C 1701-1800 1813-29 M
  (1572-1812)-1837 B 1700-99 1813-1829 [8,9,75,98]

BRIMPSFIELD M 1800-1837 [89]
BRISTOL M Bonds 1637-1700 [92]; B(I) 1707-1780 [102];
  Cathedral 1669-1837 [31] ; All Saints M 1800-1837
  [30]; Christchurch M 1800-1837 [30]; Holy Trinity
  and St Philip M 1800-1837 [84]; St Augustine
  1577-1700 [32] M 1800-1837 [29]; St James M
  1800-1837 [84]; St John M 1800-1837 [30]; St Mary
  le Port M 1800-1837 [30]; St Mary Redcliffe M 1800-
  1837 [30]; St Michael M 1800-1837 [29];St Nicholas
  M 1800-1837 [30]; St Paul M 1800-1837 [85]; St
  Peter M 1800-1837 [84]; Ss Philip and Jacob M
  1800-1837 [84]; St Stephen M 1800-1837 [30]; St
  Thomas M 1800-1837 [29]; St Werburgh M 1800-
  1837 [30]; St Joseph Rom Cath C 1777-1808 M
  1799-1809 B 1795-1808 [CRS3]; Episc French C
  1687-1762 M 1688-1744 B 1688-1751 [HS20];
  Temple M(I) 1800-1837 [30]; Arnos Vale Rom Cath
  Cem B 1894-1903 [88]; SFrs M 1800-1837 [84]
BROADWELL M 1605-1837 [76,89]
BROCKWORTH M 1800-1837 [81]
BROMESBERROW* M 1558-1837 [79]
BROOKTHORPE* M (1617-1812)-37 [10,75]
BUCKLAND C 1539-1804 M (1539-1812)-1837 B
  1551-1804 [33,66,89]
BULLEY 1639 1683-1837 [11]
CAM* M (1569-1812)-37 [8,9,70]; Cong C 1702-39 1776-
  1836 [100]
CERNEY, NORTH M 1800-1837 [89]
CERNEY, SOUTH M 1800-1837 [89]
CHARFIELD M 1585-1837 [1,3,4,6]
CHARLTON ABBOTS M 1802-1837 [89]
CHARLTON KINGS CB 1538-1634 M 1538-1837
  [34,65,89]
CHEDWORTH M 1653-1837 [64,89]
CHELTENHAM M 1558-1837 [69,89]
CHERINGTON M 1569-1837 [74,89]
CHILD'S WICKHAM M 1560-1837 [66,89]
CHIPPING CAMDEN Mf 1616-1929 M 1616-1973 B 1616-
  1942
CHIPPING SODBURY C 1629-1759 M 1629-1837 B
  1629-1714 [7,8,9,35,73] Mf C 1607-1784
CHURCHAM M 1541-1837 [11]
CHURCHDOWN M 1800-1837 [89]
CIRENCESTER Mf C 1560-1908 M 1560-1903 B
  1560-1858
CLEARWELL Mf C 1830-1958 M 1856-1958 B 1856-1961
CLIFFORD CHAMBERS M 1538-1812 [67]
CLIFTON 1538-1681 CB 1722-1760 M 1722-1766
  [93,103]
COALEY* M (1625-1812)-37 [8,67]
COATES 1801-1837 [89]
COBERLEY M 1813-1837 [89] Mf 1539-1979
CODRINGTON M(I) 1664-1837 [12]
COLD ASHTON M(I) 1813-1837 [11]
COLD ASTON* M 1728-1837 [79,89] (formerly known as
  ASTON BLANK qv)
COLESBOURN M 1801-1837 [89]
COLN ROGERS* M 1755-1837 [74,89]
COLN ST ALDWYN M 1801-1836 [89] Mf C 1650-1727
  1775-1870 M 1650-1727 B 1650-1727 1775-1928
COLN ST DENIS M 1801-1835 [89]
COMPTON ABDALE M 1800-1837 [89] Mf C 1813-1978
  M 1838-1979 B 1813-1979
CONDICOTE M 1802-1836 [90] Mf 1688-1806
CORSE M 1800-1837 [90] Mf C 1661-1766 1784-1874 M
  1661-1837 B 1661-1766 1784-1919
COWLEY M 1802-1835 [90] Mf C 1596-1732

CRANHAM* M 1800-37 [10,90]
CROMHALL M 1571-1837 [1,3,4,6]
CUTSDEAN M 1800-1837 [90]
DAGLINGWORTH M 1800-1837 [90]
DEAN, LITTLE Mf 1684-1714 M 1813-36
DEERHURST M 1800-1837 [90]
DIDBROOK M 1800-1837 [90]
DIDMARTON* M (1568-1812)-37 [8,9,73]
DODINGTON M Ext 1661-1837 [12]
DONNINGTON M 1800-1835 [90] Mf C 1754-1812 M
    1755-1812 B 1765-1809
DORSINGTON* M 1602-1812 [65]
DOWDESWELL M 1800-1836 [90] Mf C 1575-1892 M
    1575-1726 M 1760-1836 Banns 1824-1951 B 1575-
    1970
DOWN AMPNEY 1603-1979 [36]
DOWN HATHERLEY M 1800-1837 [83]
DOYNTON M(l) 1813-37 [11]
DRIFFIELD M 1801-1837 [83] Mf CB 1561-1810 M 1561-
    1737 1754-1835
DRYBROOK Mf C 1817-1926 M 1845-1921 B 1817-65
DUMBLETON M 1800-1837 [90]
DUNTISBOURNE ABBOTS* M 1607-1837 [74]
DUNTISBOURNE KNIGHTS see DUNTISBOURNE ROUS
DUNTISBOURNE ROUS* M (1549-1837) [79] Mf CB
    1545-1812 M 1545-1837 Banns 1824-1941
DURSLEY* M (1639-1812)-1837 [8,9,67] Mf C 1639-1896
    M 1639-1888 B 1639-1884
DYMOCK* CB 1538-1788 M 1538-1790 1800-1837
    [37,90]
DYRHAM see HINTON
EASTINGTON* M (1558-1812)-37 [8,9,75] Mf C 1558-
    1903 M 1558-1939 B 1558-1954
EASTLEACH MARTIN M 1801-1837 [90] Mf C 1538-1913
    M 1538-1837 B 1538-1812
EASTLEACH TURVILLE M 1800-1837 [90] Mf 1654-1745
    C 1779-1863 M 1760-1837 B 1779-1964
EBRINGTON* M (1653-1812)-1837 B Ext 1570-1633
    [18,68,90]
EDGEWORTH* M (1554-1812)-1837 [74,90] Mf C 1556-
    1735
ELBERTON M(l) 1683-1837 [11]
ELKSTONE M 1592-1837 [68,90]
ELMORE M 1560-1837 [1,3-5]
ELMSTONE HARDWICKE M 1801-1835 [90]
ENGLISH BICKNOR M 1800-1837 [90]
EVENLODE M 1800-1837 [90]
FAIRFORD* M 1619-1837 [78]
FARMINGTON M 1800-1837 [90]
FILTON* M 1653-1812 [75]
FLAXLEY M 1800-1837 [83]
FORTHAMPTON M 1687-1837 [63,90]
FRAMPTON COTTERELL M 1813-37 [11]
FRAMPTON ON SEVERN* M (1625-1812)-37 [8,9,69]
FRETHERNE M 1618-1837 [1,3-5]
FROCESTER* M 1559-1837 [8,9,76] Mf 1559-1620 1681-
    1812 C 1813-1972 M 1813-1909 B 1813-1971
GLOUCESTER* Cathedral C 1661-1872 M 1661-1754
    [38,82]; Christchurch M 1825-1836 [90]; Holy
    Trinity M 1558-1730 [39]; St Aldate M 1800-1837
    [81]; St Catherine M 1605-1737 [39]; St John the
    Baptist M 1800-1837 [81]; St Mary de Crypt M
    1800-1837 [90] Mf CB 1653-1802 M 1653-1754; St
    Mary de Lode 1656-1837 [40]; St Michael M 1800-
    1837 [81]; St Nicholas M 1558-1837 [39]; St Peter's
    Abbey Mf CB 1717-1812 M 1717-1754 1862 1903-4
    1914

GUITING POWER M 1560-1837 [66,90]
HAILES M 1813-1837 [83]
HAMPNETT M 1737-54 1801-1835 [90,P]
HAMPSTONE HARDWICKE see ELMSTONE
    HARDWICKE
HANHAM* with OLDLAND 1584-1681 [41]
HARDWICKE* M (1566-1812)-37 [10,74]
HARESCOMBE* M 1744-1837 [10,72] Mf CB 1742-1812
    M 1756-1913 D 1857-59
HARESFIELD M 1800-1837 [10,90] Mf C 1558-1964 M
    1558-1836 Banns 1823-99 B 1558-1906
HARNHILL M 1802-1835 [90] Mf CB 1730-1812 M 1730-
    1844
HARTPURY M 1800-1837 [90]
HASFIELD M 1800-1837 [90]
HATHEROP* M (1578-1837) [79] Mf M 1813-1913
HAWKESBURY* M (1603-1812)-37 [8,9,67]
HAWLING M 1800-1837 [90]
HAZLETON M 1800-1836 [90] Mf CB 1597-1797 M 1597-
    1978
HEMPSTED Mf CB 1558-1797 M 1558-1742 1756-1809
HENBURY* C 1582-1761 M 1554-1812 B 1669-1777
    [78,104] with AUST Ext 1538-1648 [18]
HEWELSFIELD M 1801-1837 [90]
HILL* M (1653-1812)-37 [8,9,72]
HINTON ON THE GREEN* M (1735-1812) 1815-1837
    [66,90]; with DYRHAM M(l) 1813-37 [11]
HORSLEY* M (1591-1812)-37 [8,9,74] Mf C 1813-86 M
    1813-81 B 1813-1909
HORTON* M (1567-1812)-37 [8,9,75]; Rom Cath Chapel
    C 1772-1787 [CRS66]
HUNTLEY* M 1583-1837 [78]
ICOMBE* M (1563-1812)-1837 [75,90]
IRON ACTON M Ext 1660-1837 [12]
KEMBLE M 1814-1837 [90]
KEMERTON CB 1572-1948 M 1575-1948 [42,66]
KEMPLEY C 1661-1903 M 1666-1850 B 1637-1850 [43]
KEMPSFORD C 1653-58 M 1653-57 CMB 1695-1700 M
    1800-1837 [44,90]
KINGS STANLEY M 1573-1837 [10,63]
KINGSCOTE* M (1652-1812)-37 [8-10,70]
KINGSWOOD* M (1598-1812)-37 [8,9,11,71]
LASBOROUGH* M 1832-1837 [81] Mf C 1559-1812
    1826-85 M 1757-1844 B 1559-1812
LASSINGTON M 1800-1837 [83]
LEA M 1800-1837 [90]
LECHLADE M 1800-1837 [90]
LECKHAMPTON Mf C 1679-1959 M 1679-1978 B 1679-
    1961 Mfc C 1686-97 1714 1737-1833 M 1738-1812
    B 1686-1714 1737-1847
LEIGHTERTON* C 1701-1800 M (1572-1812)-1833 B
    1700-1799; with BOXWELL CB 1813-29 M 1813-33
    [75,98]
LEMINGTON, LOWER* M 1701-1833 [66,90]
LEONARD STANLEY* M 1570-1837 [10,64]
LITTLEDEAN M 1800-1837 [90]
LITTLETON ON SEVERN M(l) 1684-1837 [11]
LITTLETON, WEST* see TORMARTON
LONGBOROUGH M 1800-1837 [90] Mf C 1676-1908 M
    1680-1964 B 1677-1876
LONGHOPE M 1800-1837 [81]
LONGNEY M 1660-1837 [1,3-5]
LYDNEY M 1800-1837 [90] Mf 1628-1741
MAISEMORE* C 1600-63 M 1557-1837 B 1538-99
    [10,76]
MANGOTSFIELD M(l) 1762-1837 [11]
MARSHFIELD 1559-1693 M(l) 1813-37 [11,45]

MARSTON, LONG* M 1680-1837 [72,90]
MARSTON, SICCA see MARSTON, LONG
MATSON* M 1553-1837 [65,81]
MEYSEY HAMPTON CM 1570-1979 Banns 1824-1979 B
1570-1966 [46]
MICKLETON* M (1594-1812)-1837 CMB Ext 1594-1752
[18,65,90]
MINCHINHAMPTON* M (1566-1812)-37 [8,73] Mf M
1754-1828
MINSTERWORTH* M 1633-1837 [10,79]
MISERDEN M 1801-1837 [90]
MITCHELDEAN M 1680-1837 [71,81]
MORETON IN THE MARSH CB 1607-40 C 1643-1780 M
1621-40 1672-1837 [47/8,67,90]; Ind Chapel C
1801-1837 [98]
MORETON VALENCE M 1605-1837 [1,3-5]
NAUNTON M 1545-1837 [77,90]
NEWENT M 1800-1837 [90]
NEWINGTON BAGPATH M 1599-1837 [8,9,69,74]
NEWNHAM M 1547-1837 [1,3,4,19]
NEWNTON, LONG M 1800-1837 [90]
NIBLEY, NORTH M 1567-1837 [2-4,49,50]
NORTHLEACH M 1800-1837 [90]
NORTON 1686-1724 M 1800-1837 [51,90]
NOTGROVE M 1800-1837 [90]
NYMPSFIELD M 1609-1837 [8,9,63,74]
ODDINGTON C 1676-1812 M 1676/7 1685-1768 1800-
1837 B 1549-1618 1676-1812 [52,90]
OLDBURY ON SEVERN* M 1538-1733 M(l) 1813-37
[9,77]
OLDBURY ON THE HILL* M (1568-1750)-37 [8,9,73]
OLDLAND see HANHAM
OLVESTON* M (1560-1812)-37 [11,76]
OWLPEN M 1687-1897 [8,9,63/4] Mf 1686-1764
OXENHALL M 1800-1837 [83]
OXENTON M 1800-1837 [90] Mf C 1679-1735 1775-79 M
1679-1734 1755-1906
OZLEWORTH* M (1698-1812)-37 [8,9,74]
PAINSWICK* M 1547-1837 [70,90]]
PAUNTLEY M 1800-1837 [83]
PEBWORTH* M 1595-1700 1800-1837 [83]
PITCHCOMBE* M 1709-42 1800-1837 [91]
POULTON CB 1695-1979 M 1703-1977 1813-1837
[91,WL/R37]
PRESTBURY* M 1633-1837 [77]
PRESTON (Cirencester) M 1800-1837 [91]
PRESTON (Ledbury) M 1801-1832 [91]
PRESTON UPON STOUR* M (1541-1812)-37 [66,83] Mf
C 1873-1907 M 1873-1913
PUCKLECHURCH M(l) 1813-37 [11]
QUEDGELEY M 1559-1837 [10,63,83]
QUENINGTON M 1800-1837 [83]
QUINTON* M (1548-1812)-37 [68,91]
RANDWICK M 1800-1837 [81] Mf 1662-93
RANGEWORTHY M 1663-1837 [1,3,4]
REDMARLEY D'ABITOT M 1800-1837 [91] Mf C 1539-
1965 M 1539-1969 B 1539-1905
RENDCOMBE M 1566-1837 [3,91]
RISSINGTON, GREAT* M 1538-1913 [79]
RISSINGTON, LITTLE* C 1544-1812 M (1544-1837) B
1548-1812 [79,80]
ROCKHAMPTON M 1563-1837 [1,3,4,6]
RODBOROUGH M 1620-1638 1661-1837 [8,9,98]
RODMARTON M 1800-37 [8,9,11,83]
RUARDEAN M 1800-1837 [81]
RUDFORD M 1800-1837 [83]
SAINTBURY* M (1585-1812)-37 Ext CB 1617-1713

[18,66,91]
SALPERTON M 1800-1837 [81]
SANDHURST M 1800-37 [10,91]
SAPPERTON M 1800-1812 [91]
SAUL 1583-1837 [1,3-5]
SEVENHAMPTON* M 1605-1837 [77]
SHENINGTON M 1813-1837 [91]
SHERBORNE M 1800-1836 [91]
SHIPTON MOYNE* M (1587-1812)-37 [8,9,71]
SHIPTON OLLIFFE M 1802-1836 [91]
SHIPTON SOLLARS see SHIPTON OLLIFFE
SHORNCOTE M 1800-1837 [91]
SHURDINGTON M 1800-1837 [91]
SIDDINGTON M 1801-1837 [91]
SISTON 1576-1641 M 1813-1837 [11,62]
SLAUGHTER, LOWER* M 1813-37 [79]
SLAUGHTER, UPPER* M 1538-37 [79]
SLIMBRIDGE M 1571-1837 [8,9,63]
SNOWSHILL M 1593-1603 1815-1837 [66,91] Mf ZC
1606-38 1667-1812; see also STANTON
SODBURY, LITTLE M 1800-1837 [1,3,61]
SODBURY, OLD* CB 1605-95 M 1605-(1684-1812)-37
[7,8,71]
SOMERFORD KEYNES M 1800-1837 [91]
SOUTHROP M 1656-1837 [75]
ST BRIAVELS M 1800-1837 [91] Mf C 1618-1812
STANDISH* M (1559-1812)-37 [10,68] Mf C 1559-1978 M
1559-1836 B 1559-1916
STANTON C 1572-1735 M 1572-1837 B 1561-1735
[53,66,91] Mf ZC 1612-25 1660-1812
STANWAY M 1800-1837 [91]
STAUNTON (Coleford) M 1802-1837 [91]
STAUNTON (Ledbury) M 1800-1837 [81]
STAVERTON M 1800-1837 [91] Mf C 1538-1976 M 1538-
1836 B 1538-1966
STINCHCOMBE CB 1582-1812 M 1583-1837
[8,9,53,64,68]
STOKE GIFFORD M(l) 1748-1837 [11]
STONE C 1594-1793 M 1594-1837 B 1594-1791
[8,9,54,65]
STONEHOUSE* M (1558-1812)-37 [8,9,64]; French C
1692-1791 M 1693-1748 B 1692-1788 [HS20]
STOW ON THE WOLD M 1800-1837 [91]
STRATTON M 1800-1837 [91]
STROUD M 1580-1837 [55]
SUDELEY M 1801 [83]
SUTTON-UNDER-BRAILES M 1578-1837 [66,91] Mf C
1605-1812 M 1605-1837 B 1715-1812
SWELL, LOWER* M (1686-1812)-37 [65,91]
SWELL, UPPER M 1800-1837 [91]
SWINDON M 1638-1837 [63]
SYDE* M (1686-1812)-37 [74,83]
SYSTON see SISTON
TAYNTON M 1800-1837 [83]
TEMPLE GUITING* M (1676-1771) 1813-1837 [66,91] Mf
M 1580 1612-1777 1813-1837
TETBURY* M (1631-1812)-37 [72,91]
TEWKESBURY M 1800-1837 [91]
THORNBURY* M (1550-1812)-37 [8,9,77]
TIBBERTON M 1800-1837 [83] Mf C 1764-1858
TIDENHAM 1708-54 M 1800-1837 [91]
TIRLEY* M 1655-1812 1813-1837 [76,91]
TODDINGTON M 1800-1836 [91]
TODENHAM* M (1721-1812)-37 [66,91]
TORMARTON* with LITTLETON, WEST M (1600-1812) (l)
1813-37 [11,75]
TORTWORTH* M (1620-1812)-37 [8,9,74]

TREDINGTON M 1800-1837 [91] Mf C 1762-1812
TURKDEAN* M 1572-1837 [76] Mf C 1763-1812
TWYNING* M (1674-1812)-37 [75,91]
TYTHERINGTON M 1662-1837 [1,3,4] Mf C 1731-1812
ULEY* M (1668-1812)-37 [8,9,64] Mf M 1599-1813
UPLEADON M 1800-1837 [83] Mf C 1813-1857
UPTON ST LEONARDS M 1800-37 [10,81]; Mf 1736-83
WALTON CARDIFF M 1800-1837 [91] Mf C 1677 1705-48 1779-1812 M 1697-1855
WAPLEY & CODRINGTON M 1664-1837 [12]
WASHBOURNE, GREAT M 1800-1837 [91]
WELFORD ON AVON M 1813-1837 [91] Mf C 1561-1922 M 1561-1844 Banns 1824-1934 B 1561-1881
WESTBURY ON SEVERN M 1538-1837 [56]
WESTBURY ON TRYM* 1559-1713 [57]
WESTCOTE* M (1630-1812)-37 [76,91]
WESTERLEIGH M 1660-1837 [12]
WESTON BIRT* M (1596-1812)-37 [8,9,68]
WESTON ON AVON* M 1690-1810 1814-1836 [66,91]
WESTON SUBEDGE* M (1612-1812) 1814-1837 B Ext 1658-1708 [18,66,91]
WHADDON* M (1620-1812)-37 [10,75]
WHEATENHURST M 1538-1837 [1,3-5]
WHITMINSTER see WHEATENHURST
WHITTINGTON M 1801-1836 [91] Mf C 1774-1812
WICK & ABSON M 1813-37 [11]
WICKWAR* CB 1664-88 M 1637-40 1664-(1689-1812)-37 [7-9,73]
WIDFORD see OXFORDSHIRE
WILLERSEY* M (1723-1812)-37 Ext 1606-1731 [18,68,91]
WINCHCOMBE C 1539-1812 M 1539-1837 B 1539 1543-1812 [58/9,71,91]
WINDRUSH M 1800-1837 [91] Mf C 1791-1813
WINSON M 1801-1836 [91]
WINSTONE* M 1540-1837 [78]
WINTERBOURNE M 1800-37 [11]
WITCOMBE, GREAT M 1800-1837 [91]
WITHINGTON M 1800-1837 [91]
WOODCHESTER M 1813-37 [10]
WOOLASTON M 1696-1837 [76] Mf C 1688-1878 M 1688-1837 B 1688-1864
WOOLSTONE M 1800-1837 [91]
WORMINGTON* M (1719-1812)-37 [66,91]
WOTTON UNDER EDGE M 1571-1837 [2-4,60] Mf C 1571-1900 M 1571-1898 B 1571-1874
WYCK RISINGTON* M 1605-1837 [75]
YANWORTH M 1800-1836 [91]
YATE M 1660-1837 [1,3,4]

HAMPSHIRE

ABBOTTS ANN 1561-1649 1653-1756 C 1715-1812 M 1754-1812 Banns 1754-1820 B 1757-1811 [1,111,119]
ALDERSHOT* M (1590-1812)-1837 [88,119]
ALRESFORD, OLD Mfc C 1728-1866 M 1728-1837 B 1678-1909
ALTON CB 1711-59 M 1711-53 [2]
ALVERSTOKE CM 1559-1579 B 1559-1569 [119]; Haslar Hospital C 1829-1862 B 1827-1852 [105]
AMPORT M 1665-1812 [88]
ANDOVER Mfc C 1587-1853 M 1587-1837 B 1587-1876
ANMORE see HAMBLEDON

ARRETON IoW M 1654-1837 [83]
ASHE 1606-1887 [3,4]
ASHMANSWORTH Mfc C 1811-1965 M 1813-1818 B 1811-1818
AVINGTON Mfc CB 1609-1812 M 1609-1920
BADDESLEY, NORTH Mfc C 1682-1926 M 1682-1837 B 1682-1967
BARTON STACEY MfC C 1713-1861 M 1713-1838 B 1713-1896
BASING* C 1671-76 (M 1655-1812) [89,105]
BASINGSTOKE* C(M)B 1638-1812 [5,6,91]
BAUGHURST* C(M)B 1678-1812 [40,91]
BEAULIEU C 1653-1745 1813-1838 M 1654-1745 1813-1838 B 1653-1734 1813-1838 [7,115]
BENTLEY* CB 1538-1838 M (1541-1812)-1838 [8-10,95,119]
BENTWORTH* M 1603-1837 [97]
BINSTEAD IoW C 1708-1796 M 1709-1837 B 1711-1781 [111]
BINSTED (near ALTON) C 1653-1659 1784-1813 MB 1653-1812 [11,119]
BISHOPS SUTTON Mfc C 1711-1855 MB 1711-1912
BISHOPS WALTHAM M 1780-1812 [27]
BISHOPSTOKE C 1657-1812 M 1661-1812 [12]; Ind Diss C 1817-28 [113]
BLENDWORTH CM 1780-1812 B 1780-1871 [113]
BOARHUNT Mfc C 1654-1909 M 1654-1836 B 1654-1805
BOLDRE* M 1596-1812 [97]
BONCHURCH IoW M 1754-1836 [83,86,113]
BOSSINGTON Mfc CB 1763-1812 M 1817-1832
BOTLEY CB 1679-1837 M 1680-1837 [13,14]
BRADING IoW* (1547-1812) C Ext 1706-1812 B Ext 1598-1868 [98,117]
BRADLEY CB 1725-1812 M 1725-1753 [112]
BRAMBRIDGE later HIGHBRIDGE Rom Cath C 1766-1869 M 1769-1860 D 1769-1867 [CRS27]
BRAMLEY 1580-1812 [15,87]
BRAMSHOTT with HEADLEY SFrs Z 1638-1722 M 1664-1729 B 1661-1739 [113]
BRAMSHAW see BRAMSHAW Wiltshire [WL/R 60]
BRANSGORE CB 1822-40 [103]
BREAMORE 1675-1840 [16]
BROCKENHURST M 1629-1811 [103] Mfc C 1594-1940 M 1594-1912 B 1594-1911
BROCKHAMPTON Rom Cath C 1733-1855 M 17885-1826 B 1758-1817 [CRS44]
BROOK IoW M 1654-70 1696-1776 Banns 1823-38 [103,113]
BROUGHTON Mfc C 1639-1856 M 1639-1837 B 1639-1868
BROWN CANDOVER Mfc C 1612-1889 M 1612-1837 B 1612-1812
BULLINGTON* M 1754-1812 [87]
BURGHCLERE* M 1559-1812 [94]
BURSLEDON C 1648-1715 1724-1837 M 1671-1717 1726-1837 B 1671-1709 1724-1837 [17,119] Mfc C 1760-1791 M 1759-1812 B 1759-1801
CALBOURNE IoW* M (1559-1812)-37 [83,98]
CARISBROOKE IoW M 1572-1837 [80,86]
CHALE IoW M 1699-1837 [83]
CHERITON Mfc C 1742-1854 M 1742-1837 B 1742-1885
CHILBOLTON CB 1774-1812 [113]
CHILTON CANDOVER Mfc C 1672-1847 M 1672-1837 B 1672-1877
CHILWORTH C 1722-1837 M 1721-1837 B 1723-1837 [30]
CHRISTCHURCH C 1682-1812 M Ext 1576-1609 M

1680-1762 1780-1812 B 1780-1812 [19,109,113]; Ind CB 1780-1816
CHURCH OAKLEY* CB 1559-1812 (M 1565-1812) [89,105]
CLANFIELD CM 1742/3-1802 B 1678-1802 [113]
CLIDDESDEN* M 1636-1812 [87]
COLMER 1563-1812 [47]
COMPTON M 1695-1837 [107]
COOMBE* C 1597-1827 M (1560-1812)-35 B 1562-1812 [3,88]
COWES, EAST IoW M 1836 [83]
COWES, WEST IoW M 1680-1703 [83]; Rom Cath C 1796-1856 [CRS59]
CRAWLEY* M 1675-1812 [97]
CRONDALL* C 1569-1867 M (1576-1812)-1970 B 1570-1837 [20-25,90] Mf C 1569-1837 M 1576-1653 1695-1837 B 1570-1653 1754-1837
DEANE* CB 1659-1840 M (1679-1812)-40 [26,87]
DIBDEN Mfc C 1784-1854 M 1731-1837 B 1784-1812
DOGMERSFIELD* CB 1675-93 M 1677-(1695-1812)-35 [2,89,113]
DUMMER* M 1541-1812 [87]
DURLEY Mfc C 1561-1850 M 1561-1836 B 1561-1914
EASTROP* M (1759-1807) [26,91]
ECCHINSWELL and SYDMONTON 1610-1673 1780-1837 [2,40]
ELING* C 1538-1655 (M 1539-1812) B 1537-1660 [27,93]
ELLISFIELD Mfc C 1606-1941 M 1606-1952 B 1606-1812
ELVETHAM* M 1639-1812 [89]
EMSWORTH see WARBLINGTON
ESSE see ASHE
EVERSLEY* M 1559-1812 [89]
EWHURST* C 1684-1838 (M 1682-1823) B 1687-1839 [31,94]
EXBURY Mfc C 1813-1913 M 1756-1861
FACCOMBE* CB 1586-1812 M (1586-1812)-1836 [3,88]
FARNBOROUGH* M (1584-1812)-1837 [89,113]
FAWLEY Mfc C 1673-1857 M 1673-1837 B 1673-1842
FORDINGBRIDGE 1642-1840 [29,55]; Ind ZC 1795-1837 [113]
FRESHWATER IoW* M (1576-1812)-37 [83,98]
FROYLE Mfc C 1653-1846 M 1653-1836 B 1653-1868
GATCOMBE IoW C 1673-1769 M 1560-1835 B 1673-1685 [86,105]
GODSHILL IoW M 1678-1837 B 1678-1715 [81,86]
GOODWORTH CLATFORD Mfc C 1538-1812 M 1538-1837 B 1538-1906
GOSPORT Rom Cath C 1759-1852 M 1830-1848 [CRS49]
GRATELEY Mfc C 1740-1957 M 1740-1855 B 1740-1812
GREYWELL M 1799-1806 1826-37 [113] Mfc C 1604-1908 M 1604-1837 B 1604-1979
HALE Mfc C 1626-1862 M 1626-1837 B 1626-1950
HAMBLE LE RICE C 1674-1837 M 1730-1837 B 1679-1837 [30] MFc C 1674-1717 1792-1873 M 1814-1835 B 1674-1717 1792-1920
HAMBLEDON Bapt Anmore Chapel Z 1820-1837 [113]
HANNINGTON* CB 1771-1837 (M 1768-1837) [31,97] Mfc C 1813-1867 M 1768-1839 B 1813-1962
HARBRIDGE C 1679-1837 M 1616-1837 B 1571-1840 [32/3]
HARDWAY see Winchester, Romsey and Hardway (French Chapel)
HARTLEY MAUDITT C 1672-1812 M 1673-1811 B 1679-1812 [77]
HARTLEY WESPALL* M 1558-1812 [95]
HARTLEY WINTNEY* M 1658-1812 [89]

HASLAR HOSPITAL see ALVERSTOKE
HAVANT C 1653-1845 M 1653-1837 Banns 1824-1856 B 1653-1854 [34/5]
HAYLING, NORTH M 1571-1812 [105]
HAYLING, SOUTH M 1676-1812 [105]
HEADLEY C 1540-1895 M 1539-1897 B 1539-1915 [36/7]; Sfrs see BRAMSHOTT
HECKFIELD* M 1538-1812 [92]
HERRIARD* M (1701-1812)-1837 [94,119]
HIGHBRIDGE see BRAMBRIDGE
HIGHCLERE* M 1656-1813 [94]
HOLYBOURNE Mfc C 1690-1854 M 1690-1837 B 1690-1885
HOUGHTON Mfc C 1669-1889 M 1669-1835 B 1669-1930
HOUND C 1660-1837 MB 1667-1837 [38,106] Mfc C 1760-1791 M 1759-1812 B 1759-1801
HUNTON* M 1575-1812 [95]
HURSLEY M 1600-1838 [107] Mfc C 1599-1666 C 1706-1852 M 17062-1838 B 1706-1858
HURSTBOURNE PRIORS* C 1620-1838 M (1604-1812)-37 B 1604-1837 [3,87]
HURSTBOURNE TARRANT* 1546-1812 [87]
HYTHE C 1823-1837 [114]
IBSLEY 1654-1840 [39]
ITCHEN STOKE Mfc C 1719-1920 M 1719-1836 B 1719-1986
KINGSCLERE 1780-1837 [40] Mfc C 1538-1920 M 1538-1885 B 1538-1766 1813-1906
KINGSLEY MfC 1568-1871 M 1568-1812 B 1568-1949
KINGS SOMBORNE Mfc C 1672-1858 M 1672-1837 B 1672-1888
KINGSTON IoW CB 1647-1795 M 1647-1832 [83,114]
KINGSWORTHY* M 1538-1812 [97]
KNIGHTS ENHAM* M 1683-1812 [87]
LANDPORT see PORTSEA
LAVERSTOKE* CB 1657-1837 (M 1657-1812)-37 [41,95]
LINKENHOLT* M 1579-1812 [95]
LIPHOOK Rom Cath C 1850-1908 B 1891-1902 [119]
LITCHFIELD* CB 1624-1837 (M 1627-1812) [41,94]
LONGPARISH 1654-1837 [41]
LYMINGTON C 1658-1812 M 1665-1812 B 1662-1886 [79]; Rom Cath (Pylewell House Chapel) C 1805-1840 M 1806-1837 [CRS14]
MAPLE DURWELL* M 1629-1837 [95]
MARTYR WORTHY 1560-1630 [114]
MEDSTEAD 1560-1812 [107]
MEON, EAST Mfc 1560-1676 C 1743-1954 M 1743-1963 B 1743-1874
MEON, WEST* M 1538-1800 [93]
MILLBROOK 1633-1837 [27,43,106]
MILFORD-ON-SEA Rom Cath (Rook Cliff Chapel) C 1806-1817 MB 1813-1815 [CRS14]
MINSTEAD C 1682-1837 M 1688-1837 [42]
MONK SHERBORNE M 1618-1812 [106]
MONXTON* M 1716-1812 [87]
MORESTEAD C 1549-1980 M 1550-1925 B 1553-1978 [114] Mfc CB 1549-1811 M 1549-1851
MOTTISTONE IoW M 1680-1835 [83]
NATELEY SCURES* (M 1684-1812)-3 [97,114]
NEWCHURCH IoW M 1692-1786 see also RYDE
NEWNHAM (M 1754-1812)-1836 [94,114]
NEWPORT IoW* M (1541-1837) [100]; Rom Cath C 1792-1856 M 1807-1855 D 1839-1857 1887 [CRS59]; Prot Diss Mting Hse Z 1739-1837 [114]
NEWTOWN* M 1679-1812 [94]
NITON IoW* M (1561-1812)-37 [83,98]

NORTHINGTON Mfc C 1579-1906 M 1579-1836 B 1579-1812

NORTHWOOD IoW C 1544-1656 M 1538-1837 B 1539-1656 [82,84,86,103]

NURSLING Mfc C 1617-1841 M 1617-1837 B 1617-1856

NUTLEY M 1758-1812 [119]

OAKLEY, EAST see WOOTTON ST LAWRENCE

ODIHAM* M 1538-1812 [92]

OVERTON* M 1640-1812 [88]

PAMBER M 1661-1812 [103]

PENTON MEWSEY* M 1649-1812 [87]

POPHAM* M 1628-1812 [95]

PORTSEA C 1828-38 M 1780 [112,114]; Orange St Cong CZ 1785-1838 [46]; Rom Cath C 1794-1846 M 1828-1847 [CRS49]

PORTSMOUTH* St Thomas a Becket C 1770-1776 M (1653-1812)-37 [44/5,96,101]; Bapt St Thomas Street CB 1785-1836 [114]; Royal Garrison Church B 1741-1842 [104]

PRESTON CANDOVER* M 1584-1812 [95]

PRIORS DEAN 1538-1812 [47]

RINGWOOD 1561-1840 [48/9,50/1]; Presb later Unit Upper Meeting Hse C 1748-1838 B 1815-40; Presb later Cong Lower Meeting Hse C 1790-1835 B 1820-39 [114]

ROMSEY Mfc C 1569-1852 M 1569-1837 B 1569-1856; Rom Cath see Winchester, Romsey and Hardway (French Chapel)

ROTHERWICK* M 1560-1812 [97]

ROWNER* CB 1780-1812 M (1590-1812) M(I) 1590-1922 [52,94,106]

RYDE IoW C 1719-1787 1829-1837 M 1692-1754 1756-1786 1811 1819-37 B Ext 1758-1811 [81,86,112,117,119] see also NEWCHURCH

ST LAWRENCE IoW M 1747-1836 [81,86]

ST MARY BOURNE* CB 1661-1837 M (1663-1812) [28,87]

ST NICHOLAS IoW M 1723-54 [83]

SHALFLEET IoW C 1608-1762 M 1604-1837 B 1621-1762 [53,81,86,107]

SHANKLIN IoW C 1724-1841 M 1754-1858 B 1766-1913 [81,86,117]

SHERBORNE, EAST /ST JOHN* CB 1652-1837 M 1652-(1653-1812)-37 [54,89]

SHERFIELD UPON LODDON* M 1574-1812 [95]

SHORWELL IoW M 1676-1838 B 1585-1698 [81,86,104,112,114,119]

SILCHESTER* M 1653-1812 [93]

SOPLEY* M 1682-1812 [93]; Rom Cath C 1803-1866 M Ext 1693-1788 (in C of E register) B 1787-1837 [CRS43]

SOUTHAMPTON* All Saints 1723-1812 B 1861-65 [65,104]; Holy Rood 1653-1812 CB 1838-58 [27,62-4,104]; St Lawrence & St John CB 1768-1836 M 1754-1836 [64]; St Mary 1675-1837 [57/8]; St Mary Extra Jesus Chapel 1681-1837 [59]; St Michael 1552-75 1589-1604 1618-52 1664-1837 [59-61]; French Chapel see Holy Rood; Ind C 1674-1837 B 1821-37 Deaths 1726-1809 [64]; Wes C 1798-1812 [64]; Rom Cath St Joseph C 1792-1848 M 1837-1849 M Ext 1805-1823 [56,106]; Walloon C 1567-1779 M 1567-1756 B 1567-1722 [HS4]

STEEP CB 1610-44 1653-73 1695-1840 M 1610-44 1668-73 1696-1837 [67,119]

STEVENTON* C 1604-1886 M (1604-1812)-74 B 1607-1891 [26,87,107]

STOKE CHARITY* M 1542-1812 [95]

STONEHAM, NORTH 1640-1837 [69]

STONEHAM, SOUTH 1663-1837 [68,70]

STRATFIELD SAYE* M 1539-1812 [91]

STRATFIELD TURGIS* M 1672-1809 [92]

SUTTON, LONG* M (1561-1812)-36 [91,114]

SWARRATON C 1584-1694 M Ext 1606-1616 [115]

SYDMONTON see ECCHINSWELL and SYDMONTON

TADLEY* C 1683-1812 (M 1691-1812) B 1695-1812 [71,92]

TANGLEY* M 1703-1812 [88]

THORLEY IoW M 1614-1837 [81,86]

THRUXTON C 1702-1840 M 1721-1847 B 1721-1812 [3]

TICHBORNE Rom Cath C 1785-1837 [CRS43]

TIMSBURY M 1564-1812 [106]

TISTED, EAST Mfc C 1538-1946 M 1538-1832 B 1538-1987

TITCHFIELD CB 1763-1812 [72]

TUFTON* CB 1716-1838 M (1754-1812)-37 [41,87,94]

TWYFORD* 1626-1837 [73]; Rom Cath B Ext 1628-1767 (in C of E register) [CRS27]

UP NATELEY* M (1695-1750)-1837 [88,114]

VERNHAM DEAN* C 1642-61 (M 1607-1812) B 1598-1630 [3,88]

WALLOP, NETHER Mfc C 1628-1851 M 1628-1837 B 1628-1864

WALTHAM, NORTH* M 1654-1812 [89]

WARBLINGTON with EMSWORTH Ext 1644-1930 [SX/R.123]

WARNBOROUGH, SOUTH* M 1539-1812 [92]

WEEKE M 1573-1837 [107]

WELLOW, EAST & WEST (I) 1570-1880 [76]

WESTON PATRICK 1780-1820 [74]

WEYHILL* M 1564-1812 [97]

WHIPPINGHAM IoW M 1728-1837 [84,86]

WHITCHURCH* CB 1605-1838 M (1605-1812)-38 [78,94]

WHITWELL IoW* M 1699-1837 [98]

WICKHAM M 1780-1782 [119]

WIELD C 1539-1781 M 1539-1812 B 1539-1781 [107]

WINCHESTER* Cathedral (1599-1812) [90]; College (C 1726-1861 M 1699-1745 B 1678-1903) [97]; St Bartholomew Hyde (M 1563-1837) [102]; St Clement (M 1685-1837) [102]; St Faith (M 1674-1837) [102]; St John in the Soke M 1578-1837 [107]; St Lawrence (M 1754-1812) [91]; St Maurice (M 1538-1837) [99]; St Michael in the Soke (M 1632-1812) [91]; St Peter Cheesehill (M 1597-1837) [102]; St.Swithin (CB 1562-1695 M 1564-1812) [90]; St Thomas (M 1685-1837) [102]; Rom Cath (St Peter) CM 1721-1826 [CRS1] CB 1826-1855 [CRS42]

WINCHESTER, ROMSEY & HARDWAY (French Chapel) Rom Cath CMD 1795-1801 [CRS42]

WINCHFIELD* M (1660-1812)-37 [89,114]

WINNALL M 1697-1837 [107]

WINSLADE* M 1723-1812 [88]

WOLVERTON* CB 1717-1837 M (1717-1812)-37 [40,94]

WONSTON* M 1570-1812 [95]

WOODHAY, EAST* M 1618-1812 [95]

WOODMANCOTE* M 1772-1812 [95]

WOOTTON IoW M 1760-1833 (I) 1825-37 [84,86]

WOOTTON ST LAWRENCE* C 1607-1812 M (1560-1812) [87,104]

WORLDHAM, EAST C 1690-1850 M 1692-1854 B 1690-1844 [75,77]

WORLDHAM, WEST C 1649-1840 M 1654-1845 B 1653-1844 [75,77]

WORTING* M 1604-1812 [91]

YARMOUTH IoW M 1614-1812 [84,86]
YATELEY* M 1636-1812 [88]
YAVERLAND IoW* M (1632-1812)-36 [84,98]

HEREFORDSHIRE

ABBERLEY Mf 1638 1662-1856
ABBEYDORE Mf C 1634-1874 M 1634-1854 Banns 1823-1928 B 1634-1864
ACONBURY Mf C 1665-1971 M 1665-1911 B 1665-1867
ACTON BEAUCHAMP Mf C 1577-1980 M 1577-1835 B 1577-1803
ALLENSMORE Mf C 1664-1877 M 1664-1832 Banns 1825-1888 B 1698-1877
ALMELEY 1596-1681 1745-71 [4] Mf 1596-1860 Banns 1792-1821
ASHPERTON Mf C 1538-1863 M 1538-1843 Banns 1813-1887 B 1538-1899
ASTON Mf CB 1692-1812 M 1692-1840
AVENBURY Mf C 1661-1919 M 1661-1931 B 1661-1940
AYLTON see LEDBURY
AYMESTRY Mf 1568-1897
BACTON Mf 1660-1846
BADGER Mf 1602-1836
BALLINGHAM Mf 1595-1855
BARROW Mf 1811-25
BARTESTREE Mf CB 1813-1884 M 1811-1884
BAYTON Mf 1638-1858
BIRCH, LITTLE Mf M 1557-1912 1949-1963 B 1557-1812
BIRCH, MUCH Mf 1599-1688 C 1669-1966 M 1699-1837 B 1669-1900
BISHOPS FROME Mf C 1564-1874 M 1564-1924 B 1564-1913
BISHOPSTONE Mf 1727-1845
BLAKEMERE Mf 1662-1839 B 1840-1848
BOCKLETON Mf 1638-1871
BODENHAM Mf C 1574-1921 M 1584-1961 B 1584-1904
BOLSTONE Mf CB 1758-1854 M 1813-1854
BOSBURY C 1559-60 1708-26 B 1559-1624 [1,31]
BRAMPTON ABBOTTS Mf C 1561-1937 M 1561-1837 B 1561-1960
BRAMPTON BRYAN Mf 1638 1663-1849 Banns 1823-1976
BREDENBURY Mf 1603-1858
BREDWARDINE 1660-1933 [5,6] Mf 1660-1871; with BROBURY C 1723-1890 M 1723-1837 B 1723-1908
BREINTON Mf C 1662-1973 M 1662-1980 B 1662-1980
BRIDGE SOLLERS 1615-1812 [9] Mf 1615-1853
BRIDSTOW Mf C 1560-1918 M 1660-1844 B 1844-1896
BRILLEY CB 1580-1837 M 1581-1837 [7] Mf C 1580-1860 M 1580-1837 Banns 1837-1923 B 1580-1903
BRINSOP Mf 1660-1862
BROBURY 1660-1933 Mf 1660-1871 C 1872-1922 M 1872-1882 B 1872-1907; see also BREDWARDINE with BROBURY
BROCKHAMPTON (Ross) Mf C 1598-1852 M 1590-1635 1661-1852 B 1600-1639 1661-1852
BROCKHAMPTON (Bromyard) Mf C 1817-1841
BROMYARD 1538-1837 [15/6,37-9] see also BROCKHAMPTON (Bromyard) Mf 1538-1757 M 1837-1869 Banns 1875-1947 B 1730-1866; Ind C 1696-1836 B 1763-1831 [13]
BULLINGHAM Mf 1682-1764 C 1796-1918 M 1765-1837 Banns 1825-1888 B 1796-1933

BURGHILL Mf 1655-1890 M 1891-1929
BURRINGTON Mf 1541-1854 Banns 1836-1969
BYFORD Mf 1660-1852
BYTON Mf 1822-1866
CALLOW Mf 1576-1636 1660-1850
CANON FROME Ext 1660-79 CB 1680-1812 M 1680-1811 [8] Mf 1660-1861 M 1862-1968
CANON PYNE 1660-1829
CLEHONGER Mf C 1670-1925 M 1670-1855 Banns 1826-1940 B 1670-1890
CLIFFORD 1662-1837 [35]
CLODOCK and LONGTON Mf 1714-1885 M 1885-1943 B 1885-1906
CODDINGTON Mf 1660-1849
COLLINGTON Mf 1566-1872
COLWALL Mf C 1553-1896 M 1553-1933 B 1553-1863
COWARNE, LITTLE Mf 1563-1812 M 1813-1953 Banns 1954-57
COWARNE, MUCH Mf C 1559-1939 M 1559-1954 B 1559-1914
CRADLEY Mf C 1560-1875 M 1560-1928 Banns 1822-1946 B 1560-1872; Lady Hunt Conn ZC 1818-37 [13]
CREDENHILL Mf C 1662-1965 MB 1662-1858 Banns 1824-1941
CROFT Mf 1565-1846 Banns 1887-1961
COURTFIELD see Monmouthshire
CUSOP 1662-1899 [35] Mf 1662-1862
CWM Prim Meth ZC 1828-37 [13]
CWMYOY see LLANDILOPORTHOLE Monmouthshire
DEWCHURCH, LITTLE Mf 1660-1869 C 1870-1925
DEWCHURCH, MUCH Mf C 1558-1869 M 1558-1837 Banns 1837-1915 B 1558-1893
DEWSALL Mf CB 1582-1812 M 1582-1837
DILWYN 1558-1639 [27] Mf C 1559-1902 M 1559-1947 Banns 1890-1948 B 1559-1854
DINEDOR Mf C 1750-1943 M 1750-1838 B 1750-1812
DINMORE see HOPE UNDER DINMORE
DONNINGTON C 1755-1840 M 1754-1835 B 1756-1841 [31] Mf 1828-1884
DORSTONE Mf CB 1660-1847 M 1660-1853
DORMINGTON Mf 1828-1884
DOWNTON Mf CB 1660-1830 M 1660-1837
DULAS Mf 1818-1839 1848-1850
EARDISLAND Mf C 1560-1858 M 1560-1968 B 1560-1933
EARDISLEY Mf C 1669-1938 M 1669-1964 B 1669-1930
EATON BISHOP Mf C 1588-1896 M 1588-1920 B 1588-1906
EDVIN LOACH Mf CB 1576-1754 M 1576-1832
EDVIN RALPH Mf CB 1651-1812 M 1651-1835
ELTON Mf CB 1657-1812 M 1675-1836
EVESBATCH Mf CB 1700-1812 M 1700-1834 Banns 1834-1921
EWYAS HAROLD Mf C 1734-1881 M 1734-1975 B 1734-1896
EYE 1573-1718 [10] Mf C 1573-1893 M 1573-1837 Banns 1824-1906 B 1573-1868
FAWLEY Bapt C 1827-1935 Ext 1837-1851; seec also FOWNHOPE
FELTON Mf C 1639-1961 M 1639-1837 Banns 1824-1957 B 1639-1794
FORD CHAPEL Mf 1743-1812
FOWNHOPE C 1560-1624/5 M 1538-1673 B 1618-68 [32] Mf 1566-1911 M 1566-1969 B 1566-1897; FAWLEY Chapelry C 1539-1886 [32]
FOY Mf 1661-1861

GANAREW Mf 1661-1876
GARWAY Mf CM 1661-1871 B 1661-1943
GOODRICH Mf 1661-1874
GORSLEY Bapt Z 1831-37 [13]
GRENDON BISHOP Mf CB 1662-1946 M 1662-1945
HAMPTON BISHOP 1670-1740 [45] Mf 1669-1862
HANLEY WILLIAMS Mf Ext 1662-1847
HANWOOD Mf 1660-1886
HARDWICK Mf CB 1851-1884
HAREWOOD 1671-1812 [12] Mf C 1813-1943 M 1759-
1906 B 1813-1896
HAREWOOD END Mf 1772-1838
HATFIELD C 1615-1812 M 1617-1774 B 1616-1812 [2]
Mf CB 1615-1876 M 1615-1835
HENTLAND Mf 1558-1643 C 1674-1859 M 1674-1837 B
1674-1894
HEREFORD All Saints Mf 1639 1662-1820; Holy Trinity
Mf C 1885-1931 M 1902-1938; St James Mf C 1870-
1886 M 1870-1920; St John Mf C 1838-1860 B
1827-1860; St Martin Mf 1559-1637 C 1672-1910 M
1672-1932 Banns 1948-51 B 1672-1855 1875-1908;
St Nicholas Mf CB 1556-1925 M 1556-1922; St
Owen Mf C 1626-1911 M 1626-1704 1813-1906 B
1626-1921; St Peter Mf C 1556-1883 M 1556-1640
1678-1870 B 1556-1641 1678-1921; Bapt Z 1832-
1837; Ind C 1690-1836 B 1827-35; Lady Hunt Conn
ZC 1813-36; Prim Meth with PILLAWELL ZC 1831-
37 [13]; SFrs Z 1826-1909 B 1839-1908 [1]; Wes ZC
1821-37 Ext 1843-47 [13]
HEREFORD, LITTLE Mf C 1667-1877 M 1667-1847
Banns 1824-1937 B 1667-1938
HOLME LACY Mf C 1561-1921 M 1561-1835 B 1561-
1812
HOLMER Mf C 1712-1978 M 1712-1980 B 1712-1957;
Huntington Chapelry Mf 1718-1857 M 1932-50
HOPE MANSELL Mf C 1560-1644 1678-1887 M 1602-14
1678-1837 B 1560-1629 1665-1812
HOPE under DINMORE Mf C 1701-1900 M 1701-1837
Banns 1824-1964 B 1701-1881
HUMBER Mf 1660-1867
HUNTINGTON (Holmer) see HOLMER (Huntington
Chapelry)
HUNTINGTON Mf CB 1754-1812 M 1754-1837
HUNTINGTON (Kington) CB 1661-1833 1836 M 1661-
1837 [7] Mf 1661-1846
IVINGTON Mf 1843-1849
KENCHESTER Mf 1663-1848 Banns 1828-1945
KENDERCHURCH Mf 1661-1856
KENTCHURCH Mf CB 1661-1849 M 1661-1962
KILPECK Mf C 1661-1916 MB 1661-1856
KIMBOLTON 1565-1678 1708-1837 [2]
KINGS CAPEL Mf 1661-1857
KINGSLAND Mf C 1539-1964 M 1539-1974 B 1539-1877
KINGS PYON Mf C 1538-1870 M 1538-1881 Banns 1824-
1945 B 1538-1812
KINNERSLEY Mf 1626-1680 CB 1714-1812 M 1714-1837
KINSHAM Mf 1599-1699
KINGTON 1660-1837 [36,42]; Bapt Z Ext 1791-1815 Z
1816-1837; Wes Circuit ZC 1805-37 [13] Mf C 1667-
1951 M 1667-1957 B 1667-1917; see also
HUNTINGTON (Kington)
KNILL Mf CB 1585-1811 M 1585-1836
LAYSTERS see LEYSTERS
LEA Mf 1581-1650 C 1706-1895 M 1706-1837 Banns
1823-1924 B 1706-1812
LEDBURY* C (1556-76)-1812 M (1556-76) 1686-1812 B
(1556-1576)-1642 1647-1807 [18-23] Mf 1556-1576

1857-1865 C 1871-1880; Ind C 1785-1837; Wes ZC
1817-37 [13]
LEINTHALL EARLS Mf M 1830-1880
LEINTHALL STARKES Mf 1660-1869
LEINTWARDINE Mf C 1547-1925 M 1547-1920 B 1547-
1872
LEOMINSTER Bapt Z 1733-1836 B 1702-1837; Ind C
1829-34; Moravian ZC 1786-1837 DB 1784-1837;
SFrs B 1826-37 [13]
LETTON Mf C 1762-1972 M 1754-1837 B 1762-1812
LEYSTERS CB 1703-1789 M 1703-1754 [31]
LINGEN MF C 1751-1958 M 1755-1837 B 1751-1812
LINTON see GORSLEY
LLANCILLO Mf CB 1707-1839 M 1707-1910
LLANDINABO 1596-1812 [12] Mf 1660-1863
LLANGARROW Mf 1569-1633 MB 1661-1883 C 1661-
1951
LLANROTHAL Mf C 1663-1937 M 1663-1932 B 1663-
1847
LLANWARNE Mf C 1660-1909 M 1660-1837 B 1660-
1834
LONGTOWN see CLODOCK and LONGTOWN
LUCTON Mf C 1711-1869 M 1711-1967 B 1711-1812
LUDLOW Wes Circuit C 1817-1836; Prim Meth Circuit C
1825-1834 [13]
LUGWARDINE CB 1538-1783 M 1538-1758 [24] Mf CM
1538-1858 B 1538-1930
LYDE see PIPE and LYDE
LYONSHALL Mf CM 1660-1858 Banns 1823-1882 B
1660-1904
MANSELL GAMAGE Mf 1664-1728 C 1782-1954 M 1782-
1946 B 1782-1967
MANSELL LACY Mf C 1714-1956 M 1714-1837 B 1714-
1812
MARCLE, LITTLE Mf C 1863-1969 MB 1660-1863 Banns
1858-1880
MARCLE, MUCH Mf C 1556-1886 M 1556-1837 B 1556-
1812
MARDEN Mf C 1600-1886 M 1600-1837 1864-66 B 1600-
1865
MARSTOW M 1813-1837 [45] Mf 1662-1853
MATHON Mf 1631-1808
MICHAELCHURCH Mf 1662-1852 see also TRETIRE and
MICHAELCHURCH
MIDDLETON ON THE HILL CB 1650-1838 M 1650-1806
1813-37 [11] Mf 1660-1871
MOCCAS Mf CB 1660-1847 M 1660-1977
MONKLAND 1660-1856
MONMOUTH Wes Circuit ZC 1815-1837 [13]
MORDIFORD C 1744-1812 MB 1744-1788 [43/4]
MORETON JEFFERYS Mf M 1670-1872
MORETON ON LUGG Mf 1681-1835
MUNSLEY* 1662-1812 [28] Mf 1662-1812
NEWENT see LEDBURY
NORTON CANON Mf 1661-1861
OCLE PYCHARD Mf C 1660-1916 MB 1660-1861 Banns
1823-1956
ORLOP Mf C 1672-1863 M 1672-1837 Banns 1824-1895
B 1672-1889
PEMBRIDGE M 1564-1677 CB 1642-77 [3] Mf C 1564-
1859 M 1564-1920 Banns 1823-1960 B 1564-1876;
Ind C 1822-36 [13]
PENCOMBE Mf C 1538-1872 M 1538-1837 1855 B 1538-
1913
PENCOYD CB 1564-1812 M 1564-1810 [12] Mf 1563-
1851
PETERCHURCH Mf 1661-1846

PETERSTOW Mf C 1538-1892 M 1538-1850 Banns 1824-1938 B 1538-1945
PILLAWELL see HEREFORD
PIPE AND LYDE 1558-1812 [30] Mf CB 1558-1812 M 1558-1966
PIXLEY Mf 1660-1869
PRESTON WYNNE Mf C 1730-1980 M 1730-1836 B 1730-1978
ROLLSTONE Mf 1702-1841
ROSS Mf CB 1671-1889 M 1671-1887; Ind C 1732-1837; SFrs B 1829-59 [13]; see also BROCKHAMPTON (Ross)
ROWLESTONE Mf CB 1727-1812 M 1727-1954
ST DEVEREUX 1660-1812 [14] Mf C 1669-1928 M 1669-1836 Banns 1853-1975 B 1669-1812
ST WEONARD Mf C 1624-1864 M 1624-1852 B 1624-1876
SARNESFIELD* CB 1660-1897 M 1660-1895 [29] Mf 1660-1897
SELLACK Mf 1566-1678
SHOBDON Mf C 1566-1869 M 1566-1835 B 1566-1903
STANFORD BISHOP Mf CB 1699-1812 M 1699-1837
STAUNTON ON ARROW Mf C 1558-1913 M 1558-1837 B 1558-1936
STAUNTON ON WYE Mf C 1677-1944 M 1677-1836 B 1677-1926
STOKE EDITH CB 1539-1839 M 1539-1838 [41] Mf CB 1538-1812 M 1538-1838
STOKE LACY Mf C 1567-1889 M 1567-1969 B 1567-1927
STOKE PRIOR Mf C 1678-1891 M 1678-1753 1813-1836 B 1678-1912
STRETFORD Mf C 1712-1970 M 1712-1968 B 1712-1958
STRETTON GRANDISON Mf C 1558-1912 M 1558-1944 B 1558-1976
STRETTON SUGWAS Mf C 1733-1945 M 1733-1836 B 1733-1946
SUTTON Mf CB 1539-1814 M 1539-1837
TARRINGTON 1561-1812 [17] Mf C 1561-1937 M 1561-1837 B 1561-1895
TEDSTONE WAFER Mf C 1729-1812 M 1729-1836 B 1729-1759
THORNBURY Mf C 1538-1953 M 1538-1837 B 1538-1812
THRUXTON Mf CB 1582-1812 M 1582-1754 1817-1835
TITLEY 1570-1678 [25] Mf CB 1540-1812 M 1540-1899
TRETIRE and MICHAELCHURCH Mf CB 1586-1812 M 1586-1942
ULLINGSWICK Mf C 1561-1913 M 1561-1839 Banns 1829-1919 B 1561-1809
UPTON BISHOP Mf C 1571-1910 M 1571-1839 B 1571-1880
WACTON Mf CM 1660-1877 B 1660-1812
WALTERSTONE Mf CB 1783-1812 M 1813-1835
WELLINGTON Mf C 1559-1973 M 1559-1838 Banns 1823-1883 B 1559-1935
WELLINGTON HEATH Mf C 1842-1885 B 1842-1949
WELSH NEWTON Mf C 1800-1895 M 1758-1878 Banns 1824-1917 B 1800-1947
WEOBLEY Mf 1635-1654 C 1682-1885 M 1682-1836 B 1682-1856
WESTHIDE C 1588-1839 M 1575-1840 B 1580-1601 1660-1841 [1] Mf CB 1575-1812 M 1575-1835 Banns 1857-1971
WESTON BEGGARD Mf C 1587-1928 M 1587-1932 B 1587-1812
WESTON UNDER PENYARD Mf C 1568-1914 M 1568-1956 B 1568-1874; Bapt Z 1787-1837 B 1791-1836 [13]
WHITCHURCH Mf C 1813-1883 M 1761-1838 Banns 1803-1951 B 1813-1951; Ind C 1820-33 [13]
WHITNEY CB 1660-1837 M 1662-1835 [7] Mf C 1740-1894 M 1740-1835 B 1740-1965
WIGMORE Mf C 1572-1812 M 1572-1837 Banns 1824-1964 B 1572-1905
WILLERSLEY Mf C 1836-1962 M 1819-1836 B 1819
WINFORTON Mf CB 1690-1812 M 1690-1835 Banns 1824-1959
WITHINGTON CB 1573-1839 M 1573-1840 [1,31] Mf C 1670-1898 M 1670-1837 Banns 1825-30 1858-1950 B 1670-1876
WOLVERLOW Mf Banns 1824-1933
WOOLHOPE C 1561-1812 M 1559-1812 B 1558-1812 [26,33/4]
WORMBRIDGE 1611-1812 [14] Mf 1612-1812
WORMESLEY Mf C 1749-1969 M 1749-1754 1785-1966 Banns 1829-1967 B 1749-1812
YARKHILL 1563-1840 [1] Mf C 1562-1876 M 1562-1837 Banns 1813-1918 B 1562-1912
YARPOLE Mf C 1561-1857 M 1562-1837 B 1561-1869
YAZOR Mf CB 1621-1783 1813-1839 M 1621-1836

HERTFORDSHIRE

ABBOTS LANGLEY M 1538-1837 [61] Mf 1538-1653 C 1677-1839 1851-1882 M 1677-1837 B 1673-1904
ALBURY M 1558-1837 [61] Mf C 1558-1911 M 1558-1837 B 1558-1868
ALDBURY* M 1604-1618 (1694-1812)-1896 [49,61] Mf C 1694-1875 M 1694-1896 B 1694-1871
ALDENHAM* C (1559-1812)-1816 MB (1559-1812)-1837 [11,12,53,61] Mf M 1837-1894 B 1813-1895
AMWELL, GREAT* (CB 1600-1657) M (1559-1657)-1836 [61,P] Mf CM 1558-1658 C 1683-1812 1857-1942 M 1683-1887 B 1558-1657 1688-1881
AMWELL, LITTLE Mf C 1864-1899 B 1864-1927
ANSTEY M 1540-1836 CMB(I) 1540-1837 [55,61] Mf C 1540-1857 M 1540-1837 B 1540-1923
ARDELEY* M (1546-1812)-36 [5,50,61] Mf C 1546-1880 M 1546-1837 B 1546-1872
ASHWELL C 1604-1836 M 1604-1837 B 1604-1863 [13,52,61] Mf C 1686-1837 1857-1968 M 1686-1891 B 1678-1889
ASPENDEN CM 1559-1837 [57,61] Mf C 1559-1948 M 1559-1873 B 1559-1888
ASTON M 1558-1837 [61] Mf C 1558-1901 M 1558-1922 B 1558-1902
AYOT ST LAWRENCE M 1583-1836 [61] Mf CB 1562-1812 M 1583-1836
AYOT ST PETER M 1615-19 1686-1836 [61] Mf C 1686-1895 M 1686-1836 B 1686-1812
BALDOCK M 1559-1837 [61] Mf C 1559-1880 M 1558-1878 B 1558-1883
BARKWAY M 1538-1837 [61] Mf C 1836-1967 M 1805-12 1837-95 Banns 1805-1823 B 1813-1916
BARLEY* M (1560-1812)-37 [49,61,GCI] Mf C 1559-1837 M 1560-1836 B 1560-1894
BARNET Mf C 1605-1672 M 1560-1652 B 1592-1626
BARNET, EAST M 1566-1837 [61]
BAYFORD M 1538-1837 [61] Mf CB 1538-1870 M 1538-1842
BENGEO M 1539-1837 [61] Mf C 1539-1850 1869-1893

M 1539-1895 B 1539-1879; see also TONWELL

BENNINGTON M 1694-1798 1813-37 [61] Mf C 1538-1885 M 1538-1837 B 1538-1881

BERKHAMSTEAD, LITTLE* M (1609-1812)-37 [51,61] Mf C 1604-08 1647-1900 M 1609-41 1647-1837 B 1647-1913

BERKHAMSTEAD, GREAT Mf Ind C 1787-1837; see also BERKHAMSTED St Peter

BERKHAMSTED* St Mary 1604-1839 [14/5,61] Mf 1606-41 C 1660-1810 1813-1861 M 1660-1839 B 1660-1810 1813-1886; St Peter CB 1538-1839 (M 1754-1839) [16-18,61] Mf M 1538-1812 B 1866-1882; Bapt C 1799-1837 B 1801-83 [52]; Ind C 1787-1837 [15]; SFrs Ext Z 1663-1955 M 1841-1968B 1818-1955 [52]

BISHOP STORTFORD St Michael C 1561-1961 M 1561-1837 B 1561-1976 [7] Mf C 1561-1961 M 1561-1895 B 1561-1976; Holy Trinity M 1859-1872 M 1860-1894; All Saints see HOCKERILL

BOURNE END Mf C 1855-1908 B 1855-1915

BOVINGDON C 1674-1843 M 1604-1841 B 1674-1840 [4,19,62] Mf C 1674-1895 M 1674-1753 1760-1895 B 1674-1905

BRAMFIELD M 1559-1840 [62] Mf C 1559-1958 M 1559-1892 B 1559-1768

BRAUGHING M 1565-1837 [62] Mf C 1563-1925 M 1565-1894 B 1565-1881

BRENT PELHAM M 1551-1837 [62] Mf C 1538-1932 M 1551-1855 B 1539-1855

BROXBOURNE M 1688-1837 [62] Mf C 1688-1851 M 1692-1837 B 1688-1906

BUCKLAND M 1663-1837 [62] Mf C 1661-1922 M 1664-1837 B 1663-1898

BUNTINGFORD see LAYSTON

BUSHEY* M 1560-(1581-1837) [51,62] Mf C 1684-1891 M Ext 1590-1683 M 1684-1886 B 1684-1894; United Reformed C(I) 1816-37 B(I) 1818-1920 [20]

BYGRAVE M 1614-1834 [62] Mf M 1766-1834 B 1805-1808

CALDECOTE M 1726-1834 [62] Mf C 1726-1970 M 1726-1889 B 1726-1964

CHESFIELD C 1592-1717 M 1572-1728 B 1591-1731; see also GRAVELEY cum CHESFIELD

CHESHUNT M 1559-1836 [62] Mf C 1559-1895 M 1559-1891 B 1559-1910

CHIPPERFIELD Mf C 1838-1882 M 1842-1895 B 1839-1909

CHIPPING BARNET CB 1814-24 M 1560-1642 1815-24 [57,62] Mf C 1603-74 1705-1876 M 1560-1652 1678-1894 B 1592-1629 1678-1891

CLOTHALL M 1605-1837 [62] Mf C 1717-1813 M 1717-1837 B 1717-1812

CODICOTE C(I) 1559-1846 M(I) 1558-1837 B(I) 1558-1867 [53,57]

COLNEY see also LONDON COLNEY

COLNEY HEATH Mf C 1847-1908 M 1847-1894 B 1846-1911

COTTERED M 1558-1837 [62] Mf C 1563-1971 M 1558-1837 Banns 1779-1864 B 1558-1918

CROSS, HIGH Mf C 1846-1924 M 1847-1959

DATCHWORTH* M (1570-1812)-37 [50,62] Mf C 1570-1786 1813-1892 M 1570-1895 B 1570-1786 1813-1888

DIGSWELL M 1614-1837 [62] Mf C 1538-1911 M 1575-1971 B 1775-1812

EASTWICK* M 1556-1837 [49,GCI] Mf C 1556-1879 M 1556-1836 B 1556-1930

ELSTREE* (CMB 1655-1757) M 1575-1837 [21,51,62]

ESSENDON M 1604-41 1653-1837 [62] Mf C 1653-1954 M 1653-1895 B 1653-1948

FLAMSTEAD C 1548-1847 M 1548-1838 B 1548-1869 [22,23,57,62] Mf C 1548-1864 M 1548-1838 B 1548-1869

FLAUNDEN M 1613-1837 [62] Mf C 1729-1949 M 1731-65 1834-1848 Banns 1782-1926 B 1732-1949

FURNEAUX PELHAM C 1561-1812 M 1561-1812 B 1561-1812 [24]

GADDESDEN, GREAT CM 1559-1840 B 1558-1840 [5,25,26,63] Mf M 1814-1894

GADDESDEN, LITTLE C 1681-1848 M 1604-1984 B 1681-1841 [57,63]

GILSTON* M (1559-1812)-1836 [51,63] Mf C 1558-1896 M 1558-1894 B 1558-1806

GRAVELEY cum CHESFIELD* M (1556-1812)-37 [50,63] Mf C 1555-1880 M 1567-1837 Banns 1813-1912 B 1855-1946

HADHAM, LITTLE* (1559-1812)-37 [4,63] Mf C 1559-1871 M 1560-1837 B 1560-1860

HADHAM, MUCH C 1559-1813 M 1559-1837 B 1559-1808 [36-38,63] Mf C 1813-1857 M 1813-1837 B 1813-1882

HARPENDEN CB 1562-1812 M 1562-1837 [5,27,63] Mf C 1813-1858 M 1813-1879 B 1813-1855

HATFIELD M 1604-1837 B 1678-1736 [5,28,63]; Ind & Bapt Park Street ZC 1823-54 B 1846-1920 [57]

HEMEL HEMPSTEAD M 1558-1837 [29] Mf C 1566-1949 M 1558-1948 B 1558-1944

HERTFORD All Saints C 1559-1647 M 1560-1837 B 1559-1641 [30,63] Mf M 1837-1881; St Andrew M 1561-1837 [63] Mf C 1848-1883 M 1755-1812 1837-78 Banns 1760-1816 B 1868-1927; St John M 1621-1638 1831-1835 [5,63]; SFrs M 1658-1746 [63]

HERTINGFORDBURY M Ext 1545-1637 M 1604-1836 [57,63] Mf M 1541-1641 C 1679-1848 M 1679-1951 B 1679-1865

HEXTON M 1813-1837 [63] Mf C 1538-1927 M 1538-1898 B 1538-1812

HINXWORTH M 1567-1836 [52,63] Mf C 1558-1871 M 1558-1738 1754-1837 B 1558-1963

HITCHIN M 1604-1836 [5,63] Mf C 1562-1904 M 1562-1883 B 1562-1943; Holy Saviour Mf C 1865-1878 M 1866-1894

HOCKERILL Mf C 1852-1953 M 1852-1895

HODDESDON Mf M 1844-1890 B 1844-1870

HOLWELL M 1560-1837 [63] Mf C 1560-1939 M 1560-1935 B 1560-1812

HORMEAD, GREAT 1538-1900 [32] Mf C 1538-1844 M 1538-1956 B 1538-1872

HORMEAD, LITTLE C 1588-1886 M 1598-1850 B 1591-1916 [31] Mf CM 1588-1886 B 1588-1812

HUNSDON* 1546-1837 [32] Mf C 1546-1863 M 1546-1895 B 1546-1890

ICKLEFORD M 1604-1748 1813-1837 [63] Mf C 1749-1894 M 1749-1760 1813-1895 B 1749-1877

IPPOLLITTS see ST IPPOLLITTS

KELSHALL M 1539-1836 [64] Mf C 1538-1916 M 1538-1837 B 1538-1812

KENSWORTH* M 1605-(1615-1812)-1836 [49,64,GCI]

KIMPTON M 1568-1837 [64] Mf C 1840-1890

KINGS LANGLEY C 1558-1902 M 1558-1922 B 1558-1909 [33,64]; Ind CZ 1834-37 [34] Mf C 1588-1902 M 1588-1912 B 1588-1922

KINGS WALDEN M 1558-1836 [64] Mf C 1842-1899 B 1813-1864

KNEBWORTH* CB 1596-1837 M 1596-(1606-1812)-1837 [8,35,50,57] Mf 1596-1837
LANGLEYBURY Mf C 1864-1909 M 1865-1894
LAYSTON M 1563-1836 [64] Mf C 1563-1930 M 1563-1894 B 1564-1910
LETCHWORTH* M 1601-74 (1696-1805)-37 [49,64,GCI] Mf C 1695-1812 M 1696-1899 M(I) 1838-1937 B 1695-1748
LILLEY M 1605-1618 1710-1737 [64] Mf 1609-40 C 1660-1895 M 1660-71 1710-1837 B 1660-1897
LONDON COLNEY Mf C 1826-1898 M 1838-1940 B 1828-1904
MARSTON, LONG M 1609-37 [64] Mf 1606-41 C 1820-1871 B 1820-1828
MEESDON M Ext 1738-53 1813-37 [64] Mf CB 1737-1810 M 1813-1837
MIMMS, NORTH M 1604-40 1669-73 1682-1637 [64] Mf C 1565-68 1647-1901 M 1660-1894 B 1663-1897
MINSDEN Mf 1609-1641
MUNDEN, GREAT M 1558-1837 [64] Mf C 1588-1871 B 1588-1939
MUNDEN, LITTLE M 1604-1837 [64] Mf C 1680-1852 M 1680-1895 B 1680-1890
MUNSDON Mf C 1860-1931
NETTLEDEN M 1742-1783 [64] Mf C 1741-1843 M 1742-1836 B 1687-1841; see also GADDESDEN, GREAT
NEWNHAM M 1574-98 1678-1837 [64] Mf C 1581-1812 M 1581-1750 1814-1898 B 1581-1805
NORTHAW M 1564-1750 1754-1837 [64] Mf C 1562-1881 M 1562-1880 B 1562-1768
NORTHCHURCH M 1604-24 1655-1839 [64]; St John Chapel Mf M 1855-1915; see also BERKHAMSTED St Mary
NORTON* C 1579-1950 M 1579-(1581-1812)-1946 B 1579-1919 [39,40] Mf C 1579-1950 M 1579-1946 B 1579-1919
OFFLEY* M 1604-40 (1654-1812)-1837 [49,64,GCI] Mf C 1654-1876 M 1654-1895 Banns 1754-1943 B 1654-1908
PIRTON M 1560-1837 [64] Mf C 1562-1908 M 1560-1909 B 1558-1914
PUTTENHAM M 1605-1674 1681-1837 [64] Mf CB 1610-1812 M 1610-1837
RADLETT Mf C 1864-1907 M 1866-1894
RADWELL M 1602-1835 [64] Mf C 1590-1812 M 1602-1754 1839-1896 B 1602-1812
REDBOURN M 1560-1598 1626-1837 [64] Mf C 1581-1839 M 1581-1876 B 1581-1856
REED M 1540-1837 [64,52] Mf C 1539-1768 1813-1966 M 1540-1837 B 1539-1766
RICKMANSWORTH* M 1562-(1569-1812)-36 [51,64] Mf 1569-99 1629 C 1653-1886 M Ext 1569-1630 M 1653-1864 B 1653-1885
RIDGE M 1561-1836 [64] Mf C 1562-1932 M 1563-1836 B 1559-1932
ROYSTON M 1662-1837 [52,65] Mf C 1662-1875 M 1662-1895 B 1662-1901
RUSHDEN M 1604-1837 [65] Mf C 1607-1910 M 1604-1754 1794-1837 B 1607-1812
SACOMBE M 1604-1836 [5,65] Mf C 1726-1903 M 1726-1979 B 1726-1937
ST ALBANS Abbey CM 1558-1689 B 1558-1837 [41,52,65] Mf 1558-1708 CB 1743-1812 M 1837-1895; Christ Church Mf M 1860-1895; St Michael M 1572-1592 1643-1837 [65] Mf C 1572-1899 M 1572-1894 B 1572-1857; St Peter M 1558-1837 [65] Mf C 1558-1899 M 1558-1879 B 1558-1877; St Stephen M 1558-1837 [65] Mf C 1561-1654 1693-1695 1717-1929 M 1558-1646 1693-1837 B 1558-1657 1679-1695 1724-1837 1887-1962; SFrs Mf B 1702-21
ST IPPOLLITTS M 1604-1837 [65] Mf C 1625-1894 M 1625-1924 B 1625-1872
ST PAUL'S WALDEN M 1559-1837 [65] Mf C 1559-1905 M 1559-1926 B 1558-1903
SANDON M 1604-1837 [52,65] Mf C 1697-1879 M 1678-1976 B 1678-1879
SANDRIDGE CB 1558-1840 M 1593-1840 [4] Mf Ext 1561-1696 M 1837-1934
SARRATT M 1562-1836 [65] Mf C 1560-1966 M 1560-1970 B 1560-1882
SAWBRIDGEWORTH M 1561-1837 [65] Mf C 1558-1920 M 1558-1794 1805-1837 Banns 1775-1808 B 1558-1929; see also WYCH, HIGH
SHENLEY M 1604-1837 [65] Mf C 1652-1900 M 1604-1920 B 1654-1894
SHEPHALL* C 1560-1840 M (1561-1811)-37 B 1561-1832 [50,53,66] Mf CMB Ext 1581-1696 M 1653-1811 B 1653-1958
STANDON M 1578-1837 [66] Mf C 1671-1926 M 1672-1907 B 1671-1899
STANSTEAD ABBOTS M 1754-1837 [66] Mf C 1695-1728 1752-1901 M 1754-1923 B 1678-1711 1777-1901
STANSTEAD ST MARGARET M Ext 1704-1820 [66] Mf 1703-1717 C 1762-1840 M 1757-1820 B 1762-1828
STAPLEFORD M 1579-1837 [66] Mf C 1813-1928 M 1839-1972
STEVENAGE CB 1653-1726 M 1538-1837 [42,66] Mf 1606-1726 M 1837-1875 Banns 1833-1857 B 1813-1856
STOCKING PELHAM M 1695-1837 [66] Mf C 1695-1975 M 1756-1837 Banns 1754-1812 B 1696-1812
TEWIN M 1559-1837 [66] Mf C 1559-1926 M 1560-1727 1755-1837 Banns 1754-1925 B 1559-1901
THERFIELD M 1538-1837 [52,66] Mf C 1538-1864 M 1538-1961 B 1538-1948
THORLEY M 1539-1837 [66] Mf C 1539-1942 M 1539-1961 B 1539-1925
THROCKING CB(I) 1558-1670 M 1608-1836 [57,66] Mf C 1612-1975 M 1612-1836 Banns 1754-1873 B 1616-1809
THUNDRIDGE CB 1556-1738 M 1556-1837 [43,66] Mf C 1556-1913 M 1556-1668 1682-1915 B 1556-1885
TOTTERIDGE* (1570-1837) [44,66] Mfc B 1837-1937; Diss ZC 1788-1837 [52] Mf CM 1570-1836 B 1569-1837
TOTTERIDGE & WHETSTONE Diss Mfc B 1800-85
TRING M 1566-1837 [66] Mf C 1566-1945 M 1566-1941 B 1566-1937; SFrs Ext B 1679-1709 [52]
WALKERN* CB 1559-1812 M 1559-(1681-1812)-1837 [45,46] Mf C 1559-1812 1845-1877 M 1559-1838 B 1559-1962
WALLINGTON M 1604-1637 1661-1835 [52,66]
WALTHAM CROSS Mf C 1855-1896 M 1855-1895
WARE C 1558-1812 M 1558-1718 1730-1837 B 1558-1670 [1,2,57,66] Mf C 1653-1827 1842-82 M 1653-1812 Banns 1790-1828 B 1653-1812 1852-1893; Christ Church Mf C 1858-1886
WARESIDE Mf M 1844-1959
WATFORD C Ext 1614-1846 M 1539-1837 B 1610-1846 [53,57,66] Mf C 1539-1880 M 1539-1879 B 1539-1877

WATTON AT STONE* M (1560-1812)-46 [50,53,57,66]
Mf C 1842-1925 M 1560-1812 1837-1967 B 1862-
1928
WELWYN M 1559-1563 1572-1837 [66] Mf C 1559-1876
M 1559-1900 B 1558-1934
WESTMILL M 1562-1838 [66] Mf C 1562-1867 M 1564-
1837 B 1562-1929
WESTON M 1539-1837 [66] Mf C 1539-1812 M 1539-
1903 B 1539-1897
WHEATHAMPSTEAD M 1604-1839 [48,66] Mf C 1604-1888
M 1604-1837 B 1690-1893
WIDFORD M 1558-1836 [66] Mf C 1562-1871 M 1558-
1676 1754-1836 B 1558-1894
WIGGINGTON M 1612-1633 1667-1753 1818-1837 [66]
Mf C 1611-1683 1705-1812 M 1611-1748 1818-1837
B 1611-1812
WILLIAN* (1558-1812)-1837 [40,66] Mf C 1557-1912 M
1559-1939 B 1557-1934
WORMLEY M 1685-1837 [66] Mf C 1674-1891 M 1686-
1837 B 1676-1870
WYCH, HIGH Mf C 1861-1894 M 1862-1967 B 1861-
1949
WYDDIAL M 1666-1837 [66] Mf CM 1666-1812 M 1814-
1837 B 1669-1813
WYMONDLEY, GREAT* M (1561-1812)-1837 [40,66] Mf
C 1561-1690 1710-1897 M 1563-1654 1686-90
1711-1837 B 1563-1690 1710-1812
WYMONDLEY, LITTLE* M (1629-1812)-1837 [40,66] Mf
C 1575-1629 1660-93 1721-28 1750-1964 M 1628-
29 1750-1935 B 1628-29 1752-1812
YARDLEY see ARDELEY

HUNTINGDONSHIRE

Index of Marriages in Huntingdonshire and Thorney
(Isle of Ely) 1754-1837 [1-4]

BARHAM C 1604-1619 Ext 1681-90 C 1695-1851 MB
1604-19 1698-1851 [5,19]
BLUNTISHAM cum EARITH CB Ext 1542-1837 M
1539-1650 1705-1837 [6,29]
BRAMPTON 1618-1851 [7,8]
BUCKWORTH 1604-32 C 1662-1848 M 1676-1848 B
1670-1851 [5]
BURY cum HEPMANGROVE see BURY
BURY* (I) 1561-1696 1707-1812 (M 1561-1837) [30,35]
BYTHORN (I) C 1571-1900 M 1560-1900 B 1560-1812
[35]
CATWORTH, GREAT C 1688-1851 M 1683-1851 B 1679-
1851 [9]
COLNE CM 1663-1837 B 1668-1837 [34]
CONINGTON (I) 1583-1698/9 [29]
COPPINGFOLD see UPTON
COVINGTON 1604-1851 [34]
EARITH see BLUNTISHAM
EASTON 1604-26 C 1708-1851 MB 1709-1851 [5,19]
ELLINGTON C 1608-1895 M 1608-1812 B 1608-1967
CMB(I) 1710-1851 [10,19,34]
FEN STANTON M 1612-1837 [6,23]
FENTON see PIDLEY cum FENTON
GIDDING, GREAT M 1675-1812 [19]
GODMANCHESTER 1604-1750 M 1751-1837 [11,12]
GRAFHAM (I) 1580-1851 [13]
HAMERTON 1604-1626 CB 1660-1845 M 1662-1845 [34]

HEMINGFORD ABBOTS C Ext 1692-1812 M 1693-1753
B Ext 1693-1812 [6,24,29]
HEMINGFORD GREY C Ext 1692-1789 M 1674-1837 B
1687-1791 Ext [6,24,29]
HEPMANGROVE see BURY
HILTON C Ext 1563-1711 M 1558-1812 M Ext 1813-1837
B Ext 1558-1769 [14,25,34]
HOLYWELL cum NEEDINGWORTH C(I) 1667-1742 M
1667-1812 B(I) 1667-1717 [6,15,29,35]
HUNTINGDON All Saints C 1560-1681 M 1559-1681 B
1565-1680; St John C 1585-1681 M 1586-1660 B
1589-1681; All Saints & St John C 1678-1783 M
1679-1838 B 1678-1783; St Benedict C 1576-1691
M 1575-1689 B 1582-1685; St Mary C 1605-1713 M
1593-1691 B 1595-1707; St Benedict & St Mary C
1701-1761 M 1692-1837 B 1701-1760 [16]
HURST, OLD C 1672-1812 M 1654 1670-73 1694-1836 B
1691-1812 [31]
NEEDINGWORTH see HOLYWELL
OLDHURST see HURST, OLD
ORTON LONGUEVILLE CB(I) 1696-1812 M(I) 1696-1955
[29]
PAXTON, LITTLE C 1656-1967 M 1559-1901 B 1580-
1621 1667-1966 [17]
PIDLEY cum FENTON CB 1558-1812 M 1558-1837 [27]
RAMSEY* M 1559-1837 [30]
RAVELEY, GREAT with UPWOOD M 1558-1812 [19]
RAVELKEY, LITTLE* M 1557-1839 [30]
SOMERSHAM CM 1558-1837 B 1563-1838 [32/3]
SPALDWICK 1604-1619 C 1683-1851 M 1695-1851 B
1695-1851 [18]
ST NEOTS Meth C(I) 1841-1984
ST IVES M 1561-1837 [14,36]
STAUGHTON, GREAT CM 1541-1837 B 1540-1837 [28]
STOW LONGA CB 1698-1812 M 1699-1837 [19]
STUKELEY, LITTLE M(I) 1567-1812 [19]
TOSELAND C 1567-1837 M 1567-1836 B 1581-1837 [31]
UPTON with COPPINGFOLD 1604-25 C 1660-1851 M
1664-1850 B 1662-1851 [18]
UPWOOD see RAVELEY, GREAT
WARBOYS C 1551-1654 1663-1837 M 1565-1837 B
1556-1845 [19-21,31]
WESTON, OLD (I) 1604-1851 [35]
WISTOW* M 1604-1837 [30]
WOOD WALTON M 1605-63 1754-1812 [34]
WOOLLEY C 1576-1845 M 1576-1849 B 1576-1850
[18,22]

KENT

ADDINGTON C 1562-1812 M 1568-1812 B 1563-1812
[15]
ALLINGTON C 1630-1812 M 1640-1803 B 1633-1810
[15]
APPLEDORE C 1563-1856 M 1563-1837 B 1563-1886
[45,46]
ASH (Sevenoaks) C 1560-1812 M 1562-1812 B
1553-1812 [24] Mfc 1553-1812
ASHFORD St Mary Mfc C 1570-1853 M 1570-1856 B
1570-1842
ASHURST C 1692-1812 M 1692-1754 B 1692-1806 [205]
AYLESFORD M 1653-1734 [227] Mfc 1654-1812
BADLESMERE Mfc 1563-1984

BARFREYSTONE C 1572-1900 M 1572-1936 B
1572-1899 [7]
BARMING C 1541-1611 1624-1812 M 1541-1606 1626-
1813 B 1541-1605 1624-1812 [47]
BEKESBOURNE 1558-1812 [48]
BEARSTED 1563-1641 [36]
BECKENHAM CM 1538-1851 B 1786-1851 [227,242];
Alexandra Mission District C 1869-1884 [227]
BENENDEN 1558-1940 [49-52] see also WEALD
BESSELS GREEN Bapt Z 1682-1815 M 1840-53 B
1738-1861; Diss CB 1717-1785 [227]
BETHERSDEN see WEALD
BEXLEY 1565-1812 [19]
BEXLEYHEATH Bapt B 1827-37 [227]
BIDBOROUGH C 1632-1685 1709-1837 M 1701-1753
1813-1837 B 1593-1837 [53]
BIDDENDEN C 1538-1846 M 1538-1837 B 1538-1877
[54-6] see also WEALD
BIRCHINGTON 1676-1837 [57]
BIRLING CB 1558-1840 M 1711-1836 [21,227] Mfc 1558-
1812
BLACKHEATH Morden College C 1702-1892 M 1702-
1754 B 1702-1911 [16]
BLEAN CB 1558-1812 M 1558-1774 [58]
BONNINGTON 1564-1680 [36]
BOUGHTON MALHERBE C 1665-1839 M 1671-1839 B
1671-1839 [42]
BOUGHTON under BLEAN* (1558-1625) [59] Mfc C
1784-1812
BRABOURNE C 1558-1585 M 1558-1665 B 1558-1616
1680-1693 [42]
BRASTED C 1557-1867 M 1557-1867 B 1557-1867 Ext
1868-1909 [60,61,243]
BREDHURST 1547-1837 [62]
BRENCHLEY 1560-1837 [63-65]
BROADSTAIRS see ST PETER IN THANET
BROMLEY C 1558-1928 M 1575-1934 B 1578-1941 [66-
70]
BROMPTON Mf Wes C 1796-1837
BURHAM 1626-1812 [205]
BURMARSH M 1572-1836 CB Ext 1572-1812 [41]
CANTERBURY Cathedral C 1564-1878 M 1583-1878 B
1571-1874 [71]; All Saints Mfc C 1559-1891 M
1559-1837 B 1559-1855; Holy Cross Mfc C 1563-
1880 M 1563-1837 B 1563-1812; St Alphege 1558-
1800 [72]; MfC C 1745-1846 M 1791-1837 B 1745-
1864; St Andrew Mfc C 1538-1880 M 1538-1879 B
1538-1852; St Dunstan CM 1560-1800 B 1559-1800
[73] MfC C 1559-1846 M 1559-1837 B 1559-1969;
St George the Martyr 1538-1800 [74];St Margaret
Mfc CM 1654-1942 B 1654-1885; St Mary
Bredin Mfc 1563-1840; St Mary Bredman Mfc C
1558-1868 M 1558-1837 B 1558-1812; St Mary
Magdalene 1559-1800 [75]; St Mary Northgate Mfc
C 1640-1846 M 1640-1837 B 1640-1840; St Mildred
Mfc C 1559-1839 M 1559-1837 B 1559-1950; St
Peter (1560-1800) [77] Mfc C 1794-1842 M 1755-
1836 B 1813-1863; St Paul 1562-1800 [76] Mfc C
1785-1844 M 1785-1837 B 1785-1930; Walloon C
1581-1837 M 1583-1747 D 1581-1715 [HS5]; Bapt
Blackfriars CB Ext 1780-1836; Hales Place Rom
Cath Mfc C 1793-1858 M 1793-1803 1842-1855 B
1793-1803
CAPEL C 1663-83 1702-1812 M 1663-81 1702-1812 B
1663-81 1702-87 1801-1812 [29]
CHALK 1661-1812 [22] Mfc 1661-1812

CHARING CB 1590-1686 M 1590-1685 [227]
CHARLTON (Greenwich/Woolwich) St Luke Ext 1562-
1653 C 1653-1840 M 1653-1829 B 1653-1850 [78-
84]
CHARLTON in DOVER M 1565-1837 [201]
CHART, LITTLE* 1538-1813 [198]
CHARTHAM 1558-1740 [40]
CHATHAM St Mary C 1676-1703 M(I) 1700-1704 1720-
1812 [85,228,233]; Bapt ZB 1700-1837
CHELSFIELD CM 1558-1985 B 1558-1986 [218-220] Mfc
1558-1812
CHERITON M 1563-1837 [6]
CHEVENING CM 1561-1812 B 1568-1651 1678-1812
[10] Mfc 1564-1812; see also BESSELS GREEN
CHIDDINGSTONE 1558-1836 [86,87]
CHILHAM Mf C 1558-1836
CHISLEHURST 1558-1929 [88]
CHISLET 1538-1707 [89]
COBHAM C 1655-1812 M 1676-1812 B 1668-1812 [22]
COLDRED Mfc C 1560-1812 M 1562-1836 B 1561-1812
COOLING Mfc C 1707-1812 M 1712-1812 B 1708-1812
COWDEN C 1566-1842 M 1570-1835 B 1566-1840
[206,226]
CRANBROOK C 1559-1697 1738-1840 MB 1559-1840
[43,91,92] see also WEALD
CRAY, NORTH 1538-1812 [34]
CRAYFORD 1558-1812 [34]
CUDHAM CB 1653-1851 M 1654-1840 [16,228]
CUXTON 1560-1812 [21]
DARENTH C 1678-1812 1857-1977 M 1686-1812 1837-
1922 B 1678-1812 1884-1988 [25,228,241]
DARTFORD C 1561-1577 [14] Mf C 1719-1812 M 1719-
1754 B 1634-1799 Mfc 1561-1812; Ind (Lady Hunt
Conn) C 1797-1833; Ind C 1818-1837 [93]
DAVINGTON C 1552-1836 M 1549-1831 B 1565-1837
[94]
DEAL St George Mfc C 1781-1950 M 1717-1752 1852-
1956 B 1737-1774 1809-1911; St Leonard 1559-
1837 [95-100,207,208]; Ind Mfc C 1681-1802 B
1786-98; Municipal Cemetery Mfc B 1856-1926
DEPTFORD St Nicholas Ext C 1592-1826 M 1571-1811 B
1563-1802 [13] M(I) 1822-1829 [228]; St Paul M
1730-1763 [243] Mfc B(I) 1788-1812; Bapt B 1824-
34
DITTON 1663-1812 [21]
DODDINGTON CM 1695-1706 B 1695-1722 [222]
DOVER St James the Apostle CM 1591-1842 B 1596-
1836 M 1557-1843 B 1558-1841 [102-5,SX/R179] Mf M
1557-1843; French Church C 1646-1732 M 1647-
1692 B 1685-1721 [106]; see also CHARLTON in
DOVER
DYMCHURCH M 1624-1837 Ext C 1637-1755 B 1645-
1755 [41]
EASTCHURCH Ext 1883-1918 [147]
EASTRY Mfc C 1559-1865 M 1559-1905 B 1559-1853
EBONY CB 1578-1812 M 1578-1837 [107,228]
EDENBRIDGE Mf C 1547-1799 M 1547-1754 B 1547-
1800
EGERTON 1570-1616 Ext 1618-39 [20]
ELHAM C 1732-1811 M 1736-50 B 1733-1812 [8] Mfc C
1566-1733 1813-1865 M 1566-1918 B 1566-1733
1813-1895
ELMLEY Ext CM 1883-1901 B 1883-1893 [147]
ELMSTONE CB 1552-1812 M 1565-1810 [108]
ELTHAM 1583-1685 [206] Mfc CB 1686-1803 M 1686-
1754

ERITH Ext 1625-1753
EYNSFORD* C(M)B 1538-1812 [17,201,GCI] Mfc 1813-37
EYTHORNE Bapt Mfc Z 1723-1837 D 1797-1858
FARLEIGH, EAST 1580-1840 [110,228]
FARLEIGH, WEST* M 1558-1812 [202,GCI]
FARNBOROUGH 1558-1851 [223,243]
FARNINGHAM CB 1589-1812 M 1590-1810 [15]
FAWKHAM CB 1568-1812 M 1569-1755 [29]
FOLKESTONE 1635-1840 [1-4,209]
FOOTS CRAY CB 1559-1812 M 1567-1811 [12]
FORDWICH Mfc C 1683-1927 M 1683-1835 Banns 1754-1971 B 1683-1812
FRINDSBURY 1669-1812 [111,225,228]
FRITTENDEN see WEALD
GILLINGHAM St Mary Magd C 1558-1656 M 1558-1752 (I) 1700-1812 B 1568-1655 [112,229,233]
GODMERSHAM 1564-1812 [38]
GOODNESTONE (Faversham) CB 1813-1837 [229]
GOODNESTONE (Wingham) C 1558-1880 M 1559-1880 B 1561-1880 [113]
GOUDHURST M 1558-1714 B Ext 1561-1801 [41]; Wes Meth C 1813-1836 [229]; see also WEALD
GRAVENEY B 1813-1837 [229]
GRAVESEND Mf C 1650-1812 M 1653-1812 B 1547-1812; see also MILTON
GREENWICH 1615-1637 [114]
GREENWICH, EAST St Alfrege C 1637-1842 M 1637-1840 B 1615-1713 [115-127]; Christchurch C(I) 1868-1912
GROOMBRIDGE see SPELDHURST
HACKINGTON Mfc C 1567-1837 M 1567-1836 B 1567-1886
HADLOW 1557-1836 [128,129]
HALDEN, HIGH see WEALD
HALLING CB 1705-1840 M 1706-1836 [229]
HALSTEAD* C 1561-1813 (M 1561-1837) B 1561-1811 [32,202,GCI]
HALSTOW, HIGH Mfc C 1655-1812 MB 1654-1812
HARBLEDOWN* 1557-1800 [130]
HARRIETSHAM CMB 1538-1627 M 1703-1837 [47,229]
HARTLEY C 1713-1814 M 1713-1812 B 1712-1813 [29]
HARTY Ext 1883-1918
HAWKHURST see WEALD
HAWKINGE CB 1691-1812 M 1691-1764 [41]
HAYES 1539-1812 [29]
HEADCORN see WEALD
HERNE M 1728-40 [20]
HERNE HILL CB 1741-1837 M 1653-1837 [229]
HEVER 1632-1837 [131]
HIGHAM C 1653-1723 1728-1812 M 1653-1709 1714-24 1727-52 1755-1812 B 1653-1812 [6]
HORTON KIRBIE 1678-1812 [132]
HOUGHAM C 1661-1838 M 1750-65 [230]
HUNTON Mfc 1585-1812
HYTHE C Ext 1569-1781 M 1586-1837 B Ext 1588-1832 [5]
IFIELD C 1751-1812 M 1753-1812 B 1752-1812 [22]
IGHTHAM CB 1559-1812 M 1560-1812 [23]
KEMSING CB 1561-1812 M 1562-1812 [31]
KESTON C 1541-1812 M 1540-1812 B 1542-1685 [133] Mfc 1540-1812
KILNDOWN Ext C 1843-1912 M 1843-1930 B 1843-1915 [234]
KINGSDOWN Wrotham 1725-1812 [24]
KINGSTON 1558-1837 [134]
KNOCKOLT 1548-1812 B 1813-1851 [32,135,243]

KNOWLTON C 1640-1903 M 1641-1934 B 1640-1976 [217]
LAMBERHURST* M 1564-1837 [201,GCI]
LEAVELAND C 1558-1793 M 1554-1749 B 1553-1793 [230] Mfc 1553-1812
LEE CB 1579-1850 M 1579-1817 B 1580-1850 [136,211,230]
LEIGH C 1562-1837 M 1560-1837 B 1564-1837 [18,137]
LESSNESS Bapt Z 1807-29 D 1808-22 [231]
LEWISHAM St Mary 1558-1750 [138]
LEYBOURNE C 1560-1841 M 1560-1837 B 1560-1812 [28,231]
LEYSDOWN Ext C 1884-1908 M 1884-1913 B 1884-1912 [147]
LONGFIELD CM 1563-1812 B 1558-1812 [29]
LOOSE Mf C 1559-1943 M 1556-1966 B 1559-1811 1813-1849
LUDDESDOWN 1681-1812 [18]
LULLINGSTONE 1578-1812 [139]
LYDD C 1542-1840 M 1812-40 B 1539-1848 [140/1,213-215] Mfc C 1542-1846 M 1542-1837 B 1540-1812
LYDDEN CB 1540-1812 M 1540-1680 1687-1837 [36]
LYMINGE 1538-1837 [142]
LYMPNE M 1617-1836 [5]
MAIDSTONE* All Saints M 1542-1754 [143] Wes Mf C 1796-1837
MALLING, EAST 1570-1839 [144,212] Mfc 1570-1812
MALLING, WEST CB 1698-1840 M 1698-1830 [145/6]
MARDEN see WEALD
MARGATE St John the Baptist (Thanet) Mf 1559-1837 Mfc C 1559-1847 M 1767-1792 B 1559-1812; Rom Cath B 1823-70 [231]
MEOPHAM C 1561-1812 M 1575-1812 B 1573-1679 1709 1743-1812 [14]
MEREWORTH CM 1560-1837 B 1559-1837 [31,137]
MILSTEAD CB 1813-40 M 1754-1842 [41]
MILTON (Gravesend) Mf 1559-1812 CMB(I) 1559-1812
MILTON (Sittingbourne) Mfc C 1538-1669 B 1538-1631
MINSTER in Sheppey Ext C 1882-1918 MB 1883-1918 [147]
MINSTER in Thanet M 1557-1837 [148] see also St Mary Minster (Thanet)
MONKS HORTON C 1559-1743 M 1559-1766 B 1558-1746 [42]
MONKTON Mfc C 1700-1883 M 1700-1911 B 1700-1952
MORDEN COLLEGE see Blackheath
MURSTON B(I) 1813-1935 [243]
NETTLESTEAD 1640-1812 [32]
NEWENDEN 1559-1813 [149] see also WEALD
NEWINGTON* (Hythe) (M 1559-1837) Ext CB 1561-1876 [8,202]
NEWINGTON (Sittingbourne) Ext 1558-1848 1917-25 [204]
NONINGTON Ext CB 1538-1812 [8]
NORTHFLEET CB 1539-1812 M 1539-1748 1754-1812 [9]
NURSTEAD C 1561-1812 M 1562-1806 B 1561-1734 1754-1812 [22]
NUSTED see NURSTEAD
OFFHAM CB 1538-1837 M 1538-1852 B 1539-1837 [20,137]
ORPINGTON 1560-1935 [32,150-2,231]
OTFORD 1630-1812 [33]
PECKHAM, EAST Holy Trinity 1558-1812; St Michael CM 1813-36 B 1813-50 [28,153]
PECKHAM, WEST 1561-1812 [20]

PEMBURY CB 1813-36 M 1813-1837 [154] Mfc M 1560-1812

PENSHURST* CB 1558-1812 M 1558-(1647-1812)-36 [155,231,GCI]

PETHAM C 1634-1661 M 1634-1658 B 1634-1655 [231]

PLAXTOL CB 1648-1812 M 1649-1812 [27] Mfc 1648-1812

PLUMSTEAD CB 1783-1787 M(I) 1817-27 [224,231]

QUEENBOROUGH Ext C 1911-1918 MB 1906-1918 [147]; Ind C 1797-1840 [156]

RAMSGATE see SAINT LAWRENCE in Thanet

RAINHAM M(I) 1700-1812

RIDLEY C 1626-1812 MB 1631-1812 [24] Mfc 1626-1812

RIVER (Dover) CB 1566-1840 M 1566-1837 [157] Mfc 1566-1840

ROCHESTER Cathedral C 1657-1837 M 1669-1754 B 1661-1837; St Nicholas C 1624-73 1745-1839 M 1624-1840 B 1624-90 1705-1813 [235-8,244]; St Margaret C 1653-1882 M 1653-1837 B 1639-1885 [158-164,216,225,231]; Presb Mf C 1736-1808;

RODMERSHAM C Ext 1530-1850

ROLVENDEN C 1557-1812 M 1558-1754 B 1558-1812 [106/7,165,231] see also WEALD; Bapt ZC 1796-1834 [234]

ROMPERSHAM 1530-1850 [GCI]

RYARSH 1560-1837 [25,137]

ST LAWRENCE in Thanet* 1560-1653 [168]

ST MARY CRAY C 1579-1812 M 1580-1810 B 1580-1812 [13]

ST MARY HOO Mfc 1695-1812

ST MARY MINSTER (Thanet) Mfc C 1557-1853 M 1557-1837 B 1557-1880

ST PAUL'S CRAY C 1579-1812 M 1581-1748 1754-1837 B 1579-1830 [12,231]

ST PETER in Thanet 1582-1837 [169,170] Mf 1582-1777

SALTWOOD C Ext 1560-1768 M 1562-1837 B Ext 1569-1803 [5]

SANDHURST 1560-1840 [171] see also WEALD

SANDWICH St Peter C 1538-1600 M 1538-76 [172/3]

SEAL C 1561-1845 MB 1561-1837 [24,42]

SEASALTER C 1555-1845 M 1691-1845 B 1673-1845 [210]

SELLING CB 1558-1812 M 1560-1755 [210] Mfc 1557-1979

SEVENOAKS CB 1559-1812 M 1559-1837 Diss C 1717-85 D 1717-1785 [175-7,227] see also BESSELS GREEN

SEVINGTON Mfc C 1554-1962 M 1669-1808 1813-1832 B 1560-1961

SHEERNESS Holy Trinity 1883-1918; St Paul 1911-1918 [147]

SHELDWICH Mfc 1560-1984

SHEPHERDSWELL see SIBERTSWOLD

SHEPPEY, ISLE of see under individual parishes

SHIPBOURNE 1560-1812 [29,178]

SHOREHAM 1558-1812 [30]

SHORNE CB 1538-1812 M 1538-1623 1654-1812 [26]

SIBERTSWOLD Mfc C 1560-1909 M 1563-1837 1909-1953 B 1563-1916

SITTINGBOURNE Banns(I) 1754-1809 B(I) 1813-1851 [245] Mfc C 1538-1668 B 1538-1624

SMARDEN see WEALD

SMEETH Mfc 1569-1838

SNODLAND C 1559-1841 M 1559-1837 B 1559-1840 [179,231]; Cong ZC 1883-1907 [234]; Ind ZC 1836-1867 [234]

SOUTHFLEET 1558-1812 [30]

SPELDHURST with Groombridge CB 1588-1836 M 1559-1836 [180-2]

STANSTED C 1564-1812 M 1602-1822 B 1572-1812 [27]

STAPLEHURST CB 1596-1695 M 1538-1812 [183,202,GCI] see also WEALD

STOKE Mf M 1755-1812

STONE (Dartford) CB 1718-1812 M 1722-1812 [31]

STONE (Oxney) C 1569-1869 M 1569-1837 B 1569-1929 [184]

STOURMOUTH 1538-1812 [185]

STROOD M(I) 1700-1812 [225,231]

STURRY Mfc C 1538-1890 M 1538-1837 B 1538-1861

SUNDRIDGE 1562-1812 [33]

SUTTON (Dover) CB 1538-1812 M 1545-1812 [36]

SUTTON AT HONE 1607-1812 M(I) 1813-1837 B(I) 1813-1851 [35,243]

SUTTON VALENCE Ind ZC 1795-1837 [232]

SWANSCOMBE 1559-1812 [39]

SWANLEY VILLAGE Mfc B 1862-1981

TENTERDEN see WEALD

TESTON CM 1538-1840 B 1538-1838 [186,232]

THANET see Margate (St John the Baptist), Minster in Thanet, St Laurence in Thanet, St Mary Minster (Thanet) and St Peter in Thanet

THROWLEY Mfc 1557-1980

TILMANSTONE Mfc 1558-1900

TONBRIDGE C 1553-1812 MB 1547-1837 [187-9]

TROTTESCLIFFE 1540-1812 [27]

TUDELEY C 1663-1683 1709-60 1788-1812 M 1664-83 1709-1812 B 1663-81 1709-59 1802-1812 [29]

TUNBRIDGE WELLS St Charles the Martyr C 1729-1812 [232,SX/R74]

WALMER Mfc B 1560-1988

WATERINGBURY CM 1705-1844 B 1705-1847 [23,191]

WEALD Mfc CMB : all entries before 1601 for the parishes indicated

WESTBERE Mfc C 1577-1934 M 1577-1836 Banns 1824-1932 B 1577-1947

WESTERHAM* C 1559-1601 (M 1559-1837) [201,232,GCI] Mf C 1559-1878 M 1559-1902 B 1559-1916

WICHLING* M 1577-1837 [202,GCI]

WICKHAM, EAST CM 1730-1812 B 1715-1812 [25]

WICKHAM, WEST 1558-1900 [232,GCI]

WICKHAMBREUX C 1563-1611 M 1558-1651 B 1558-1650 [192]

WILLESBOROUGH* M 1538-1837 [202,GCI]

WILMINGTON C 1684-1845 M 1685-1837 B 1683-1860 [15,193/4]

WITTERSHAM C 1550-1839 M 1550-1840 B 1550-1860 [44] see also Weald

WOMENSWOLD 1754-1812 [197]

WOODCHURCH see WEALD

WOOLWICH St Mary Magdalene CB 1719-1730 M 1719-1729 C(I) 1800-03 [232,234]

WOULDHAM C 1538-1852 M 1569-1760 1813-39 B 1538-1683 1722-1839 [195]

WROTHAM C 1813-1842 M 1813-1837 B 1813-1870 CMB(I) 1558-1842 [41,196] Mfc 1558-1812

WYE Mfc CB 1538-1812 M 1545-1805

WYMYNGEWELD see WOMENSWOLD

YALDING 1559-1812 [199,200]

LANCASHIRE

ACCRINGTON Mfc M(l) 1813-1837; Machpelah Bapt Chapel Mfc B 1834-1864
AINSWORTH Presb Unit ZC 1641-1901 B 1717-1960 [157/8]
ALDINGHAM* with CONISTON C 1561-1694 1765-1837 M 1542-1694 1754-1837 B 1558-1695 1756-1837 [30,195] Mfc CB 1695-1756 M 1658-1756
ALSTON LANE Rom Cath C 1782-1840 [CRS31]
ALTCAR Mfc M(l) 1800-58 Mfc CB 1663-1810 M 1664-1812
ALTHAM* 1596-1695 [36] Mfc M(l) 1813-1837
ASHTON IN MAKERFIELD C 1698-1755 M 1700-53 [123] Mfc C 1698-1755 M 1700-1753
ASHTON UNDER LYNE* C 1824-1837 M(l) 1754-1800 B 1825-1837 [124,196] Mf C 1720-1765 1816-1824
ASHWORTH Mfc M(l) 1824-40
ATHERTON Mf C 1724-1849
AUGHTON* 1541-1764 [81]
BECCONSALL Chapelry (Croston) Mfc M(l) 1813-46 see also HESKETH
BELTHORNE Ind Chapel Mfc Grave registers (l) 1861-1983 ZC 1824-1983
BENTHAM C 1673-1812 M 1668-1812 B 1666-1812 [69]
BILLINGE ZC 1696-1812 M 1699-1810 B 1699-1812 [181] Mfc M(l) 1813-26 1830-36
BISPHAM* with LYTHAM C 1599-1754 MB 1631-1754 [33]
BLACKBURN* 1600-60 C 1646-1680 MB 1653-1680 [41,93]; St Mary Mfc M(l) 1813-1837; Islington Part Bapt Mfc C 1786-1837 B 1764-1837; Presb Chapel Mf C 1811-1868
BLACKLEY 1655-1753 CB 1754-1783 [39,196]
BLACKROD* CB 1606-1701 M 1614-1700 [36] Mf C 1701-1860 M 1701-1754 B 1701-1853
BLAWITH* CB 1728-1837 M 1730-1837 [94,125]
BOLTON BY BOWLAND Mfc M(l) 1813-1837
BOLTON LE MOORS Mfc M(l) 1813-37
BOLTON LE SANDS* 1655-1736 [42]
BOLTON* 1573-1660 [50]; SFrs B 1821-56 [178]; Union Workhouses Z 1839-1887 [159] Mfc 1887-1914; Bridge St Meth C(l) 1844; St John Lum St Mfc C 1849-54; St Peter Mfc M(l) 1838-50
BRETHERTON Chapelry Mfc M(l) 1843-46
BRINDLE* 1558-1714 [11]; Rom Cath C 1721-1816 M 1722-1834 B 1720-1840 [CRS23]
BROUGHTON IN FURNESS C 1634-1812 MB 1662-1837 [90,174,195]
BROUGHTON (Salford)* CB 1653-1804 M 1653-1759 [48]
BURNLEY* 1562-1653 Mfc M(l) 1813-1837
BURTONWOOD* C 1668-1837 M 1683-1750 B 1697-1837 [84]
BURY* (1590-1698) [1,10,24] Mf 1699-1837 Mfc M(l) 1800-1837; Cong Ind Chapel Mfc 1796-1837; Wes Brunswick Mfc C(l) 1835-82; Meth Union Street Mfc C(l) 1839-68
CARTMEL* 1559-1723 [28,96]; Priory Mfc C 1724-1778 M 1724-1790 B 1724-1771; includes CARTMEL FELL M 1754-1790 and LINDALE 1754-1790
CATON* 1585-1718 [59]
CHAPEL LE DALE 1607-1813 [71]
CHILDWALL* (1557-1680)-1753 [106,122]; Holy Trinity WAVERTREE 1794-1840 [178]

CHIPPING* C 1559-1693 M 1599-1692 B 1599-1694 [14]; Rom Cath see LEAGRAM & CHIPPING
CHORLEY* (1548-1653)-1708 [38,196]
CHORLTON CUM HARDY M 1639 1737-1837 M 1737-1751 B 1753-1837 [183]
CHURCH KIRK 1600-1747 [102] Mfc M(l) 1813-1837
CLAUGHTON 1701-1813 [59] Mf 1716-1862; Rom Cath C 1771-1834 [CRS20]
CLAYTON LE MOORS Rom Cath see DUNKENHALGH & ENFIELD; New Jerusalem CM 1868-1983 [177]
CLIVIGER see HOLME
COCKERHAM* 1595-1657 [21]
COLNE* C (1599-1653) 1679-1734 1774-1812 M (1599-1644) B (1599-1650) 1654-1679 1774-1812 [17,127/8,190/1,197] Mf C 1774-1812 Mfc M(l) 1813-1837
COLTON* 1623-1812 [129,130] Mfc 1623 1626-1812
CONISTON* 1599-1700 [30] see also ALDINGHAM
COTTAM (Preston) Rom Cath C 1783-1834 [CRS15]
CROFT B 1833-1920 [160]; with SOUTHWORTH (Chapelry of Winwick) CB 1833-1841 [178]; Unit C 1787-1884 B 1808-99 [155]
CROSBY, GREAT C 1749-1893 B 1854-85 [176,200]
CROSTON* C 1543-1727 M 1538-1685 B 1538-1684 MB 1690-1727 [6,20]; Mfc 1538-1900; see also BECCONSALL, BRETHERTON, MAWDSLEY
CROXTETH PARK (Liverpool) (Fr Worthington) C 1713-1717 [CRS13]
CULCETH Rom Cath C 1791-1825 [CRS13]
DALTON* (1565-1691) 1813-1837 [100,104,195]
DARWEN, LOWER Mfc Chapel C 1751-1794 B 1785-1793
DARWEN, OVER Mfc New Diss Meeting House C 1793-1826 B 1793-4
DEANE* 1604 1613-1750 [53/4] Mfc M(l) 1813-1837; see also BOLTON Workhouses
DENDRON Chapelry of Aldingham B 1803-1812 [195]
DENTON* 1695-1741 [47] Mf C 1758-1837
DERBY, WEST* C 1688-1837 M 1698-1837 [110]
DIDSBURY* 1561-1751 [8] Mf M Ext 1656-1804
DIMPLE Walmsley Old Chapel Mfc C 1789-1840 B 1793-1840
DOWNHAM 1606-1837 [118]
DUNKENHALGH and ENFIELD Rom Cath C 1770-1837 M 1831-37 D 1833 [CRS36]
ECCLES* C 1564-1665/6 M 1565-1664 B 1563-1663 [25,201] Mf C 1564-1726 1756-1805 1813-1841 M 1565-1709 1754-1837 B 1563-1721 1765-1838
ECCLESTON IN THE FYLDE, GREAT* Rom Cath C 1771-1832 [CRS15]
ECCLESTON* 1603-94 [15]
EDENFIELD Mfc C 1813-1927 M 1837-1907 B 1839-1934
ENFIELD Rom Cath see DUNKENHALGH & ENFIELD
EUXTON C 1734-81 [198]
FARNWORTH* CB 1538-1812 C 1895-1920 M (1538-1698)-1837 1897-1920 [80,97,161/2,172/3,175] see also BOLTON Workhouses
FERNYHALGH Rom Cath C 1771-1833 B 1802-56 [CRS31]
FLIXTON C 1570-1787 M 1570-1812 [131/2]
FORMBY* Chapel 1620-1780 [112] Mfc 1781-1837
GARSTANG* (1567-1734) C 1881-1962 M 1881-1955 B 1881-1982 [63,68,180]; Rom Cath C 1788-1824 M 1791-1822 B 1798-1824 [CRS16] Mf Rom Cath C 1788-1824
GOOSNARGH CB 1639-1753 M 1639-1812 [64] Mf C 1813-1876; Rom Cath C 1777-1855 M 1848 1850

1856 [CRS31] Rom Cath Hill Chapel C 1770-1777 [CRS12/4]

GORTON CHAPEL Mf C 1599-1803 B 1651-1807 D 1743-1809

GORTON* C 1599-1741 M Ext 1601-1672 M 1672-1741 B 1650-1741 [47] Mf C 1741-1901 M 1741-54 1838-1901 B 1741-1894

GREENACRES Ind Mfc C 1816-60 B 1836-60

GREENMOUNT United Reform Mfc C 1865-1900; see also TOTTINGTON

GRESSINGHAM* CB 1676-1812 M 1691-1828 [59]

HAGGATE Bapt Chapel Mfc Z 1762-1841 B 1786-94 1811-1857

HALE* CB 1572-1740 M 1572-1754 [92]

HALSALL* 1606-1754 [105] Mfc M(I) 1813-1837 see also MELLING (Chapel)

HALTON* 1592-1725 1727-1837 [44,188] Mfc M(I) 1813-37

HAMBLETON* CB 1695-1812 M 1695-1757 [82]

HARWOOD, GREAT C 1547-1812 MB 1560-1812 [75] Mfc M(I) 1813-1837

HASLINGDEN Mfc M(I) 1813-1837

HAWKSHEAD* 1568-(1705-1837) [133-6,163]

HEATON NORRIS* St Thomas C 1769-1845 B 1767-1850 [121] Mf C 1769-1845 B 1767-1851

HESKETH with BECCONSALL Mfc M(I) 1823-29

HEYSHAM* 1658-1813 [44]

HEYWOOD Mf C 1745-1844 B 1765-1846

HOLCOMBE Emmanuel Mfc(I) 1726-1812; Mf C 1726-1858 B 1726-1845

HOLLINFARE* C 1654-1837 M 1705-44 B 1709-1837 [120]

HOLLINWOOD Mf C 1769-1855 M 1836-37 B 1769-1840 Mfc M(I) 1836-43

HOLME (Cliviger) Holme Chapel CB 1742-1841 M 1742-57 1839-40 [183]

HOLME-ON-SPALDING-MOOR Rom Cath C 1744-1840 M 1744-1791 B 1765-1816 [CRS4]

HORNBY* (C 1742-90 M 1743-48 B 1763-89) [59] Mf Ext 1742-1862; Rom Cath (Parish of Melling) M 1763-1798 1813 D 1762-1798 1812-1818 [CRS32]

HORWICH Mf 1695-1753 C 1753-1841 B 1754-1838

HUYTON* (1578-1727) M 1821-37 [85,194]

INGLETON and CHAPEL-LE-DALE Rom Cath 1807-1813 [71]

IRELETH Chapel C 1745-1784 M 1745-1753 [193]

ISLINGTON see BLACKBURN

KELLET, OVER C 1648-1812 MB 1653-1812 [42]

KIRKBY St Chad Chapel (Parish of Walton-the-Hill) 1610-1839 [164/5]

KIRKBY-in-FURNESS C 1634-1837 MB 1662-1837 [43,193]

KIRKHAM* 1539-1653 [83,99]

LANCASTER CB 1599-1786 M 1599-1754 [32,57,88]; Rom Cath C 1784-1837 M 1785-98 1800-1837 D 1799-1841 [CRS20]

LANGHO C 1725-1837 M 1837 B 1765-1837 [200]

LATHOM CHAPEL see ORMSKIRK

LEA IN THE FYLDE Rom Cath see SALWICK HALL & LEA

LEAGRAM and CHIPPING Rom Cath C 1780-1840 M 1837-1856 B 1827-1857 [CRS36]

LEE HOUSE CHAPEL Rom Cath see THORNLEY

LEIGH* 1558-1625 [136,Mfc] Mf C 1560-1885 M 1560-1845 B 1560-1856

LEIGHTON HALL and YEALAND Rom Cath C 1762-1839 B 1764-84 1818-35 1847-55 D 1824-44 [CRS20]

LEVER Chapel (Bolton-le-Moors) CB 1791-1840 [126]

LEYLAND Ext 1622-41 1653-1710 M(I) 1711-1783 [137]

LINDALE see CARTMELL PRIORY

LIVERPOOL St Nicholas C 1660-1725 MB 1673-1725 [35,101]; St Peter Mfc C 1704-15; Register of births kept by Henry Park 1769-1830 [171]; Kaye St Presb Mf C 1697 1709-1769; Rom Cath St Mary (Highfield Street) CM 1741-1773 [CRS9]; Rom Cath (Ford, Yew Tree, Ainsdale Cemeteries) Mfc B 1859-1989; Rom Cath see also CROXTETH PARK

LONGTON Mfc B 1895-1990

LOWICK* C 1718-1837 M 1727-1837 B 1758-1837 [94,138]

LYTHAM* CB 1679-1761 M 1679-1754 [33]; Rom Cath C 1753-1829 M 1753-1803 [CRS16]

MAGHULL Mfc C 1663-1812 M 1660-1754 B 1663-1844 Mf C 1813-1875

MANCHESTER* Cathedral (1573-1666) M Ext 1573-1750 [31,55,56,89,139]; St John Mf C 1769-1878; St Mary C 1756-1888 M 1806-37 B 1754-1871 [77] Mf M 1806-21 1865-88; Ind Mosley Street C 1792-99 1837 [191]; Platt Chapel Mf C 1687-1807 1858-1965 M 1865-1863 B 1786-1807 1861-1919 1946-53

MARTON (Blackpool) Mfc C 1826-64 B 1806-1900

MAWDSLEY Mfc M(I) 1871-83 Chapelry (Croston) Mfc M(I) 1843-46

MELLING C 1625-1721 M 1636-1752 B 1629-1721 [40] Mf 1677-1853; Chapel (Halsall) CB 1607-1812 M 1603-1837 [108;

MEOLS, NORTH* C 1594-1837 MB 1600-1837 [66,72,198] Mfc 1761-1806 1808-1838

MIDDLETON* (1541-1752) [12,18,49] Mf C 1752-1838 MB 1752-1837 see also ASHWORTH and BOLTON UNION

MOWBRECK HALL with KIRKHAM Rom Cath C 1775-1827 B 1814-39 [CRS15]

NEWCHURCH (Pendle) Mfc M(I) 1813-1837

NEWCHURCH (Rossendale)* 1653-1723 [45]

NEWCHURCH (Winwick) C 1559-1841 M 1607-1751 B 1607-1841 CB(I) 1813-1841 [22,179,194] Mfc with CROFT with SOUTHWORTH C 1813-42 B 1813-41

NEWHOUSE (Preston) Rom Cath C 1774-1834 B 1808-1834 [CRS15]

NEWTON Chapelry Mf B 1756-88

NEWTON HEATH Mf C 1655-1722 1761-92 M 1729-54 B 1678-1728 1783-92

OLDHAM St Mary 1558-1661 [197] Mf C 1662-1744 MB 1666-1733 Mfc M(I) 1813-1830; St Mary Mfc M(I) 1831-67; St Peter Mfc M(I) 1836-37; Waterhead Cong Mfc C 1856-1963

ORMSKIRK* (1557-1626)-1678 [13,98] Mf CMB Ext 1604-1687 CMB 1690-1739 1741-1804 1806-36 includes LATHOM CHAPEL from 1758 and SKELMERSDALE from 1782; Diss C 1743-1837 [194]

PADIHAM* 1573-1653 [16] Mfc M(I) 1813-1837

PENDLEBURY Mf CB 1776-1787

PENDLETON Mf C 1776-1856 B 1776-1860

PENNINGTON* C (1613-99)-1837 M (1616-89) 1695-1837 B (1612-1702)-1837 [29,174,193] Mf C 1707-1812

PENWORTHAM* 1608-1753 [52] Mfc M(I) 1813-1837

PILLING* C 1630-1721 M 1630-1719 B 1685-1718 [39]

POULTON LE FYLDE* (1591-1677) [19]; Rom Cath C 1814-30 B 1815-51 [CRS16]

PRESCOT C 1580-1694 M 1538-41 1575-1693 B 1573-1694 [76,114,176]; see also RAINFORD and ST HELEN'S

PRESTON* 1611-35 [48]

PRESTON, LONG Mfc Bapt M(I) 1884-1957 B 1836-1985

PRESTWICH 1603-1712 [34,49] Mf CB 1712-1843 M 1713-1837 Mfc M(I) 1754-1800

RADCLIFFE* CB 1557-1783 M 1560-1761 [60,61]

RAINFORD* CB (1702-1812)-37 M (1704-1812)-37 [119,166/7]; Ind Chapel CB 1746-1837 [168]; see also PRESCOT and ST HELEN'S

RIBCHESTER C 1598-1801 M 1598-1736 B 1598-1761 [26,141] Mfc CM 1695-1735 B 1694-1736; Rom Cath C 1783-1837 M 1806-1811 [CRS36]

RINGLEY Mf C 1770-1841 B 1770-1812

RISLEY (Warrington) Chapel C 1787-1884 B 1808-99 [155]; Presb ZC 1838-1845 DB 1838-1868 [197]

RIVINGTON Mf C 1703-1836 M 1706-1836 B 1702-1873; Non Conf Chapel CB 1747-1836 [189]

ROBERT HALL Rom Cath see TATHAM

ROCHDALE* (1582-1700 M 1701-1801) [58,62,142/3] Mf C 1701-1841 1877-1899 M 1799-1843 1894-1906 B 1701-1843 Mfc 1582-1616 M(I) 1813-1837; Hope Chapel Mfc M 1844-1926

RUFFORD* 1632-1812 [115]

ST HELENS* CB 1713-1812 M 1723-(1788-1837) [107,111]; Ind C 1734-1837 B 1812-37 Communicants 1711-30 [169]; see also PRESCOT and RAINFORD

ST MICHAEL-ON-WYRE B 1662-1708 [27] Mf C 1813-1875

SALFORD B 1834-1888 [194]

SALWICK* with LEA IN FYLDE Rom Cath C 1775-1813 1820-37 M 1811-13 B 1776-80 1814-37 [CRS15]

SAMLESBURY Rom Cath C 1721-1837 M 1754-1810 1830-37 B 1829-35 [CRS23]

SANKEY, GREAT Mfc C 1728-1837 M 1730-53 B 1735-1839

SCORTON (Garstang) Rom Cath C 1774-89 1795-1835 [CRS20]

SEATHWAITE C 1684-1836 M 1737-1836 B 1736-1837 [193]

SEFTON C 1597-1780 M 1600-1783 B 1600-1780 [86]

SHAW Mfc M(I) 1836-7

SKELMERSDALE Mfc C(I) 1817-1920 M(I) 1859-1980 B(I) 1822-1975 see also ORMSKIRK

SOUTHPORT Christchurch Mf C 1820-35 1837-9 M 1820 1824-35 1837 B 1820-22 1824-35 1837-9; Holy Trinity Mf CB 1874-5; St Paul Mf C 1881; St Stephen CB 1878-1880

SOUTHWORTH see CROFT

SOUTHWORTH HALL Rom Cath C 1795-1827 [CRS13]

STALMINE* 1583-1724 [51]

STANDISH* C 1560-1653 M 1558-1650 B 1558-1652 [46] Mf CB 1558-1812 M 1558-1754; Borwick Hall Chapel Rom Cath C 1728 [CRS25]

STOCKPORT Mfc M(I) 1799-1837

STRETFORD Mf C 1598-1871 M 1598-1769 1835-1883 B 1598-1855

SWINTON Mf C 1791-1825

TATHAM FELLS* CB 1745-1837 M 1746-1754

TATHAM* 1558-1837 [59,78]; Robert Hall Chapel Rom Cath CM 1757-1811 D 1757-58 [CRS4,CRS32]

THORNLEY Lee House Chapel Rom Cath C 1800-1840 B 1829-1846 [CRS36]

THORNTON in LONSDALE 1576-1812 [67]

THURNHAM Rom Cath C 1785-1838 B 1825-1849 [CRS20]

TODMORDEN* C 1670-1780 M 1669-1780 B 1666-1780 [117]

TORVER* (1599-1792)-1837 [43,170]

TOTTINGTON* CB 1799-1837 [116]; Greenmont Unit Ref Ch Mfc C 1865-1900

TOWNELEY HALL Rom Cath C 1706-26/7 M 1705-27 [CRS2]

TUNSTALL* 1626-1812 [40]

TURTON* C 1720-27 1770-1812 B 1720-30 1770-1812 [82]

ULVERSTON Mfc 1545-1812; Holy Trinity C 1832-37 M 1836-37 B 1835-37; St Mary C 1812-1837 MB 1813-1837 [145]; Rom Cath C 1812-1842 M 1822-1844 [CRS20]

UNSWORTH Mf C 1730-1840 M 1730-1753 B 1732-1840 Mfc C 1730-96 M 1730-36 1753 B 1732-96 [194]

UPHOLLAND* (C 1607-1735 M 1600-1735 B 1619-1735) [23] Mfc M(I) 1813-37

URSWICK* (1608-95) CB 1694-1837 M 1692-1837 [29,195,202]

WALNEY Chapel C 1744-1858 M 1837-1900 B 1745-1856 [194]

WALTON LE DALE* CB 1609-1808 M 1609-1812 [37]

WALTON ON THE HILL St Mary C 1586-1748 M 1586-1746 1813-18 B 1586-1745 [5,91,194]; St Anne, Stanley, West Derby C 1831-52 M 1837-52 B 1832-52 [179]; see also FORMBY Chapel, KIRKBY (St Chad Chapelry) and DERBY, WEST

WARRINGTON 1591-1706 C 1709-1868 M 1709-1841 B 1709-1837 [70,95,184,194]; Unit Cairo Street ZC 1724-1853 ZD 1788-1960 [153,182]; Bank St Wes Meth ZC 1809-1837; St John Chapel (Lady Hunt Conn) ZC 1806-1837; Stepney Cong ZC 1798-1837

WARTON IN AMOUNDERNESS Mfc 1726-85 M 1726-33 B 1726-82

WARTON* 1568-1813 [73]

WAVERTREE see CHILDWALL

WESTBY (Kirkham)* Rom Cath C 1763-1816 [CRS15]

WESTHOUGHTON Mf C 1732-1852 M 1732-1839 B 1733-1754

WHALLEY* 1538-1601 1605-1653 [7,74] Mfc M(I) 1813-1837

WHITECHAPEL C 1818-38 B 1818-1903 [194]

WHITTINGTON* C 1538-1764 M 1558-1764 B 1546-1764 [3]

WHITTLE-LE-WOODS Mf 1843-1845

WIDNES St Ambrose C 1884-1972 [185-7]; see also FARNWORTH

WIGAN* CB 1580-1625 M 1594-1625 [4] Mf 1746-83 1813-1829

WINWICK C 1563-1837 M 1600-1841 B 1600-1837[109,113,147-152] Mfc C 1661-1837 M 1661-1841 B 1661-1837 see also NEWCHURCH; Unit Park Lane C 1786-1837 B 1800-37 [154]

WOODLAND Chapel C 1735-1837 B 1748 [193]

WOODPLUMPTON* 1604-1784 [27,103]

WOOLSTON (Warrington)* Rom Cath C 1771-1834 [CRS17]

YEALAND* see LEIGHTON HALL

LEICESTERSHIRE

AB KETTLEBY* Mfc C 1580-1891 M 1580-1753 B 1580-
1910; with HOLWELL (M 1580-1812) [71]
ALLEXTON M 1570-1621 [23] CMB 1636-1836
ANSTEY Mfc C 1571-1892 M 1556-1837 B 1557-1812
see also THURCASTON
APPLEBY MAGNA C 1572-1862 M 1573-1837 B
1572-1906 [24/5]
ARNESBY Ext 1566-1640 [14,87]
ASFORDBY* M 1564-1837 [80]
ASHBY DE LA ZOUCHE M 1561-1754 B 1561-1673 [26]
ASHBY FOLVILLE* CB 1584-1812 (M 1584-1837) [5,75]
Mf C 1813-1876
ASHBY MAGNA M 1576-1836 [86] Mf M 1586-1754
ASHBY PARVA* M 1589-1837 [74]
ASTON FLAMVILLE* Mf C 1763-1812; Turville Chapel
Rom Cath C 1759-67 [CRS13]
AYLESTONE* with GLEN PARVA and LUBBESTHORPE
M 1561-1837 [81,86]
BAGGRAVE see HUNGERTON
BAGWORTH see THORNTON
BARKBY* M 1586-1812 [71]
BARKESTONE* M 1569-1837 [73] Mfc CMB 1569-1682
CB 1780-1817
BARLESTONE Mfc C 1652-1943 M 1652-1837 B 1652-
1812
BARROW ON SOAR* M 1563-1837 [76] Mfc 1563-1658
C 1689-1966 M 1689-1727 B 1689-1812
BARSBY see ASHBY FOLVILLE
BARWELL 1563-1640 [27]
BEEBY* M 1538-1837 [75] Mfc C 1538-1807 MB 1538-
1812
BELGRAVE* C 1565-1838 M 1565-(1653-1837) B
1565-1851 [10-13,79]
BIRSTALL* C1561-1838 M 1561-(1574-1837) B 1561-
1837 B Ext 1838-1873 [1,13,79] Mf C 1562-1565
BITTESWELL* M 1558-1837 [74] Mfc C 1558-1887 M
1558-1754 B 1558-1936
BLABY* C(I) 1569-1921 (M 1568-1837) [81,87]
BLACKFORDBY Ext C 1655-1744 M 1562-1734 B 1561-
1747 [10] Mfc 1653-1854 M 1653-1738 1832-33 B
1653-1815
BLASTON Mfc C 1676-1845 1902 M 1676-1837 B 1676-
1812
BOTTESFORD* M 1563-1812 [70]
BOWDEN GREAT Mfc C 1559-1880 M 1564-1837 B
1560-1857 Mf M 1813-32
BRANSTON* (M 1591-1839) [73] Mf C 1813-77
BRAUNSTON* M 1561-1837 [81]
BREEDON M 1685-1690 [87]
BRENTINGBY* see THORPE ARNOLD
BRINGHURST with DRAYTON M 1604-38 [14] Mfc C
1640-1812 M 1640-1800 B 1672-1812
BROOKSBY* M 1767-1812 [71] Mfc CMB 1767-1811
BROUGHTON, NETHER* M 1577-1837 [80]
BRUNTINGTHORPE Mfc C 1574-1897 M 1574-1837 B
1574-1969 M 1608-1836 [86]
BURROUGH ON THE HILL* M 1612-1837 [74] Mfc CB
1612-1819 M 1612-1752
BURTON LAZARS* M 1762-78 [72]
BURTON-ON-THE-WOLDS see PRESTWOLD
BUSHBY see THURNBY
CARLTON CURLIEU M 1571-1678 [14]
CARLTON Market Bosworth 1714-1812 [28] see also

MARKET BOSWORTH
CASTLE DONINGTON Ext CB 1693 1696 1702 M 1672-
1692 [87]
CATTHORPE* M 1573-1837 [74]
CHADWELL* see WYKEHAM
CLAWSON, LONG* M 1558-1837 [80]
CLAYBROOKE CB 1563-1637 CB Ext 1701-05 M 1563-
1836 [9,29,86]
COLD NEWTON* see LOWESBY
COLD OVERTON Ext C 1556-1726 M 1606-72 B 1574-
1770 [10]
COLEORTON Mfc C 1611-1878 M 1611-1837 B 1611-
1962
CONGERSTONE* M 1608-99 (1756-1812) [14,70]
COSSINGTON* C 1649-59 (M 1754-1837) [14,75] Mf M
1813-31 Mfc CB 1544-1812 M 1544-1837
COSTON M 1561-1812 [70] Mfc CB 1561-1812 M 1561-
1749
COTES see PRESTWOLD
COTESBACH Mfc CB 1558-1812 M 1558-1752
CRANOE Mfc CB 1653-1812 M 1653-1837
CROFT M 1548-1837 [86]
CROPSTON* see THURCASTON
CROXTON KERRIAL* M 1558-1837 [73]
CROXTON, SOUTH* CB 1662-1770 M 1561-1634 (1662-
1837) [6,14,75]
DALBY, GREAT* (M 1581-1812) B Ext 1591-1689 [14,72]
Mf C 1565-1812
DALBY, LITTLE* M 1559-1812 [72]
DALBY ON THE WOLDS or OLD DALBY* 1633-39 M
1725-1837 [12,80] Mf C 1813-77
DESFORD M 1559-1837 CMB Ext 1629-99 [14,21] Mf M
1799-1837
DISEWORTH M 1564-1639 B Ext 1683 [14,87] Mf M
1813-36 Mfc C 1656-1872 M 1656-1754 B 1656-
1907
DONINGTON see HUGGLESCOTE
DRAYTON see BRINGHURST
DUNTON BASSETT Mf C 1813-76 M 1810-76
EARL SHILTON M 1552-1837 [22]
EASTON, GREAT Mf C Ext 1572-1812
EASTWELL* CB Ext 1612-1677 (M 1588-1837) [75,87]
EATON* M 1724-1837 [73]
EDMUNDTHORPE Mfc 1560-1812 Banns 1754-1909
ENDERBY C 1559-1656 M 1560-1837 B 1567-1656
[3,22]
EVINGTON* M 1601-1837 [71] Mfc C 1601-1950 M
1601-1812 B 1601-1940
FENNY DRAYTON 1570-1850 [30]
FOSTON Mfc CB 1690-1812 M 1690-1836
FOXTON 1715-1722 [85] Mf M 1754-1837
FREEBY* M 1601-1775 [72]
FRISBY ON THE WREAKE* CB 1561-1840 M 1561-
(1659-1837)-40 [31,71] Mf M 1754-1836
FROLESWORTH* M 1538-1837 [74]
GADDESBY* C 1568-1641 1647-1747 (M 1569-1812) B
1569-1747 [7,14,70]
GALBY Mf M 1815-36
GARENDON Rom Cath Mfc M 1873
GILMORTON* CB 1561-1812 M 1562-(1611-1837)
[32,74]
GLEN, GREAT Mfc C 1687-1962 M 1687-1956 B 1687-
1921
GLEN PARVA* see AYLESTONE
GLENFIELD* C 1566 1568 1604-1837 (M 1604-1837) B
1568/9 1605-1837 [81,89]
GOADBY M 1604-95 [14]

GOADBY MARWOOD* M 1657-1837 [80] Mf M 1813-1854

GRIMSTON* M 1635-1837 [75]

GUMLEY C 1596-1630 M 1566-1687 B 1595-1632 [14,85]

HALLATON Mfc C 1563-1864 M 1563-1837 B 1563-1877

HARBY* (M 1700-1837) B Ext 1637 [73,87] Mfc C 1700-1850 M 1700-72 B 1700-1962

HARSTON* M 1707-1837 [73]

HATHERN Mf C Ext 1563-1757 [122]; Rom Cath Mfc C 1862-82

HIGHAM ON THE HILL 1563-1850 [33]

HINCKLEY (I) 1554-1786 Mf M 1561-1834; Rom Cath C 1797 1805 1814-43 M 1830-46 B 1826-58 [34-36] Mfc C 1843-89 D 1862-95

HOBY* CB 1562-1686 (M 1562-1812) [6,71]

HOLWELL see AB KETTLEBY

HORNINGHOLD M 1582-1639 [14]

HOSE* M 1688-1837 [73] Mfc C 1688-1894 M 1688-1754 B 1688-1974

HOTON* M 1653-1837 [14,77]

HOUGHTON ON THE HILL* CB 1582-1639 (M 1584-1837) [79,G2]

HUGGLESCOTE with DONINGTON-LE-HEATH and IBSTOCK Chapelries C 1580-1804 M 1580-1807 B 1580-1742 [2]

HUMBERSTONE* CB 1557-1678 M 1557-(1559-1837) [37,78]

HUNGERTON* M 1614-1837 [75] with BAGGRAVE, INGERSBY and QUENBY

HUSBANDS BOSWORTH Mf C 1813-77; Rom Cath C 1794-1876 [85]

IBSTOCK see HUGGLESCOTE

ILSTON ON THE HILL M 1607-91 [14]

INGERSBY* see HUNGERTON M 1614-1837 [75]

KEGWORTH B Ext 1676/7 [87]

KEYHAM* 1563-1750 M (1568-1837) [76,87]

KILBY Mfc C 1570-1886 M 1570-1837 B 1570-1812

KILWORTH, SOUTH 1559-1830

KIMCOTE and WALTON 1565-1710 [39]

KIRBY BELLARS* M 1563-1636 (1713-1837) [14,71] Mf Ext C 1563-1804

KIRBY MUXLOE* CB 1561 1566 1597-1837 M 1561 1597-(1619-1837) [40,81]

KIRKBY MALLORY M 1571 1585 1599-1837 [21] Mfc C 1598-1953 M 1598-1794 B 1598-1811

KNIGHTON* M 1672-1837 [81]

KNIPTON* C Ext 1562-1695 (M 1562-1837) B Ext 1562-1682 [6,73] Mfc C 1561-1885 M 1561-1752 B 1561-1972

LANGTON Mfc CB 1779-97

LANGTON, EAST & WEST Mfc CB 1646-1812 M 1646-1837

LAUGHTON M 1803-1837 [87] Mfc CB 1754-1813 M 1754-1802

LEICESTER M(I) 1801-1837 [84]; All Saints Ext 1571-1812 B 1827-31 [14,42]; St George C 1827-1830 B 1827-31 [14,85]; St Leonard Ext 1622 1695-1781 B 1827-31 [14,87]; St Margaret Ext 1617-1670 C 1780-1837 M 1754-1837 B 1784-1855 Ext CMB 1615-1783 [14,42-49,87]; St Martin Ext 1656-1722 B 1827-31 [14,87]; St Mary 1600-1738 Ext 1738-1812 B 1827-31 [14,42,50/1]; St Mary de Castro 1800-1837 [52-4]; St Nicholas Ext 1634-1812 B 1827-31; Bapt Archdeacon Lane C 1820-1836 B 1821-1853 [14]; Bapt Dover Street Z 1813-37; Bapt Friar Lane Z 1785-1837 B 1787 1789; Bapt Harvey Lane Z 1784-1832 B 1805-37 [41]; Bapt Upper Charles Street DB 1831-1837; Ind Bond Street CZ 1801-1836 B 1824-1836; Indep Gallowtree Gate CZ 1817-1837 B 1824-1837; Ind Salem,Freeschool Lane Z 1804-1833 C 1813-1833; Prim Meth ZC 1811-37; Wes ZC 1792-1837 B 1773-1838 [41]; Presb Great Meeting C 1711-1838 Z 1785-1838 B 1711-1729 [41]; Grace Dieu Rom Cath Mfc C 1859-73 M 1861-69; Holy Cross Rom Cath Mfc C 1815-35 1843-1908 M 1841-1908; St Peter Rom Cath Mfc C 1896-1908; Sacred Heart Rom Cath Mfc C 1884-96; St Patrick Rom Cath Mfc C 1873-1907 D 1880-1901

LEIRE* (M 1559-1837) [74] Mfc C 1559-1883 M 1559-1802 B 1559-1932

LONG CLAWSON* M 1558-1837 [80]

LOUGHBOROUGH Ext 1633-1789 [87]; Burial Ground B(I) 157-1877 [87]; St Mary Rom Cath C 1833-1908 M 1841-55 D 1839-40 1855-1907 B 1843-55

LOWESBY* with COLD NEWTON M 1561-(1658-1837) [14,79] Mfc CB 1653-1812 M 1653-1753

LUBBESTHORPE* see AYLESTONE

LUTTERWORTH 1564-1640 [14] Mf C 1757-1855

MARKET BOSWORTH CB 1567-1670 M 1567-1699 [9,13,14,87] see also CARLTON

MARKET HARBOROUGH Mfc C 1584-1951 M 1584-1837 B 1584-1800

MARKFIELD CB 1571-1812 M 1569-1812 [10,56]

MEASHAM Rom Cath Mfc C 1882-1909

MELTON MOWBRAY* M 1546-1812 [72] Mfc C 1791-1880 M 1754-1885 B 1791-1892; St John Rom Cath Mfc C 1843-97

MISTERTON CB(I) 1558-1812 M 1558-1838 [57,86]

MOUNTSORREL* CB 1600-1746 M 1600-(1677-1837) [13,14,58,76,87]

MUSTON* CB 1561-1730 (M 1561-1812) [59,70]

NEVILL HOLT Rom Cath Mfc C 1772-1854

NEWBOLD FOLVILLE see ASHBY FOLVILLE

NEWBOLD SAUCEY see OWSTON

NEWTON HARCOURT see WISTOW

NEWTON LINFORD 1654-1812 [14,60]

NORTON JUXTA TWYCROSS M 1573-1681 [14] Mf C Ext 1564-1685

OADBY M 1569-1639 1655-1837 [61]

OSGATHORPE 1608-78 [14] Mfc C 1683-1888 MB 1683-1812

OWSTON with NEWBOLD SAUCEY* M 1701-1837 [77] Mfc C 1701-1982 M 1701-1810 B 1701-1983

PACKINGTON with SNIBSTON C 1676-1765 M 1574-1747 B 1676-1754 [8,61]

PEATLING MAGNA M 1565-1836 [22] Mf C 1565-1785

PECKLETON M 1567-1837 [21]

PICKWELL* M 1570-1841 [74]

PLUNGAR* Ext 1561-1703 M 1695-1837 [73,87]

PRESTWOLD* M 1560-1837 [77] with BURTON-ON-THE-WOLD and COTES

QUENBY see HUNGERTON

QUENIBOROUGH* (M 1562-1837) Ext CB 1536-1690 [14,75]

QUORN 1576-1746 [7]

QUORNDON* M 1576-1837 [78]

RAGDALE* CB 1604-38 M 1604-38 (1668-1837) [13,71] Mfc CB 1668-1766 M 1668-1753

RATBY* CB 1624-38 1695-1710 M 1624-(1695-1812) [G2,14,70]

RATCLIFFE CULEY Mf C 1816-1874

RATCLIFFE ON THE WREAKE* M 1578-(1698-1837) [14,75]

REARSBY* M 1653-1837 [77]
REDMILE* 1653-1837 [73]
ROTHERBY* C 1561-1668 (M 1561-1812) B 1565-1642
 [6,71]
ROTHLEY* M 1562-1837 [76]
SADDINGTON CM 1538-1681 B 1543-1681 [85] Mfc C
 1767-1836
SALTBY Mfc C 1565-1878 M 1565-1836 B 1565-1807
SAPCOTE Mfc C 1564-1921 M 1579-1812 B 1579-1918
SAXBY* M 1593-(1680-1837) [14,80]
SAXELBYE* with SHOLEBY M 1555-1837 [80]
SCALFORD* M 1558-1812 [71]
SCRAPTOFT* M 1539-1812 [70] Mfc C 1572-84 1604-39
 1672-1721
SEAGRAVE* M 1561-(1682-1837) [14,75]
SHACKERSTONE 1558-1650 1661-67 [9,13,29]
SHANGTON Mfc CB 1580-1653 1680-1812 M 1580-1653
 1680-1829
SHARNFORD* M 1595-1837 [74]
SHEEPY MAGNA 1561 1570 1574 1576 1585 1605-06
 1607-1837 [62] Mf C Ext 1561-1742
SHEPSHED Ext 1660-1800 [87] Mfc C 1538-1878 M
 1538-1854 B 1538-1896; Rom Cath Mfc C 1837-
 1908 D 1854-94
SHOLEBY see SAXELBYE
SIBSON/SIBBESDON* 1559-1812 (M 1569-1812)
 [14,63,70]
SILEBY* CB 1563-1714 M 1563-(1568-1837) [64,77]
SNARESTONE see SWEPSTONE
SNIBSTON see PACKINGTON
SOMERBY* CB 1590-1715 (M 1601-1812) [14,29,71]
SPROXTON M 1581-1639 [14]
STANTON UNDER BARDON see THORNTON
STAPLEFORD* M 1577-(1655-1837) [14,80]
STATHERN* C 1604-1812 (M 1567-1837) B 1567-1812
 [13,73]
STOCKERSTON Mfc CB 1574-1812 M 1574-1837
STOKE GOLDING 1561-1850 [65]
STOUGHTON* M 1537-1837 [79]
STRETTON 1585-1837
SWEPSTONE cum SNARESTONE Mfc C 1561-1884 M
 1578-1837 B 1578-1891
SWINFORD Mfc C 1560-1646 1706-1900 M 1561-1632/3
 1752-1837 B 1559-1600 1621-33 1700-1923
SWITHLAND* Ext 1616-1703 (M 1624-1837) [42,74]
SYSTON* M 1562-1639 (1663-1837) [14,75] Mfc C 1644-
 1885 M 1663-1889 B 1660-1952
THORNTON with BAGWORTH and STANTON UNDER
 BARTON 1559-1778 [66]
THORPE ARNOLD* with BRENTINGBY M 1558-1840
 [80]
THORPE LANGTON Mfc CB 1606-1812 M 1606-1837
THORPE SATCHVILLE see TWYFORD
THRUSSINGTON* M 1565-(1660-1812) [14,71]
THURCASTON* Ext 1606-1763; with CROPSTON (m
 1561-1837) [79]
THURLASTON M 1566 1583 1588-1837 [22]
THURMASTON* CB Ext 1561-1719 M 1561-(1719-1837)
 [67,79]
THURNBY* with BUSHBY M 1564-1837 [79]
TILTON* M 1561-(1631-1837) [14,79] Mf C 1763-1861
TUGBY Mfc C 1568-1895 MB 1568-1812
TUR LANGTON M Ext 1612 [87] Mfc C 1693-1914 M
 1693-1760 B 1693-1793
TWYCROSS 1583-1728 [68] see also NORTON JUXTA
 TWYCROSS
TWYFORD* with THORPE SATCHVILLE M 1562-1812

[70] Mf C 1766-1853
WALTHAM ON THE WOLDS Mf C Ext 1577-1808
WALTON see KIMCOTE
WALTON ON THE WOLDS* M 1568-1837 [78]
WANLIP* C 1561-1838 (M 1563-1837) B 1570-1837
 [4,78]
WARTNABY* M 1633-1838 [75] Mfc CB 1633-1812 M
 1633-1752
WELHAM M 1575-1697 [14]
WHATTON, LONG Ext 1671-1750 [87] Mfc 1549-1742 C
 1813-1852 M 1754-1837 B 1813-1837
WHETSTONE M 1571-1837 [86,87]
WHITWICK Rom Cath Mfc C 1843-1909
WIGSTON MAGNA* M 1567-1837 [81] Mfc C 1567-1909
 M 1567-1754 B 1567-1888
WILLOUGHBY WATERLESS M 1559-1837 [86]
WISTOW and NEWTON HARCOURT Mfc C 1588-1940
 1588-1837 B 1588-1810
WITHCOTE* M 1681-1837 [77] Mfc CB 1679-1809 M
 1679-1754
WOODHOUSE* CB Ext 1625-1702 (M 1623-1837) [78]
WYFORDBY* M 1558-1837 [80] Mfc C 1557-1783 M
 1557-1754 B 1557-1796
WYKEHAM/WYCOMBE with CHADWELL M 1633-1837
 [76]
WYMESWOLD* M 1560-1837 [77] Mfc C 1560-1909 M
 1560-1812 B 1560-1959
WYMONDHAM Mfc C 1538-1946 M 1538-1811 Banns
 1796-1865 B 1538-1962

LINCOLNSHIRE

ABY Mf C 1643-1718 M 1663-1698 B 1654-1725
ADDLETHORPE M 1561-1837 [52] Mf C 1565-1812 M
 1565-1837 B 1565-1969
AISTHORPE M(I) 1754-1812 Mfc CB 1593-1812 M 1606-
 1966
ALFORD CB 1538-1680 [5] M 1538-1837 [49] Mf C 1561-
 1654 1684-1904 M 1538-1654 1684-1972 B 1538-
 1654 1678-1944; Wes Mf C 1805-1837; see also
 CLAXBY by ALFORD
ALGARKIRK M(I) 1754-1812
ALKBOROUGH Mf C 1538-1985 M 1538-1837 B 1538-
 1918
ALLINGTON, EAST M 1559-1812 [43]
ALLINGTON, WEST M 1559-1812 [43]
ALTHORPE Mf C 1672-1941 M 1672-1975 B 1672-1933
ALVINGHAM Mf C 1583-1964 M 1583-1978 B 1583-1965
AMCOTTS Mf C 1836-1930 M 1836-1973
ANCASTER M(I) 1754-1812
ANDERBY M 1561-1837 [52] Mf C 1563-1916 M 1564-
 1837 B 1564-1812
ANWICK M(I) 1754-1812
APLEY Mf CB 1561-1812 M 1561-1763 1817
APPLEBY Mf C 1626-1950 M 1626-1984 B 1626-1901
ASGARBY M(I) 1754-1812
ASGARBY by SPILSBY Mf C 1595-1816 M 1595-1834 B
 1596-1816
ASHBY by PARTNEY Mf CB 1770-1812 M 1754-1837
ASHBY de la LAUNDE M(I) 1754-1812
ASHBY, WEST Ext C 1571-1824 M 1561-1837 B
 1561-1826 [11] Mf C 1561-1889 M 1561-1837 B
 1561-1959

ASHBY cum FENBY M(I) 1754-1812 Mf C 1723-1936 M
1723-1926 B 1723-1989
ASHBY PUERORUM Mf C 1653-1812 M 1659-1806 B
1653-1812 Mf M 1815-1838
ASHBY ST PAUL Mf C 1913-1942 M 1926-1938
ASLACKBY 1558-1661 [13] Mf 1558-1661 C 1730-1861
M 1730-1836 B 1730-1929
ASSERBY see BILSBY
ASTERBY Mf C 1668-1909 M 1668-1837 Banns 1775-
1862 B 1668-1812
ASWARBY M(I) 1754-1812 Mf M 1753-1962
AUBOURN M 1562-1837 [44] Mf C 1749-1896 M 1749-73
1777-1978 B 1749-1975
AUNSBY M(I) 1754-1812
AUTHORPE Mf CB 1561-1812 M 1561-1833
AYLESBY M(I) 1754-1812 Mf M 1813-1835
BARDNEY Mf CB 1653-1951 M 1653-1976
BARHOLME Mf C 1726-1812 M 1728-1836 B 1726-1808
BARKWITH, EAST Mf C 1695-1943 M 1695-1981 B 1695-
1983
BARKWITH, WEST Mfc C 1681-1965 M 1681-1924 B
1681-1812
BARKSTON M(I) 1754-1812
BARLINGS M(I) 1754-1812 Mfc C 1626-1876 M 1626-
1842 B 1626-1938
BARNETBY LE WOLD Mf CB 1754-1944 M 1753-1974
BARNOLDBY LE BECK M(I) 1754-1812 Mf CB 1571-1812
M 1571-1837
BARROWBY M 1538-1837 [53]
BARROW ON HUMBER Mf CM 1560-1943 B 1576-1937
BARTON ON HUMBER St Mary Mf C 1570-1974 M
1570-1980 B 1570-1857; St Peter M 1566-1837
[GCI] Mf C 1566-1966 M 1566-1967 B 1566-1968; St
Augustine Rom Cath Mfc C 1845-1898 M 1871-1876
BASSINGHAM M 1572-1812 [45] Mf C 1572-1968 M
1573-1812 1814-1967 B 1572-1949
BASSINGTHORPE M(I) 1754-1812 Mf C 1541-1719 M
1541-1718 1755-1835 B 1542-1719
BASTON Mf C 1558-1898 M 1558-1937 B 1558-1760
1813-1931
BAUMBER Mf C 1691-1897 M 1691-1959 B 1691-1977
BECKINGHAM M(I) 1754-1812
BEELSBY M(I) 1754-1812 Mf C 1559-1983 M 1566-1985
B 1559-1981
BEESBY M 1565-1837 [49] Mf CB 1743-1812 M 1749-
1811 see also HAWERBY cum BEESBY
BELCHFORD Mf C 1698-1985 M 1698-1837 B 1698-1899
BELLEAU Mf C 1697-1861 M 1697-1837 B 1697-1932
BELTON in AXHOLME M(I) 1754-1812 Mf C 1542-1855
M 1542-1881 B 1542-1884
BENINGTON in HOLLAND Mf C 1567-1652 1697-1737
1753-1812 M 1559-1645 1697-1738 1755-1970 B
1559 1697-1738 1753-1899
BENNINGTON, LONG Mf C 1799-1913 M 1777-1933 B
1799-1901
BENNINGTON, LONG with FOSTON M 1560-1837 [47]
Mf C 1560-1799 M 1560-1777 B 1560-1799
BENNIWORTH Mf C 1691-1865 M 1691-1837 B 1691-
1812 (gap)
BICKER C 1561-1726 M 1561-1633 M(I) 1754-1812 [14]
Mf M 1920-1979
BIGBY Mf C 1697-1953 M 1697-1837 B 1697-1812
BILLINGHAY M(I) 1754-1812
BILLINGSBOROUGH Mf C 1561-1963 M 1561-1919 B
1561-1812
BILSBY with ASSERBY and THURLBY M 1561-1837
[52]

BILSBY Mf C 1669-1979 M 1669-1981 B 1669-1814
1884-1966
BINBROOK ST GABRIEL M(I) 1754-1812 Mf CB 1749-
1847 M 1750-1837
BINBROOK ST MARY M(I) 1754-1812 Mf C 1694-1899 M
1700-1911 B 1699-1906
BISCATHORPE Mf C 1688-1806 M 1689-1753 1813-1837
B 1689-1806
BITCHFIELD M(I) 1754-1812 Mf C 1674-1812 M 1674-
1838 B 1674-1812
BLOXHOLM M(I) 1754-1812
BLYBOROUGH Mf C 1785-1867 M 1754-1836 B 1785-
1812
BLYTON Mf 1571-1812 B 1924-1933
BOLINGBROKE, NEW Mf C 1854-1902
BOLINGBROKE, OLD Mf C 1561-1882 M 1559-1837 B
1538-1894
BONBY Mf 1649-1680 C 1724-1988 M 1724-1989 B
1724-1983
BOOTHBY GRAFFOE C 1563-1975 M (1562-1837)-1954
B 1563-1977 [50,59,62] Mf C 1720-1812 M 1720-
1794 B 1720-1812
BOOTHBY PAGNELL M(I) 1754-1812 Mf CB 1559-1811
M 1559-1953
BOSTON 1557-1638 [1,3]; St Aiden Mf B 1822-1850; St
Botolph Mf C 1557-1599 1684-1976 M 1564-1598
1655-1848 1872-1983 B 1559-1599 1678-1886 1896-
1963; St Botolph Cemetery Mf B 1964-1970; St
James Mf C 1893-1967; Grove Street Ind Mf C
1820-1837; St Mary Rom Cath Mf C 1825-94 M
1830-38 1853-71 D 1854-1902
BOTTESFORD 1599-1717 [15] Mf C 1603-1840 M 1603-
1928 B 1603-1921
BOULTHAM M 1562-1837 [50] Mf CB 1561-1812 M
1561-1836
BOURNE 1562-1650 [7] Mf C 1563-1888 M 1564-1888 B
1562-1938; Wes Mf C 1814-1837 see also MORTON
by BOURNE
BOXBY Ext 1698-1738 [54]
BRACEBOROUGH Mf C 1593-1812 M 1593-1912
BRACEBRIDGE M 1562-1837 [50] Mf C 1663-1882 M
1663-1910 B 1633-1892
BRACEBY M(I) 1754-1812 Mf CB 1779-1812 M 1759-
1837
BRADLEY M(I) 1754-1812 Mf M 1813-1987
BRANSTON Mf C 1680-1734 M 1680-1784 B 1625-76
1680-1734
BRANT BROUGHTON M(I) 1754-1812
BRATOFT Mf CB 1685-1812 M 1689-1839
BRATTLEBY M(I) 1754-1812 Mfc C 1685-1811 M 1685-
1966 B 1686-1812
BRAUNCEWELL CB 1626-1840 M 1627-1837 Banns
1800-1855 [59]
BRIGG Mf C 1843-1931 M 1840 1867-1927 B 1872-1919;
Ind Mf C 1794-1816; Wes Mf C 1815-1837; St Mary
Rom Cath Mfc C 1875-1908; see also BROUGHTON
by BRIGG, SOMERBY by BRIGG, WORLABY by
BRIGG and WRAWBY by BRIGG
BRIGSLEY M(I) 1754-1812 Mf CB 1722-1812 M 1722-
1961
BRINKHILL Mf CB 1561-1813 M 1561-1753 1814-1944
BROCKLESBY 1538-1837 [16] Mf 1538-1571 C 1672-
1812 M 1672-1836 B 1673-1812
BROTHERTOFT M(I) 1754-1812
BROUGHTON by BRIGG Mf C 1538-1846 M 1538-1849
B 1538-1857

BROXHOLME Mf C 1642-1987 M 1642-1978 B 1642-1812

BUCKNALL Mf C 1708-1895 M 1709-1956 B 1708-1812

BULLINGTON see GOLTHO cum BULLINGTON

BURGH LE MARSH Mf C 1538-1864 M 1538-1837 B 1538-1854

BURGH ON BAIN Mf CB 1578-1812 M 1578-1835

BURTON by LINCOLN M(I) 1754-1812 Mfc C 1559-1812 M 1558-1839 B 1558-1839 Mf C 1558-1812 M 1558-1839 B 1558-1813

BURTON COGGLES M(I) 1754-1812 Mf C 1813-1929 M 1754-1837

BURTON PEDWARDINE CB 1561-1574 1763-1970 M 1562-1574 1754-1832 [54]

BURTON UNDER STATHER Mf CMB 1567-1673 C 1678-1919 M 1678-1929 B 1678-1870

BURWELL Mf C 1586-1976 M 1586-1971 B 1586-1812

BUSLINGTHORPE Mfc C 1760-1766 1814-1981 M 1762-1979 B 1760-1766 1816-1963

BUTTERWICK Mf C 1697-1876 M 1697-1837 B 1697-1812

BUTTERWICK, WEST Mf C 1825-1895 B 1844-1914

BYTHAM, CASTLE see CASTLE BYTHAM

BYTHAM, LITTLE 1681-1837 [10] Mf C 1681-1930 M 1681-1926 B 1681-1849

CADEBY see WYHAM cum CADEBY

CADNEY Mf C 1563-1885 M 1563-1951 B 1563-1931

CAENBY M(I) 1754-1812 Mfc C 1712-1954 M 1712-1934 B 1712-1951

CAISTOR Mf C 1885-1923 Mfc CMB 1632-1699 C 1742-1885 M 1742-1761 1778-1892 B 1742-1907

CALCEBY Mf C 1621-1723 M 1621-1719 B 1621-1718

CAMMERINGHAM M(I) 1754-1812 Mfc CB 1662-1812 M 1662-1937 1899-1978

CANDLESBY Mf C 1753-1947 M 1755-1837 B 1755-1812

CANWICK Mf C 1681-1812 M 1681-1837 B 1681-1812

CAREBY M(I) 1754-1812 Mf C 1562-1811 M 1562-1837 B 1562-1810

CARLBY Mf CB 1668-1812 M 1668-1836

CARLTON, GREAT Mf C 1561-89 1653-67 1700-13 1739-1904 M 1561-88 1654-65 1700-13 1739-1971 B 1561-89 1653-66 1700-13 1739-1812

CARLTON LE MOORLAND M 1561-1812 [45] Mf CMB 1561-1685 C 1732-1896 M 1732-1977 B 1732-1812

CARLTON, LITTLE Mf C 1726-1978 M 1726-1837 Banns 1833-1968 B 1727-1975

CARLTON, NORTH M(I) 1754-1812 Mfc C 1653-1812 M 1653-1836 B 1653-1971

CARLTON SCROOP M(I) 1754-1812

CARLTON, SOUTH M(I) 1754-1812 Mfc CB 1655-1813 M 1655-1863

CASTLE BYTHAM M(I) 1754-1812 M 1755-1812 [59] Mf C 1567-1885 M 1567-1837 B 1567-1812

CASTLE CARLTON Mf C 1571-1913 M 1571-1876 B 1571-1886

CAWKWELL Mf C 1683-1886 M 1695-1886 B 1692-1900

CAWTHORPE, LITTLE Mf M 1759-1836

CAYTHORPE M(I) 1754-1812

CHAPEL ST LEONARD Mf 1665-1677 B 1828-1978

CHERRY WILLINGHAM M(I) 1754-1812 Mf C 1662-1812 M 1662-1809 B 1663-1812 Mfc C 1678-1961 M 1678-1978 B 1678-1985

CLAXBY Rom Cath C 1755-59 [CRS13]

CLAXBY by ALFORD (M 1561-1837) [52]; Mf C 1699-1973 M 1699-1927 B 1699-1978

CLAXBY by NORMANBY Mfc 1566-1652 C 1694-1961 M 1694-1962 B 1694-1812

CLAXBY PLUCKACRE Mf C 1561-1873 M 1562-1730 B 1561-1789 (gaps); see also MOORBY with CLAXBY PLUCKACRE

CLAYPOLE M(I) 1754-1812 M 1538-1837 [47]

CLEE, NEW St John Mf M 1800-1962; St John the Evangelist Mf C 1879-1929; St Stephen Mf C 1904-1962 M 1915-1974; Mission Chapel Mf C 1873-1880

CLEE, OLD M(I) 1754-1812 Mf C 1562-1875 M 1562-1876 B 1562-1859

CLEETHORPES St Aidan Mf C 1900-1973 M 1906-1963 B 1939-1952

COATES by STOW Mf CB 1664-1812 M 1664-1956

COATES, GREAT M(I) 1754-1812 Mf C 1653-1939 M 1653-1932 B 1653-1961

COATES, LITTLE M(I) 1754-1812 Mf C 1726-1946 M 1726-1933 B 1729-1914; Good Shepherd Mission Mf C 1912-1935 M 1914-1931 1971

COATES, NORTH Mf C 1659-1917 M 1705-1771 1793 1814-1979 B 1660-1966

COCKERINGTON, NORTH Mf C 1645-1964 M 1645-1949 B 1645-1963

COCKERINGTON, SOUTH Mf CB 1670-1812 M 1670-1837

COLD HANWORTH M(I) 1754-1812 Mfc C 1725-1973 M 1726-1966 B 1726-1974

COLEBY* (1561-1812) [17] Mf C 1561-1875 M 1562-1738 1742-1966 B 1563-1927

COLSTERWORTH M(I) 1754-1812 Mf C 1571-1900 M 1571-1642 1662-1930 B 1571-1642 1660-1916

CONINGSBY Mf C 1561-1963 M 1561-1941 B 1561-1907

CONISHOLME Mf CB 1559-1812 M 1559-1951

CORBY GLEN M(I) 1754-1812 Mf C 1564-1890 M 1564-1837 B 1564-1896

CORRINGHAM Mf C 1647-1859 MB 1647-1812

COVENHAM ST BARTHOLOMEW Mf C 1566-1924 M 1566-1974 B 1566-1812

COVENHAM ST MARY Mf CB 1596-1813 M 1596-1921

COWBITT M 1561-1850 [46] Mf 1595 C 1699-1907 M 1700-1932 B 1699-1875

CRANWELL C 1650-1813 M 1560-1676 1702-1752 1815-1837 B 1650-1812 [54,62]

CREETON M(I) 1754-1812 Mf C 1692-1812 M 1694-1833 B 1692-1812

CROFT Mf C 1548-1981 M 1548-1979 B 1548-1890

CROSBY Mf C 1913-1961 M 1923-1971 B 1914-1924

CROWLAND Mf C 1639-1873 M 1639-1772 1807-1973 Banns 1773-1812 B 1629-1972

CROWLE 1561-1662 [59] Mf C 1561-1973 M 1582-1959 B 1563-1931; St Norbert Rom Cath Mfc C 1872-1905

CROXBY Mfc M 1775-1812 1838-1969

CROXTON Mf 1562-1812

CUMBERWORTH M 1561-1837 [52] Mf C 1561-1976 M 1562-1980 B 1557-1989

CUXWOLD Mf CB 1683-1811 M 1683-1753 Mfc M 1837-1978

DALBY Mf CB 1721-1812 M 1721-1832

DALDERBY Mf C 1690-1730 M 1690-1730 1738 B 1690-1742 see also SCRIVELSBY with DALDERBY

DEEPING ST. JAMES Mf C 1674-1759 1803-1878 M 1674-1919 B 1674-1759 1803-1913

DEEPING ST. NICHOLAS Mf C 1846-1977 M 1847-1981 B 1846-1974

DEEPING, WEST Mf C 1657-1894 M 1657-1837 B 1657-1812

DEMBLEBY M(I) 1754-1812

DENTON M 1558-1837 [53]

45

DEXTHORPE with WELL M 1566-1837 [52]

DIGBY M(I) 1754-1812

DODDINGTON see WESTBOROUGH cum DODDINGTON

DODDINGTON PIGOT CB 1562-1812 M 1562-1837 [18,45] Mf C 1690-1911 M 1690-1978 B 1690-1856

DONINGTON ON BAIN Mf C 1655-1887 M 1655-1837 B 1655-1812 (gaps)

DONINGTON IN HOLLAND C 1642-1761 MB 1653-1761 [19]

DORRINGTON M(I) 1754-1812

DOWSBY Mf C 1731-1930 M 1731-1811 B 1731-1812

DRAX see MIDDLE RASEN

DRIBY Mf C 1622-1965 M 1629-1959 B 1623-1779 1815-1941

DUNHOLME M(I) 1754-1812 Mf C 1582-1881 M 1581-1840 B 1582-1811

DUNSTON Mf C 1564-1624 1690-1895 M 1587-1603 1605-39 1690-1812 1814-1977 B 1564-76 1605-24 1690-1905

DUNSBY Mf CB 1538-1812 M 1538-1837

EAGLE M 1588-1837 [45] Mf C 1588-1955 M 1588-1837 B 1588-1895

EASTVILLE Mf M 1840-1890

EDENHAM Mf 1654-1769 C 1705-1914 M 1705-1964 B 1705-1852

EDLINGTON Mf C 1561-1813 M 1561-1837 B 1561-1812 (gaps)

ELFORD Mf C Ext 1813-1864

ELKINGTON, NORTH Mf C 1701-1970 M 1701-1974 B 1702-1974

ELKINGTON, SOUTH Mf C 1701-1904 M 1702-1766 1813-1965 B 1701-1975

ELSHAM Mf C 1566-1876 M 1566-1989 B 1566-1924

ENDERBY, BAG Mf CB 1562-1812 M 1562-1837

ENDERBY, MAVIS Mf C 1579-1812 M 1580-1837 B 1579-1811

ENDERBY, WOOD Mf C 1561-1812 M 1563-1965 B 1561-1979 (gaps)

EPWORTH Mf C 1538-1601 1710-1903 M 1564-92 1710-1881 B 1538-92 1711-1945

EVEDON 1587-1813 CB 1560-1861 M 1561-1837 [54,56]

EWERBY M 1661-1838 [59]

FALDINGWORTH Mfc 1560-1622 C 1654-1908 1956-1961 M 1654-1978 B 1654-1812

FARFORTH with MAIDENWELL Mf C 1784-1812 M 1784-1837 B 1787-1808

FARLESTHORPE 1562-1837 [52] Mf CB 1608-1789 M 1608-1837

FENBY see ASHBY cum FENBY

FENTON M(I) 1754-1812

FERRIBY, SOUTH Mf C 1594-1911 M 1583-1971 B 1538-1954

FILLINGHAM M(I) 1754-1812 Mfc C 1661-1948 M 1661-1837 B 1661-1813

FIRSBY by SAXBY Mfc C 1813-1840

FIRSBY by SPILSBY Mf C 1717-1812 M 1719-1810 B 1717-1812

FISHTOFT Mf C 1696-1921 M 1697-1963 B 1696-1887

FISKERTON M(I) 1754-1812 Mfc C 1539-1863 M 1539-1842 B 1529-1906

FLEET M 1561-1812 [43] Mf C 1652-1928 M 1656-1913 B 1657-1904

FLIXBOROUGH Mf C 1660-1730 1733 1735-1947 M 1660-1751 1754-1835 1837-1925 B 1660-1730 1735-1812

FORDINGHAM see ULCEBY cum FORDINGHAM

FOLKINGHAM M 1562-1565 1576-1577 1583-1656

1754-1812 [59]

FOSDYKE M(I) 1754-1812

FOSTON M 1646-1657 1776-1837 [47]

FOTHERBY Mf C 1568-1973 M 1568-1837 B 1568-1812

FRAMPTON M(I) 1754-1812 Mf C 1774-1812 1852-1946

FREISTON Mf C 1657-1895 M 1653-1837 B 1658-1891

FRIESTHORPE Mfc C 1620-1833 M 1620-1811 1837-1971 B 1620-1812

FRISKNEY Mf C 1559-1932 M 1559-1936 B 1559-1908

FRITHVILLE Mf C 1823-1851 M 1822-1837 B 1828-1886

FRODINGHAM M 1703-1812 M Ext 1653-1836 B 1751-1812 [20,59] Mf 1636-1812

FULBECK M(I) 1754-1812

FULLETBY Mf CB 1750-1947 M 1750-1812

FULNETBY see RAND cum FULNETBY

FULSTOW Mf C 1586-1865 M 1586-1837 B 1586-1890

GAINSBOROUGH 1564-1640 [6] Mf 1649-1760; All Saints Mf C 1564-1834 M 1564-1899 B 1564-1912; Holy Trinity Mf C 1844-1973 M 1844-1910 B 1844-1941;St John Mf B 1919-1971; St Michael Mf C 1897-1876; St Thomas Rom Cath Mfc C 1844-55 M 1848-53 D 1849-84

GATE BURTON Mf C 1735-1812 M 1735-53 1755-1809 1813-1837 B 1735-1810

GAUTBY Mf CB 1570-1812 M 1570-1837(gaps) Banns 1755-1835 1878-1980

GAYTON LE MARSH Mf C 1687-1926 M 1687-1837 B 1687-1812

GAYTON LE WOLD Mf CB 1773-1812 M 1778-1837

GEDNEY Mf C 1558-1894 M 1558-1923 B 1558-1921

GEDNEY DROVE END Mf C 1856-1897

GEDNEY HILL Mf C 1694-1851 M 1693-1858 B 1693-1812

GLENTHAM M(I) 1754-1812 Mfc C 1690-1859 M 1690-1837 B 1690-1812

GLENTWORTH Mf C 1586-1917 M 1586-1947 B 1586-1812

GOLTHO cum BULLINGTON Mf C 1672-1952 M 1672-1882 B 1672-1951

GONERBY, GREAT M 1560-1837 [53]

GOSBERTON Mf C 1659-1982 M 1659-1974 B 1656-1983

GOULCEBY Mf C 1690-1922 M 1690-1836 B 1690-1812

GOXHILL Mf C 1572-1932 M 1572-1985 B 1572-1987

GRAINSBY 1561-1676 1712-1745 CB 1745-1813 M 1745-1835 [11,56] Mf C 1561-1844 M 1561-1676 1714-1835 B 1574-1813

GRAINTHORPE Mf C 1654-1858 M 1653-1837 B 1653-1880

GRANTHAM (1562-1632) [4]; St Wulfram M (I) 1813-37 [35] M C 1700-1859 M 1700-1853 B 1700-1884; Rom Cath St Mary C 1831-1844 M 1841-2 [59] Mfc C 1831-56 M 1841-2 see also NOTTINGHAM

GRASBY Mf C 1653-1835 M 1653-1837 B 1653-1834

GREATFORD Mf CB 1770-1812 M 1775-1837 see also WILSTHORPE

GREETHAM Mf C 1653-1812 M 1670-1812 B 1654-1812

GREETWELL M(I) 1754-1812 Mfc C 1813-1985 M 1755-1978 B 1814-1984

GRIMOLDBY Mf C 1577-1837 M 1558-1974 B 1558-1967

GRIMSBY, GREAT St James 1538-1812 [22] Mf C 1538-1961 M 1538-1983 B 1538-1910; All Saints Mf C 1888-1928 M 1905-27 B 1898-1941; St Andrew Mf C 1870-1961 M 1871-1961 B 1871-1958; St Augustine Mf C 1905-1962 M 1912-1962 B 1951-61; St Barnabas Mission Mf C 1876-1954 M 1951-54; St Hugh Mf C 1911-68 M 1944-51;

GRIMSBY, GREAT (continued) St Luke Mf C 1877-1965 M 1913-1969; St Martin Mf C 1922-1953; St Paul Mf C 1888-1971 M 1908-1969; St Mary Rom Cath Mfc C 1856-1907 M 1875-99 D 1856-95

GRIMSBY, LITTLE Mf C 1593-1606 1685-1812 M 1593-1603 1688-1835 B 1596-1605 1680-1811

GUNBY ST NICHOLAS M(I) 1754-1812 Mf C 1560-1812 M 1561-1837 B 1564-1812

GUNBY ST PETER Mf C 1724-1812 M 1725-1832 B 1724-1810

HABROUGH M(I) 1754-1812 Mf CB 1538-1844 M 1538-1837

HACCONBY Mf C 1703-1884 M 1703-1837 B 1703-1941

HACEBY M(I) 1754-1812

HACKTHORN M(I) 1754-1812 Mfc CB 1653-1812 M 1653-1944

HADDINGTON M 1562-1837 [44]

HAGNABY Mf CB 1683-1812 M 1683-1836

HAGWORTHINGHAM Mf C 1562-1861 M 1562-1837 B 1562-1907

HAINTON Mfc C 1932-1961 M 1632-1837 B 1623-1812; Rom Cath Mfc C 1772-1836 M 1856-98 D 1860-1909

HALE, GREAT M(I) 1754-1812

HALLINGTON Mf 1654-1742 see also RAITHBY cum HALLINGTON and MALTBY

HALTHAM Mf CM 1561-1974 B 1561-1813

HALTON, EAST C 1574-95 1653-58 1716-1864 M 1654-58 1716-1837 B 1653-58 1716-1892

HALTON HOLGATE Mf C 1701-1869 M 1701-1837 B 1701-1912

HALTON, WEST Mf C 1598-1897 M 1598-1950 B 1598-1942

HAMERINGHAM Mf CB 1777-1812 M 1744-1837

HANNAH cum HAGNABY M 1560-1837 [49] Mf C 1559-1812 M 1560-1961 B 1559-1811

HAREBY Mf CB 1587-1812 M 1587-1836

HARLAXTON M 1559-1837 [53] Mf C 1558-1808 1813-75 M 1559-1645 1653-1705 1708-1837 B 1558-1645 1653-1808 1813-1901

HARMSTON M 1563-1837 [50] Mf C 1563-1870 M 1563-1979 B 1563-1949

HARPSWELL Mf C 1559-1812 M 1559-1836 B 1559-1811

HARRINGTON Mf CB 1697-1812 M 1697-1837

HATCLIFFE 1695-1755 M(I) 1754-1812 [11] Mf C 1696-1908 M 1696-1984 B 1695-1987

HATTON Mf CB 1552-79 1659-1812 M 1554-79 1659-1811 1813-1837

HAUGH Mf C 1764-93 M 1762-1810 1817-1836 B 1763-1810

HAUGHAM Mf CB 1766-1813 M 1756-1947

HAWERBY cum BEESBY M(I) 1754-1812 Mf C 1596-1960 M 1596-1951 B 1597-1949

HAXEY Mf C 1556-1864 M 1571-1901 B 1559-1922

HAYDOR M 1650-1675 1688-1837 [59]

HEALING M(I) 1754-1812 Mf C 1571-1939 M 1571-1937 B 1571-1963

HEAPHAM Mf CB 1558-1812 M 1558-1837

HECKINGTON M 1561-1837 [45]

HEIGHINGTON see WASHINGBOROUGH

HELPRINGHAM M(I) 1754-1812

HEMINGBY Mf CB 1578-1872 M 1579-1896 (gaps)

HEMSWELL Mf C 1688-1885 M 1684-1836 B 1683-1963

HEYDOUR M 1650-1675 1688-1837 [59]

HIBALDSTOW Mf C 1631-1891 M 1631-1945 B 1631-1878

HOGSTHORPE M 1559-1837 [52] Mf C 1559-1886 M 1559-1837 B 1559-1940

HOLBEACH 1613-41 Mf C 1831-1946 M 1813-1893 B 1813-1964; Wes C 1837-40 [24,59]

HOLTON cum BECKERING Mfc 1560-1629 C 1660-1963 M 1660-1975 B 1660-1812

HOLTON LE CLAY CB 1753-1811 M 1754-1800 [62] Mf C 1753-1920 M 1754-1837 B 1753-1966

HOLTON LE MOOR Mfc M 1813-1971

HOLYWELL M(I) 1754-1812 M 1814-1835 [59] Mf C 1558-1981 M 1558-1969 B 1558-1889

HONINGTON M(I) 1754-1812

HORBLING 1653-1837 [25] Mf C 1653-1955 M 1653-1961 B 1653-1909

HORNCASTLE CB (1559-1639 1684-1727 1739-77) M (1559-1639 1684-1727 1739-1812) 1825-37 [26-30,60] Mf C 1559-1794 M 1559-1754 B 1559-1793; St Mary Mf 1695-1739 C 1794-1959 M 1754-1965 B 1794-1934 see also LANGTON by HORNCASTLE, MARTIN by HORNCASTLE and THORNTON by HORNCASTLE

HORSINGTON Mf C 1558-1875 M 1558-1836 B 1558-1812

HOUGH ON THE HILL M 1562-1836 [54]

HOUGHAM M 1756-1838 [55]

HOWELL M(I) 1754-1812

HOWSHAM Mf M 1899-1973

HUMBERSTON M(I) 1754-1812 Mf M 1958-65 B 1813-1943

HUNDLEBY Mf C 1707-1878 M 1707-1953 B 1707-1891

HUTTOFT M 1562-1837 [51] Mf 1562-64 C 1613-1859 M 1613-1919 B 1613-1912

HYKEHAM, NORTH and SOUTH M 1562-1837 [44] Mf C 1694-1936 M 1694-1844 B 1694-1812

HYKEHAM, NORTH Mf C 1855-1910 M 1858-1944 B 1856-1926

IMMINGHAM M(I) 1754-1812 Mf C 1724-1961 M 1724-1963 B 1724-1925

INGHAM M(I) 1754-1812 Mfc C 1567-1929 M 1567-1978 B 1567-1902

INGOLDMELLS M 1561-1837 [52] Mf C 1728-1944 M 1728-1837 B 1728-1812

INGOLDSBY M(I) 1754-1812 Mf C 1566-1878 M 1566-1838 B 1566-1812

IRBY IN THE MARSH Mf C 1545-1813 M 1540-1836 B 1542-1812

IRBY UPON HUMBER 1558-1785 M(I) 1754-1812 [31] Mf CB 1560-1812 M 1560-1811

IRNHAM M(I) 1754-1812 Mf CM 1559-1968 B 1559-1812; Rom Cath C 1765-1784 1797-1845 M 1765-1800 1824-1855 D 1765-1784 1824-1855 1858-1859 [62] Mfc C 1765-1859 M 1765-1800 1824-55 D 1765-84 1824-47

KEAL, EAST Mf C 1707-1878 M 1707-1837 B 1707-1941

KEAL, WEST Mf 1642-84 C 1707-1859 M 1707-1837 B 1707-1901

KEDDINGTON Mf C 1563-1976 M 1566-1672 1695-1977 B 1563-1674 1695-1949

KEELBY M(I) 1754-1812 Mf C 1565-1891 M 1565-1952 B 1565-1939

KELSEY, SOUTH St Mary (M 1559-1812) [44] Mfc C 1560-1770 1813-49 M 1560-1978 B 1560-1770 1813-1894; St Nicholas (M 1559-1812) [44] Mfc 1559-1656 C 1708-1801 M 1708-1791 B 1708-1802

KELSEY, NORTH Mf 1612-86 C 1712-1849 M 1712-1944 B 1712-1869

KELSTERN M(I) 1754-1812 Mf C 1651-1879 M 1651-1837 B 1651-1812

KEXBY see UPTON cum KEXBY

KETTLETHORPE Mf C 1653-1948 M 1655-1836 B 1653-1923

KILLINGHOLME M(I) 1754-1812 Mf C 1564-1870 M 1564-1837 B 1564-1897

KINGERBY (I) 1562-1646 [32] Mfc C 1765-1954 M 1776-1962 B 1770-1893; Rom Cath MB Ext 1641-1780 [CRS22]

KIRKBY cum OSGODBY Mfc C 1558-1869 M 1558-1979 B 1558-1915

KIRKBY, EAST Mf C 1583-1865 M 1583-1839 B 1583-1821

KIRKBY GREEN Mf C 1722-1812 M 1722-1810 1821-35 1837-1973 B 1723-1812

KIRKBY LAYTHORPE/KIRKBY LA THORPE M 1556-1641 1660-1837 [54,60,63]

KIRKBY ON BAIN C 1693-1920 MB 1562-1922 [11] Mf C 1562-1880 M 1562-1837 B 1562-1897

KIRKBY UNDERWOOD 1558-1753 [33] Mf CB 1558-1812 M 1558-1838

KIRKSTEAD Ext C 1663-1799 M 1690-1785 B 1677-1763 [60] Mf C 1677-1970 M 1677-1965 B 1677-1814

KIRMINGTON Mf C 1697-1891 M 1697-1836 B 1697-1965

KIRMOND LE MIRE Mfc CB 1751-1812 M 1756-1808 1838-1968

KIRTON IN HOLLAND M(I) 1754-1812

KIRTON IN LINDSEY Mf C 1708-1898 M 1708-1837 1855-1900 B 1708-1947

KNAITH Mf C 1732-98 1800-1812 M 1739-1809 1814-1837 B 1732-97 1799-1806

KYME, SOUTH M(I) 1754-1812

LACEBY M(I) 1754-1812 Mf C 1538-1968 M 1538-1963 B 1538-1977

LANGTOFT Mf C 1649-1980 M 1666-1977 B 1666-1900

LANGTON by HORNCASTLE Mf CB 1753-1812 M 1767-1837; St Andrew Mf C 1869-1919 M 1859-1944 B 1869-1930

LANGTON by PARTNEY Mf CB 1558-1812 M 1558-1837

LANGTON by WRAGBY Mf C 1653-1903 M 1663-1987 B 1653-5 1729 1741-1812 (gaps)

LAUGHTON Mf C 1566-1881 M 1566-1837 B 1568-1812

LAVINGTON see LENTON

LEA Mf C 1600-80 1709-1812 M 1600-80 1709-1837 B 1600-80 1709-1812

LEADENHAM 1558-1698 1721-39 [54] M(I) 1754-1812

LEASINGHAM 1575-1837 [34] M(I) 1754-1812

LEGBOURNE Mf C 1711-1868 M 1718-1837 B 1711-1919

LEGSBY Mf C 1563-1970 M 1563-1973 B 1563-1812

LENTON M(I) 1754-1812 Mf C 1576-1921 M 1576-1838 B 1576-1812

LEVERTON Mf C 1562-1908 M 1562-1980 B 1562-1887

LIMBER, GREAT Mf CB 1561-1812 M 1561-1814

LINCOLN* St Andrew Mf C 1878-1967 M 1884-1964; St Benedict M (1562-1753) (I) 1754-1837 [9,35] Mf C 1645/6-1854 1933-4 1938-41 1943 1947-8 M 1662-1752 1819-1859 B 1662-1854 (united with St Peter at Arches:1876); St Botolph (M 1652-1753) (I) 1754-1837 [9,35] Mf C 1561-1912 M 1561-1925 B 1561-1876; St Faith Mf C 1899-1947 M 1899-1959 B 1899-1963; St John Newport C 1708-1814 (M 1743-53) 1748-1803 [9,60] Mf C 1708-1861 B 1748-1803; St Margaret in the Close (1538-1837) [2] Mf C 1538-1930 M 1538-1754 B 1538-1871 (united with St Peter in Eastgate:1949); St Mark M (1561-1754) (I) 1754-1812 1828-1837 [9,35] Mf C 1660-1969 M 1660-1754 1828-1969 B 1660-1877;St Martin M (1548-1754) (I) 1754-1837 [9,35] Mf C 1548-1952 M 1546-1627 1687-1968 B 1548-1868; St Mary Magd M (1602-1753) (I) 1754-1837 [9,35] Mf C 1665-1958 M 1665-1964 B 1665-1912; St Mary le Wigford M (1562-1754) (I) 1754-1837 [9,35] Mf C 1622-1964 M 1562-1971 B 1562-1916; St Michael on the Mount M (1562-1754) (I) 1754-1837 [9,35] Mf C 1562-1951 M 1562-1753 1808-1963 B 1562-1891; St Nicholas Newport CB 1736-1812 M (1602-1753)-1812 [9,60] Mf C 1740-1901 M 1840-1879 1891-1933 B 1742-1923; St Paul in the Bail M (1565-1753) (I) 1754-1837 [9,35] Mf C 1695-1968 M 1695-1965 B 1695-1889; St Peter at Arches M (1561-1753) (I) 1754-1837 [9,35] Mf C 1561-1930 M 1561-1927 B 1561-1856 (united with St Peter in Eastgate M (1562-1753) 1813-37 (I) 1754-1837 [9,35,60] Mf C 1662-1956 M 1662-83 1753 1886-1948 B 1662-1958 (united with St Margaret in the Close:1949); St Peter at Gowts CB (1538-1837) M (1538-1753) (I) 1754-1812 1826-1837 [8,9,35] Mf C 1540-1911 M 1538-1672 1688-1753 1826-1898 B 1538-1874; St Swithin M (1562-1753) (I) 1754-1837 [9,35] Mf C 1686-1951 M 1686-1753 1803-1961 B 1686-1907; St Hugh Rom Cath Mfc C 1764-1909 D 1794-1818 1834 1845-66; Workhouse C 1827-41 B 1828-37 [60]; Quarry Maternity Home Mf C 1944-69; see also BURTON by LINCOLN

LINWOOD Mfc CB 1705-1812 B 1705-1935

LISSINGTON Mfc C 1563-1928 M 1563-1978 B 1563-1812

LOUTH Holy Trinity Mf C 1866-1955 M 1867-1956 Banns 1959-74 B 1841-1904; St James Mf C 1538-1851 1861-1943 M 1538-1646 1685-1942 B 1538-1941; St Michael Mf C 1863-1964 M 1863-1946 B 1863-1936; see also WORLABY by LOUTH

LUDBOROUGH Mf C 1598-1938 M 1598-1842 B 1598-1812

LUDDINGTON C 1700-1784 1812-1927 M 1700-1976 B 1700-1784 1813-1941

LUDFORD Mf C 1696-1947 M 1696-1837 B 1696-1962

LUSBY Mf C 1690-1812 M 1691-1836 B 1691-1812

LUTTON Mf C 1548-1856 M 1538-1941 Banns 1947-51 B 1538-1874

MABLETHORPE (M 1561-1837) [51] Mf C 1648-1967 M 1648-1971 B 1648-1951

MAIDENWELL see FARFORTH with MAIDENWELL

MALTBY see RAITHBY cum HALLINGTON and MALTBY

MALTBY LE MARSH M 1561-1837 [49] Mf CB 1644-49 1686-1812 M 1644-49 1686-1837

MANBY CB 1679-1812 M 1679-1758 1778 [55] Mf C 1679-1973 M 1679-1968 B 1679-1894

MANTON Mf C 1813-1905 M 1754-1811

MAREHAM LE FEN Mf 1561-1639 C 1661-1988 M 1662-1928 B 1661-1907

MAREHAM ON THE HILL Mf C 1572-1700 1712-1812 M 1572-1699 1708 1712-1743 1754-1812 1814-1837 B 1572-1698 1712-1743 1766-1812

MARKBY M 1558-1837 [49] Mf CB 1558-1761 M 1558-1967

MARKET DEEPING Mf CM 1709-1983 B 1709-1976

MARKET RASEN Mf C 1671-75 1690-1708 M 1671-74 1693-1708 B 1671-75 1692-1708 Mfc C 1560-1659 1712-1948 M 1560-1663 1709-1946 B 1560-1661 1708-1950; Rom Cath C 1792-1840 [CRS22] Mfc C 1797-1908 M 1848-64

MARKET STAINTON Mf CB 1689-1812 M 1690-1837

MARSH CHAPEL Mf C 1589-1916 M 1589-1838 B 1589-1886
MARSTON M(I) 1754-1812
MARTIN by HORNCASTLE* C 1561-1836 M 1561-1836 B 1561-1836 [36,60] Mf CB 1561-1812 M 1561-1835 (gaps)
MARTIN BY TIMBERLAND Mf C 1876-1936 M 1878-1963
MARTON Mf C 1651-1964 M 1651-1836 B 1651-1907
MELTON ROSS Mf 1568-1812 C 1813-1950 M 1754-1837
MESSINGHAM Mf C 1560-1629 1646-1872 M 1560-1629 1646-1885 B 1558-1629 1646-1875
METHERINGHAM Mf C 1538-1975 M 1538-1977 B 1538-1948
MIDDLE RASEN Mfc C 1813-1902 M 1837-1978 B 1813-1923
MIDDLE RASEN DRAX Mfc CB 1772-1812 M 1755-1843
MIDDLE RASEN TUPHOLME Mfc CB 1708-1812 M 1710-1843
MIDVILLE Mf C 1821-1923 M 1822-39
MININGSBY Mf CB 1695-1971 M 1697-1958
MINTING Ext 1581-1813 [11] Mf C 1562-1876 M 1562-1837 B 1562-1812(gaps)
MOORBY Mf CB 1561-1812 M 1561-1811 1837-1970: with CLAXBY PLUCKACRE Mf C 1813-1970 M 1813-36 B 1813-1975
MOORHOUSES St Laurence Chapel of Ease Mf C 1875-1937 see also REVESBY
MOULTON M 1558-1837 [46] Mf C 1558-1967 M 1558-1962 B 1560-1950
MORTON by BOURNE Mf C 1549-1951 M 1549-1972 B 1549-1858
MUCKTON Mf C 1695-1965 M 1695-1959 B 1695-1812
MUMBY M 1562-1837 [51] Mf 1573-1708 C 1737-1868 M 1737-1837 B 1737-1929; MUMBY Chapel M 1565-1692 [51]
NAVENBY M 1562-1837 [50] Mf C 1681-1972 M 1681-1979 B 1681-1908
NETTLEHAM M(I) 1754-1812 Mfc C 1283-1968 M 1583-1959 B 1582-1904
NETTLETON Mf C 1813-1927 M 1755-1812 1814-1978 B 1813-1955 Mfc C 1684-1807 M 1684-1754 B 1684-1808
NEWTON by TOFT Mfc CB 1630-1812 M 1630-1974
NEWTON on TRENT Mf C 1656-1909 M 1656-1837 B 1656-1812
NEWTON LE WOLD see WOLD NEWTON
NOCTON Mf C 1582-1812 M 1582-1754 1837-1969 B 1582-1812
NORMANBY by SPITAL M(I) 1754-1812 Mfc C 1654-1865 M 1654-1837 B 1654-1812
NORMANBY LE WOLD Mfc CB 1561-1812 M 1561-1975
NORMANTON M(I) 1754-1812
NORTHORPE Mf CB 1593-1985 M 1593-1983
NORTON BISHOP Mf 1587-1703 C 1744-1964 M 1744-1953 B 1744-1924
NORTON DISNEY M 1578-1812 [44] Mf C 1578-1670 1680-1983 M 1578-1669 1681-1810 1813-1976 B 1578-1671 1680-1757 1760-1983
ORBY Mf C 1726-1911 M 1725-1836 B 1725-1989
ORMSBY HALL Private Chapel Rom Cath Mfc C 1868
ORMSBY, NORTH Mf C 1813-1973 MB 1813-1974
ORMSBY, SOUTH Mf C 1561-1920 M 1561-1836 B 1561-1812
OSBOURNBY M 1561-1812 [56]
OSGODBY see KIRKBY cum OSGODBY
OWERSBY Mfc C 1559-1894 M 1559-1976 B 1559-1812

OWMBY by SPITAL M(I) 1754-1812 Mfc CB 1700-1812 M 1700-1837
OWSTON FERRY Mf C 1638-1926 M 1659-1923 B 1668-1852
OXCOMBE Mf C 1787 1813-1978 M 1790-99 1822-1956 B 1788
PANTON by WRAGBY M 1754-1837 [55] Mf C 1736-1955 M 1737-1953 B 1737-1956
PARTNEY Mf C 1699-1881 M 1700-1836 B 1699-1965 see also ASHBY by PARTNEY
PICKWORTH M(I) 1754-1812
PILHAM Mf C 1677-1812 M 1677-1749 1756-1810 1814-1837 B 1677-1812
PINCHBECK M 1560-1812 [43] Mf C 1560-1940 M 1560-1921 B 1560-1878
PINCHBECK, WEST Mf C 1957-1973 M 1851-1976 B 1850-1936
PONTON, GREAT M(I) 1754-1812 Mf 1622-74 C 1686-1941 M 1686-1951 B 1686-1890
PONTON, LITTLE M(I) 1754-1812 Mfc C 1713-1812 M 1729-1837 B 1729-1811
POTTER HANWORTH Mf C 1683-1875 M 1684-1977 B 1663-1918
QUADRING Mf C 1583-1653 1681-1943 M 1583-1652 1681-1979 B 1583-1652 1681-1928
QUARRINGTON with OLD SLEAFORD C 1611-1875 M 1561-1837 B 1611-1890 [37,63] Mf M 1561-1659
RAITHBY by LOUTH Mf CB 1664-1975 M 1664-1836
RAITHBY by SPILSBY Mf CB 1558-1812 M 1559-1837
RAITHBY cum HALLINGTON and MALTBY see RAITHBY by LOUTH
RANBY Mf C 1569-1812 M 1569-1811 B 1569-1813 (gaps)
RAND cum FULNETBY Mf CB 1661-1812 M 1661-1966
RASEN, WEST Mf C 1561-1812 Mfc C 1683-1812 M 1683-1978
RAUNCEBY M(I) 1754-1812
RAVENDALE M(I) 1754-1812 Mf C 1723-1983 M 1740-1837 B 1732/3-1987
RAVENDALE, EAST Mf M 1838-1988
REDBOURNE Mf C 1558-1971 M 1558-1968 B 1558-1976
REEPHAM M(I) 1754-1812 Mfc C 1653-1881 M 1653-1848 B 1653-1890
RESTON, NORTH Mf CB 1563-1812 M 1563-1829
RESTON, SOUTH Mf CB 1766-1814 M 1757-1837
REVESBY Mf C 1594-1937 M 1597-1837 B 1594-1879
RIBY M(I) 1754-1812 Mf C1560-1956 M 1560-1836 B 1560-1812
RIGSBY with AILBY and ALFORD CB 1561-1680 M 1620-1837 [5,49] Mf 1686-1743 C 1753-1812 M 1754-63 1836/7 B 1754-1812
RIPPINGALE Mf C 1633-1849 M 1633-1943 B 1633-1876
ROPSLEY M 1754-1812 [60] Mf C 1558-1944 M 1561-1930 B 1558-1961
ROTHWELL Mfc C 1561-1915 M 1561-1838 1911-62 B 1561-1825
ROUGHTON Mf C 1564-1813 M 1564-1835 B 1564-1811
ROWSTON M(I) 1754-1812
ROXBY cum RISBY 1689-1738 [60] Mf C 1689-1894 M 1689-1953 B 1689-1926
RUCKLAND Mf CB 1758-1812 M 1757-1836
RUSKINGTON M(I) 1754-1812
SALEBY with THORESTHORPE M 1555-1837 [49] Mf CB 1554-1812 M 1554-1837
SALMONBY Mf CM 1558-1965 B 1558-1812

SALTFLEETBY All Saints Mf CB 1558-1812 M 1558-
1836; St Clement Mf M 1756-1835; St Peter Mf C
1653-1928 M 1653-1939 B 1653-1812
SAPPERTON M(I) 1754-1812 Mf M 1813-1833
SAUSTHORPE Mf CB 1565-69 1745-1812 M 1565-69
1745-1837
SAXBY ALL SAINTS M(I) 1754-1812 Mf C 1719-1988 M
1719-1975 B 1719-1812; SAXBY with OWMBY Mfc
CB 1666-1812 M 1666-1754
SAXILBY Mf C 1563-1921 M 1563-1911 M 1563-1865
SCAMBLESBY Mf C 1569-1863 M 1569-1836 B 1569-
1900
SCAMPTON M(I) 1754-1812 Mf C 1695-1706 M 1695-
1705 B 1678-79 1695-1706 Mfc C 1548-1955 M
1548-1970 B 1548-1812
SCARLE, NORTH M (1564-1812) [43] Mf C 1571-1865 M
1571-1837 B 1571-1901
SCARTHO 1562-1837 [38] Mf 1565-1618 C 1686-1948 M
1686-1953 B 1686-1942
SCAWBY Mf C 1558-1948 M 1599-1935 B 1559-1954
SCOPWICK Mf C 1695-1897 M 1695-1752 1754-84 1814-
1978 B 1695-1947
SCOTHERN M(I) 1754-1812 Mfc C 1630-1930 M 1630-
1843 B 1630-1891
SCOTTER Mf C 1561-1947 M 1561-1985 B 1561-1945
SCOTTON 1671-1812 [63] Mf C 1560-1869 M 1560-1924
B 1561-1952
SCREDINGTON C 1561-1692 1738-1850 M 1561-1615 B
1561-1692 1738-1970 [39] M(I) 1754-1812
SCREMBY Mf CB 1716-1812 M 1716-1836
SCRIVELSBY with DALDERBY Mf C 1753-1812 M 1753-
1836 B 1752-1812
SCUNTHORPE St John Mf C 1889-1960 M 1891-1983
SEARBY Mfc CB 1558-1812 M 1558-1836
SEDGEBROOK M 1559-1812 [43] Mf C 1559-1650 1654-
1962 M 1559-1650 1657-1836 B 1559-1649 1654-
1812
SEMPRINGHAM Mf C 1558-1920 M 1558-1974 B 1558-
1897
SIBSEY Mf C 1565-1846 M 1565-1923 B 1565-1918
SILK WILLOUGHBY 1625-1812 [40]
SIXHILLS Mfc CB 1672-1812 M 1672-1974; Rom Cath C
1772-1785 1795-1852 [55]
SKEGNESS St Clement Mf C 1653-1959 M 1653-1949 B
1653-1946; St Matthew Mf C 1885-1959 M 1880-
1945
SKELLINGTHORPE M 1563-1812 [45] Mf CMB 1563-
1684 C 1707-53 1784-1811 1813-1965 M 1748-54
1837-1978 B 1707-53 1784-1811 1897-1916
SKENDLEBY Mf C 1723-1904 M 1724-1836 B 1723-1812
SKIDBROOK with SALTFLEET Mf C 1563-1897 M 1563-
1964 B 1563-1951
SKILLINGTON C 1541-1595 1605-37 1669-73 1680-1753
M 1665-67 1701-1753 M(I) 1754-1812 B 1622-45
1649-1653 [45,63] Mf C 1542-1866 M 1665-1837 B
1583-1867
SKINNAND M 1589-1749 [44] Mf C 1813-1955 B 1813-
1911
SKIRBECK Mf C 1661-1938 M 1661-1918 B 1661-1940
SLEAFORD M 1561-86 1654-70 1683-1699 [63] M(I)
1754-1812; Our Lady of Good Counsel Rom Cath
Mfc C 1881-1903
SLEAFORD, OLD see QUARRINGTON
SLOOTHBY see WILLOUGHBY cum SLOOTHBY
SNARFORD Mfc C 1718-1875 M 1718-1973 B 1720-1845
SNELLAND Mfc CB 1653-1812 M 1653-1719 1813-1977
SNITTERBY Mf C 1858-1989 M 1858-1964 B 1860-1990

SOMERBY by GRANTHAM M 1562-1837 [53]
SOMERBY by BRIGG Mf C 1661-1808 M 1663-1965 B
1662-1800
SOMERCOTES, NORTH Mf C 1563-1929 M 1563-1930 B
1563-1957
SOMERCOTES, SOUTH Mf C 1558-1884 M 1558-1963 B
1558-1958
SOMERSBY Mf CB 1573-1812 M 1573-1836
SOTBY Mf C 1658-1972 M 1659-1980 B 1658-1976
SPALDING (M 1550-1812) [42]; Wes C 1823-40 [60]; SS
Mary & Nicholas Mf C 1538-1961 M 1550-1985 B
1538-1987; Immaculate Conception & St Norbert
Rom Cath Mfc C 1876-1902
SPANBY M(I) 1754-1812
SPILSBY Mf C 1562-1938 M 1562-1908 B 1562-1814 see
also ASGARDBY by SPILSBY, FIRSBY by SPLISBY
and RAITHBY by SPILSBY
SPRIDLINGTON M(I) 1754-1812 Mfc C 1560-1922 M
1560-1837 B 1686-1812
SPRINGTHORPE Mf CB 1558-1812 M 1558-1837
STAIN see WITHERS with STAIN
STAINBY M(I) 1754-1812 Mf CB 1653-1812 M 1660-1836
STAINFIELD Mf C 1680-1961 M 1680-1967 B 1680-1872
STAINTON by LANGWORTH M(I) 1754-1812 Mfc CB
1720-1837 M 1720-1863
STAINTON LE VALE Mfc 1703-5 C 1757-1813
STAINTON, MARKET see MARKET STAINTON
STALLINGBOROUGH Mf C 1588-1876 M 1561-1837 B
1558-1908
STAMFORD All Saints Mf C 1560-1860 M 1560-1883 B
1560-1877; St George Mf C 1559-1977 M 1561-1980
B 1559-1903; St John Mf C 1561-1634 1664-1856 M
1561-1635 1665-1837 Banns 1823-1862 B 1561-
1633 1664-1874; St Mary Mf CB 1569-1812 M 1569-
1837; St Michael Mf C 1560-1949 M 1560-1958 B
1560-1928; St Mary & Augustine Rom Cath Mfc C
1833-52
STAPLEFORD M 1563-1809 [45] Mf C 1695-1755 1757-
1982 M 1695-1908 1813-1975 B 1695-1755 1757-
1984
STEEPING, GREAT Mf C 1711/2-1945 M 1712-52 1754-
1837 B 1711/2-1812
STEEPING, LITTLE Mf C 1559-1881 M 1560-1836 B
1559-1812
STENIGOT Mf C 1562-1834 M 1562-1836 B 1562-1812
STEWTON Mf C 1700-1978 M 1712-1956 B 1713-1977
STICKFORD Mf C 1662-1835 M 1662-1836 B 1662-1812
STICKNEY Mf C 1648-1941 M 1653-1978 B 1653-1882
STIXWOULD Mf C 1547-1955 M 1565-1837 B 1548-1811
(gaps)
STOKE ROCHFORD M(I) 1754-1812 Mf C 1663-94 1724-
1887 M 1665-93 1726-1957 B 1664-94 1724-1958
STOKE, SOUTH M C 1740-1841
STOW see COATES by STOW, WILLOUGHBY by STOW
STOW IN LINDSEY Mf 1651-1944 M 1651-1977 B 1651-
1920
STRAGGLETHORPE M(I) 1754-1812
STRUBBY with WOODTHORPE M 1558-1837 [49] Mf C
1558-1947 M 1558-1837 B 1558-1812
STUBTON 1562-1837 [47]
STURTON, GREAT 1679-1762 [60] Mf CB 1679-1812 M
1679-1837 (gaps)
SUDBROOKE M(I) 1754-1812 Mfc 1579-1651 CB 1722-
1812 M 1722-1843
SURFLEET M 1562-1812 [44] Mf C 1662-1978 M 1662-
1971 B 1665-1928

SUTTERBY Mf C 1560-1800 1825-1959 M 1560-1800 1823-1951 B 1560-1800
SUTTERTON M(I) 1754-1812
SUTTON BRIDGE Mf C 1841-1928 M 1845-1936 B 1843-1927
SUTTON IN THE MARSH M 1561-1837 [49] Mf C 1813-1901 M 1814-1983 B 1813-1944
SUTTON, LONG Mf C 1669-1871 M 1670-1866 B 1669-1873
SUTTON ST EDMUND Mf C 1706-1846 M 1706-1977 B 1706-1864
SUTTON ST JAMES Mf C 1706-1942 M 1706-1974 B 1706-1907
SUTTON ST MARY see SUTTON, LONG
SWABY Mf C 1660-1967 M 1669-1834 B 1660-1926
SWALLOW Mf C 1813-1988 M 1838-1977 Mfc CB 1672-1812 M 1672-1836
SWARBY M 1561-1640 [60] M(I) 1754-1812
SWATON M(I) 1754-1812 Mf C 1686-1812
SWAYFIELD M(I) 1754-1812 Mf C 1724-1912 M 1724-1836 B 1724-1812
SWINDERBY M (1562-1812) [44] Mf C 1568-1974 M 1568-1751 1754-1978 B 1568-1911
SWINESHEAD M(I) 1754-1812 Mf C 1561-1812
SWINHOPE CB 1697-1812 M 1700-1835
SWINSTEAD M(I) 1754-1812 Mf C 1733-1871 M 1733-1910 B 1733-1934
SYSTON M(I) 1754-1812 Mf C 1783-1873
TALLINGTON Mf M 1690-1837
TATHWELL Mf C 1761-1812
TATTERSHALL M 1754-1836 [55] Mf C 1568-1886 M 1568-1969 B 1568-1918
TEALBY Mfc C 1714-1986 M 1714-1874 B 1714-1941
TEMPLE BRUER Mf M 1882-1975
TETFORD Mf Ext 1579-1677 1709-59 C 1760-1847 M 1754-1837 B 1790-1872
TETNEY M(I) 1754-1812 Mf C 1730-1849 M 1730-1837 B 1730-1866
THEDDLETHORPE ALL SAINTS Mf C 1560-1908 M 1560-1971 B 1650-1812
THEDDLETHORPE ST HELEN Mf C 1566-1916 M 1566-1836 B 1566-1932
THORESBY, NORTH C 1552-1662 1726-1854 M 1552-1662 1726-1982 B 1552-1662 1726-1880 [56] Mf CM 1552-1663 C 1726-1854 M 1726-1837 B 1552-1662 1726-1880
THORESBY, SOUTH Mf C 1660-1812 M 1662-1836 B 1661-1812
THORESTHORPE see SALEBY
THORESWAY Mfc C 1726-1812 M 1727-1978 B 1727-1812
THORGANBY M(I) 1754-1812
THORNTON CURTIS Mf C 1568-1975 M 1569-1837 B 1567-1918
THORNTON by HORNCASTLE 1561-1812 [36] Mf CB 1561-1812 M 1561-1839 (gaps)
THORNTON LE MOOR Mf C 1774-1845 Mfc CB 1711-1812 M 1711-1974
THORPE ON THE HILL M (1563-1835) [45] Mf C 1694-1897 M 1694-1752 1754-1812 1824-1835 B 1694-1812
THORPE ST PETER Mf C 1653-1963 M 1653-1978 B 1653-1920
THORPE SATCHVILLE see TWYFORD
THRECKINGHAM M(I) 1754-1837
THURLBY by BILSBY see BILSBY
THURLBY by BOURNE C 1561-1849 M 1564-(1576-1812) 1837-1841 B 1561-1844 [41,44,60] Mf C 1560-1907 M 1564-1837 B 1561-1941
THURLBY by LINCOLN Mf C 1575-1643 1649-54 1669-1982 M 1575-1641 1655 1669-1710 1715-82 1801-10 1813-1978 B 1575-1643 1649-55 1669-1984
TIMBERLAND Mf C 1660-1908 M 1660-1964 B 1660-1890
TOFT by NEWTON Mfc CB 1653-1812 M 1653-1976
TORKSEY Mf C 1576-1890 M 1577-1610 1657-1837 B 1575-1610 1653-1968
TORRINGTON, EAST Mfc CB 1593-1646 1674-1812 M 1593-1646 1674-1955 Mf C 1740-1835
TORRINGTON, WEST Mf C 1771-1828 Mfc 1638-69 CB 1721-1812 M 1721-1836
TOTHILL Mf C 1608-1958 M 1609-1950 B 1608-1963
TOYNTON ALL SAINTS Mf C 1689-1925 M 1691-1955 B 1689-1925
TOYNTON, HIGH Mf C 1715-1813 M 1719-1934 B 1715-1870
TOYNTON, LOW Mf C 1585-1959 M 1585-1955 B 1585-1959
TOYNTON ST PETER Mf C 1562-1640 1662-1926 M 1562-1970 B 1742-1812
TRIMBLEBY Mf C 1695-1916 M 1695-1836 B 1695-1980
TRUSTHORPE M 1562-1837 [51] Mf C 1669-1909 M 1665-1836 B 1665-1952
TUPHOLME see MARKET RASEN
TYDD ST MARY Mf C 1540-1894 M 1540-1986 B 1540-1967
UFFINGTON Mf C 1562-1774 1799-1863 M 1813-1837 B 1799-1812
ULCEBY by BARTON Mf C 1718-1836
ULCEBY cum FORDINGHAM Mf C 1733-1846 M 1749-1837 B 1752-1801
ULCEBY cum GRIMSBY Mf C 1567-1851 M 1567-1837 B 1567-1920
UPTON cum KEXBY Mf C 1563-1860 M 1563-1836 B 1563-1812
USSELBY Mfc CB 1564-1812 M 1564-1933
UTTERBY Mf CB 1695-1812 M 1695-1980
WADDINGHAM Mf C 1653-1990 M 1653-1961 B 1653-1953
WADDINGTON M (1563-1837) [50] Mf C 1675-1952 M 1675-1970 B 1675-1918
WADDINGWORTH Mf C 1593-1959 M 1593-1884 B 1593-1949
WAINFLEET All Saints Mf C 1679-1867 M 1679-1967 B 1679-1927; St Mary Mf C 1611-1852 M 1611-1837 B 1611-1882
WAITHE C 1763-1979 M 1762-1974 B 1763-1976 [56] Mf C 1693-1979 M 1693-1981 B 1693-1976
WALCOT by FOLKINGHAM M(I) 1754-1812
WALESBY Mfc C 1562-1918 M 1562-1978 B 1562-1812
WALTHAM M(I) 1754-1812 Mf C 1561-1889 M 1561-1837 B 1561-1876
WASHINGBOROUGH Mf C 1564-1880 M 1564-1748 1754-1837 B 1564-1883
WELBOURN M(I) 1754-1812
WELBY M 1755-1812 [60] Mf C 1813-1834
WELL M 1566-1837 [52] Mf CB 1649-1812 M 1649-1955
WELLINGORE M (1602-1837) [50] Mf C 1653-1920 M 1657-1987 B 1653-1859
WELTON by LINCOLN M(I) 1754-1812 Mfc C 1568-1973 M 1568-1963 B 1568-1938
WELTON LE MARSH Mf C 1558-1869 M 1558-1837 B 1558-1944

WELTON LE WOLD Mf C 1558-84 1612-1894 M 1554-1969 B 1554-1614 1654-1812

WESTBOROUGH cum DODDINGTON M 1564-1837 [54] Mf C 1562-1745

WESTON Mf CB 1678-1948 M 1678-1957

WESTON SAINT MARY M 1562-1837 [46]

WHAPLODE Mf CB 1559-1678 C 1688-1890 M 1560-1679 1688-1754 1809-1944 B 1559-1678 1688-1953

WHAPLODE DROVE Mf CB 1713-1900 M 1713-1901

WHITTON Mf C 1546 1562-1852 M 1545 1562-1836 B 1546 1562-1812

WICKENBY Mfc C 1558-1925 M 1558-1976 B 1558-1812

WIGTOFT M(I) 1754-1812

WILKSBY Mf C 1562-1812 M 1562-1835 B 1562-1979

WILLINGHAM by STOW Mf C 1562-1873 M 1562-1980 B 1562-1919

WILLINGHAM, NORTH Mfc CB 1658-1812 M 1568-1972

WILLINGHAM, SOUTH Mfc C 1711-1920 M 1711-1835 B 1711-1812

WILLOUGHBY M 1538-1837 [51]

WILLOUGHBY cum SLOOTHBY Mf C 1538-1965 M 1538-1980 B 1538-1968

WILLOUGHTON Mf C 1599-1858 M 1599-1836 1844-1847 B 1599-1898

WILSFORD M(I) 1754-1812 Mf C 1562-1774

WILSTHORPE Mf CB 1770-1812 M 1754-1836 see also GREATFORD

WINCEBY Mf C 1579-1954 M 1579-1942 B 1579-1962

WINTERINGHAM Mf C 1562-1976 M 1562-1981 B 1562-1933

WINTERTON Mf C 1559-1638 1653-1948 M 1558-1638 1664-1950 B 1558-1638 1654-1947

WINTHORPE Mf C 1561-1918 M 1588-1837 B 1551-1960

WISPINGTON Mf CB 1662-1815 M 1662-1963(gaps)

WITHAM, NORTH M(I) 1754-1812 Mf C 1592-1813 M 1592-1837 B 1591-1812

WITHAM ON THE HILL Mf C 1670-1932 M 1670-1942 B 1670-1893

WITHAM, SOUTH M(I) 1754-1812 Mf CM 1687-1837 B 1687-1812

WITHCALL Mf CB 1579-1812 M 1754-1940

WITHERN M 1560-1837 [51] Mf C 1558-1872 M 1558-1837 B 1558-1929

WITHERN with STAIN Mf C 1561-1765

WOLD NEWTON M(I) 1754-1812 Mf C 1578-1812 M 1578-1836 B 1578-1809

WOODHALL Mf C 1562-1955 M 1562-1951 B 1562-1970

WOODHALL SPA Mf C 1919-1966 M 1944-1987 B 1930-1972 see also LANGTON by HORNCASTLE

WOOLSTHORPE M 1562-1837 [53]

WOOTTON Mf C 1563-1919 M 1563-1837 B 1563-1879

WORLABY by BRIGG Mf C 1559-1951 M 1559-1989 B 1559-1919

WORLABY by LOUTH Mf C 1870-1961

WRAGBY M 1661-1837 [55] Mf C 1567-1924 M 1567-1977 B 1567-1882

WRAWBY Mf CB 1715-1895 M 1561-1918

WRAWBY cum BRIGG Ind Mf C 1816-1837

WROOT Mf C 1573-1651 1653-1888 M 1573-1644 1653-1812 1814-1967 B 1573-1968

WYBERTON M(I) 1754-1812 Mf C Ext 1561-1744

WYHAM cum CADEBY 1695-1772 M 1816-1821 [63] Mf C 1696-1772 1813-1978 M 1695-1772 1816-1976 B 1696-1772 1817-1974

YARBURGH Mf C 1561-1976 M 1561-1975 B 1561-1978

LONDON

PARISHES OUTSIDE THE BOUNDARIES OF THE CITY OF LONDON ARE LISTED UNDER THE ANCIENT COUNTIES IN WHICH THEY WERE SITUATED :- Essex, Kent, Middlesex and Surrey.

LONDON (CITY of)

ALDGATE see HOLY TRINITY MINORIES

ALDERSGATE (formerly St MARY AXE) Wes ZC 1827-37 [262]

ALLHALLOWS THE GREAT C 1668-1840 M 1671-1720 B 1667-1853 [87,92,94-6]; united with ST MICHAEL PATERNOSTER ROYAL(1893); see also St James, Duke's Place

ALLHALLOWS THE LESS C 1558-1812 B 1558-1853; united with ALLHALLOWS THE GREAT (1670) [87,92-96,99,100,221]

ALLHALLOWS BREAD STREET C 1538-1892 M 1539-1876 B 1538-1851 [43]; united with ST MARY LE BOW(1876)

ALLHALLOWS HONEY LANE M 1538-1837 B 1814-51 [44/5]; united with ST MARY LE BOW(1670)

ALLHALLOWS LOMBARD STREET M 1553-1837 B 1813-53 [88,291]; united with ST EDMUND THE KING AND MARTYR (1937)

ALLHALLOWS LONDON WALL 1559-1675 Ext CB 1675-1729 M 1675-1712 B 1813-49 [97/8]

ALLHALLOWS STAINING C 1642-1870 M 1653-1753 B 1813-1853 [88,221,282]; united with ST OLAVE HART STREET

ALL SAINTS SKINNER STREEET united with ST BOTOLPH BISHOPSGATE(1869)

AUSTIN FRIARS Dutch Ref 1571-1874 [101]

BEVIS MARKS EC3 Synagogue M 1657-1901 [JR/REG]

BISHOPSGATE Bapt Z 1789-1811; Irvingite C 1829-40 [263]

BRIDEWELL CHAPEL M 1665-1837 [84]; united with ST BRIDE FLEET STREET(1864)

CHRISTCHURCH GREYFRIARS see CHRISTCHURCH NEWGATE STREET

CHRISTCHURCH NEWGATE STREET 1538-1754 [21] Mf 1724-1812; united with ST SEPULCHRE HOLBORN(1954)

FLEET PRISON and RULES OF THE FLEET 1691-1702 Ext M 1686-1754 [115,270-2]; see also OLD RED HAND and MITRE CHAPEL

FRENCH CHURCH see THREADNEEDLE STREET

GUILDHALL CHAPEL M 1620-83 [116]; Chapel demolished (1822)

HOLY SEPULCHRE WITHOUT NEWGATE see ST SEPULCHRE HOLBORN

HOLY TRINITY GOUGH SQUARE united with ST BRIDE FLEET STREET(1906)

HOLY TRINITY MINORIES B 1813-52 Mfc M 1676-1683 M(I) 1683-1868/7; united with ST BOTOLPH ALDGATE(1893)

HOLY TRINITY THE LESS M 1755-1830 B 1813-52 [83]; united with ST MICHAEL QUEENHITHE(1670) and with ST JAMES GARLICKHYTHE(1875)

LAMB'S CHAPEL MONKWELL STREET Ext CM.1618-1753 [176]

MITRE CHAPEL see OLD RED HAND & MITRE CHAPEL

OLD RED HAND and MITRE CHAPEL M 1750-54 [88]

RULES OF THE FLEET see FLEET PRISON
ST ALBAN WOOD STREET 1629-30 C 1662-1852 M
1662-1836 B 1662-1786 1800-49 [91,151]; united
with ST VEDAST FOSTER LANE(1954)
ST ALPHAGE LONDON WALL B 1813-51 Mf C 1813-
1875; united with ST GILES CRIPPLEGATE(1954);
see also ST MARY ALDERMANBURY
ST ANDREW HOLBORN M 1754-1764 [282]
ST ANDREW HUBBARD CM 1538-1600 M 1639-40 [83]
B 1813-46; united with St MARY AT HILL(1670)
ST ANDREW UNDERSHAFT B 1813-49; united with ST
MARY AXE (c1561)
ST ANDREW BY THE WARDROBE Mf C 1558-1838 M
1558-1797; see also ST ANN BLACKFRIARS
ST ANN BLACKFRIARS Mf M 1726-1812; united with ST
ANDREW BY THE WARDROBE(1670)
ST ANNE & ST AGNES B 1813-53 [221]; united with ST
VEDAST FOSTER LANE(1954); see also ST JOHN
ZACHARY
ST ANTHOLIN BUDGE ROW C 1538-1840 M 1538-1837
B 1538-1853 [8,154,262]; united with ST JOHN THE
BAPTIST WALBROOK(c1670) and ST MARY
ALDERMARY(1873)
ST AUGUSTINE WATLING STREET B 1813-53 united
with ST FAITH UNDER ST PAUL(c1674) and ST
MARY LE BOW(1954)
ST BARTHOLOMEW BY THE EXCHANGE M 1558-1837
[83,89] B 1813-38; united with ST MARGARET
LOTHBURY(1839); demolished(1841) and
rebuilt(1850) as St Bartholomew Moor Lane
ST BARTHOLOMEW MOOR LANE united with ST GILES
CRIPPLEGATE(1966)
ST BARTHOLOMEW THE GREAT B 1843-53
ST BARTHOLOMEW THE LESS C 1547-1894 M 1547-
1837 Banns 1754-1941 B 1547-1853
ST BENET FINK M 1538-1845 [155] B 1813-45; united
with ST PETER LE POER(1842) and ST MICHAEL
CORNHILL(1906)
ST BENET GRACECHURCH M 1558-1837 [88] B 1813-
52; united with ALLHALLOWS LOMBARD
STREET(1864) and ST EDMUND THE KING AND
MARTYR(1937); see also ST LEONARD EASTCHEAP
ST BENET PAUL'S WHARF CM 1619-1837 B 1619-1853
[38-41,262]; united with ST NICHOLAS COLE
ABBEY(1879); see also ST PETER PAULS WHARF
Welsh congregation from 1879
ST BENET SHEREHOG 1516-1754 [49/50,176]; united
with ST STEPHEN WALBROOK(1670)
ST BOTOLPH (WITHOUT) ALDERSGATE M 1640-1755
[156]
ST BOTOLPH BILLINGSGATE 1629-1640 C 1685-1840
M 1813-37 B 1685-1845 [86]; united with ST
GEORGE BOTOLPH LANE(1670) and ST MARY AT
HILL(1901)
ST BOTOLPH (WITHOUT) BISHOPSGATE C 1558-1690
M 1558-1753 B 1558-1752 [168-170] Mf 1717-1741
ST BRIDE FLEET STREET Mf CM 1587-1653 B 1587-95
ST CHRISTOPHER LE STOCKS CB 1558-1780 M 1558-
1837 [83,172/3,GCI]; united with ST MARGARET
LOTHBURY(1781)
ST CLEMENT EASTCHEAP CM 1539-1839 B 1539-1853
[67/8,87]; see also ST MARTIN ORGAR
ST DIONIS BACKCHURCH C 1538-1754 M 1538-1837 B
1538-1754 1813-49 [3,88,291]; united with
ALLHALLOWS LOMBARD STREET(1876) and ST
EDMUND THE KING AND MARTYR (1937)
ST DUNSTAN IN THE EAST C 1558-1758 M 1558-1754

B 1558-1766 1813-53 [69,81/2,221]; united with
ALLHALLOWS BARKING BY THE TOWER(1960)
ST DUNSTAN IN THE WEST Ext C 1601-49 M 1602-
1762 B 1650-1777 [91]
ST EDMUND THE KING AND MARTYR C 1670-1840 M
1670-1837 B 1670-1850 [87,174] see also ST
NICHOLAS ACONS, ALLHALLOWS LOMBARD
STREET, ST LEONARD EASTCHEAP, ST BENET
GRACECHURCH and ST DIONIS BACKCHURCH
ST ETHELBURGA BISHOPSGATE C 1671-1914 M 1679-
1754 1792-1915 B 1672-1849 [175/6,GCI]
ST EWIN united with CHRISTCHURCH NEWGATE
STREET(1547)
ST FAITH UNDER ST PAUL M 1677-1837 [89] B 1813-
53; united with ST AUGUSTINE WATLING
STREET(1670) and ST MARY LE BOW(1954)
ST GABRIEL FENCHURCH M 1572-1683 1814-37 [83] B
1813-51; united with ST MARGARET PATTENS
(1670)
ST GEORGE BOTOLPH LANE M 1653-60 1685-1720
[262] B 1813-48 Mf C 1813-1875; united with ST
MARY AT HILL(1901)
ST GILES CRIPPLEGATE Mf C 1627-1640; see also ST
BARTHOLOMEW MOOR LANE, ST ALPHAGE
LONDON WALL and ST MARY ALDERMANBURY;
includes (from 1966) ST LUKE OLD STREET, ST
MARY CHARTERHOUSE and ST PAUL PEARTREE
STREET (all Middlesex)
ST GREGORY BY ST PAUL CB 1813-21 M 1559-1700
1813-21 [157,176]; united with ST MARY
MAGDELEN OLD FISH STREET(1670) and ST
SEPULCHRE HOLBORN(1954)
ST HELEN BISHOPSGATE CM 1575-1837 B 1575-1853
[31,262]
ST JAMES DUKE'S PLACE C 1747-1840 M 1664-1837 B
1747-1853 [87,216-219,GCI]; united with ST
KATHERINE CREE (1873)
ST JAMES GARLICKHYTHE M 1754-1837 B 1813-53
[83,221]; see also HOLY TRINITY THE LESS and ST
MICHAEL QUEENHITHE
ST JAMES IN THE WALL see LAMB'S CHAPEL
MONKWELL STREET
ST JOHN THE BAPTIST WALBROOK 1629-30 C 1682-
1812 M 1682-1754 [8,154]; united with ST
ANTHOLIN BUDGE ROW(1670) and ST MARY
ALDERMARY(1873)
ST JOHN THE EVANGELIST FRIDAY STREET 1653-
1822 [43]; united with ALLHALLOWS BREAD
STREET(1670) and ST MARY LE BOW(1876)
ST JOHN ZACHARY M 1665-6 1755-1837 [85] B 1813-
49; united with ST ANNE & ST AGNES(1670) and
ST VEDAST FOSTER LANE(1954)
ST KATHERINE COLEMAN M 1563-1754 [88] B 1813-
53; united with ST OLAVE HART STREET(1921)
ST KATHERINE CREE M 1639-40 1663-1837 [84]; see
also ST JAMES DUKE'S PLACE
ST LAWRENCE JEWRY 1538-1676 C 1677-1842 M
1677-1837 B 1677-1853 [70/1,262]; see also ST
MARY MAGDALEN MILK STREET and ST MICHAEL
BASSISHAW
ST LAWRENCE POUNTNEY M 1538-1837 Ext C 1538-
1770 B 1538-1813 [89,91,291] B 1813-53; united
with ST MARY ABCHURCH(1670)
ST LEONARD EASTCHEAP M 1538-1705 [88]; united
with ST BENET GRACECHURCH STREET(1670)
ALLHALLOWS LOMBARD STREET(1864) and ST
EDMUND THE KING & MARTYR(1937)

ST LEONARD FOSTER LANE united with
CHRISTCHURCH NEWGATE STREET(1670) and ST
SEPULCHRE HOLBORN(1954)
ST MAGNUS THE MARTYR M 1557-1712 Ext C 1560-
1720 B 1560-1712 1813-1853 [98,158,291]; see also
ST MARGARET NEW FISH STREET HILL and ST
MICHAEL CROOKED LANE
ST MARGARET LOTHBURY M 1558-1837 [83,89,171] B
1813-1853; see also ST CHRISTOPHER LE STOCKS,
ST BARTHOLOMEW BY THE EXCHANGE, ST
OLAVE JEWRY, ST MARTIN POMEROY, ST
MILDRED POULTRY, and ST MARY COLECHURCH
ST MARGARET MOSES 1559-1812 [42] B 1813-1850;
united with ST MILDRED BREAD STREET(1670) and
ST MARY LE BOW(1954)
ST MARGARET NEW FISH STREET 1629-1640 [176];
united with ST MAGNUS THE MARTYR (1670)
ST MARGARET PATTENS M 1650-1837 [83] B 1813-53;
see also ST GABRIEL FENCHURCH
ST MARTIN LUDGATE M 1754-1837 [84]; see also ST
MARY MAGDALEN OLD FISH STREET and ST
GREGORY BY ST PAUL
ST MARTIN ORGAR CB 1625-1812 M 1625-1738
[67,68,88]; united with ST CLEMENT
EASTCHEAP(1670)
ST MARTIN OUTWICH C 1664 1670-1873 MB 1670-1873
[32,91,176]; united with ST HELEN
BISHOPSGATE(1873)
ST MARTIN POMEROY M 1539-1647 [83,159] B 1813-
48; united with ST OLAVE JEWRY(1670) and ST
MARGARET LOTHBURY(1886)
ST MARTIN VINTRY C 1617-1840 M 1617-1648 B 1617-
1850 [12,87,176/7,186-188] B 1813-49; united with
ST MICHAEL PATERNOSTER ROYAL(1670)
ST MARY ABCHURCH Ext C 1558-1779 M 1558-1754 B
1558-1812 [91,160] B 1813-53; see also ST
LAWRENCE POUNTNEY
ST MARY ALDERMANBURY CM 1538-1837 B 1538-1859
[61,62,65,221]; united with ST ALPHAGE LONDON
WALL(1917) and ST GILES CRIPPLEGATE(1954)
ST MARY ALDERMARY C 1558-1840 M 1558-1837 B
1558-1851 [5,86]; see also ST THOMAS THE
APOSTLE, ST ANTOLIN BUDGE ROW and ST JOHN
THE BAPTIST WALBROOK
ST MARY AT HILL C 1558-1750 M 1558-1702 B 1558-
1805 Ext CM 1538-1600 B 1558-1850 [152,291]; see
also ST ANDREW HUBBARD
ST MARY BOTHAW Mf C 1536-1653 M 1536-1657 1754-
1812 B 1536-1653; united with ST SWITHIN
LONDON STONE (1670) and ST STEPHEN
WALBROOK(1954)
ST MARY AXE united with ST ANDREW
UNDERSHAFT(c1561); see also ALDERSGATE
ST MARY LE BOW CB 1538-1852 M 1538-1837 [44/5];
see also ALLHALLOWS HONEY LANE, ST PANCRAS
SOPER LANE, ALLHALLOWS BREAD STREET and
ST JOHN THE EVANGELIST FRIDAY STREET
ST MARY COLECHURCH Ext 1558-1654; united with ST
MILDRED POULTRY(1670), ST OLAVE JEWRY(1871)
and ST MARGARET LOTHBURY(1886)
ST MARY MAGDALEN MILK STREET C 1558-1677 M
1559-1666 B 1559-1665 [72,89]; united with ST
LAWRENCE JEWRY(1670)
ST MARY MAGDALEN OLD FISH STREET M 1539-1638
1664-1837 B 1813-53 [85,161,291]; united with ST
MARTIN LUDGATE(1890)
ST MARY MOUNTHAW C 1568-1837 M 1568-1835 B

1568-1849 [58]; united with ST MARY SOMERSET
and ST NICHOLAS COLE ABBEY(1886)
ST MARY SOMERSET CM 1558-1837 B 1557-1853
[59,60]; united with ST NICHOLAS COLE
ABBEY(1866); see also ST MARY MOUNTHAW
ST MARY STAINING 1629-31 C 1673-1820 M 1754-1820
B 1805 1807-12 [151]; united with ST MICHAEL
WOOD STREET(1670), ST ALBAN WOOD
STREET(1884) and ST VEDAST FOSTER
LANE(1954)
ST MARY WOOLCHURCH HAW C 1558-1699 M 1559-
1666 1813-37 B 1558-1666 1813-1848 [183,184];
united with ST MARY WOOLNOTH(1670)
ST MARY WOOLNOTH C 1538-1760 1813-30 M 1538-
1754 1813-37 B 1538-1760 1813-52; see also ST
MARY WOOLCHURCH HAW [183/4]
ST MATTHEW FRIDAY STREET C 1538-1840 M 1538-
1836 B 1538-1846 [63,86,89]; see also ST PETER
WESTCHEAP; united with ST VEDAST FOSTER
LANE(1882)
ST MICHAEL BASSISHAW C 1538-1892 M 1538-1837 B
1538-1853 [72-74,89,221]; united with ST
LAWRENCE JEWRY(1897)
ST MICHAEL CORNHILL C 1546-1840 M 1546-1837 B
1546-1853 [7,87]; see also ST PETER LE POER and
ST BENET FINK
ST MICHAEL CROOKED LANE M 1539-1779 [163] B
1813-52; united with ST MAGNUS THE
MARTYR(1831); see also ST MARGARET NEW FISH
STREET
ST MICHAEL LE QUERNE C 1685-1837 B 1685-1849
[29,30,176,262]; united with ST VEDAST FOSTER
LANE
ST MICHAEL PATERNOSTER ROYAL C 1558-1840 M
1558-1837 B 1558-1850 [96,177,189,262,291]; see
also ST MARTIN VINTRY
ST MICHAEL QUEENHITHE M 1639-40 1754-1837 [83]
B 1813-52; united with HOLY TRINITY THE
LESS
ST MICHAEL WOOD STREET C 1559-1663 1800-20 M
1559-1661 1754-1820 B 1559-1660 [151] B 1813-20;
see also ST MARY STAINING; united with ST ALBAN
WOOD STREET(1894) and ST VEDAST FOSTER
LANE(1954)
ST MILDRED BREAD STREET 1629-1631 1639-1640
1658-1853 [42,176]; see also ST MARY LE BOW
MOSES; united with ST MARY LE BOW(1954)
ST MILDRED POULTRY Ext 1538-1667 M 1754-1837
[84] B 1813-52; see also ST MARY COLECHURCH;
united with ST OLAVE JEWRY(1871) and ST
MARGARET LOTHBURY(1886)
ST NICHOLAS ACONS C 1539-1840 M 1539-1837 B
1539-1850 [87,182]; united with ST EDMUND THE
KING & MARTYR(1670)
ST NICHOLAS COLE ABBEY CB 1538-1812 M 1584-
1837 1873 [84,185,283,GCI] B 1813-51; see also ST
NICHOLAS OLAVE, ST MARY SOMERSET, ST MARY
MOUNTHAW, ST BENET PAUL'S WHARF and ST
PETER PAUL'S WHARF
ST NICHOLAS OLAVE C 1704-1840 M 1705-20 1813-36
B 1704-1852 [86]; united with ST NICHOLAS COLE
ABBEY(1670)
ST NICHOLAS SHAMBLES united with CHRISTCHURCH
NEWGATE STREET(1547)

ST OLAVE HART STREET 1563-1754; Ext 1563-1893
[46,88] see also ALLHALLOWS STAINING and ST
KATHERINE COLEMAN
ST OLAVE OLD JEWRY M 1538-1837 [83,164]; see also
ST MARTIN POMEROY, ST MILDRED POULTRY and
ST MARY COLECHURCH; united with ST MARY
LOTHBURY(1886)
ST OLAVE SILVER STREET C 1813-1852 M 1666-1836
Ext CB 1562-1770 M 1662-1770 [91,151]; united
with ST ALBAN WOOD STREET(1670) and ST
VEDAST FOSTER LANE (1954)
ST PANCRAS SOPER LANE M 1538-1837 B 1813-49;
united with ST MARY LE BOW(1670)
ST PAUL'S CATHEDRAL C 1875-1897 M 1697-1899 B
1760-1899 [26]; see also ST GREGORY BY ST PAUL
ST PETER CORNHILL C 1538-1840 M 1538-1837 B
1538-1853 [1,4,87]
ST PETER LE POER M 1561-1837 [166]; united with ST
MICHAEL CORNHILL(1906); see also ST BENET
FINK
ST PETER PAUL'S WHARF C 1607-1837 M 1607-1834 B
1607-1849 [38,40/1,262]; united with ST BENET
PAUL'S WHARF(1670) and ST NICHOLAS COLE
ABBEY(1879)
ST PETER WESTCHEAP C 1813-1840 B 1813-1846
[86,88]; united with ST MATTHEW FRIDAY
STREET(1670) and ST VEDAST FOSTER
LANE(1887)
ST SEPULCHRE HOLBORN C 1663-1714 M 1662-1761
B 1662-1723 B(I) 1813-57 1900-04 [89,91,283]
ST STEPHEN COLEMAN STREET M 1538-1754 [88];
united with ST MARGARET LOTHBURY(1954)
ST STEPHEN WALBROOK 1559-1860 [49,50]; see also
ST BENET SHEREHOG
ST SWITHIN LONDON STONE C 1675-1840 B 1666-
1935 [90] Mf C 1615-75 M 1619-65 B 1614-66; see
also ST MARY BOTHAW; united with ST STEPHEN
WALBROOK(1954)
ST THOMAS THE APOSTLE C 1558-1840 M 1558-1837
B 1558-1849 [6,86]; united with ST MARY
ALDERMARY(1670)
ST THOMAS IN THE LIBERTY OF THE ROLLS united
with ST DUNSTAN IN THE WEST(1886)
ST VEDAST FOSTER LANE C 1558-1836 M 1559-1837 B
1558-1853 [29,30,262]; see also ST MICHAEL LE
QUERNE, ST MATTHEW FRIDAY STREET and ST
PETER WESTCHEAP
TEMPLE CHURCH C 1629-1853 M 1629-1760 B 1628-
1853 [180,191] B 1813-53
THREADNEEDLE STREET French Church C 1600-1840
M 1600-1752 [HS9,HS13,HS16,HS23]
WELSH CONGREGATION see ST BENET PAUL'S
WHARF
WHITEFRIARS PRECINCT see ST BRIDE FLEET STREET
and ST DUNSTAN IN THE WEST; united with HOLY
TRINITY GOUGH SQUARE(1842)

MIDDLESEX

ACTON M 1566-1812 [248,GCI]
ASHFORD M 1629-39 1696-1837 B(I) 1699-1929 B 1949-
1963 [214,251,291,GCI]
ASKE'S HOSPITAL (Hoxton) see SHOREDITCH

BAVARIAN EMBASSY CHAPEL see WESTMINSTER
BAYSWATER French C 1889-1943 M 1877-1932 [104]
BEDFONT, EAST M 1659-1754 [281]
BELL LANE E1 see SPITALFIELDS
BERWICK STREET W1 see WESTMINSTER
BETHNAL GREEN M 1746-54 (I) 1829-37 [281,263]; Ind
C 1704-55 [263]; Diss Cambridge Road C 1771-
1836 [263]; Virginia Chapel C 1825-37 [263]
BEVIS MARKS EC3 see LONDON (CITY of)
BRENTFORD, NEW* C 1619-20 1653-1805 M 1618-1836
B 1618-1805 [214,280,105,279,251,GCI]
BRENTFORD, OLD Albany Chapel Mfc ZC 1831-37
BROMLEY St Leonard M 1639-40 [214]
BROWN'S LANE see SPITALFIELDS
BUNHILL FIELDS see FINSBURY
CAREY STREET WC2 see WESTMINSTER
CHAPELS ROYAL see WESTMINSTER (St James's)
CHARTERHOUSE see ISLINGTON
CHELSEA St Luke C(I) 1813-1818 M 1639-40,1704-1800
[106,107,214,291]; All Souls Rom Cath Mfc B 1845-
58
CHISWICK* C 1678-1872 M 1678-1837 B 1678-1850
[108-112]
CLERKENWELL St James C 1551-1754 (I) 1778-1780
MB 1551-1754 [9,10,13,17,19,20]; Northampton
Tabernacle ZC 1835-37 [262]; Wilderness Row Wes
ZC 1824-37 [262];
COVENT GARDEN see WESTMINSTER (St Paul, Covent
Garden)
COWLEY* M 1563-1812 [214,249,GCI]
CRANFORD M 1564-1834 [214,213]
CRISPIN STREET E1 see SPITALFIELDS
DRAYTON, WEST* M 1568-1837 [249,213,GCI]
EALING* M 1582-1837 [214,255]
EDGWARE M 1630 1639 1717-1840 [214,213]; see also
STANMORE LITTLE
EDMONTON* C 1558-1715 (M 1557-1837) B 1557-1727
[212,214,253]; Winchmore Hill Chap Mfc Z 1819-36
C 1822-37 B 1831-2; Tottenham & Edmonton Chap
Mfc C 1818 1830-37 Z 1829-36 B 1821-36
ENFIELD* M 1550-1837 [252]; Baker Street Chap Mfc C
1727-1837; Chase Side Chap Mfc ZC 1790-1840 B
1831-54; Ind Chap Mfc ZC 1808-1836; Ponders End
Ind Chap Mfc Z 1796-1836 C 1805-1836; Ponders
End United Reform C 1769-1803 [283]
FELTHAM* M 1634-1837 [251,213,GCI]
FINCHLEY* M 1560-1837 [254]; Whetstone & Totteridge
Ind Mfc C 1788-1804,1819,1831-37 Z 1788-
1804,1819,1824-37 B 1800,1835-37
FINSBURY St Barnabas B (I) 1842-54; St Luke Old Street
C 1742-65 C (I)1813-1818 M 1742-64 M(I) 1783-
1800 [178,220,281,291,GCI]; St Mark Myddleton Sq
C 1828-40 B 1830-56 [263]; St Paul Bunhill Row Z
1820-40 C 1839-89; St Paul Pear Tree Court Z 1829-
40 C 1865-81; St Peter St John St Road C 1871-80;
St Silas Penton St Z 1803-35 C 1865-80 [263]; St
Thomas Goswell Street B (I) 1846-54 [281];
Wesley's Chapel City Rd B 1779-1854 [292] Mfc B
1799-1854; Bunhill Fields B 1823-1854 [210,211];
see also PENTONVILLE
FRIEN BARNET M 1675-1837 [213]
FULHAM M 1614 [214]
GLASSHOUSE STREET W1 see WESTMINSTER
GRAYS INN see HOLBORN
GREENFORD M 1539-1812 [248,GCI]; see also
PERIVALE

HACKNEY St John C(I) 1545-1820 C Ext 1556-1823 M
1540-1754 M(I) 1589-1820 B Ext 1595-1808 [117-
119,209,212,GCI]
HACKNEY, WEST St Barnabas M 1824-37 [281]
HADLEY see MONKEN HADLEY
HAGGERSTON M 1830-37 [281]
HAMMERSMITH Rom Cath C 1710-1838 [CRS26]; Ind
Ebenezer Mfc Z 1760-1835 C 1773-1835 B 1786-87;
Bapt Trinity Chap, West End Mfc ZC 1780-1837 B
1784-1837; George Yard Chap Mfc ZC 1758-1837;
Wes Chap, Waterloo St Mfc Z 1797-1837 C 1807-37
B 1814-54
HAMPSTEAD St John Ext C 1600-1747 M 1601-1750 B
1560-1773 [214,212]
HAMPTON* C 1554-1812 M 1629-30 1657-1837 B 1554-
1677 1723-1812 [120/1,213/4,250,263,267,GCI]
HANWELL M 1570-1812 [214,248,GCI]
HANWORTH* M 1629-30 1639 1732-1837 [214,251,GCI]
HAREFIELD* M 1546-1837 Ext C 1565-1812 M 1575-
1871 B 1569-1851 [179,252]
HARLINGTON* C 1540-1845 M 1540-1853 B 1540-1841
[214,248,269,GCI]
HARMONDSWORTH M 1629-31 1671-1837
[213,214,291]
HARROW ON THE HILL* CMB 1558-1840
[122,123,282]; Bapt Mfc Z 1826-36 C 1831-36
HAYES* CMB 1557-1840 [249,273,GCI]
HENDON St Mary M 1630,1653-1837; Ind Mill Hill Mfc
ZC 1784-1830 [214,260]
HESTON* M 1559-1819 [214,248,281,GCI]
HIGHGATE C 1633-1848 M 1635-1757 1832-37 B 1633-
1903 [285] Mfc B 1633-1903; Salem (New) Chap
Mfc C 1785-89 1810-36 Z 1809-36; Highgate School
Chap C 1636-1750 M 1635-1846 B 1633-1888 [212]
HILLINGDON C 1559-1861 M 1559-1866 B 1559-1855
[249,274-6,GCI]
HOLBORN* Grays Inn Chap C Ext 1704-1862 M Ext
1633-1754 M 1695-1850 [91]; Holy Trinity Mfc B
1839-1856; St Andrew see LONDON (CITY of); St
George the Martyr C 1710-1768 M 1706-1800
[203,GCI]; St Giles in the Fields M 1561-1650 [88];
Lincolns Inn Chap Ext C 1722-1806 M 1695-1754 B
1695-1789 [91]; Lincolns Inn Fields Rom Cath C
1731-1772 M 1734-1822 1824-1831 [CRS19]
HORNSEY M 1654-1812 [214]
HOUNSLOW* M 1708-1812 [251,GCI]; Ind Ship Lane
Chap Mfc ZC 1827-36 B 1829-33
HOXTON Hug C 1751-83 M 1748-53 [HS45]
HUNGERFORD MARKET see WESTMINSTER
ICKENHAM* M 1558-1837; Ext C 1558-1874 M 1567-
1886 B 1622-1890 [213,214.249,124,GCI] Mf C
1813-74
ISLEWORTH C 1566-1807 M 1566-1812 Banns 1800-16
B 1566-1747,1782-1812 [125,126,282]; Rom Cath C
1748-1835 [CRS13]
ISLINGTON Charterhouse C 1695-1837 M 1671-1890 B
1695-1854 [18]; Holy Trinity M 1830-37; St John
Evangelist Upper Holloway Rd B 1829-54; St Mary
C (I) 1831-36 M(I) 1784-1812; Liverpool Rd Wes ZC
1828-37
KENSAL GREEN Catholic Cemetery Mfc B 1858-1876
KENSINGTON* Holy Trinity Knightsbridge C 1658-93 M
1658-1739 [143-146,282]; St Mary Abbotts C 1539-
1850 M 1539-1837 B 1539-1853 [16,128-141]; Ind
Hornton Street Mfc ZC 1825-37 [214]
KENTISH TOWN St John Baptist B(I) 1790- 1970 [282]
KINGSBURY M 1639 [214]

KNIGHTSBRIDGE see KENSINGTON
LALEHAM C 1538-1692 1789-1839 M 1539-1683 1754-
1838 Ext 1630-39 B 1538-1690 1789-1842 [214,286]
LEICESTER FIELDS see WESTMINSTER
LINCOLN'S INN see HOLBORN
LITTLETON C 1579-1852 M 1564-1810 B 1562-1851
[147,214,262]
LITTLINGTON see LITTLETON
MARCHES (Eglise du) see SPITALFIELDS
MARYLEBONE see ST MARYLEBONE
MIDDLESEX HOSPITAL see ST MARYLEBONE
MILK ALLEY W1 see WESTMINSTER
MILL HILL Ind Grammar School Mfc Z 1828-37 C 1831-
37; see also HENDON
MIMMS, SOUTH M 1558-1837 [254] Mfc B 1900-83
MONKEN HADLEY* M 1619-1837 [254] Mfc B(I) 1775-
1952
NORTHOLT* M 1575-1812 [214,249,GCI]
NORWOOD M 1654-1837 [214]
OXFORD CHAPEL (Vere School) see ST MARYLEBONE
PADDINGTON St James M 1630 1784-92; St John the
Evangelist B(I) 1833-54 [214,283]
PEARL STREET E1 see SPITALFIELDS
PENTONVILLE St James B 1790-1798 [263] Mf C 1810-
1876
PERIVALE C 1707-1855 M 1720-1844 B 1720-1952
[214,283]
PICCADILLY see WESTMINSTER
PINNER* M 1654-1837 [251,GCI]
PONDERS END see ENFIELD
POPLAR All Saints C (I) 1728-33 1775-6 1802-12 M
1670-1754 [209,283]
PORTUGUESE EMBASSY CHAPEL see WESTMINSTER
RIDER COURT MEWS see WESTMINSTER
RUISLIP C 1685-1840 M 1629-31,1694-1840 B 1695-1875
[104,214]
ST GEORGE IN THE EAST C 1836-37 M(I) 1737-95 B
1760-64 [261/2,284] Mf ZC 1729-79
ST KATHERINE BY THE TOWER CB 1584-1695 M 1584-
1726 [75-79]
ST LUKE OLD STREET see FINSBURY
ST MARY CHARTERHOUSE see LONDON (CITY of)
ST MARYLEBONE* M 1629 1668-1812 (I) 1815
[47,48,51-57,288]; Middlesex Hospital Lying-in ZC
1747-1807 [148-150,195]; Oxford Chapel, Vere St M
1736-54 [47]; Christ Church, Cosway St M 1825-28
[288]; Wes Salisbury Street ZC 1828-37 [262];
Protestant Mtg Hse Z 1782-1819 [282]
ST PANCRAS St Pancras C 1660-1752 (I) 1830 M 1660-
1752 (I) 1836-37 B 1689-1752 (I) 1796-1807
[193,195,265]
ST PAUL PEAR TREE STREET see LONDON (CITY of)
ST THOMAS IN THE LIBERTY OF THE ROLLS see
LONDON (CITY of)
SHADWELL M 1671-1700 [185]
SHEPPERTON C 1574-1846 M 1574-1850 B 1574-1866
[214,181]
SHOREDITCH St Leonard C 1694-1709 [284]; Aske's
Hospital C 1731-1839 M 1696-1754 B 1724-1852
[104]; see also HAGGERSTON
SNOW HILL (HOLBORN) B(I) 1813-1837 1900-04
SOHO see WESTMINSTER
SOMERSET HOUSE Chapel M 1714-1776 [GCI]; see
also WESTMINSTER
SOUTHGATE Chase Side Chap Mfc ZC 1812-36

SPITALFIELDS Christ Church C (I) 1767-95 M (I) 1805-28 [265] Mfc Banns(I) 1833-1861; Bell Lane Hug Chapel C 1709-16 [HS45]; Brown's Lane Hug Chap C 1719-40 [HS45]; Chareton Hug C 1701-05 M 1701-04; Crispin St Hug C 1694-1715 M 1696-1753 [HS32]; Eglise du Marche Hug C 1719 [HS45]; Pearl St C 1700-1701 [HS32]; St Jean Hug C 1687-1823 M 1687-1751 [HS39]; Church of the Artillery Hug C 1691-1786 M 1691-1754 [HS42]; La Patente de Spitalfields Hug C 1689-1785 M 1689-1753 [HS11]; Princes St Synagogue M(I) 1897-1907 [284]; Repertoire General Hug C 1689 [HS]; Sir George Whele's Chap M 1720-52 [262] Swanfields Hug C 1731-35 M 1722-31 [HS45]; West St Hug C 1706-43 M 1706-41 [HS32]; Wheeler St Hug C 1703-1741 M 1704-41 [HS45]
STAINES C 1644-94 MB 1653-60 [197]; Ind Chap ZC 1785-1837 [SR/R21]
STANMORE, GREAT* M 1599-1837 [214,252]
STANMORE, LITTLE Edgware Chap Mfc 1829-36 C 1834-37 B 1835
STANWELL* M 1632-1837 [214,251]; Ind Poyle Z 1796-1837 C 1823-37 B 1826-35 [SR/R21]
STEPNEY* St Dunstan C(I) 1745-72 M 1568-1754 (I) 1791-2 1807-1824 [198-201,261] Mfc M 1719-54; Ind Mtg Hse, Bull Lane M 1646-77 [262] Mfc B 1790-1853
STOKE NEWINGTON St Mary M 1560-1812 [202]
STRATFORD LE BOW M 1629 [214]
SUNBURY ON THAMES* M 1566-1837 [213,214,251] Mf C 1784-1875
SWANFIELDS see SPITALFIELDS
TEDDINGTON* M 1560-1837 [250]
TOTTENHAM* M 1558-1837 [214,256]; Wes Chap Mfc Z 1817-37 C 1821-37 B 1819-37; see also EDMONTON
TOTTERIDGE see FINCHLEY
TWICKENHAM* C 1538-1831 M 1538-1837 B 1538-1838 [205-208,213,214,250]
UXBRIDGE* M 1538-1694 [252]; Providence (Ind & Presb) Chapel ZC 1789-1806 1812-26 1824-1837 B 1812-1837 1847-1855; Providence Cong Church C 1884-1954 [290]
WAPPING St John C 1617-65 Extracts 1666-97 MB 1620-65 [287]; see also SPITALFIELDS
WARWICK STREET W1 see WESTMINSTER
WEMBLEY St John the Evangelist C 1846-1913 M 1847-1915 B 1846-98 [289] Mfc M(I) 1846-1915
WEST STREET E1 see SPITALFIELDS
WESTMINSTER Abbey CB 1607-1875 M 1655-1875 [190]; Bavarian Embassy Rom Cath C 1748-70 M 1747-79 [103]; Castle Street or Hungerford Market Hug C 1688-1754 M 1688-1753 [HS31]; Chapel Royal St James Hug C 1738-56 M 1700-54 [HS28]; Rom Cath M 1662-71 [CRS38]; Chapel Royal Somerset House Rom Cath M 1671-1700 [196, CRS38]; Dutch C 1694-1775 M 1692-1754 B 1689-1774; La Patente de Soho Hug C 1682-1782 M 1689-1753 [HS45]; Le Carre & Berwick Street Hug CM 1690-1788 [HS25]; New Court Carey Street Ind Chapel Mf C 1707-1837; Portuguese Embassy Rom Cath C 1740-41 M 1695-1849 B 1740-41 [288, CRS38]; Probate Registry ZM 1709-11; Rider Court Hug C 1700-38 M 1700-47 [HS30]; St Anne Soho C 1789-1808 Ext 1686-1752 M Ext 1686-1753 B 1788-1808 [153,212]; St George Hanover Sq M 1725-1845 [11,19,22,24,209];

St George Hyde Park C 1741-54 M 1737-54 [209]; St George Mayfair CM 1735-54 [15]; St James Piccadilly B 1754-62 [194]; Sainte Chapelle (Chappelle Francais) Little George Street SW1 Rom Cath Mf C 1842-1909 M 1846-1910; St Margaret Westminster C 1539-1688 M 1539-1699 B 1539-1673 [64,192,204,259]; St Martin in Fields Trafalgar Square CMB 1550-1636 B(I) 1806-37 [25,66,288] Mf C 1798-1812 Mfc B 1806-56; St Mary le Strand M 1625-1754 [162]; St Paul Covent Garden C 1653-1837 B 1653-1752 [33-7]; St Peter see Abbey; Somerset House Chapel C 1732-75 M 1714-58 B 1720-70 [196,288]; Spring Gardens the Savoy & des Grecs Hug C 1703-1900 M 1684-1753 [HS26]; Swallow Street Hug C 1690-1708 M 1691-1709 [HS28]; Tabernacle Milk Alley/ Glasshouse Street/Leicester Fields Hug CM 1688-1783 [HS29]; Westminster Cath Rom Cath Mf Ext C 1729-1827 M 1729-54 (includes entries for Oxon, Yorks, Staffs and Mont.)
WHEELER STREET see SPITALFIELDS
WHETSTONE see FINCHLEY
WHITECHAPEL St Mary C 1558-1570 1792-1802 MB 1558-1576 [215,291]
WILLESDEN C 1569-1614 M 1569-1838 B 1572-1614 [167,288]
WINCHMORE HILL see EDMONTON

NORFOLK

ACLE M 1664-1815 [56,GCI] Mf C 1664-1847
ALBY Mf C 1558-1983 M 1558-1725 1754-1837 B 1558-1975
ALDBOROUGH Ext 1725-1812 M(I) 1747-1811
ALDEBY Mf Ext C 1560-1649 M 1558-1793 B 1566-1811
ALDERFORD Mfc C 1723-1812 M 1727-1837 B 1726-1812
ANMER M 1600-1837 [67]
ANTINGHAM Ext 1726-1812 [89] Mf CB 1679-1812 M 1680-1753
ARMINGHALL Mf C 1560-1735 M 1560-1754 B 1560-1698
ASHBY BY LODDON Mf Ext C 1620-1743 M 1623-1744 B 1624-1742
ASHBY ST MARY Mf C 1620-1874 M 1621-1839 B 1623-1812
ASHWICKEN with LEZIATE* M 1717-1837 [65]
ASMANHAUGH Mf C 1562-1812 M 1562-1836 B 1562-1811
ATTLEBRIDGE Mfc C 1712-1812 M 1725-1835 B 1716-1812
ATTLEBOROUGH 1552-1840
AYLMERTON C 1725-1812 M 1725-1811 B 1725-1811 [87] Mfc C 1696-1903 M 1696-1924 B 1696-1900
BABINGLEY* M 1662-1812 [57,GCI]
BACONSTHORPE 1710-11 1747-1812 [86] Mf 1682-1725
BACTON Mf 1558-1812
BAGTHORPE* M 1562-1837 [67]
BALE (I) 1540-1962 [83]
BARMER see SYDERSTONE
BARNEY Mf C 1538-1712 M 1542-1710 B 1538-1689
BARNINGHAM NORTH see BARNINGHAM NORWOOD

57

BARNINGHAM NORWOOD Ext 1726-1810 1813-1900
[86] Mf CB 1538-1812 M 1560-1812 Mfc C 1538-
1665 1676-89 1714-1907 M 1539-1644 1666-88
1723-54 1848-1901 B 1538-1648 1661 1665-85
1710-1812
BARSHAM, NORTH* M 1557-1837 [61]
BARSHAM, EAST* M 1658-1837 [61]
BARSHAM, WEST* C 1756-1851 M 1813-1851 B 1764-
1851 [61,83] C 1756-1851 M 1813-1851 B 1764-
1851
BARTON BENDISH 1691-1837 [49] Mf CB 1695-1733 M
1695-1763
BARTON TURF* M 1558-1836 [59]
BARWICK see STANHOE
BATCHLEY see BALE
BAWBURGH Mf C 1555-1802 M 1565-1812 Banns 1754-
1819 B 1557-1809
BAWSEY* CB 1539-1773 (M 1539-1771) [57,72,GCI] Mf
Ext 1539-1773
BECKHAM, WEST* CB 1724-1812 (M 1689-1836)
[58,87]
BEDINGHAM* M 1561-1812 [59]
BEECHAMWELL C 1558-1901 M 1558-1836 B
1558-1812 [8, 47] Mf M 1558-1642 1738-1836
BEESTON ST LAWRENCE Mf C 1558-1713 M 1558-
1712 B 1559-1712
BEESTON by MILEHAM Ext 1538-1693 [20] Mf M 1538-
1753
BEESTON Mf C 1558-1812 M 1558-1801 1813-1838 B
1558-1809
BEESTON REGIS CB 1743-1810 M 1743-1812 [25] Mf
1723, 1739-40
BEETLEY Ext 1539-1779 [20]
BEIGHTON by SELE Mf Ext C 1602-1878 M 1602-1834
B 1591-1880
BEIGHTON Mf Ext 1559-1837
BERGH APTON Mf M 1556-1753
BESSINGHAM 1724-1811 [87] Mf C 1695-1707 1733-
1837 M 1695-1707 1733-1832 Banns 1754-1843 B
1695-1707 1734-1838
BESTHORPE Mf C 1559-1725 M 1559-1640 1677-1725 B
1559-1649 1677-1725
BEXWELL 1558-1837 [85]
BILLINGFORD Mf 1739-40
BILLOCKBY* M 1561-1748 [62] Mf Ext C 1563-1805 M
1561-1748 B 1570-1811
BILNEY, WEST* M 1562-1837 [65]
BINHAM Mfc C 1559-1653 1702-49 1782-1876 M 1560-
1643 1702-48 1754-1837 B 1559-1644 1702-49
1782-1903
BINTREE Mfc C 1582-1710 1713-1899 M 1593-1667
1681-1706 1713-1836 Banns 1686-1903 B 1558-
1706 1713-99 1813-1903
BIRCHAM TOFTS* M 1698-1837 [67]
BIRCHAM ST MARY* M 1669-1837 [67]
BIRCHAM NEWTON* CB 1562-1743 M 1562-1837
[48,67]
BIXLEY Mf Ext C 1575-1809 M 1563-1732 B 1578-1796
BLAKENEY Ext 1696-1789 [87]
BLICKING Mf C 1559-1811 M 1567-1823 B 1560-1677
BLO NORTON Mf CB 1562-1725 M 1562-1630 1658-
1812 Banns 1758-1847
BLOFIELD 1515-1783 [GCI] Mf C 1554-1812 Mfc C 1545-
1901 M 1547-1915 B 1546-1901
BODHAM Ext 1729-1812 [89]
BODNEY* 1563-1837 [49] Mf 1735-1740
BOOTON* M 1560-1812 [58]

BOUGHTON 1691-1837 [49]
BRADENHAM, WEST Mf CB 1538-1812 M 1538-1646
1676-1789 Mfc C 1538-1901 M 1539-1902 B 1643-
1690 1813-1902
BRADENHAM, EAST Mf C 1691-1812 M 1714-1812 B
1695-1812
BRADFIELD Ext 1725-1812 [89] Mf C 1726-1812 MB
1725-1812
BRAMERTON Mf C 1551-1751 M 1551-1739 B 1551-
1733
BRAMPTON C 1732-1812 M 1732-50 1753-1812 B 1732-
1811 [6]
BRANDISTON Mfc C 1562-1901 M 1565-1900 B 1562-
1900
BRAYDESTON* 1623-1812 [56]
BRIDGHAM Mf C 1558-1737 M 1558-1736 B 1558-1728
BRUMSTEAD Mf CM 1561-1812 B 1561-1845 Mfc C
1562-1812 M 1561-1949 B 1561-1812
BRUNDALL* M 1563-1812 [56,GC]
BUCKENHAM, OLD 1560-1649 [68] Mf 1537-1691
BUCKENHAM PARVA (alias TOFTS) see TOFTS, WEST
BURGH ST MARGARET* M 1813-1837 [62] Mf 1746-47
1769-70 C 1787-1852 M 1822-37 B 1797-1863
BURLINGHAM ST PETER* M 1546-1812 [56,GCI] Mf CB
1560-1884 M 1560-1834
BURLINGHAM ST ANDREW* M 1540-1812 [56,GCI] Mf
CB 1538-1884 M 1538-1837
BURNHAM DEEPDALE Mf M 1538-1753
BURNHAM ULPH and SUTTON* M 1653-1837 [59]
CAISTOR next YARMOUTH Mf Ext C 1593-1812 M
1572-1831 B 1565-1812
CAISTOR ST EDMUND Mf 1557-1719
CAISTOR ON SEA* M 1563-1837 [62] Mf C 1558-1737 B
1550-1812
CALTHORPE* M 1558-1812 [56]
CANTLEY CB 1813-37 M 1813-35 [83]
CARLTON COLVILLE Mfc C 1710-1906 M 1710-1912 B
1710-1857
CARLETON RODE* M 1560-1812 [59]
CARLTON next LANGLEY Mf Ext C 1562-1812 M 1564-
1846 B 1566-1797
CASTLE RISING* C 1573-1840 (M 1573-1837) B 1627-
1840 [64,72]
CASTLEACRE* M 1600-1707 1710-1813 [56,60] see also
NEWTOWN by CASTLEACRE
CASTON* M 1539-1700 [10] Mf 1538-1720
CATFIELD Mf CB 1559-1812 M 1559-1837
CATTON Mf C 1688-1812 M 1695-1753 B 1691-1812
CHEDGRAVE* M 1550-1812 [57,GCI] Mf 1550-1812
Banns 1759-1889
CLAXTON Mf CB 1691-92 CMB 1713-14 1717-18
CLEY Mf C 1539-1667 1686-1743 M 1560-1667 1687-
1744 B 1558-1667 1686-1744
COCKLEY CLEY 1691-1837 [49]
COCKTHORPE C 1560-1812 M 1560-1812 B 1560-1812
[74,87] Mfc CB 1560-1812 M 1560-1802 1817-34
1858-1902 Banns 1823-1854
COLBY Mf CB 1553-1812 M 1553-1755
COLNEY 1705/6-1837 [85]
COLTISHALL C 1558-1808 M 1558-1754 B 1558-1812
[74]
COLVESTON see DIDLINGTON with COLVESTON
CONGHAM* M 1581-1837 [64] Mf CB 1580-1812 M
1581-1812
CORTON Mfc C 1579-1861 M 1580-1836 Banns 1754-
1811 1824-1930 B 1579-1912
COSSEY see COSTESSEY

COSTESSEY Mf CB 1538-1812 M 1539-1812; Rom Cath C 1769-70 1785-1821 M 1799 [CRS22]

CRANWICH 1691-1837 [49]

CREAKE, SOUTH* CB 1538-1840 M 1550-1837 [9,63]

CREAKE, NORTH 1538-1840 [72]

CRESSINGHAM, LITTLE 1691-1837 [85]

CRESSINGHAM, GREAT* M 1557-1812 [58]

CRIMPLESHAM Mf Ext 1561-1672

CRINGLEFORD* CB 1561-1840 (M 1561-1837) [60,85] Mf C 1561-1854

CROSTWICK Mf M 1561-1654 1673-80 1701-19 1730-53

CROSTWIGHT Mf CB 1698-1812 M 1698-1836

CROWNTHORPE Mfc C 1700-1912 M 1700-1920 Banns 1754-1872 1911-25 B 1701-1812

DEREHAM, EAST Mf C 1679-1838 MB 1679-1837

DEREHAM, WEST Mf Ext 1559-1786 M 1558-1753

DERSINGHAM* C 1653-1667 M 1653-1837 B 1687 [11,67]

DICKLEBURGH Mf M 1540-1754

DIDLINGTON with COLVESTON 1691-1837 [49]

DILHAM Mf C 1563-1882 M 1563-1839 B 1566-1812

DISS Mf 1551-1837

DITCHINGHAM* M 1559-1812 [18,60] Mf C 1559-1726 M 1640-1707 B 1559-1729

DOCKING with SOUTHMERE* M 1558-1837 [67]

DOUGHTON see DUNTON

DOWNHAM MARKET Mf C 1541-1726 M 1557-1726 B 1554-1726; Wes ZC 1814-1837

DUNHAM MAGNA M 1538-1812 [57,GCI]

DUNSTON 1557-1837 [49]

DUNTON with DOUGHTON* M 1784-1837 [63]

EARLHAM 1621-1837 [85] Mf C 1621 1635-1746 M 1634-1754 B 1639-1748

EATON Mf C 1557-1812 M 1558-1698 B 1558-1660 MB 1722-1812

ECCLES Mf CB 1538-1704 M 1538-1694 see also HEMPSTEAD cum ECCLES

ELLINGHAM Mf Ext C 1671-1810 M 1588-1810 B 1557-1809

ELMHAM, NORTH* 1538-1631 Ext to 1791 [19,20]

EMNETH M 1681-1949 M 1681-1968 B 1751-1920

FAKENHAM* M 1719-1837 [61] Mfc C 1719-1901 M 1719-1788 1804-1901 B 1720-1910; Prim Meth Ext C 1835-38 [83]

FELBRIGG CB 1725-1812 M 1731-1812 [86] Mf C 1568-1812 MB 1556-1812

FELTHORPE Mf CB 1744-1812 M 1754-1812

FERSFIELD Mf CB 1565-1735 M 1565-1732

FILBY* M 1561-1837 [62] Mf 1561-1726 CB 1727-1812

FINCHAM St Martin M 1543-1812; St Michael M 1587-1745 [47]

FLITCHAM* M 1755-1837 [64]

FLORDON Mf 1558-1724

FORDHAM 1573-1837 [49] Mf C 1563-1729 1786-91 MB 1577-1729 B 1786-91

FORNCETT ST PETER 1561-1837 [GCI]

FORNCETT ST MARY 1688-1812 [GCI]

FOULSHAM Mf M 1559-1686

FRAMLINGHAM EARL Mf 1707-18

FRAMLINGHAM PIGOT Part Bapt B 1808-36

FRANSHAM, GREAT Ext 1559-1811 [20]

FRANSHAM, LITTLE Ext 1538-1737 [20]

FRENZE C 1654-1852 M 1662-1852 B 1651-1877 [49]

FRETTENHAM Mf C 1801-2 B 1785-1809

FRING* M 1700-1812 [60]

FRITTON 1558-1728 [7]

GARBOLDISHAM C 1813-47 M 1813-37 B 1813-81 [87]

Mf 1609-1812

GATELEY Mf 1683-1812

GAYTON King's Lynn* M 1702-1837 [65]

GAYTON THORPE* M 1575-1837 [65]

GAYWOOD* M 1653-1837 [69]

GIMINGHAM Ext 1725-1811 [89] Mf C 1565-1812 M 1558-1845 B 1558-1812

GISLEHAM Mfc CB 1559-1812 C 1823-1905 M 1559-1750 1759-1812 1824-1901

GISSING Mf 1691-99 1713-14 1739-40 1796

GLANDFORD Ext 1687-1812 [89]

GOODERSTONE 1563-1837 [85]

GRESHAM* Ext 1725-35 1737-1812 (M 1690-1812) [59] Mf CB 1559-1783 M 1559-1751

GRIMSTON* M 1552-1837 [64]

GUIST Mf B 1813-1838 Mfc C 1557-1707 1710-1877 M 1561-1706 1722-1836 B 1558-1812

GUNTHORPE see BALE

GUNTON Mfc C 1723-1927 M 1724-1832 1848-1902 Banns 1759-1940 B 1723-1963

HACKFORD Mfc C 1584-1901 M 1559-1647 1660-1771 1813-1901 B 1559-1901

HADDISCOE Mf M 1655-1753

HALVERGATE Mf CB 1550-1784 M 1551-1760

HANWORTH Ext 1727-1812 [89]

HAPPISBURGH Mf CB 1558-1812 M 1558-1837

HARDLEY Mf 1708-09 1713-14

HARDWICK Mf C 1561-1787 MB 1516-1812

HARGHAM Mf 1561-1741

HARLING, WEST Mf 1538-1598 Mfc CM 1539-1721 1728 C 1788-1812 M 1759-1906 B 1539-1812

HARLING, EAST Mf 1544-1730

HAUTBOIS, LITTLE see LAMMAS

HAVERINGLAND 1600-1837 [85]

HEACHAM* M 1558-1812 [57,GCI]

HEDENHAM* M 1559-1812 [59]

HEIGHAM M 1813-37 [P]

HELHOUGHTON* M 1539-1837 [63] Mfc C 1539-1921 M 1539-1899 B 1539-1905

HELLINGTON Mf 1563-1812

HEMBLINGTON* M 1551-1837 [66,GCI] Mf Ext C 1563-1869 M 1568-1833 B 1664-1877

HEMPNALL Mf C 1694-1743 M 1560-1731 B 1560-1725

HEMPSTEAD by HOLT Ext 1730-1812 [89] Mf C 1558-1839 M 1558-1835 B 1558-1812

HEMPSTEAD cum ECCLES Mf CB 1707-1812 M 1707-1837

HEMSBY* (M 1556-1837) [62] Mf 1556-1812 Banns 1815-1823

HERRINGBY see STOKESBY with HERRINGBY

HERRINGFLEET Mfc CB 1706-1812 M 1709-1812 Banns 1754-1808 1825-1914

HETHERSETT Mf C 1617-55 1694-1838 M 1620-1652 1695-1837 B 1617-1650 1696-1837

HEVINGHAM C 1600-1839 M 1601-1836 B 1600-1837 [44]

HICKLING* M 1657-1812 [59] Mf C 1653-1716 MB 1654-1716

HINDOLVESTON 1693-1747 [24]

HILGAY Mf M 1583-1760

HILLINGTON* M 1695-1837 [64]

HINGHAM 1600-1845 [12] Mfc C 1600-66 1683-1912 M 1600-64 1683-1812 1828-1903 Banns 1754-1910 B 1600-52 1683-1905

HOCKERING Mf CB 1561-1725 M 1562-1735

HOCKWOLD cum WILTON M 1662-1837 [13]

HOLKHAM* M 1542-1812 [57,GCI]

HOLME NEXT THE SEA* M 1705-1812 [60] Mf CB 1704-1812 M 1705-1811
HOLME HALE* M 1539-1837 [60]
HOLT see HEMPSTEAD by HOLT
HOLT MARKET Mf 1557-1605 Ext 1676-95
HONING Mf CB 1630-1813 M 1630-1836
HONINGHAM Mfc C 1563-1725 M 1563-1723 B 1563-1674 1724-27
HOPTON Mfc C 1673-1882 M 1675-80 1695-1783 1799-1810 Banns 1755-83 1795-1901 B 1674-1903
HORNING Mf M 1558-1754 Ext 1558-1837
HORNINGTOFT* M 1539-1837 Ext 1542-1757 [20,63]
HORSEY Mf CB 1559-1812 M 1571-1824 Ext C 1813-70 M 1755-1812 B 1813-68
HORSTEAD* M 1558-1812 [58]
HOUGHTON next HARPLEY Mfc C 1654-1904 M 1654-1740 1756-1905 B 1654-1812
HOUGHTON ST GILES Mfc C 1559-1812 M 1559-1901 B 1559-1762 1783-1812
HOVETON ST JOHN Mf C 1673-1726 M 1674-1728 B 1673-1733 Mfc C 1673-1921 M 1673-1903 B 1673-1904
HOVETON ST PETER Mf 1624-1720 Mfc C 1624-1906 M 1624-1900 Banns 1755-1914 B 1625-1812
HOWE Mf 1708-09 1717-1718
HUNSTANTON Ext C 1538-1730 M 1542-1721 B 1538-1810 [83]
HUNWORTH Ext 1729-1812
ICKBURGH 1693-1837 [85]
ILLINGTON Mfc C 1673-1770 1783-1812 M 1673-1836 Banns 1846-1913 B 1675-1772 1783-1812
INGHAM Mf 1713-97 (gaps) C 1800-124 MB 1801-12
INGOLDISTHORPE* M 1754-1837 [67] Mf CM 1739-40
INGWORTH* M 1559-1812 [56]
INTWOOD Mfc C 1538-1726 M 1698-1719 B 1558-1726
IRSTEAD Mf 1538-1581 1620 1626-7
ISLINGTON Mf Ext 1540-1651
KENNINGHALL Mf C 1558-1727 M 1558-1724 B 1558-1717
KERDISTON see REEPHAM
KETTERINGHAM Mf 1695-1732
KINGS LYNN St Margaret Mf C 1559-1766 1777-1838 M 1559-1754 1777-1837 B 1559-1840; St Nicholas Mf C 1628-1738 M 1562-1738 1734-1837 B 1562-1841
KNAPTON Mf C 1687-1813 MB 1687-1836
LAKENHAM, OLD M 1801-37 [73] Mf C 1605-1812 M 1571-1812 B 1572-1808 Mfc C 1601-1901 M 1568-74 1602-44 1664-94 1754-1901 B 1568-74 1602-1808 1813-1902
LAMMAS with LITTLE HAUTBOIS 1539-1894 [21]
LANGFORD 1692-1837 [85]
LANGHAM* M 1695-1812 [58] Mfc C 1695-1702 1707-1880 M 1710-51 1755-1837 B 1695-1700 1711-1812
LANGHAM BISHOPS or EPISCOPI see LANGHAM
LANGLEY with CARLTON M 1695-1812 [56] see also CARLTON next LANGLEY
LARLING Mfc C 1723-52 1756-1812 M 1723-53 1755-1839 B 1678-83 1723-54 1756-1812 Banns 1824-1901
LESSINGHAM Mf CB 1557-1812 M 1557-1837
LETHERINGSETT Ext 1714-1812 [89] Mf 1601-36 CB 1653-1759 M 1662-1752
LEXHAM, EAST* M 1541-1812 [56]
LEZIATE see ASHWICKEN
LIMPENHOE Mf CM 1662-1793 Banns 1762-1810 B 1662-1790
LINGWOOD Mf C 1562-1838 M 1562-1757 B 1562-1812

LITCHAM* M 1555-1812 [20,57,GCI]
LODDON see ASHBY by LODDON
LONGHAM Ext 1564-1761 [20]
LUDHAM Mf Ext 1583-1853
LYNN, WEST Mf C 1737-1838 M 1695-1837 B 1715-1838
MARHAM Mf C 1562-1730; Ext 1539-1837
MARSHAM 1538-1836 [69]
MASSINGHAM, LITTLE* M 1559-1837 [63]
MASSINGHAM, GREAT* M 1564-1837 [65]
MATLASKE Mf 1558-1726
MATTISHALL Cong ZC 1772-1837; Prim Meth ZC 1832-37
MAUTBY* M 1663-1834 [60] Mf 1600-36 1663-1812 M 1813-1837 Mfc CB 1664-1802 M 1663-1730 1758-1810 1816-34 Banns 1798-1802 1805-1826
MELTON, LITTLE 1734-1837 [85] Mf 1724-25
METHWOLD Mf 1683-1726
METTON C 1731-1812 M 1738-1803 B 1731-1811 [86] Mf C 1738-1770 M 1738-1754 B 1738-1812
MIDDLETON* M 1560-1839 [65]
MILEHAM Ext 1569-1787 [20] see also BEESTON by MILEHAM
MORNINGTHORPE Mf C 1557-1727 MB 1562-1727
MORSTON CB 1689-1811 M 1689-1810 Mfc C 1700-1811 1837-1842 M 1701-1837 1839-1915 B 1700-1812 Banns 1754-1812; see also STIFFKEY with MORSTON
MORTON ON THE HILL Mfc CB 1559-1812 M 1561-1753 1775-1837 Banns 1755-1812 1824-1904
MOULTON, LITTLE (Great Yarmouth) Mfc C 1539-1901 M 1539-1654 1663-1723 1739-52 1755-1901 B 1539-1725 1735-1905 Banns 1754-1812 1824-1912
MUNDESLEY* M 1724-1812 [58] Mf C 1756-1801 M 1726-1744 B 1756-1812
MUNDFORD 1699-1739 [83]
NARBURGH* (M 1558-1812) Ext C 1538-1730 M 1542-1721 B 1538-1810 [56]
NARFORD M 1559-1812 [57,GCI]
NEATISHEAD Mf 1676-1727
NECTON Mf 1558-1812
NEEDHAM Mf M 1644-1750
NEWTON, WEST M 1561-1837 [60]
NEWTON by CASTLEACRE C 1559-1822 M 1561-1724 B 1559-1799 [31] Mf 1752-3
NORTHWOLD Mf C 1637-1727 M 1656-1727 B 1693-1727
NORWICH All Saints M 1813-17 (I) 1818-37; Cathedral M 1697-1754 [35] Mf C 1702-1811 M 1697-1754 B 1703-1837 ; St Andrew M 1813-37; St Augustine Mf CB 1558-1837 M 1558-1812 ; St Benedict C 1586-1840 M 1562-1837 B 1563-1840 [33]; St Clement M 1813-37; St Edmund M 1813-37; St Ethelreda M 1813-37; St George Colegate M 1813-37 [83] Mf C 1538-1838 MB 1538-1837; St George Tombland C 1538-1840 M 1538-1837 B 1538-1856 [29,30]; St Giles CB 1538-1840 M 1540-1837 [4]; St Gregory M(I) 1813-37; St Helen C 1708-1841 M 1708-1836 B 1678-1856 [5]; St James with Pockthorpe C 1556-1840 M 1556-1837 B 1556-1855 [2,3]; St John Maddermarket M(I) 1813-37; St John Sepulchre M(I) 1813-37; St John Timberhill M(I) 1813-37; St Julian M (I) 1813-37; St Lawrence M 1813-37; St Margaret CB 1560-1840 M 1559-1837 [38/9]; St Martin at Oak C 1560-1840 MB 1628-1843 [40-42]; St Martin at Palace M 1538-1837 B 1538-1838 [36/7];

NORWICH (continued) St Mary Coslany CB 1813-37 M
1557-1837 [58,34]; St Mary in Marsh M (I) 1813-37;
St Michael Coslany M(I) 1813-37 Mf CB 1558-1653
M 1558-1837; St Michael at Plea 1538-1695 M(I)
1813-37 [46] Mf 1538-1696; St Michael at Thorn
M(I) 1813-37; St Paul M 1813-37; St Peter Hungate
M 1813-37; St Peter Mancroft M 1538-1738 (I) 1813-
37 [27]; St Peter Mountergate M(I) 1813-37; St
Peter Southgate M(I) 1813-37; St Saviour C 1555-
1856 M 1555-1837 B 1556-1840 [43]; Ss Simon and
Jude C 1539-1840 M 1539-1837 B 1539-1856 [1]; St
Stephen M(I) 1813-37; St Swithin M(I) 1813-37; Ind
Old Meeting House C 1657-81; Walloon (1565-
1832); see also THORPE next NORWICH

OBY* M 1563-1718 [62]

ORMESBY, GREAT Mf Ext 1667-1837

ORMESBY St Margaret M 1601-1837; St Michael M
1591-1837 [62]; Mf Ext 1568-1773

OVERSTRAND CB 1725-1812 M 1726-1812 [86]

OXBURGH* Rom Cath 1791-1811 [CRS7] Mf M 1538-
1743

OXNEAD Mf 1573-1731 1780-3

PALLING and WAXHAM Mf CB 1779-1813

PALLING Mf 1616-1711 C Ext 1780-1870 B Ext 1779-
1870

PANXWORTH Mfc C 1847-1906 M 1847-1900 B 1848-
1900 see also WOODBASTWICK

PASTON Mf 1538-1631 1720-1812

PENTNEY* M 1731-1837 [65]

PLUMSTEAD, LITTLE Mf 1559-1724

PLUMSTEAD, GREAT Mf Ext C 1558-1807 M 1558-1752
B 1561-1807

POSTWICK Mf Ext 1570-1812

POTTER HEIGHAM Mf Ext 1538-1812

PULHAM Mf 1539-1754

QUIDENHAM Mf 1538-1725

RACKHEATH* 1645-1837 [49]

RANWORTH* M 1559-1812 [58] Mf Ext C 1561-1795 M
1559-1795 B 1558-1795 Mfc C 1558-1915 M 1559-
1837 B 1559-1812 Banns 1763-1816 1823-1902

RAYNHAM, EAST see RAYNHAM ST MARTIN

RAYNHAM ST MARTIN CB 1627-1716 [28] Mf 1691-2
1708-09

RAYNHAM, SOUTH* M 1601-1837 [66]

RAYNHAM, WEST CB 1539-1653 M 1538-1764 [53,66]

REDENHALL Mf Ext 1558-1653

REEDHAM Mf 1691-1709(gaps) Ext CB 1758-1837 M
1754-1837

REEPHAM with KERDISTON Mfc C 1538-1723 1813-
1902 M 1539-1714 1754-1901 B 1539-1723 1813-
1863

REPPS Mf Ext 1563-1812

REPPS, NORTH 1725-1812 [86]

REPPS, SOUTH 1725-1812 [86]

RIDLINGTON Mf CB 1559-1812 M 1559-1838

ROCKLAND ST MARY Mf C 1539-1725 M 1539-1728 B
1539-1744

ROLLESBY Mf C 1561-1812 M 1559-1812 B 1564-1808

ROUGHAM Mf 1769-70 Mfc C 1663-1739 1804-37 1840-
88 M 1663-1737 B 1663-1739 1803-34 1840-1922

ROUGHTON 1562-1837 B(I) 1813-1922 [17,45,87]

ROXTON see RYSTON cum ROXTON

ROYDON (Diss) CMB 1559-1837 [85]

ROYDON (Kings Lynn)* C(M)B 1721-1835 M CB 1721-
1835 M 1721-1833

RUDHAM, EAST* M 1562-1837 [63]

RUDHAM, WEST* M 1565-1837 [63]

RUNCTON, NORTH CB 1563-1652 M 1563-1837
[51,66,83] Mfc C 1563-1876 M 1563-1651 1653-
1741 1754-1837 B 1563-1812 Banns 1754-1903

RUNHAM* M 1538-1812 [60] Mf 1539-1812 Mfc C 1539-
1901 M 1539-1775 1785 1805-1900 B 1539-1812

RUNTON Mfc C 1744-1901 M 1744-54 1813-1924 B
1743-1902 Banns 1754-1842 1850-1871

RUSHALL Mf 1562-1754

RUSTON, EAST Mf 1558-1812 Mfc C 1558-1900 M 1558-
1683 1693-1900 B 1558-1889 Banns 1754-1812
1824-1945

RUSTON, SOUTH see SCO RUSTON

RYSTON cum ROXTON 1687-1837 [49]

SALL Mf C 1560-1812 M 1558-1753 B 1558-1812

SANDRINGHAM* M 1561-1812 [57,GCI]

SANTON 1707 1769-1837 [49]

SAXLINGHAM by HOLT Ext 1721-1812 [89] Mfc C 1558-
1666 1709 1711-14 1717-1901 M 1558-1674 1683-
95 1710-14 1718-1901 B 1558-1696 1708-12 1717-
1812

SAXLINGHAM NETHERGATE with SAXLINGHAM
THORPE Mf 1556-1790; Part Bapt Z & Reg 1793-
1837

SAXLINGHAM THORPE see SAXLINGHAM
NETHERGATE

SAXTHORPE Mf C 1695-1791 M 1696-1754 B 1696-1791

SCARNING Ext 1539-1778 [20]

SCO RUSTON C 1707-1837 M 1726-1837 B 1723-1837
[85] Mf C 1707-1812 M 1726-1835 B 1723-1812 Mfc
C 1707-1901 M 1726-51 1758-1835 1838-1904 B
1723-1806 1814-1900

SCULTHORPE* M 1561-1837 [61] Mf 1562-1726

SEDGEFORD* M 1560-1837 [67,73]

SELE see BEIGHTON by SELE

SHARRINGTON Mf 1672-1812

SHELFANGER 1686-1837 [85]; Bapt B 1795-1837

SHELTON Mf 1557-1633 C 1683-1812 M 1636-1812 B
1678-1795

SHEREFORD* 1722-1837 [63]

SHERINGHAM 1670-1858 [25] Mf M 1754-1812

SHERNBORNE* M 1755-1838 [67]

SHINGHAM 1708-1837 [47,49] Mf M 1762-1836

SHIPDHAM Mf C 1558-1812 M 1558-1740 B 1558-1804;
Ind Chapel C 1833-1837 [86]

SHOTESHAM All Saints Mf M 1561-1753; St Mary Mf C
1690-1783 M 1687-1754 B 1687-1781

SHOULDHAM Mf C 1654-1725 MB 1653-1725

SHROPHAM Mfc C 1721-1875 M 1721-1836 B 1721-
1918 Banns 1754-1900

SIDESTRAND 1735-1812 [86]

SLOLEY Mf 1560-1812

SMALLBURGH* Mf CB 1561-1812 M 1561-1837

SNETTERTON Mf 1669-1729 Mfc C 1669-1932 M 1670-
1812 1818-1911 B 1669-1812

SNETTISHAM* M 1682-1812 [57,GCI]

SNORING PARVA* M 1559-1837 [61]

SNORING MAGNA* M 1560-1837 [61]

SOMERTON, EAST see WINTERTON cum EAST
SOMERTON

SOMERTON, WEST* M 1737-1837 [62] Mf Ext C 1736-
1811 M 1737-1752 B 1726-1812

SOUTHACRE* M 1576-1812 [56]

SOUTHMERE see DOCKING*

SPROWSTON Mf C 1690-1836 MB 1721-1837

STALHAM Mfc C 1562-1742 M 1562-1740 B 1562-1725

STANFIELD Ext 1560-1752 [20]

STANFORD with STURSTON 1699-1837 [85] Mfc C 1769-1902 M 1755-1807 1813-35 1838-1902 B 1769-1904

STANHOE with BARWICK* M 1567-1837 [67]

STARSTON Mf M1561-1753

STIFFKEY with MORSTON Mfc CMB 1548-1710 C 1715-1865 M 1715-1919 B 1715-1902

STOKE HOLY CROSS Mf CB 1538-1812 M 1538-1812

STOKESBY* M 1560-18612 [60]; with HERRINGBY Mf 1538-1812 Banns 1775-1842 Mfc C 1560-1880 M 1562-1645 1653-1731 1733-1837 B 1560-1643 1652-1927 Banns 1824-1900

STRADSETT Mf 1559-1740

STRATTON ST MICHAEL Mf 1558-1725; Cong ZC 1825-1837

STRATTON ST MARY Mf 1547-1653 C 1671-1742 M 1671-1726 B 1671-1696

STRUMPSHAW* M 1562-1812 [56]

STURSTON see STANFORD with STURSTON

SUFFIELD M 1739-1810 [83]

SURLINGHAM Mf C 1574-1899 ZMB 1561-1890

SUTTON Mf C 1576-1812 M 1559-1802 1815-36 B 1564-1812 see also BURNHAM ULPH and SUTTON

SWAFFHAM M 1559-1837 [66] CB Extacts 1587-1682 [20] Mf CB 1559-1812 M 1559-1829

SWAFIELD* M 1660-1812

SWAINSTHORPE C 1559-1734 M 1558-1733 B 1558-1731

SWANNINGTON Mf C 1539-1812 M 1540-1812 B 1538-1812 Mfc C 1541-1751 1812-1882 M 1540-1837 B 1538-1812 Banns 1824-1913

SWANTON ABBOT Mf CB 1538-1812 M 1538-1641 1676-1838

SWARDESTON Mf C 1538-1754 M 1538-1730 B 1538-1697

SYDERSTONE* CB 1585-1840 M (1585-1837)-1840 [23,63,72]

TASBURGH Mf 1558-1724

TATTERFORD* M 1561-1837 [61] Mf C 1561-1765 MB 1561-1730 Mfc C 1560-1756 1765-1812 M 1560-1753 1761-1811 1814-1954 B 1560-1756 1765-1812 Banns 1762-1861

TATTERSETT* M 1755-1837 [61] Mfc C 1760-1811 1813-1902 M 1755-1812 1835-1900 B 1760-1811 1813-1902 Banns 1755-1832

TAVERHAM 1601-1837 [49]

THETFORD St Mary with St Cuthbert and St Peter Mf C 1640-1669 MB 1653-1669; St Cuthbert Mf C 1672-1837 M 1673-1837 B 1737-1837 Mfc 1653-1672; St Mary Mf CM 1666-1837 M 1653-1726 1733-1913 M 1653-1714 1724-7 1733-1913 B 1653-1726 1733-1901; St Peter Mf C 1672-1838 MB 1672-1837 Mfc 1653-1672

THOMPSON Mf CB 1538-1812 M 1538-1754

THORNAGE Ext 1696-1812 [89]

THORPE see also SAXLINGHAM THORPE

THORPE ABBOTTS Mf 1560-1727

THORPE NEXT NORWICH Mf C 1642-1812 M 1671-1812 B 1673-1812

THORPE MARKET 1762-1812 [87] Mf C 1538-1739 M 1537-1733 B 1554-1739

THREXTON 1602/3-1837 [49]

THRIGBY* M 1539-1812 [60] Mf 1539-1812 Mfc C 1539-1684 1687-94 1695-1717 1721-30 1747-1812 M 1540-1680 1690 1695-9 1708-26 1739-41 1747 1750-1811 1813-1836 B 1539-1677 1688-92 1696-1700 1705-14 1726-7 1749-1804 Banns 1786-1815

1844 1898-1952

THURGARTON Mf M 1744-1811

THURLTON CB 1558-1840 M 1558-1836 [45] Mf M 1538-1714 1744-1811

THURNE with OBY and ASHBY* M 1559-1837 [62]

THURSFORD* M 1692-1837 [61]

THWAITE ST MARY* M 1539-1837 [60]

TOFTS, WEST with BUCKENHAM PARVA (alias TOFTS) 1705-1837 [85] Mfc C 1734-1902 M 1755-1901 B 1733-1901 see also STANFORD with STURSTON, also TOFTS,WEST

TOFTREES* M 1754-1837 [20,61] Mf 1739-40 1746-7

TOPCROFT* M 1557-1813 [60]

TRIMINGHAM CB 1557-1840 M 1557-1837 [45,87] Mf CB 1557-1840 M 1557-1836

TROWSE Mf C 1706-1724 B 1696-1724

TRUNCH Mf 1558-1812 M 1813-37

TUDDENHAM, EAST C 1561-1752 M 1561-1747 B 1561-1751 [32]

TUDDENHAM, NORTH Mf C 1560-1788 M 1560-1754 B 1560-1723

TUNSTALL Mf CB 1557-1812 M 1593-1644 1695-1754

TUNSTEAD Mf 1677-1725 Mfc C 1678-1900 M 1678-1901 B 1678-1908

ULPH see BURNHAM ULPH and SUTTON

UPTON* (M 1558-1812) [56,GCI] Mf CM Ext 1558-1698 B 1558-1701

WACTON Mfc C 1560-1607 1610-53 1657-1778 1781-1901 M 1560-1607 1610-46 1650 1661-1700 1717-50 1754-1836 B 1553-1651 1655 1659-1703 1715-78 1781-1812 Banns 1754-1811 1824-1882

WALCOT* Mf CB 1558-1812 M 1558-1836

WALSHAM, SOUTH St Lawrence Mf C 1551-1756 M 1550-1812 B 1550-1785; St Mary Mf C 1551-1743 M 1550 1643 1708-1743 B 1551-1743

WALSHAM, NORTH Mf C 1557-1812 M 1541-1837 B 1541-1812

WALSINGHAM, GREAT Mfc C 1558-1870 M 1559 1566-1900 B 1558-1898

WALSINGHAM, LITTLE Mfc C 1558-1734 1873-1876 M 1558-1733 1788-1812 1837-1900 B 1558-1678 1873-75 1885-1900 Banns 1788-1832 1873-75

WALSOKEN Mf C 1582-1850 M 1582-1868 Banns 1822-1874 B 1582-1975

WALTON, EAST* M 1560-1837 [65] Mf 1560-1750 CB 1750-1782

WATERDEN* C 1730-1837 M (1743-1812)-1850 B 1747-1836 [63,83]

WATTON Prim Meth 1832-37; Ind Chapel C 1822-1837 [86]; see also MATTISHALL

WAXHAM Mf CB 1780-1812 Ext C 1785-1854 M 1758-1834 B 1789-1825 see also PALLING and WAXHAM

WEASENHAM ALL SAINTS Mf C 1568-1812 M 1561-1812

WEASENHAM ST PETER Mf C 1581-1750 1783-1809 M 1581-1812 B 1581-1740 1783-1812

WEETING* M 1558-1812 [59]

WELLINGHAM Mf 1746-47 Mfc C 1756 1777-80 1782-1915 M 1765-81 1784-1811 1813-1900 B 1756 1778-1901

WELNEY M 1813-1895 [86]

WENDLING 1539-1677 Ext [20]

WEREHAM M 1553-1758

WESTACRE* M 1665-1837 [65] Mf 1665-1812

WESTWICK Mf CB 1642-1812 M 1642-1836

WEYBOURNE Ext 1729-1812 [89]

WHISSONSETT* M 1700-1837 [63]

WHITWELL Mfc CB 1559-1783 C 1813-1887 M 1559-1902 B 1813-1908
WIGGENHALL ST MARY 1558-1654 [50] Mf Ext 1538-1782
WILBY Mf CB 1541-1730 M 1543-1730
WILTON see HOCKWOLD cum WILTON
WINCH, EAST* M 1690-1837 [65]
WINCH, WEST Mf 1559-1812
WINTERTON cum EAST SOMERTON* M 1747-1837 [62] Mf C 1717-1812 M 1747-1813 B 1747-1812
WITTON by BLOFIELD* M 1582-1812 [56,GCI]
WITTON Mf 1558-1903
WOLVERTON* M 1653-1812 [57,GCI]
WOODBASTWICK with PANXWORTH M 1561-1813 [58] Mfc C 1560-1920 M 1561-1840 B 1558-1813
WOOD DALLING Mf 1653-1812
WOODRISING C 1561-1783 M 1562-1748 B 1564-1782 [52]
WOODTON* M 1538-1812 [54,60]
WOOTTON, NORTH* M 1655-1837 [64]
WOOTTON, SOUTH* M 1556-1837 [64]
WORMEGAY Mf 1565-1642
WORSTEAD Mf C 1562-1767 M 1562-1752 B 1600-1767 Mfc C 1558-1659 1661-1900 M 1558-1658 1661-1752 1754-1900 B 1558-1667 1678-1884
WRAMPLINGHAM Mf M 1566-1725
WRETHAM, EAST Mfc C 1748-81 1783-1812 B 1748-1812
WRETHAM, WEST Mf 1745-46 Mfc C 1783-1793 B 1783-1791
WRETHAM, EAST and WEST Mfc C 1813-1891 M 1754-1811 1813-1837 Banns 1754-1818 1823-1901
WRETTON M 1697-1770
WYMONDHAM M 1813-37 [73]; Ind/Cong C 1754-1822 B 1754-1838 [83]
YARMOUTH, GREAT 1721-54 [14-16,84] Mf C 1559-1782 M 1558-1782 1799-1835 B 1558-1691 1824-30 D 1786-1835; Ind CB 1643-1705; St Nicholas Mf Ext C 1570-1781 M 1559-1716 see also CAISTOR next YARMOUTH
YAXHAM Mf C 1688-1723 1782 M 1695-1734 B 1686-1729

NORTHAMPTONSHIRE

ASHTON C 1682-1910 M 1682-1837 B 1707-1773, 1778-1944 [36]
BARBY Ext 1573-1621 [16]
BARNACK Ext 1591-1721
BOUGHTON B 1600-1657 1671 [36]
BUCKBY, LONG 1558-1689 [2] Mf C 1570-1689
BURTON LATIMER C 1538-1812 M 1538-1757 B 1538-1733 [3,36]
BYFIELD CMB 1688-1772 [38]
CASTOR M 1538-1812 [32]
CHACOMBE Ext 1566-1812 [OX/R 26]
CLAYCOTON 1541-1614 [4]
COLD ASHBY CM 1560-1733 B 1559-1733
COLLINGTREE Mf M 1754-1837
COURTEENHALL 1538-1812 [1]
CRANFORD ST. JOHN Mf M 1692-1752
CROUGHTON M 1663-1812 [33]
CULWORTH C 1563-1841 MB 1610-1841 [5]

DINGLEY 1580-1812 [6] Mf M 1583-1811
DODFORD C 1581-1720 M 1581-1812 B 1581-1667 [32,38]
EASTON NESTON with HULCOTE 1707-1861 [35]
EASTON ON THE HILL C 1598-1842 M 1578-1646, 1653-1843 B 1583-1859 [1]
ETTON 1701-1804 [7]
EVERDON M 1558-1812 [33]
EYDON B 1538-1906 [2]
FARNDON, EAST C 1562-1644 M 1562-1656 B 1581-1641 [38]
FARTHINGSTONE M 1544-1812 [33]
FAXTON M 1570-1837 [32] Mf C 1578-1649 M 1570-1640 B 1568-1642
GAYTON CM 1558-1744 B 1558-1743 [2]
GLINTON Ext CB 1701-1812 M 1567-1814 [8,32]
GREATWORTH Mf M 1583-1813
HARDWICK C 1561-1780, 1782-1839 M 1561-1835 B 1559-1774, 1782-1839 [G1]
HARPOLE M 1538-1812 [33]
HARRINGWORTH CB Ext 1695-1804
HARTWELL C 1684-1867 M 1684-1964 B 1684-1910 [37]
HELPSTON 1701-1807 [9]
HEYFORD M 1558-1837 [32]
HIGHAM FERRERS Meth C 1811-37 [10]
HINTON IN THE HEDGES Mf 1558-1754
HULCOTE see EASTON NESTON
ISHAM C 1701-1805 M 1701-1754 B 1701-1805 [38]
KELMARSH 1559-1837 [1]
KETTERING Bapt CB Ext 1785-1837; Ind Ext C 1714-1813 B 1785-1836 [11]
KING'S CLIFFE Catholic Mission ZC 1773-1855 M 1777-1831 [38]
KINGS SUTTON M 1570-1811 [12]
LAMPORT M 1587-1837 [33]
LICHBOROUGH Mf M 1732-1812
LUTTON C 1653-1812 M 1654-1812 B 1655-1812 [13-15]
MAIDWELL Ext 1570-1696 [16]
MARSTON SAINT LAWRENCE C 1671-1707 1813-40 M 1700-1837 B 1664-72 [35]
MAXEY C 1538-1812 MB 1538-1812 [17-20]
MIDDLETON CHENEY Ext 1558-1614 [OX/R 26]
MOULTON 1565-1812 [21]
NASEBY CM 1563-1840 B 1564-1840 [34/35]
NORTHAMPTON St Peter M 1578-1812 [33]
NORTHBOROUGH CB 1712-1809 M 1538-1812 [22,32]
NORTON (Daventry) CMB 1678-1752 [38]
OAKLEY, GREAT C 1562-1718 M 1564-1718 B 1564-1695 [35]
PEAKIRK CB 1701-1811 M 1617-1812 [23,32]
PETERBOROUGH St John Ext C 1598-1848 M 1795-1893 B 1598-1899 [G1]; St Peter & All Souls Rom Cath C 1848-1900 MB 1859-1900
PYTCHLEY Ext 1559-1692 [16] Mf M 1695-1812
RAUNDS C 1581-1617 1623-28 1706-1837 M 1581-1617 1624-31 1706-1837 B 1583-1616 1625-27 1706-1837 [24,38]
RINGSTEAD C 1589-95 1605-55 M 1607-20 B 1608-20 1636 [38]; Part Bapt Z 1811-36 [25]
ROCKINGHAM 1562-1721 [26]
ROTHWELL Ext 1614-1706 [16]; Ind M 1692-1701 [25]
RUSHTON 1538-1837 [27]
SPRATTON 1538-1653 [28]
STOKE BRUERNE M 1561-1812 [32]
STOWE NINE CHURCHES M 1560-1837 [33]
SUTTON BASSETT see WESTON BY WELLAND
TANSOR Mf M 1639-1837

THENFORD Ext 1567-1670 [OX/R 26]
THORNHAUGH-cum-WANSFORD Mf M 1654-1836
Banns 1756-1837
THRAPSTON Bapt Z 1795-1837 C 1795-1807 B 1794-
1837 [25]
TIFFIELD 1559-1840 [36]
UFFORD 1712-1812 [29]
WANSFORD see THORNHAUGH cum WANSFORD
WARKWORTH CB 1813-40 [36] see also
BANBURY,SOUTH Oxon
WEEDON LOIS 1705-1812 [30]
WELLAND see WESTON by WELLAND
WELLINGBOROUGH Bapt ZC 1795-1837 DB 1792-1836
[25]; SFrs C 1653-1836 M 1760-1835 B 1658-1836
[31];
WESTON BY WELLAND M 1576-1812 [32]
YARWELL Mf C 1813-47

NORTHUMBERLAND

ALLENDALE CM 1662-1684 B 1662-1851 [55]
ALNHAM* C (1688-1812) M (1705-1812)-37 B (1727-
1812) [17,53]
ALNWICK C 1645-69 M(I) 1813-37 [18,53]
ALWINTON 1719-1812 M(I) 1813-1837 [6,53]; Holystone
Chapelry B 1816-1842 [NU/M1]; Biddlestone Hall
Rom Cath CD 1767-1840 M 1767-18348 [CRS14];
see also HARBOTTLE
ANCROFT M(I) 1813-37 B 1813-37 [51,53]
BAMBOROUGH see BAMBURGH
BAMBURGH C 1654-1762 M 1653-1758 M(I) 1813-1837
B 1652-1809 CMB 1813-37 [7,53]
BEADNELL CB 1766-1812 M 1767-1781 [19]
BELFORD 1701-1812 M(I) 1813-37 [2,53]
BELLINGHAM Rom Cath CM 1794-1837 [CRS2]
BERWICK ON TWEED CM 1574-1700 M(I) 1813-1837
[20/1,53] Mf C 1572-1812 M 1572-1754 B 1572-
1841; United Pres M 1782-1812 [52]; Shaws Lane
Dissent M 1778-1791 1810 [52]
BIDDLESTON HALL see ALWINTON
BLANCHLAND 1753-1851 M(I) 1753-1837 [52,68]
BOTHAL* 1680-1812 [22] see also HEBBURN
BRANTON (Eglingham) Presb C 1785-1837 [23]
BRANXTON 1736-1812 M(I) 1813-37 [1,53]
BYRNESS CB 1797-1812 [8,52]
BYWELL ST ANDREW M(I) 1685-1837 [52]
BYWELL ST PETER M(I) 1663-1837 [52]
CALLALY CASTLE Rom Cath CM 1796-1839 D 1797-
1881 [CRS7]
CAPHEATON Rom Cath with KIRKWHELPINGTON Rom
Cath C 1760-84 M 1782 D 1772-85 [CRS14]
CARHAM M 1815-36 [52/3]
CHATTON* (1712-1812) M(I) 1813-37 [24,53]
CHILLINGHAM M(I) 1813-37 [53]
COCKSHAW Rom Cath C 1753-1832 M 1766 1826 1830
D 1807 1813-1824 [CRS26]
CORBRIDGE* (1654-1812)-1851 [25,49]; Halton Chapel
CB 1813-1851 [59]
CORSENSIDE C 1715-1843 M 1738-1843 B 1726-1843
[54]
CORNHILL M(I) 1813-1837 [53]
CROOKHAM Presb Z 1732-87 C 1777-1833 [26]
DODDINGTON CB 1697-1812 M 1697-1812 M(I) 1813-

1837 [1,52,53]
EDLINGHAM* 1658-1812 M(I) 1813-1837 [27,53]
EGLINGHAM* (1662-1812) M(I) 1813-1837 [28,53]; see
also BRANTON
ELLINGHAM CB 1695-1819 M 1695-1804 M(I) 1813-1837
[29,53]; Diss Z 1751-1806 [29]
ELSDON 1672-1812 [48]
EMBLETON M(I) 1813-37 [53]
ETAL Presb C 1751-1828 [51]
FELTON M(I) 1813-37 [53]; Felton Park Rom Cath C
1792-1858 [51]
FORD 1683-1812 M(I) 1813-37 [3,53]
GLANTON Presb ZC 1784-1837 [51]
HAGGERSTON Rom Cath D 1790-1856 [30]
HALTON* CB 1654-1812 M 1654-1769 [31]
HALTWHISTLE C 1691-1750 M 1691-1719 B 1656-1723
[16,58]
HARBOTTLE (Alwinton) Presb C 1735-1802 [54]
HAYDON BRIDGE 1654-1812 [4] Mf B 1881-1903
HEBBURN* 1680-1812 M(I) 1887-1935 [22,52] see also
BOTHAL
HEDDON ON THE WALL* C 1671-1710 B 1698-1705
[45]
HESLEYSIDE see BELLINGHAM
HEXHAM M 1579-1851 B 1754-1851 [46,63/4,66]; Rom
Cath C 1715-1826 M 1716-1806 B 1715-1754
[CRS26]; see also STONECROFT; Bapt C 1651-1680
[32]; Ebenezer Indep C 1787-1837 [51]; Wes C
1797-1836 [51]
HOLYSTONE see ALWINTON
HOLY ISLAND 1578-1958 [33,52/3]; Ch of Scotland M
1799-1822 [33]
HOUGHTON, LONG 1646-1812 M(I) 1813-1837 [36,53]
HOWICK M(I) 1813-37 [53]
HUMSHAUGH C 1818-1851 B 1819-1851 [58]
ILDERTON* (1724-1812) M(I) 1813-1837 [24,53]
INGRAM* (1696-1812) M (1684-1812)-37 B (1682-
1812) [34,52/3]
KIRKHARLE CB 1695-1875 M 1692-1875 [51]; Diss C
1775-1875 [51]
KIRKHAUGH M(I) 1761-1837 [52]
KIRKHEATON see KIRKHARLE
KIRKNEWTON C 1770-1787 M 1770-1788 M(I) 1813-
1837 B 1762-1788 [53,58]
KIRKWHELPINGTON Rom Cath see CAPHEATON
KNARESDALE Ext C 1741-1851 M 1743-1851 B 1742-
1851 M(I) 1695-1837 [51/2]
KYLOE M 1813-1837 [52/3]
LAMBLEY C 1697-1701 M 1701-1837 B 1701-1732
[51/2]; see also KNARESDALE
LEE C 1664-1851 [69]
LESBURY* (1690-1812) M(I) 1813-1837 [35,53]
LONG FRAMLINGTON M(I) 1813-1837 [53]
LONGBENTON C 1670-1812 M 1653-1812 M(I) 1653-
1837 B 1669-1812 [5,59]
LOWICK 1716-1812 M(I) 1813-37 [1,53]
MELDON* C 1706-1812 M 1727-1812 B 1716-1812 [37]
MINSTERACRES Rom Cath C 1795-1840 [38]
MORPETH Mf 1719-1812
NETHERWITTON Mf CB 1696-1812 M 1706-1812; Rom
Cath C 1789-1803 B 1796-1801 [51]
NEWBIGGIN Mf C 1662-1812 M 1665-1782 B 1665-1812
NEWBROUGH see WARDEN
NEWBURN M(I) 1659-1837 [52] Mf C 1660-1739 M 1659-
1739 B 1660-88;

NEWCASTLE UPON TYNE All Saints C 1713-1830 M
1600-1830 [10-14] M 1813-1837 [39] Mf C 1600-
1902 M 1600-1872 B 1600-1924; St Andrew M(I)
1597-1837 [47]; St Nicholas M 1574-1812 [41]; St
Andrew Rom Cath C 1765-1843 B 1765-1806
[40,CRS35]; Brunswick Meth C 1837-1937 [59];
Hanover Sq Unit 1774-1898 [8]
NORHAM M(I) 1813-37 [53]; Presb C 1753-1854 M 1763-
1856 [54]
OVINGHAM 1679-1812 M(I) 1769-1837 [9,52]
RENNINGTON C 1768-1812 M 1769-1779 B 1769-1812
[8]
ROCK C 1769-1812 M 1771-1780 B1768-1812 [8]
ROTHBURY C 1653-1812 M 1658-1812 B 1654-1812
[15,16]
SHILBOTTLE see WHITTINGHAM
SHOTLEY C 1675-1812 M 1670-1812 M(I) 1813-1837 B
1690-1797 [16,42,52]
SIMONBURN CMB 1681-1851 [60]
SLALEY C 1703-1851 M 1722-1851 M(I) 1722-1837 B
1720-1851 [52,57]
STONECROFT Rom Cath see HEXHAM
SWINBURNE CASTLE Rom Cath C 1828-59 M 1830-
1845 B 1833-1849 [51]
THROCKINGTON C 1715-1850 M 1736-58 1770-75
1813-1850 B 1736-52 1762-1851 [57]
TWEEDMOUTH M(I) 1813-37 [53]
WARDEN CB 1695-1725 M 1695-1724 [16]; Newbrough
Chapelry CB 1695-1980 M 1695-1753 1869-1976
[16,50]; Rom Cath C 1774-1796 M 1784-1795 B
1775-1796 [54]
WARKWORTH 1667-1812 [43]
WHALTON 1661-1812 [44]
WHITFIELD C 1611-1812 M 1605-1812 M(I) 1600-30
1698-1840 B 1612-1812 [8,52]
WHITLEY C 1764-1851 M 1765-1851 B 1764-1851 [49]
WHITTINGHAM M(I) 1813-1837 [53]
WOODHEAD Rom Cath C 1774-96 M 1784-1795 D 1775-
1796 [51]
WOOLER M(I) 1813-37 [53]
WOOLER, WEST Presb C 1749-1785 [51]

NOTTINGHAMSHIRE

ANNESLEY* M (1599-1812) M(I) 1813-1837 [48,79] Mfc
1599-1900
ARNOLD* (M 1546-1812) M(I) 1813-1837 [52,66] Mfc CB
1544-1900
ASKHAM* (M 1538-1831) M(I) 1813-1837 [57,67,GCI]
Mfc 1538-1900
ASHFIELD see KIRKBY IN ASHFIELD
ASLOCTON see WHATTON
ATTENBOROUGH* (M 1560-1812) M(I) 1813-1837
[45,67] Mfc 1559-1900
AUSTERFIELD M(I) 1754-1812 [79]
AVERHAM* Ext 1538-1719 (M 1538-1837) M(I) 1813-
1837 [35,56,66,GCI] Mfc 1538-1900
AWSWORTH* (M 1756-1812) [47] Mfc 1756-1900
BABWORTH M(I) 1754-1837 [67,79] Mfc 1623-1900
BALDERTON M(I) 1813-37 [66] Mfc 1538-1900
BARNBY M(I) 1813-1837 [66] Mfc 1593-1900
BARNSTONE see LANGAR

BARTON IN FABIS* (M 1558-1812) M(I) 1813-1837
[46,79] Mfc 1558-1900
BASFORD* (M 1568-1812) M(I) 1813-1837 [45,67] Mfc
1561-1900
BAWTRY M(I) 1754-1837 [67,79]
BECKINGHAM* (M 1618-1837) M(I) 1813-1837
[57,67,GCI] Mfc 1615-1900
BEESTON* (M 1558-1812) M(I) 1813-1837 [45,67] Mfc
CB 1558-1900
BILBOROUGH* (M 1569-1812) M(I) 1813-1837 [45,67]
Mfc 1569-1900
BILSTHORPE* (M 1654-1837) M(I) 1813-1837 [61,67]
Mfc 1654-1900
BINGHAM* (M 1598-1812) M(I) 1813-1837 [40,67] Mfc
1598-1900
BLEASBY* CB 1573-1837 M (1573-1837) M(I) 1813-1837
[55,67,70,GCI] Mfc 1573-1900
BLIDWORTH* (M 1566-1837) M(I) 1813-1837 [57,67,GCI]
Mfc 1566-1900
BLYTH M(I) 1754-1837 [67,79] Mfc 1556-1900
BOLE M(I) 1754-1837 [67,79] Mfc 1755-1900
BOTHAMSALL C 1538-1812 M 1538-1812 B 1538-1812
M(I) 1754-1837 [67,79,83]
BOUGHTON* (M 1685-1837) M(I) 1813-1837 [61,67] Mfc
1685-1900
BRAMCOTE* (M 1562-1812) M(I) 1813-1837 [45,67] Mfc
1562-1900
BRIDGFORD, EAST* (M 1614-1812) M(I) 1813-1837
[40,67] Mfc 1557-1900
BRIDGFORD, WEST* (M 1559-1812) M(I) 1813-1837
[46,67] Mfc 1559-1900
BROUGHTON SULNEY* M (1571-1812) [41] see also
BROUGHTON, UPPER
BROUGHTON UPPER M(I) 1813-1837 [79] Mfc
1571-1900
BULCOTE M(I) 1813-1837 [67] Mfc 1841-1900
BULWELL* (1635-1812) M(I) 1813-1837 [48,79] Mfc CB
1621-1900; Inghamite ZCD 1803-17 [80]
BUNNY* M (1556-1818) M(I) 1813-1837 [48,79] Mfc
1556-1900
BURTON JOYCE* (M 1559-1812) M(I) 1813-1837 [49,67]
Mfc 1559-1900
BURTON, WEST M(I) 1754-1837 [67,79] Mfc 1602-1900
CALVERTON* M (1560-1812)-37 M(I) 1813-1837
[51,67,80,GCI] Mfc 1569-1900
CAR COLSTON* M (1570-1812) M(I) 1813-1837 [40,67]
Mfc 1570-1900
CARBURTON 1528-1812 M(I) 1754-1837 [1,67,79]
CARLTON IN LINDRICK M(I) 1754-1837 [67,79] Mfc
1559-1900
CARLTON ON TRENT M(I) 1754-1837 [67,79] Mfc 1782-
1900
CAUNTON* (M 1709-1837) M(I) 1813-1837 [56,67] Mfc
1709-1900
CLARBOROUGH M(I) 1754-1837 [67,79] Mfc 1567-1900
CLAYWORTH M(I) 1754-1837 [67,79] Mfc 1540-1900
CLIFTON, NORTH* M (1654-1812) M(I) 1813-1837
[58,67] Mfc 1539-1900
CLIFTON* M (1573-1812) M(I) 1813-1837 [46,79] Mfc
1573-1900; with GLAPTON B 1573-1840 [80]
CODDINGTON M(I) 1813-1837 [66] Mfc 1676-1900
COLLINGHAM, NORTH* M 1571-1837 M(I) 1813-1837
[58,66] Mfc 1558-1900
COLLINGHAM, SOUTH* M 1558-1837 M(I) 1813-1837
[58,66] Mfc 1558-1900
COLSTON BASSETT* CB 1591-1850 M (1591-1812) M(I)
1813-1837 [2,3,41,79]

COLWICK* M (1569-1754)-1812 M(I) 1754-1837
[49,67,79] Mfc 1569-1900
CORTLINGSTOCK/COSTOCK* (M 1558-1812) M(I)
1813-1837 [44,79] Mfc 1558-1900
COSSALL* C 1654-1881 M 1654-(1663-1812)-1837 M
1654-1837 [4,47,79]; C Adult 1851-1880 [4]
COSTOCK see CORTLINGSTOCK
COTGRAVE* (M 1559-1812) M(I) 1813-1837 [41,79] Mfc
1569-1900
COTHAM M(I) 1813-1837 [66] Mfc 1587-1900
COTTAM M(I) 1754-1837 [67,79] Mfc 1695-1900
CROMWELL* (M 1654-1837) M(I) 1813-1837 [59,66] Mfc
1650-1900
CROPWELL BISHOP* CB 1539-1850 M (1539-1812)-
1837 [5,6,41,79,80]
CROPWELL BUTLER M(I) 1813-1837 [67] see also
TYTHBY
CROPWELL, LITTLE see TYTHBY
CUCKNEY M(I) 1754-1837 [67,79]
DARLTON M(I) 1754-1837 [67,79] Mfc 1568-1900
DRAYTON, EAST M(I) 1754-1837 [67,79] Mfc 1755-1900
DRAYTON, WEST M(I) 1754-1837 [67,79] Mfc 1632-1900
DUNHAM M(I) 1754-1837 [67,79] Mfc 1654-1900
EAKRING* C 1603-1701 (M 1563-1837) B 1621-1702 M(I)
1813-1837 [61,67,75] Mfc 1563-1900
EASTWOOD* C 1689-1845 M 1692-(1711-1812)-1837 B
1690-1861 [7,50,79,GCI]
EATON M(I) 1754-1837 [67,79] Mfc 1660-1900
EDINGLEY* C(M)B 1580-1837 M(I) 1813-1837 [57,67,77]
Mfc 1580-1900
EDWALTON* (M 1538-1812) M(I) 1813-1837 [46,79] Mfc
1545-1900
EDWINSTOWE 1634-1758 M(I) 1754-1837 [8,67,79] Mf
C 1758-1877 Mfc 1634-1905
EGMANTON* (M 1653-1837) M(I) 1813-1837 [61,67] Mfc
1653-1900
ELKESLEY M(I) 1754-1837 [67,79] Mfc 1628-1900
ELSTON CHAPEL M(I) 1813-1837 [66] Mfc 1584-1878
ELSTON M(I) 1813-1837 [66] Mfc 1572-1900
ELTON-ON-THE-HILL* CB 1592-1850 M (1593-1812)-
1849 M(I) 1813-1837 [9,40,67] Mfc 1592-1900
EPPERSTON* (M 1584-1812) M(I) 1813-1837 [51,67] Mfc
1582-1900
ESTHWAITE see EASTWOOD
EVERTON* with SCAFTWORTH M 1643-1837 M(I) 1813-
1837 [60,67] Mfc 1560-1900
FARNDON 1695-1718 M(I) 1813-1837 [10,66] Mfc 1558-
1900
FARNSFIELD* (M 1572-1837) M(I) 1813-1837 [51,67]
Mfc 1572-1900
FINNINGLEY M(I) 1754-1837 [67,79] Mfc 1557-1900
FLAWBOROUGH* (M 1680-1812) M(I) 1813-1837 [43,66]
Mfc 1680-1900
FLEDBOROUGH* (M 1562-1837) M(I) 1813-1837 [59,67]
Mfc 1562-1900
FLINTHAM* (M 1629-1812) M(I) 1813-1837 [40,67] Mfc
1576-1900
GAMSTON M(I) 1754-1812 [67,79] Mfc 1544-1900
GEDLING* (M 1558-1812) M(I) 1813-1837 [49,67] Mfc
1558-1900
GIRTON* M (1680-1807) M(I) 1754-1837 [58,67,79,GCI]
Mfc 1680-1900
GLAPTON see CLIFTON
GONALSTON* M (1538-1812) M(I) 1813-1837 [51,67]
Mfc 1538-1900
GOTHAM* (M 1558-1812) M(I) 1813-37 [44,79] Mfc
1560-1900

GRANBY* with SUTTON CB 1567-1837 M (1567-1812)-
1837 M(I) 1813-1837 [11,12,40,67]
GREASLEY* CB Ext 1600-1676 (M 1600-1812) M(I) 1813-
37 [35,47,79] Mfc 1600-1900
GRINGLEY ON THE HILL M(I) 1754-1837 [67,79] Mfc
1678-1900
GROVE M(I) 1754-1837 [67,79] Mfc 1726-1900 see also
RETFORD, EAST
HABBLESTHORPE see LEVERTON, NORTH
HALAM* C(M)B 1559-1837 M(I) 1813-1837
[57,67,78,GCI] Mfc 1559-1900
HALLOUGHTON* C(M)B 1621-1837 M(I) 1813-1837
[55,67,72,GCI] Mfc 1621-1900
HARWORTH M(I) 1754-1837 [67,79] Mfc 1538-1900
HAWKESWORTH* (M 1569-1812) M(I) 1813-1837
[40,67] Mfc 1569-1900
HAWTON* (M 1564-1812) M (I) 1813-37 [43,66] Mfc
1564-1900
HAYTON* with TILNE M (1655-1838) M(I) 1813-1837
[60,67] Mfc 1655-1900
HEADON* (1566-1812) M(I) 1754-1837 [13,67,79]
HICKLING* CB 1646-1812 M (1646-1812)-1837 M(I)
1813-1837 [14,15,41,79] Mfc 1646-1900
HOCKERTON* CB 1582-1837 (M 1582-1837) M(I) 1813-
1837 [35,56,67,73]
HOLME PIERREPOINT* CB 1813-50 M (1564-1812)-38
M(I) 1754-1837 [41,67,79,80] Mfc 1564-1900
HOLME* M 1711-1837 M(I) 1813-1837 [56,66,GCI] Mfc
1711-1900
HOVERINGHAM* C 1553-1679 (M 1560-1812) B 1567-
1665 M(I) 1813-1837 [34,51,67]
HUCKNALL TORKARD* (M 1559-1812) M(I) 1813-1837
[48,79] Mfc 1560-1900; Holy Cross Rom Cath Mfc C
1880-1901
KELHAM Ext 1663-1808 M (1663-1837) M(I) 1813-1837
[35,56,66] Mfc 1663-1900
KEYWORTH* M (1657-1812) M(I) 1813-1837 [46,79] Mfc
1643-1900
KILVINGTON* (M 1538-1812) M(I) 1813-1837 [43,66]
Mfc 1538-1900
KINGSTON ON SOAR* M (1755-1811) M(I) 1813-1837
[44,79] Mfc 1657-1900
KINOULTON* CB 1606-1837 M (1569-1812)-37 M(I)
1813-1837 [16,41,79]
KIRKBY IN ASHFIELD (M 1620-1812) M(I) 1813-1837
[50,79,GCI] Mf C 1600-1811 Mfc 1620-1900 see also
HUCKNALL
KIRKLINGTON* C(M)B 1575-1837 M(I) 1813-1837
[57,67,71,GCI] Mfc 1575-1900
KIRTON* CB 1538-1777 (M 1538-1837) M(I) 1813-1837
[34,61,67]
KNEESALL* M (1682-1837) [59] M(I) 1813-1837 [67] Mfc
1682-1900
KNEETON* M (1592-1812) M(I) 1813-1837 [40,67] Mfc
1591-1900
LAMBLEY* M (1569-1812) M(I) 1813-1837 [51,67,GCI]
Mfc 1652-1900
LANEHAM* M 1566-1837 M(I) 1813-1837 [57,67,GCI]
Mfc 1538-1900
LANGAR* with BARNSTONE CB 1595-1812 M (1596-
1812)-1837 M(I) 1813-1837 [17,18,48,67]
LANGFORD* M (1703-1837) M(I) 1813-1837 [58,66,GCI]
Mfc 1669-1900
LAXTON* M (1607-1837) M(I) 1813-1837 [61,67] Mf C
1564-1609 1716-1725 Mfc 1563-1900
LEAKE, EAST* CB Ext 1600-1711 (M 1600-1812) M(I)
1813-1837 [44,79,82/3] Mfc 1600-1900

LEAKE, WEST* CB 1614-1840 M 1614-(1617-1811)-40
M(I) 1813-1837 [19,44,79,83]
LENTON* M (1540-1812) M(I) 1813-37 [45,67] Mfc CB
1598-1900
LEVERTON, NORTH with HABBLESTHORPE M(I) 1754-
1837 [67,79,80] Mfc 1669-1900
LEVERTON, SOUTH M(I) 1754-1837 [67,79] Mfc 1658-
1900
LINBY* M (1692-1837) M(I) 1813-1837 [60,79] Mfc 1692-
1900
LITTLEBOROUGH M(I) 1754-1837 [67,79] Mfc 1599-1900
LOUND see SUTTON CUM LOUND
LOWDHAM* M (1559-1812) M(I) 1813-1837 [49,67] Mfc
1559-1900z
MANSFIELD WOODHOUSE* Ext 1653-1782 M (1657-
1837) M(I) 1813-1837 [35,52,66] Mfc 1653-1900
MANSFIELD* (M 1559-1837) M(I) 1813-1837 [52/3,66]
Mfc 1559-1900; Rom Cath C 1810-12 see
SPINKHILL, Derbyshire [DE/R 46]; St Philip Rom
Cath Mfc C 1877-1906 M 1879-1906 D 1878-1906
MAPLEBECK* M (1562-1837) M(I) 1813-1837 [52,67] Mfc
1679-1900
MARKHAM, EAST C 1596-1604 M 1561-1604 B 1561-80
M(I) 1754-1837 [67,79,GCl] Mfc 1561-1900
MARKHAM, WEST M(I) 1754-1812 [79] Mfc 1651-1900
MARNHAM* M (1601-1837) M(I) 1813-1837 [59,67] Mfc
1601-1900
MATTERSEY M(I) 1754-1837 M 1813-1837 [67,79,83]
Mfc 1539-1900
MISSON M(I) 1754-1837 [67,79] Mfc 1636-1900
MISTERTON M 1679-1682 M(I) 1754-1837 [67,79,83] Mfc
1540-1900
MORTON* M (1640-1837) M(I) 1813-1837 [55,67,GCl]
Mfc 1640-1900 see also SOUTHWELL
MUSKHAM, NORTH* M (1706-1837) M(I) 1813-1837
[56,66] Mfc 1705-1900 see also SOUTHWELL
MUSKHAM, SOUTH* M (1589-1837) M(I) 1813-1837
[56,66] Mfc 1589-1900 see also SOUTHWELL
NEWARK ON TRENT (M 1599-1837) M(I) 1813-1837
[43,54,66,GCl] Mfc CB 1601-1900; Holy Trinity Rom
Cath Mfc C 1826-82 see also NOTTINGHAM
NORMANTON IN THE WOLDS see PLUMTREE
NORMANTON ON SOAR* M (1559-1812)-1837 M(I)
1813-1837 [44,79,83] Mfc 1559-1900
NORMANTON ON TRENT* M (1673-1837) M(I) 1813-
1837 [59,67] Mfc 1673-1900
NORTON CUCKNEY Mfc 1632-1900
NORWELL* M (1638-1837) M(I) 1813-1837 [59,67] Mfc
1681-1900
NOTTINGHAM* St Mary M (1566-1812) M(I) 1763-1837
[39,66,62/3] Mfc CB 1566-1900; St Nicholas M
(1562-1812) M(I) 1813-1837 [65,66] Mfc CB 1562-
1900; St Peter M (1572-1812) M(I) 1813-1837
[64,66] Mfc CB 1570-190; Bapt Paradise Place Z
1806-37 C 1831-37; Bethesda Meeting House Z
1831-1837 [83]; High Pavement Chapel/Hyson
Green Mission (I) 1872-1921; St Augustine Rom
Cath Mfc C 1880-92 1894-1903; St Barnabas Rom
Cath Mfc C 1825-1908 M 1856-96 D 1894-1906; St
Mary, Hyson Green, Rom Cath Mfc C 1882-90 D
1894-1906; St Patrick Rom Cath Mfc C 1867-1910 D
1867-96; Sacred Heart Rom Cath Mfc C 1877-1905;;
NOTTINGHAM, NEWARK & GRANTHAM Rom Cath
C 1786-1854 [83] Mfc C 1786-1826
NUTHALL* M (1663-1812) M(I) 1813-1837 [47,79] Mfc
1657-1900
OLLERTON* (1592-1812) M(I) 1754-1837 [21,67,79] Mfc

1592-1900
ORDSALL M(I) 1754-1837 [67,79] Mfc 1538-1900
ORSTON* M (1590-1812)-1837 M(I) 1813-1837
[40,67,83] Mfc 1590-1900
OSSINGTON* M (1600-1837) M(I) 1813-1837 [59,67] Mfc
1594-1900
OWTHORPE* Ext 1731-1837 M (1733-1812) M(I) 1813-
1837 [22,41,79] Mfc 1731-1900
OXTON* M (1564-1812) M(I) 1813-1837 [51,67,GCl] Mfc
1564-1900 see also SOUTHWELL
PAPPLEWICK* M (1661-1837) M(I) 1813-1837 [60,79]
Mfc 1661-1900
PERLETHORPE 1530-1811 M(I) 1754-1837
[23,67,79,GCl] Mfc 1530-1900
PLUMTREE* C(M)B 1558-1812 M(I) 1813-37 [24/5,56,79]
RADCLIFFE ON TRENT* M (1633-1812)-1837 M(I) 1813-
1837 [41,67] Mfc 1632-1900
RADFORD* Ext 1569-1721 (M 1563-1812) M(I) 1813-
1837 [48,67,P] Mfc CB 1563-1900
RAGNALL M(I) 1754-1837 [67,79] Mfc 1700-1900 see
also SOUTHWELL
RAMPTON M(I) 1754-1837 [67,79] Mfc 1565-1900
RATCLIFFE ON SOAR* M (1624-1812) M(I) 1813-37
[46,79] Mfc 1597-1900
REMPSTONE* C 1689-1989 (M 1570-1812)-1989 M(I)
1813-37 B 1689-1990 [44,79,84] Mfc 1570-1900
RETFORD, EAST M(I) 1754-1837 [67,79] Mfc 1573-1900;
with GROVE C(I) 1813-1860 [80]
RETFORD, WEST M(I) 1754-1837 [67,79] Mfc 1772-1900
ROLLESTON* M 1559-1837 M(I) 1813-1837 [56,67,GCl]
Mfc 1559-1900
RUDDINGTON* C 1636-1851 M 1653-(1655-1813)-1837
M(I) 1813-37 B 1653-1852 [35,46,79,81]
SAUNDBY M(I) 1754-1837 [67,79] Mfc 1562-1900
SCAFTWORTH see EVERTON
SCARLE, SOUTH* M (1684-1837) (I) 1813-37 [58,66] Mfc
1680-1900
SCARRINGTON* M (1571-1812) M(I) 1813-37 [40,67]
SCREVETON* M (1640-1812) M(I) 1813-1837 [40,67]
Mfc 1639-1900
SCROOBY* M (1695-1837) M(I) 1813-1837 [60,67] Mfc
1695-1900
SELSTON* M (1559-1812) M(I) 1813-37 [50,79,GCl] Mfc
CB 1557-1900
SHELFORD* M (1563-1812) M(I) 1813-1837 [41,67] Mfc
1563-1900
SHELTON* (1595-1812) M(I) 1813-37 [33,43,66] Mfc
1595-1900
SIBTHORPE* M (1720-1812) M(I) 1813-37 [43,66] Mfc
1720-1900
SKEGBY* M (1569-1812) M(I) 1813-1837 [50,66,GCl] Mfc
1569-1900
SNEINTON* M (1655-1812) M(I) 1813-1837 [49,67] Mfc
1654-1900
SOUTHWELL* Ext 1566-1732 C(M) 1559-1837 M(I) 1813-
1837 [35,55,67,80,GCl] Mfc CB 1559-1900
STANFORD ON SOAR* M (1633-1812) M(I) 1813-1837
[44,79] Mfc 1633-1900
STANTON ON THE WOLDS* M (1736-53) M(I) 1754-
1837 [56,79] Mfc 1735-1900
STAPLEFORD* (M 1656-1812) M(I) 1813-1837 [47,67]
Mfc 1656-1900
STAUNTON* M (1654-1812) M(I) 1813-37 [43,66] Mfc
1654-1900
STAUNTON Chapel* M (1663-1812) [43] Mfc 1663-1900
STOKE, EAST* M(I) 1813-1837 [66] Mfc 1538-1900 see
also ELSTON Chapel

STOKEHAM M(I) 1754-1837 [67,79] Mfc 1619-1900
STRELLEY* M (1665-1812) M(I) 1813-37 [47,67] Mfc
1654-1900
STURTON LE STEEPLE M(I) 1754-1837 [67,79] Mfc
1638-1900
SUTTON see GRANBY
SUTTON BONNINGTON* St Anne M (1560-1812) M(I)
1813-37 [44,79] Mfc 1560-1900; St Michael M
(1559-1812) M(I) 1813-1837 [44,79] Mfc 1558-1900
SUTTON CUM LOUND* M (1538-1837) M(I) 1813-1837
[60,67] Mfc 1538-1900
SUTTON IN ASHFIELD* M (1572-1837) M(I) 1813-1837 B
1577-1810 [26,50,52,66] Mfc 1577-1900
SUTTON ON TRENT* M (1584-1837) M(I) 1813-1837
[59,67] Mfc 1584-1900
SYERSTON* M (1567-1812) M(I) 1813-37 [43,66] Mfc
1567-1900
TEVERSAL* M (1572-1812) M(I) 1813-37 [50,66,GCI] Mfc
1571-1900
THORNEY* M (1561-1837) M(I) 1813-1837 [58,67,GCI]
Mfc 1562-1900
THOROTON* M (1583-1812) M(I) 1813-1837 [40,67] Mfc
1583-1900
THORPE (Newark)* M (1559-1800) M(I) 1813-1837
[43,66] Mfc 1542-1900
THRUMPTON* M (1679-1812) M(I) 1813-37 [46,79] Mfc
1679-1900
THURGARTON* CB 1721-1837 M (1654-1812) M(I) 1813-
1837 [51,67,74,GCI] Mfc 1721-1900
TILNE see HAYTON
TITHBY see TYTHBY
TOLLERTON* (M 1559-1812) M(I) 1813-37 [41,79] Mfc
1558-1900
TRESWELL M(I) 1754-1837 [67,79] Mfc 1557-1900
TROWELL* (M 1570-1812) M(I) 1813-1837 [47,67] Mfc
1567-1900
TUXFORD M(I) 1754-1837 [67,79] Mfc 1624-1900
TYTHBY* CB 1559-1684 1799-1813 M (1583-1684 1754-
1812)-37 M(I) 1813-37 [27,41,51,67] Mfc 1559-1900
see also SOUTHWELL
UPTON* M (1586-1837) M(I) 1813-1837 [55,67,GCI] Mfc
1585-1900
WALESBY* (C 1580-1792 M 1594-1752 B 1585-1791)
M(I) 1754-1837 [28,67,79] Mfc 1580-1900
WALKERINGHAM C 1613-25 1636-41 1657-1840 adults
to 1870 M 1605-51 1657-1840 B 1605-40 1657-1840
M(I) 1754-1837 [29,67,79] Mfc 1605-1900
WARSOP M(I) 1754-1837 [67,79] Mfc 1538-1900
WELLOW 1703-1812 M(I) 1754-1837 [31,67,79] Mf C
1813-1839
WESTON* M (1559-1837) M(I) 1813-1837 [59,67] Mfc
1559-1900
WHATTON* M (1538-1812) [40] Mfc 1538-1900; with
ASLOCTON M(I) 1813-1837 [67]
WHEATLEY, NORTH M(I) 1754-1837 [67,79] Mfc 1649-
1900
WHEATLEY, SOUTH M(I) 1754-1837 [67,79] Mfc 1546-
1900
WIDMERPOOL* M (1540-1812) M(I) 1813-1837 [44,79]
Mfc 1539-1900
WILFORD* M (1657-1812) M(I) 1813-1837 [46,79] Mfc
1657-1900
WILLOUGHBY ON THE WOLDS* M (1682-1812) M(I)
1813-37 [46,79] Mfc 1680-1900
WINKBURN* CB 1542-1837 M (1553-1773) 1813-1837
M(I) 1754-1837 [59,67,76,79,83]
WINTHORPE* M (1695-1812) M(I) 1813-37 [43,66] Mfc

1687-1900
WOLLATON* M (1576-1812) M(I) 1813-37 [47,67] Mfc
1576-1900
WOODBOROUGH* M (1573-1812) M(I) 1813-1837
[51,67,GCI] Mfc 1547-1900 see also SOUTHWELL
WORKSOP CB 1558-1771 M 1558-1754 M(I) 1754-1837
[32,67,79] Mfc 1558-1900
WORKSOP MANOR Rom Cath C 1772-1873 M 1785 B
1785-1806 [83]
WYSALL* M (1654-1812) M(I) 1813-1837 [46,79] Mfc
1654-1900

OXFORDSHIRE

Oxfordshire Marriage Index Mf 1538-1837

ADDERBURY 1598-1900 [18,27,170/1] Mf 1670-1683
1722-1853; see also BODICOTE; SFrs see
BANBURY
ADWELL C 1539-89 1636-1969 M 1540-89 1636-45
1671-1966 B 1539-89 1636-1974 [14,125] Mf 1639-
1675 1721-1851
ALBURY C 1639-1693 M 1653-1837 B 1653-70 1678-
1980 [28] Mf Ext 1680-1851
ALKERTON CB 1544-1986 M 1546-1975
[12,21,26,29,228] Mf 1720-1851
ALVESCOT C 1660-1950 MB 1663-1950 [201] Mf
1721-1851
AMBROSDEN C 1611-1878 M 1611-1837 Banns 1823-
1858 B 1611-1858 [14,29,30] Mf Ext 1685-1851
ARDLEY C 1700-1851 M 1713-1851 B 1680-1851 [13,31]
Mf Ext 1680-1851
ASCOT UNDER WYCHWOOD C 1569-1869 M
1570-1977 B 1572-1917 [118] Mf 1721-1851
ASTHALL with ASTHALL LEIGH CB 1667-1975 M
1667-1974 [32] Mf Ext 1667-1851
ASTON BAMPTON see BAMPTON ASTON
ASTON, NORTH CB 1565-1850 M 1565-1837 [12,159]
Mf 1722-1853
ASTON ROWANT CB 1554-1840 M 1555-1837 [120] Mf
Ext 1639-1871
BALSCOTE C 1821-1986 M 1821-1939 B 1821-1988
[125,218]; with WROXTON Mf 1813-53
BAMPTON CM 1538-1890 B 1538-1891 [33-5] Mf 1680-3
1721-1855 see also SHIFFORD
BAMPTON ASTON Mf 1843-1865
BAMPTON LEW Mf 1843-1878
BANBURY CB 1558-1838 M 1558-1837 [26,P] Mf 1606
1662-1851; Indep/Cong Church Lane C 1794-1806 :
Lady Hunt Conn C 1807-12; Meth C 1805-13; Presb
see BLOXHAM; Rom Cath C 1771-1832 [P]; SFrs Z
1632-1837 M 1648-1837 B 1655-1837 [23]
BANBURY, SOUTH M 1853-1967 [242]
BARFORD ST MICHAEL C 1643-1899 M 1718-1903 B
1678-1898 1932-1988 [24,31,37,60,206] Mf
1721-1852
BARFORD ST JOHN C 1629-1983 M 1669 1698-1928 B
1669 1695-1762 1813-1988 [18,24,211] Mf 1669
1721-37 1809-1852
BARTON WESTCOTT Mf 1719-1853
BECKLEY C 1678 1703-1979 M 1703-1979 B 1678
1703-1976 [28] Mf 1678-1851

BEGBROKE C 1671-1843 M 1664-1814 B 1666-1851 [38]
Mf C 1747-1853
BENSINGTON Ind ZB 1835-36
BENSON C 1565-1840 M 1568-1840 B 1566-1840
[14,39] Mf 1661-1858 see also BENSINGTON
BERRICK SALOME C 1609-1839 M 1609-1841 B
1609-1840 [40] Mf 1639-70 1687-96 1720-47 1768-
1853
BICESTER 1539-1840 [20,37,191/2]] Mf 1680-1685
1699-1700 1721-1834; Cong C 1695-1745 M 1695-6
[41]; Market End Ind Chapel Mf C 1786-1837
BINSEY CB 1759-1987 M 1754-1979 [195] Mf 1805-1866
BIX C 1577-1897 M 1577-1931 B 1577-1952 [226] Mf
1639 1680 1685 1721-1852
BLACK BOURTON C 1543-1840 M 1561-1840 B
1542-1864 [38] Mf 1678 1681 1721-1853
BLADON C 1545-1947 M 1545-1976 B 1545-1978
[32,239] Mf 1684 1721-1856
BLETCHINGDON 1559-1840 [13,60] Mf Ext 1713-1865
BLOXHAM C 1630-1860 MB 1630-1862 Banns 1754-
1875 [12,24,148/9,195] Mf 1721-1871; Presb (with
MILTON and BANBURY) C 1786-1837 [36,P]
BODICOTE C 1563-1988 M 1563-1753 1837-1940 M
1567-1982 [18,209] Mf 1721-1852; Crematorium B
1976-1988 [209]; with ADDERBURY M 1754-1837
[209]
BOURTON Banns 1863-1953 [125]
BOURTON, GREAT see CROPREDY
BRADWELL C 1615-1847 M 1620-1837 B 1618-1917 [38]
Mf 1721-1812 1845-1852
BRIGHTWELL see BRITWELL PRIOR
BRIGHTWELL BALDWIN CB 1546-1981 M 1547-1979
[28] Mf 1639 1696 1721-1812
BRITWELL PRIOR* Mf 1604-5 1633-39 1812; Rom Cath
CD 1765-88 [CRS13]
BRITWELL SALOME C 1574-1981 M 1575-1640
1658-1977 B 1574-1643 1650-80 1706-1982 [42] Mf
Ext 1696-1852
BRIZE NORTON CM 1538-1837 B 1568-1877 [14,38] Mf
1682 1722-1852
BROADWELL see BRADWELL
BROUGHTON M 1680-1840; with NORTH NEWINGTON
C 1683-1893 M 1683-1862 B 1683-1881 [21,194]
BROUGHTON POGGS C 1556-1849 M 1558-1836 B
1556-1855 [43] Mf 1721-1852
BUCKNELL 1653-1840 [20] Mf 1700 1721-1852
BURFORD C 1612-1858 M 1612-1888 B 1612-1937 [44-
6] Mf 1684 1721-1860
CADMORE END Mf 1851-53
CASSINGTON* C 1631-1939 C 1603-(1673-1837)-1939
B 1624-1905 [47,116] Mf 1721-1852
CAVERSFIELD C 1640-1840 M 1650-1840 B 1651-1840
[20,125]
CAVERSHAM C 1597-1849 M 1597-1837 B 1597-1867
[157] Mf 1639 1670 1682-99 1721-1859
CHADLINGTON 1565-1967 [48] Mf 1660 1721-1813
CHALGROVE C 1538-1641 1655-90 1702-1851 M
1531/2 1543-1643 1655-97 1702-1838 B 1538-1640
1655-89 1702-1851 [49] Mf Ext 1640-1845
CHARLBURY CB 1559-1900 M 1559-1890 [13,125,141-3]
Mf 1670-1684 1720-1851; SFrs Mf B 1867-1886
CHARLTON ON OTMOOR C 1572-1852 M 1568-1837 B
1562-1875 [32] Mf 1700 1721-1854
CHASTLETON C 1586-1984 M 1573-1976 B 1572-1985
[119,172,226] Mf 1682 1721-1783 1801-1852
CHECKENDON C 1719-1956 M 1720-1979 B 1719-1971
[119] Mf 1639 1722-1860

CHESTERTON C 1539-1840 M 1538-1837 B 1540-1840
[14,50] Mf Ext 1718-1855
CHINNOR C 1581-1609 1621-1978 MB 1622-1973
[14,51,121/2]; Prim Meth C 1857-1909 [132]; Ind Z
1797-1837 C 1804-37 B 1815 Mf C 1797-1837
CHIPPING NORTON* C 1563-1883 M (1560-1837)-1898
B 1560-1876 [52/3,115,132] Mf 1669-70 1680 1721-
1856; Bapt Z(I) 1767-1831 ZC 1767-1837 B(I) 1788-
1940; Wes Meth (with STOW ON THE WOLD) C
1868-1923 SFrs Mf 1869-85
CHISLEHAMPTON CB 1762-1840 M 1763-1837 [99] Mf
Ext 1769-1833 (with STADHAMPTON until 1762)
CHURCHILL 1630-1978 [14,156] Mf 1630-1904
CLANFIELD C 1633-49 1679-1839 M 1633-43 1672-1837
B 1633-43 1679-1880 [43] Mf 1721-1852
CLAYDON C 1569-1981 M 1569-1982 B 1569-1849
[22,137] Mf Ext 1605-1851
CLIFTON HAMPDEN C 1576-1641 1659-1688 1716-1840
M 1578-1651 1657-1696 1716-1837 B 1579-1688
1716-1840 [49] Mf Ext 1662-1866
COGGES C 1653-1973 M 1655-1973 B 1654-1973
[14,47] Mf Ext 1721-1852
COMBE, LONG C 1646-1851 M 1654-1837 B 1653-1874
[14,50] Mf Ext 1647-1851
CORNWELL C 1662-1982 M 1662-1980 B 1664-1983
[119] Mf Ext 1669-1853
CO(A)TE BAMPTON Bapt C 1647-1837 M 1775 1839 B
1647-1882
COTTISFORD C 1610-1942 M 1651-1977 B 1611-1977
[13,50] Mf Ext 1721-1852
COWLEY St James C 1678-1892 M 1696-1881 B 1696-
1903 [198] Mf 1721-1853; St John C 1870-1898
[231]
CRAWLEY see HAILEY
CROPREDY C 1538-1861 M 1558-1976 (I) 1539-1976 B
1538-1904 [22,54/5,195,GCI]; and GREAT
BOURTON Mf 1664-1812
CROWELL* C 1594-1978 M (1602-1837)-1970 B 1602-
1979 [42,56,115] Mf Ext 1639-1852
CROWMARSH GIFFORD C 1576-1685 1737-1840 M
1576-1685 1694-1753 Ext 1754-1812 B 1576-1685
1678-1840 [37] Mf Ext 1639-1852
CUDDESDON with WHEATLEY C 1541-1837 M 1542-
1836 B 1542-1837 [14,57/8] Mf 1724-1829
CULHAM C 1648-1987 MB 1648-1986 [14,59,218] Mf
1721-1852
CUXHAM C 1578-1982 M 1579-1982 B 1580-1981 [42]
Mf Ext 1639-1865
DAYLESFORD C 1660-1968 M 1660-1959 B 1660-1971
[125]
DEDDINGTON 1630-1837 [12,14,123] Mf 1669-1682
1721-1858
DORCHESTER B 1638-1840 [224] Mf 1661-1816
DRAYTON (Banbury) C 1577-1965 M 1578-1837 B 1577-
1987 [21,132,200] Mf 1721-1859
DRAYTON ST LEONARD C 1568-1840 M 1569-1837 B
1573-1840 [60] Mf Ext 1767-1857
DRAYTON ST PETER see DRAYTON (Banbury)
DUCKLINGTON C(I) 1550-1880 M(I) 1581-1880 B(I)
1580-1880 [61] Mf 1721-1863
DUNS TEW C 1654-1695 1721-1837 M 1654-1688 1741-
1837 B 1654-1690 1721-1837 [12,50] Mf Ext 1669-
1852
EASINGTON C 1637-1869 1911-79 M 1670 1721-1873
1908-61 B 1722-1979 [125] Mf Ext 1639-1865
ELSFIELD C 1670 1689-1979 M 1670 1686-1979 B 1670
1694-1979 [31] Mf Ext 1670-1852

EMMINGTON CB 1538-1983 M 1539-1981 [15,140] Mf
1639-40 1684 1690 1721-1852
ENSTONE C 1558-1928 M 1558-1976 B 1558-1974
[62,164,245] Mf 1670 1721-1839
EPWELL C 1577-1838 M 1580-1837 B 1584-1837 [19,26]
Mf Ext 1722-1853 see also SWALCLIFFE
EWELME C 1599-1982 M 1599-1643 1661-1979 B 1599-
1982 [63] Mf Ext 1670-1852
EYNSHAM* C 1653-1900 (M 1665-1837)-1900 B 1653-
1900 [64,116,219] Mf 1725-1844
FARINGDON, LITTLE Mf 1865-98
FIFIELD C 1670-1967 M 1670-1965 B 1659-1984 [146]
Mf Ext 1669-1851
FINMERE 1560 C 1579-1872 M 1579-94 1632-1853 B
1579-84 1592 1615-1936 [13,158] Mf 1684-1853
FINSTOCK C 1840-1920 M 1850-1920 B 1842-1907
[201] Mf 1847-51
FOREST HILL C 1564-1666 1700-1840 M 1564-1661
1681 1741-1837 B 1564-1666 1682-83 1741-1840
[40] Mf 1564-1683 1721-1852
FRINGFORD C 1596-1863 M 1586-1863 B 1588-1900
[13,40] Mf 1680 1700 1721-1849
FRITWELL 1558-1951 [15,221] Mf 1558-1691 1713-1812
FULBROOK CB 1615-1840 M 1615-1837 [162]
GARSINGTON C 1562-1853 M 1562-1693 1710-1851 B
1563-1694 1710-1855 [40]
GLYMPTON C 1567-1863 M 1567-1859 B 1567-1862
[65,125]
GODINGTON CB 1678-1840 M 1678-1837 [20]
GORING C 1673-1888 M 1676-1837 B 1673-1865 [217];
Lady Hunt Conn Z 1792-1837 C 1790-1837
GORING HEATH St Barth Chapel C 1742-1956 M 1743-
52 B 1743-1956 [66,125,206]
HAILEY C 1797-1900 B 1797-1932 [31] see also WITNEY
St Mary
HAMPTON GAY C 1662-1837 M 1657-1836 B 1662-1852
[43]
HAMPTON POYLE C 1540-1977 M 1545-1977 B 1544-
1978 [15,67]
HANBOROUGH* CB 1560-1860 M (1560-1837)-1860
[68,116]
HANWELL C 1586-1930 M 1586-1837 B 1586-1833
[21,69]
HARDWICK with TUSMORE C 1744-87 1813-1976 M
1755-92 1813-1977 B 1739-98 1813-1977 [13,125]
HARPSDEN C 1560-1928 M 1563-1910 B 1558-1878
[15,211]
HASELEY, GREAT 1538-1838 [15,70]
HEADINGTON C 1678-1896 M 1598-1886 B 1678-1900
[15,165]
HEADINGTON QUARRY C 1849-1905 M 1850-1927 B
1849-1902 [173]
HENLEY ON THAMES C 1558-1979 M 1558-1976 B
1558-1945 [71,179-84,210,236/7]
HETHE C 1679-1879 M 1700 1713-1879 B 1678-1955
[13,67]
HEYFORD LOWER 1539-1840 [23]
HEYFORD, UPPER C 1555-1702 1717-1885 M 1557-
1664 1666-1925 B 1557-1957 [13,159]
HEYTHROP C 1605-1980 M 1613-1976 B 1613-1981
[13,132,172]
HOLTON C 1633-1948 M 1633-1978 B 1633-1982
[67,194]
HOOK NORTON C 1550-1911 M 1669-1837 B 1643-1867
[12,136]; Bapt Z 1772-1837 M 1844-77 B 1841-56
HORLEY C 1540-1880 M 1538-1837 B 1539-1965
[21,26,72] see also HORNTON

HORNTON C 1704-1862 M 1703-54 1785-1837 1915-25
B 1703-1880 with HORLEY M 1754-1812 [21,69]
HORSPATH CM 1561-1900 B 1562-1900 [73,230]
HORTON CUM STUDLEY C 1880-1979 M 1882-1979 B
1880-1980 [126]
IBSTONE C 1639-1947 MB 1639-1973 [228] see also
Buckinghamshire
IDBURY C 1669-1984 M 1722-1952 B 1721-1985 [159]
IFFLEY C 1572-1981 M 1574-1971 B 1754-1986
[160,177/8]
IPSDEN CB 1569-1983 M 1569-1978 [15,74]
ISLIP C 1590-1848 M 1590-1844 B 1590-1871 [75]
KELMSCOTT C 1538-1692 1763-1845 M 1547-1645
1678-81 1765-1811 B 1538-1688 1764-1850 [43]
KENCOT C 1554-1852 M 1600-1849 B 1581-1857 [126]
KIDDINGTON C 1573-1977 M 1576-1975 B 1576-1973
[15,76]; Rom Cath C 1788-1840 [CRS17]
KIDLINGTON C 1579-1837 MB 1574-1837 [37,77]
KINGHAM C 1663-1910 M 1663-1902 B 1663-1963 [78]
KIRTLINGTON CB 1558-1699 1720-40 M 1558-1699
1754-1840 [13,15,76,194]
LANGFORD C 1538-1851 M 1589-1851 B 1538-1880
[79,126]
LAUNTON C 1648-1979 M 1671-1978 B 1681-1979
[15,196]
LEIGH, NORTH C 1572-1966 M 1574-1948 B 1573-1950
[87,127]
LEIGH, SOUTH CB 1613-1974 M 1613-1970 [64]
LEW see BAMPTON LEW
LEWKNOR C 1666-1856 M 1666-1837 B 1666-1884
[80,126]
LITTLEMORE C 1814-1925 M 1847-1936 B 1836-1929
[133] see also OXFORD St Mary the Virgin
MAPLEDURHAM C 1627-1840 MB 1627-1837 [126];
Rom Cath CB 1711-12 [CRS1]
MARCH BALDON C 1559-1840 M 1598-1837 B 1506
1597-1840 [104,127] Mf Ext 1662-1851
MARSTON C 1653-1944 M 1654-1900 B 1653-1904
[127,173]
MERTON C 1635-1964 M 1721-1837 B 1635-1972
[76,82]
MIDDLETON STONEY C 1598-1978 MB 1599-1978
[13,83]
MILCOMBE C 1562-1766 M 1562-1711 B 1562-1719 [24]
MILTON Presb see BLOXHAM
MILTON Chapelry of Adderbury C 1857-1989 M 1956-
1988 B 1857-1989 [230]
MILTON, GREAT M 1550-1840 [16,84]
MILTON UNDER WYCHWOOD C 1854-1920 M 1855-
1900 B 1854-1908 [230]
MINSTER LOVELL C 1656-1973 M 1667-1972 B 1661-
1973 [85,200]
MIXBURY C 1645-1876 M 1657-1882 B 1645-1966
[13,86]
MOLLINGTON C 1570-1897 M 1565-1959 B 1565-1979
[22,197]
MONGEWELL C 1660-1925 MB 1682-1923 [16,127]
NETTLEBED C 1641-1853 M 1654-1836 B 1653-1883
[146]
NEWINGTON 1572-1869 [43]
NEWINGTON, NORTH see BROUGHTON
NEWINGTON, SOUTH C 1538-1989 M 1538-1975 B
1538-1925 [24,246]; SFrs see BANBURY
NEWNHAM MURREN CM 1685-1840 B 1678-1835 [37]
NEWTON PURCELL C 1540-1860 M 1538-1860 B 1540-
1860 [13,127]
NOKE CB 1574-1976 M 1575-1955 [127]

NORTHLEIGH see LEIGH, NORTH
NORTHMOOR* CB 1653-1899 M (1654-1837)-40 [88,116]
NUFFIELD C 1570-1853 M 1571-1837 B 1571-1852 [128]
NUNEHAM COURTENAY CB 1715-1840 M 1717-1836 [104]
ODDINGTON C 1571-1977 M 1572-1969 B 1572-1977 [76]
OVERTHORPE see BANBURY
OXFORD All Saints CMB 1559-1895 [89,193]; Christchurch C 1633-1884 M 1642-1754 1865-1884 B 1639-1882 [16,211]; Holy Trinity CM 1845-1913 B 1849-1928 [240]; Magdalen College M 1728-54 [16]; Merton College C 1616-1892 M 1623-1888 [81]; New College C 1750 1765 M 1703-54 B 1702-1803 [90]; St Aldate CB 1538-1900 M 1840-1900 [233-5]; St Barnabas C 1869-1980 M 1869-1984 B 1871-1966 [91/2] see also St Paul; St Clement CB 1665-1865 M 1626-1867 [166]; St Cross (or Holywell) CB 1653-1852 M 1657-1852 [89,208]; St Ebbe C 1559-1851 M 1577-1837 Banns 1775-1851 B 1558-1867 [174/5]; St Giles C 1576-1891 M 1599-1900 B 1605-1862 [167-9,249]; St John's College C 1722 M 1695-1752 B 1696-1748 [16]; St John the Baptist M 1813-37 see also OXFORD, Merton College; St Martin C 1562-1893 M 1562-1895 [89,223]; St Mary Magdalen C 1577-1851 M 1754-1837 B 1565-1812 [89,187,222,227,248]; St Mary the Virgin C 1599-1931 M 1599-1900 B 1599-1962 [229] (with LITTLEMORE) M 1813-37; St Michael C 1558-1923 M 1569-1922 B 1565-1941 [89,202,244]; St Paul CB 1837-1810 [163] see also St Barnabas; St Peter le Bailey C 1585-1853 M 1585-1866 B 1585-1870 [84,212/3]; St Peter in the East C 1559-1856 M 1559-1837 B 1559-1864 [215]; Ss Philip & James C 1863-1911 M 1863-1914 B 1875-1907 1946 [244]; St Thomas C 1655-1900 M 1583-1620 1667-1900 B 1561-1900 [89,117,205/6]; Ind New Road Z 1784-1837 CB 1785-1836; Wes Z 1801-37 C 1812-37 B 1818-37; St Michael Wes Mf C 1812-37; St Clement Rom Cath CMD 1701-1834 [CRS7] CM 1729-30 [CRS14]
PIDDINGTON C 1654-1872 M 1654-1837 B 1654-1947 [16,76]
PISHILL C 1666-1889 M 1667-1836 B 1666-1938 [128]
PYRTON* (M 1568-1836) Ext C 1597-1840 B 1570-1840 [115,128]
RADSTONE Ext 1573-1684 [26]
RAMSDEN CB 1842-1920 M 1854-1920 [217]
ROLLRIGHT, GREAT C 1560-1987 M 1560-1978 B 1560-1935 [13,93/4,135]
ROLLRIGHT, LITTLE C 1721-1985 M 1721-1972 B 1721-1984 [13,176]
ROTHERFIELD GREYS C 1591-1848 M 1592-1837 B 1592-1901 [146]; Ind Free Ext Z 1753-1837 C 1719-1837 B 1685-1837 [31]
ROTHERFIELD PEPPARD C 1571-1839 M 1572-1827 B 1572-1839 [138];Cong C 1797-1877
ROUSHAM C 1543-1977 MB 1543-1978 [99]
SALFORD C 1669-1967 M 1669-1978 B 1669-1949 [95]
SANDFORD ST MARTIN C 1695-1863 M 1695-1839 B 1695-1861 [12,50]
SANDFORD-ON-THAMES C 1573-1984 M 1574-1978 B 1574-1961 [145] Mf C 1713-1875
SARSDEN C 1575-1982 M 1575-1978 B 1575-1869 [16,195]
SHENINGTON C 1613-1873 M 1613-1837 B 1613-1926

[96]
SHIFFORD 1721-1969 [206] see also BAMPTON
SHILTON C 1662-1850 M 1672-1849 B 1664-1864 [97]
SHIPLAKE CM 1639-40 C 1672-1840 M 1674-1839 B 1639 1674-1850 [225]
SHIPTON ON CHERWELL C 1653-1838 M 1654-1836 B 1653-1841 [128]
SHIPTON UNDER WYCHWOOD CB 1538-1759 1813-1899 M 1538-1899 [153/4,162]
SHIRBURN C 1587-1980 M 1590-1980 B 1598-1975 [16,129]
SHORTHAMPTON C 1646-1836 Ext 1881-1980 M 1656-1980 B 1670-1 1773-1964 [129,211]
SHUTFORD C 1698-1875 M 1702-1978 B 1699-1921 [19,135] see also SWALCLIFFE; SFrs see BANBURY
SIBFORD C 1840-1973 M 1841-1976 B 1840-1918 [225]
SIBFORD GOWER SFrs see BANBURY
SOMERTON C 1660-1979 M 1661-1979 B 1627-47 1661-1979 [13,31]
SONNING (Berks) C 1592-1836 M 1592-1837 B 1592-1846 [98,150-2]
SOULDERN C 1668-1934 M 1668-1840 B 1666-1965 [16,195,220]
SOUTHLEIGH see LEIGH, SOUTH
SPELSBURY 1541-1892 [147]
STADHAMPTON (with CHISLEHAMPTON until 1762) C 1567-1840 M 1569-1837 B 1571-1840 [16,99]
STANDLAKE* C 1559-1959 M (1559-1837)-1959 B 1560-1959 [100,116,161]
STANTON HARCOURT* C 1567-1852 M 1569-(1570-1837)-1870 B 1569-1872 [101/2,116]
STANTON ST JOHN CB 1654-1841 M 1654-1848 [16,99]
STEEPLE ASTON C 1543-1857 M 1538-1837 B 1538-1878 [12/3,103] Mf 1721-1859
STEEPLE BARTON C 1678-1853 M 1695-1837 B 1678-1868 [12,103]
STOKE LYNE C 1665-1862 M 1666-1837 B 1665-1900 [13,158]
STOKE, NORTH 1639 C 1721-1982 M 1721-1981 B 1721-1981 [16,129]
STOKE ROW Ind CZ 1818-33
STOKE, SOUTH C 1557-1941 M 1577-1897 Banns 1824-1950 B 1552-1903 [139]
STOKE TALMAGE CB 1670 1721-1980 M 1721-1973 [129]
STOKENCHURCH (Berks) 1707-1837 [51,197]; Ind Z 1812-1837 C 1830-1837
STONESFIELD C 1571-1855 M 1571-1837 B 1571-1878 [103]
STONOR Rom Cath Z 1791-1840 C 1758-1840 M 1759-1837 Deaths 1758-1839
STOW ON THE WOLD Wes Meth see CHIPPING NORTON
STRATTON AUDLEY C 1696-1874 M 1696-1841 B 1697-1952 [16,103]
STUDLEY see HORTON cum STUDLEY
SUMMERTOWN C 1833-1911 M 1833-1902 B 1833-1925 [155]
SUNNINGWELL C 1813-42 M 1813-36 B 1741-1842 [200]
SWALCLIFFE C 1558-1840 M 1566-1840 B 1577-1840 [19,26]
SWERFORD C 1577-1985 M 1579-1978 B 1578-1943 [13,176]
SWINBROOK* C 1669-1975 M 1667-(1685-1837)1970 B 1677-1976 [16,97]

SWYNCOMBE C 1573-1982 M 1568-1980 B 1569-1982 [16,130]
SYDENHAM C 1657-1980 M 1663-1981 B 1663-1980 [51,140]; Bapt Z 1821-37
TACKLEY C 1568-1900 M 1559-1900 B 1560-1900 [185]
TADMARTON C 1548-1871 M 1548-1837 B 1551-1912 [21,26,219]
TAYNTON 1538-1837 [162]
TETSWORTH C 1604-1858 M 1625-1837 B 1653-1895 [130]
TEW, GREAT C 1609-1840 MB 1606-1837 [12,37,138]
THAME CB 1667-1734 M 1601-1760 [17,51]; Bapt Z 1826-1836 D 1828-1836
TOOT BALDON C 1579-1840 M 1599-1836 B 1599-1840 [104]
TUSMORE see HARDWICK
WARBOROUGH C 1538-1648 1672-1957 M 1538-1648 1662-1974 B 1538-1871 [98,130,172]
WARDINGTON C 1572-1967 M 1571-1978 B 1566-1969 [22,216]
WATERPERRY* C 1539-1839 M 1538-1837 B 1539-1842; Waterperry Manor House Rom Cath see OXFORD St Clement Rom Cath
WATERSTOCK C 1580-1838 M 1580-1849 B 1581-1838 [17,130]
WATLINGTON C 1635-1842 M 1635-1827 B 1635-1857 [17,105]; Wes Z 1811-37 C 1824-37 B 1835
WENDLEBURY CM 1579-1860 B 1599-1860 [17,130,197]
WESTCOTE BARTON C 1559-1838 M 1561-1678 1730-1837 B 1560-1840 [12,103]
WESTON ON THE GREEN C 1591-1840 M 1599-1840 B 1598-1840 [13,131]
WESTON, SOUTH C 1586-1980 M 1559-1970 B 1558-1978 [51,131]
WESTWELL C 1602-1850 M 1576-1850 B 1577-1850 [97,106]
WHEATFIELD C 1639 1722-1980 M 1721-1973 B 1722-1977 [131]
WHEATLEY see CUDDESDON
WHITCHURCH 1585-1851 [107/8,186]
WIDFORD C 1600-1974 M 1606-1864 B 1606-1966 [131,162]
WIGGINTON C 1558-1881 M 1558-1979 B 1558-1968 [12,24,135]
WILCOTE 1755-1837 [162]
WITNEY Holy Trinity C 1849-1971 [134]; St Mary C 1551-1940 M 1605-1931 B 1583-1652 1678-1715 1709-1837 1857-1907 [109-111,131,199] see also HAILEY; SFrs Z 1612-1837 M 1686-1837 B 1708-1837 [109-111]; Meth C 1837-1951 M 1851-68 [134]; Prim Meth C 1843-73 [134]; Woodgreen Cem B 1849-1973 [200]
WIVELCOTE see WILCOTE
WOLVERCOTE 1596-1918 [112/3]
WOODEATON C 1564-1978 M 1695-1961 B 1539-1978 [131]
WOODGREEN see WITNEY
WOODSTOCK C 1653-1908 M 1653-1910 B 1653-1905 [188-190]
WOOTTON* M 1564-1837 [97,115]
WORTON, NETHER M 1813-30 [12]
WORTON, OVER CB 1328-1881 M 1629-1881 [12,195]
WROXTON C 1548-1956 M 1552-1939 B 1548-1889 [12,21,26,114,135] see also BALSCOTE with WROXTON
YARNTON* C 1569-1900 (M 1569-1836)-1900 B 1569-1897 [97,116,240]

YELFORD C 1788-1969 M 1788-1944 [195]

RUTLAND

ASHWELL Mfc CB 1595-1806 M 1595-1812
AYSTON Mfc CB 1656-1812 M 1656-1811
BARROWDEN Mfc C 1603-1858 M 1603-1837 B 1614-1892
BELTON Mfc C 1577-1885 M 1577-1836 B1577-1813
BRAUNSTON Mfc C 1558-1871 M 1558-1812 B 1558-1907
BROOKE Mfc C 1576-1812 M 1582-1836 B 1574-1779
BURLEY Mfc C 1577-1893 M 1577-1837 B 1577-1812
CASTERTON, GREAT Mf M(I) 1754-1837 Mfc C 1655-1891 M 1655-1837 B 1655-1812
CASTERTON, LITTLE Mf M(I) 1754-1837 Mfc 1559-1812
COTTESMORE with BARROW 1655-1725/6 [1] Mfc C 1655-1849 M 1655-1837 B 1655-1877
EDITH WESTON Mfc C 1585-1882 M 1585-1837 B 1585-1812
EGLETON Mfc C 1538-1812 M 1583-1836 B 1538-1813
EMPINGHAM Mfc M(I) 1754-1837
ESSENDINE Mfc C 1600-1812 M 1624-1835 B 1621-1781
EXTON with HORN Mfc C 1597-1915 M 1597-1964 B 1597-1942
GREETHAM Mf C 1576-1812 M 1700-09 1746-1812 B 1664-1709 1747-1812
HAMBLETON Mfc C 1558-1926 M 1558-1812 B 1558-1978
HORN see EXTON with HORN
KETTON Mfc C 1568-1916 M 1561-1837 B 1569-1856
LANGHAM Mfc C 1559-1974 M 1559-1812 B 1559-1935
LUFFENHAM, NORTH 1572-1812 [2] Mfc C 1572-1869 M 1572-1837 B 1572-1923
LUFFENHAM, SOUTH Mfc C 1682-1983 M 1682-1837 B 1678-1971
LYDDINGTON CB 1562-1914 M 1641-1914 [3] Mfc C 1569-1948 M 1626-1837 B 1563-1880
LYNDON Mfc CB 1580-1812 M 1580-1837
MANTON Mfc C 1573-1913 M 1573-1837 B 1573-1812
MORCOTT Mfc C 1539-1960 M 1539-1837 B 1539-1904
NORMANTON Mfc CB 1755-1801 1813-1966 M(I) 1754-1837 M 1805 1813-36
OAKHAM 1754-1837 [4] Mfc C 1564-1952 M 1564-1978 B 1564-1894
PICKWORTH Mfc C 1660-1812 M 1661-1837 B 1661-1785
PILTON Mfc C 1585-1812 M 1553-1837 B 1548-1811
RYHALL M 1674-1838 [5] Mfc C 1653-1878 M 1674-1837 B 1663-97 1727-1867
SEATON Mfc C 1561-1974 M 1538-1836 B 1538-1947
STOKE DRY Mfc CB 1559-1812 M 1559-1837
TICKENCOTE Mfc C 1574-1812 M 1574-1837 B 1574-1812
TINWELL Mfc C 1561-1939 M 1561-1837 B 1561-1812
TIXOVER Mfc CB 1754-1986 M 1754-1837
UPPINGHAM Mfc C 1571-1852 M 1571-1837 B 1571-1862
WARDLEY Mfc C 1574-1812 M 1574-1825 B 1574-1802
WHISSENDINE M 1563-1837 [5] Mfc C 1577-1875 M 1577-1812 B 1577-1867 M 1563-1837
WING Mfc C 1625-1891 M 1625-1837 B 1625-1812

SHROPSHIRE

ABDON* CB 1561-1812 M 1561-1837 [2] Mf 1638 1660-1857
ACTON BURNELL* C (1568-1812)-40 M (1568-1838) B (1568-1812) [3,109]; Rom Cath (C 1769-1838) [1]
ACTON ROUND 1638 1660 1662-1713 M 1813-1837 [109] Mf Ext 1660-1844
ACTON SCOTT Mf Ext 1638-1849
ADDERLEY* 1692-1812 [6]
ALBERBURY* 1564-1812 [4,5]
ALBRIGHTON (Shrewsbury)* (Ext 1555-1812) [6]
ALBRIGHTON (Wolverhampton)* 1555-1812 [6]
ALVELEY 1636-1735 [7] Mf C 1561-1837
ASHFORD BOWDLER 1602-1837 [8]
ASTLEY* 1695-1812 [6]
ATCHAM Ext 1619-1755 CB 1813-1840 [104,P]
BADGER* CB 1660-1812 M 1660-1836 [9] Mf 1836-1870
BARROW C 1813-1823 [112]
BATTLEFIELD* CB 1665-1812 M 1665-1774 [10,11] Mf 1665-1848
BECKBURY Mf 1610-1878
BEDSTONE* 1719-1812 [11] Mf 1638-1854
BERRINGTON* CB 1559-1812 M 1559-1837 [12] Mf 1813-1875
BILLINGSLEY* 1625-1812 [13]
BISHOPS CASTLE Ind Cong C 1814-37 [104]
BITTERLEY* 1658-1812 [13] Mf 1662-1852
BOLAS, GREAT* 1582-1812 [14]
BOBBINGTON see STAFFORDSHIRE
BONINGALE* 1698-1812 [13] Mf C Ext 1813-1875
BOURTON Mf C 1841-1847
BRIDGNORTH* St Leon M 1636-1812; St Mary Magd M 1665-1725 [15]; Bapt Castle Street (CB 1779-1836) [1]; Ind Stoneway Chapel (C 1765-1812) B 1822-37 [1,104]
BROMFIELD* 1559-1812 [11]
BROSELEY* (1570-1750) [16,17]; Bapt Birch Meadow Z 1835-37 (C 1794-1835) [1,104]
BROUGHTON* 1586-1812 [11] Mf C 1813-1856
BUCKNELL 1598-1675 [104]
BUILDWAS* CB 1665-1812 M 1665-1837 [18]
BURFORD* 1558-1812 [9,19]
CARDESTON 1663-1812 [20]
CHAPEL LAWN B 1844-1987 [109]
CHELMARSH* 1557-1812 [20]
CHETTON Mf 1538-1812
CHIRBURY* (1629-1812) [21]; Ind C 1829-36; Part Bapt Z 1829-35 [104]
CHURCH ASTON Mf C 1681 1732-1855
CHURCH PREEN 1680-1813 [114]
CHURCH STRETTON* 1661-1812 [20] Mf 1813-1865
CLAVERLEY* CB 1568-1812 M 1568-1837 [22] Mf 1720 1809-1836
CLEE Mf 1638 1663-1855
CLEE HILL* Caynham Wes C 1796-1829 [1]
CLEOBURY MORTIMER* 1601-1812 [23] Mf 1660-1678
CLIVE* (1667-1812) CB 1813-1866 [1,20]; Ind (C 1831-37) [109]
CLUN B 1660-1739 [110]
CLUNBURY CM (1574-1812)-41 B Ext 1841-1859 [25/6,109] Mf 1660-1852
CLUNGUNFORD Mf 1660-1850
COLD WESTON* C 1663-1812 M 1663-1829 B 1663-1833 [26] Mf 1660-1860

CONDOVER* 1570-1812 [27]
COUND* 1562-1812 [25]
CRICKHEATH Oswestry Ind C 1829-36 [104]
CULMINGTON Mf 1660-1850
DAWLEY GREEN Meth New Conn C 1829-37 [104]
DAWLEY MAGNA Mf 1813-1828
DEUXHILL* with GLAZELEY 1654-1812 [35]
DIDDLEBURY* 1583-1812 [29]
DITTON PRIORS* M 1813-1837 [109]; Wes (ZC 1801-34) [1]
DODINGTON Mf 1562-1812; Presb C 1814-1823
DONINGTON* 1556-1812 [29]
DORRINGTON* with LYTH HILL Ind ZC 1808-37 [1]
DOWLES Mf 1660-1845
EASTHOPE* CB 1624-1812 M 1624-1830 [30]
EATON CONSTANTINE CM 1384-1813 [115]
EATON-UNDER-HEYWOOD CMB Ext 1581-1671 CMB 1660-1837 [30]
EDGMOND* CMB Ext 1559-1651 CMB 1669-1812 [31]
EDGTON* 1660-1812 [31]
EDSTASTON* C (1712-1812)-54 M (1712-1812) B (1712-1812)-85 [31,105]
ELLESMERE* Ind C (1787-1811)-37 [1,104] Mf C 1757-1812
ERCALL, HIGH* CB 1585-1812 M 1585-1837 [32]
FELTON, WEST Ind Grimpo Chapel C 1833-36 [104]
FITZ* 1559-1812 [33]
FORD CM 1589-1812 B 1589-1793 [33,34]
FRANKTON (Whittington) Ind C 1835-37 [104]
FRODESLEY* 1547-1812 [33]
GLAZELEY see DEUX HILL
GREETE* 1663-1812 [35]
GRINSHILL* 1592-1812 [35]
HABBERLEY* (1598-1617 1670-1812) Ext 1573-1802 [36,P]
HADNALL* Ext 1751-1892 [P] Mf C 1721-1837; Ind (1798-1837) [1]
HALESOWEN Indep C 1805-1837 [112]
HALSTON* C 1668-1849 M 1713-1826 B 1700-1897 [37]
HANWOOD* 1560-1763 [37]
HARLESCOTE* Ext 1663-1807 [P]
HARLEY* CB 1590-1812 M 1746-1812 [37/8]
HODNET* 1539-1812 [36]
HOLDGATE 1651-1711 [110]
HOLLINS WOOD Shifnal Meth New Conn C 1829-37 [104]
HOPE BAGOT* CB 1714-1812 M 1714-1837 [39]
HOPE BOWDLER Mf C 1563-1837
HOPESAY* CB 1660-1812 M 1660-1837 [40]
HOPTON CASTLE 1538-1812 M 1813-1837 [37,41,109]
HOPTON WAFERS* (CB 1638-1812 M 1638-1812)-1837 [36,109]
HORDLEY* 1656-1812 [36]
HUGHLEY* 1576-1812 [37,42]
KENLEY* 1682-1812 [43]
KINLET* 1657-1840 [43]
KINNERLEY* 1677-1812 [44]
KNOCKIN* 1661-1812 [43]
LEE BROCKHURST* 1567-1838 [46]
LEEBOTWOOD* 1547-1812 [45]
LEIGHTON* 1661-1812
LLANYBLODWEL* 1597-1812 [47]; Smyrna Chapel C 1825-36 [1]
LLANYMYNECH* 1666-1812 [47]
LONGDON UPON TERN * 1692-1812 [45]
LONGNOR* 1586-1812 [45]

LOPPINGTON C 1654-1859 Ext C 1654-1746 M 1607-1742 B 1650-1708 [105,P] Mf 1722-1810
LUDLOW* 1558-1812 [48/9]; Ind Corve Street C 1802-36 B 1826-36 [1]; Old Street Prim Meth C 1824-1837 [112]; Wes Meth Broad Street C 1815-1837 [112]
LYDBURY, NORTH Mf 1660-1846
LYDHAM* 1596-1812 [45] Mf 1638 1660-1850
LYTH HILL see DORRINGTON
MADELEY Mf 1638 1660-1754
MADELEY WOOD Meth New Conn C 1829-37 [104]; Wes Meth ZC 1815-1837 [112]
MAINSTONE Mf 1813-1875
MARKET DRAYTON* Ind C 1776-1836 [1]
MAWLEY HALL* Rom Cath C 1763-1831 [1]
MELVERLEY* C 1723-99 MB 1723-1812 [51]
MEOLE BRACE* CB 1660-1812 M 1660-1837 [52] Mf 1638 1660-1849
MIDDLETON SCRIVEN* 1728-1812 [53] Mf 1660-1853
MILSON* CM 1707-1812 B 1681-1812 [54] Mf 1638 1660-1846
MINSTERLEY C 1806-1837 [1] Mf 1815-1859
MONK HOPTON* 1698-1812 [51] Mf 1638 1660-1848
MONTFORD* 1661-1812 Ext 1573-1664 [53]
MORE* 1570-1812 [51,55] Mf CB 1549-1862
MORETON CORBET* 1580-1812 [51,56]
MORETON SAY* 1690-1812 [53]
MORVILLE Mf 1660-1876
MUCH WENLOCK Ext 1558-1698 [P]
MUNSLOW* 1538-1812 [57]
MYDDLE* CB 1541-1812 M 1541-1837 [54]
NEEN SAVAGE* 1575-1812 [58]
NEEN SOLARS* C 1708-1812 M 1708-1851 B 1678-1812 [58]
NEENTON* CB 1558-1812 M 1558-1805 [53]
NESS, GREAT* CB 1589-1812 M 1589-1837 [59]
NESS, LITTLE 1605-1737 [110]
NEWPORT* Rom Cath (C 1785-1843 M 1807-46) [1,CRS13]; Prot Diss C 1828-37 [104]
NEWTOWN C 1816-1906 B 1813-1963 [106] see also WEM
NORBURY* CB 1560-1812 M 1560-1789 [61] Mf 1638 1660-1867
NORTON IN HALES* 1572-1880 [58]
OLDBURY* (1582-1812) [62,111]; Old Diss Chapel (C 1715-1813) [1]; Presb Chapel M 1812-1837 [109]
ONIBURY* CB 1577-1812 M 1577-1836 [62] Mf CB 1662-1849 M 1662-1836
OSWESTRY* (1558-1812) [63-6]; Calv Meth Castle Lane C 1819-1837 [112]; Cong Old Chapel (C 1780-1811) B 1812-1837 [1,109]; Wes C 1812-15 [1,109]
PITCHFORD* 1558-1812 [67/8] Mf C 1813-1878
PLOWDEN* Rom Cath C 1826-37 [1]
PONTESBURY* (1538-1812) [69] Mf 1638 1663-1753; Bapt CD 1828-36 [104]
PRADOE B 1907-1984 [109]
PREES* Ind Whixall C 1805-23 [1]; Prees Green Prim Meth C 1824-1837 [112]
PREESHENLLE Whittington Ind C 1833-36 [104]
PRESTON GOBALDS/GUBBALS* (CB 1560-1812 M 1560-1837) [70]; Ind Zions Hill C 1827-37 [104]
PULVERBATCH 1542-1812 [71]
PRYSHENLLE see PREESHENLLE
QUATFORD Ext 1636-1811 [109]
QUATT MALVERN Mf C 1662-64
RATLINGHOPE* (CB 1794-1812 M 1755-1813) [68,107]

RICHARD'S CASTLE M 1813-37 B Ext 1813-1890 72 [109]
RODINGTON* 1678-1837 [26,116]
RUYTON IN THE ELEVEN TOWNS* 1719-1812 [68]
SAINT MARTINS* CB 1601-1812 M 1601-1837 [72]
SELATTYN* 1556-1812 [73]
SHAWBURY Ext 1561-1711 [P]
SHEINTON* 1558-1812 [74,81]
SHERIFFHALES* 1557-1812 [75]
SHIFNAL Bapt Z 1811-36 [104] see also HOLLINS WOOD
SHIPTON* 1538-1812 [76,81]
SHREWARDINE* Ext 1645-1812 [P]
SHREWSBURY* Holy Cross Ext 1542-1854 [P]; St Chad (1616-1812) [77-9]; St Julian Ext 1559-1812 B 1841-81 [P,104]; St Mary (1584-1812) [80]; Swan Hill Ind Chapel (C 1767-1812) B 1768-1836 [1,109,111]; Bapt Claremont Z 1808-1825 (C 1766-1808) [1,104,112]; Meth New Conn C 1835-37 [104]; Presb High Street C (1692-1812) 1813-37 [1,104]; Prim Meth Castle Court C 1822-3 [104]7; Wes Meth St John CZ 1812-37 [104]; Rom Cath (C 1775-1837) [1]; SFrs (1657-1834) [1]
SIBDON CARWOOD* 1583-1812 [81/2] Mf 1583-1812
SIDBURY* 1560-1811 [84]
SILVINGTON 1663-1837
SMETHCOTE* 1612-1812 [81,83]
STANTON LACY* 1561-1812 [84]
STANTON ON HINE HEATH 1655-1682 [111]
STAPLETON* 1546-1812 [81,85]
STIRCHLEY 1658-1812 [84]
STOKE ON TERN Ext C 1662-1709 M 1654-1717 B 1661-1689 [109]
STOKE ST MILBOROUGH* CB 1654-1812 M 1654-1837 [86]
STOKESAY* CB 1559-1812 M 1559-1837 [68]
SUTTON Shrewsbury Ext 1709-1870 [P]
TASLEY* 1563-1813 [87]
TIBBERTON* 1719-1812 [88]
TONG* 1629-1812 [87]
UFFINGTON* 1578-1812 [89]
UPPINGTON* 1650-1812 [89]
UPTON CRESSETT CB 1637-1840 M 1637-1837
WATERS UPTON* CB 1547-1815 M 1547-1811 [90]
WELLINGTON* C (1628-1700) (I) 1800-1825 [91,108]; Tanbank Ind C(I) 1829-37 [109]
WEM* C (1582-1812)-40 C Adult 1841-80 M (1582-1812)-37 B (1582-1812)-40 [92-4]; Ind Chapel Street (C 1785-1836) [1]; Presb C (1755-1814) [1]; Chapelry of NEWTOWN (1779-1812) [60]
WESTBURY* 1637-1812 [95]; Ind (C 1806-37) [1]
WESTON UNDER RED CASTLE* 1565-1812 [96]
WHITCHURCH* C 1633-1797 M 1627-1797 B 1630-1797 [97-9]; Presb (C 1708-1812) 1814-1823 [1,109]; Wes Meth C 1813-1830 [112]
WHITE LADIES* B 1816-44 [100]
WHITTINGTON* 1591-1812 [101]
WHIXALL* Ind ZC 1805-37 [1]
WILLEY* C 1644-1812 MB 1665-1811 [90]
WISTANSTOW* CB 1661-1812 M 1661-1837 [90]
WITHINGTON* 1591-1812 [100]
WOLSTASTON* 1601-1812 [100]
WORFIELD 1562-1812 [102]
WORTHEN* 1558-1812 [103]
WROCKWARDINE* B (1591-1812) [100]; Wes Meth C 1818-37 [SH/M3]

WROCKWARDINE WOOD Prim Meth C 1822-37 [111];
  Trench Wes C 1827-37 [111]
WROXETER 1613-1812 [96]

SOMERSET

ABBAS COMBE 1597-1812 [87,90]
AISHOLT* 1598-1812 [87,90,107]
ALFORD* 1594-1811 [90]
ALLER* CB 1598-1811 M 1560-1812 [90,102]
ALLERTON* 1598-1810 [90]
ALMSFORD see ANSFORD
ANGERSLEIGH 1595-1811 [87,90,108]
ANSFORD C 1554-1837 M 1559-1837 B 1555-1837
  [5,90]
ASHBRITTLE CB 1599-1812 M 1563-1812 [87,90,112]
ASHCOTT* 1599-1812 [90]
ASHILL CB 1598-1757 M 1558-1815 [87,90,105,GCI]
ASHINGTON 1572-1812 [91]
ASHPRIORS 1595-1812 [87,91,109]
ASHTON, LONG* 1623-79 [88]
ASHWICK 1598-1812 [87,91]
AXBRIDGE 1597-1812 [87,91]
BABINGTON 1607-1812 [87,91]
BABCARY 1598-1812 [87,91]
BACKWELL 1598-1813 [87,91]
BADGWORTH 1598-1813 [91]
BAGBOROUGH, WEST* M 1565-1812 [115]
BALTONSBOROUGH 1599-1668 [87]
BARRINGTON* M (1654-1812)-37 [105,126,GCI]
BARROW GURNEY CB 1617-22 M 1593-1812 [87,103]
  Mfc C 1590-1900 M 1754-1899 B 1591-1900
BARROW, NORTH 1598 [87]
BARROW, SOUTH Ext 1605-1786 [91]
BARTON ST DAVID 1607-79 [87]
BATCOMBE 1597-1669 [87]
BATH Abbey (Ss Peter and Paul) 1569-1840 [18-20] B (at
  WIDCOMBE) 1784-1840; St James CB(I) 1569-1812
  M(I) 1718-1812 CMB 1813-1840 B (at WIDCOMBE)
  1784-1840 [15,20,21] see also LYNCOMBE and
  WIDCOMBE; St Michael CB 1569-1840 M 1559-1840
  B Ext 1569-1839 [16,22,23,88,123/4]; Ext (Ss Peter
  and Paul, St James, St Michael, St Mary of the Stall,
  Widcombe) 1603-95 1704-58 1768-1802 [93,95];
  Rom Cath C 1759 1780-1825 M 1781-1824 D
  1780-1819 [CRS66]; Jewish M 1838-1901 [P]
BATHAMPTON C 1600-1760 1765-1980 M 1599-1752
  1841-1980 B 1599-1980 [24,25,117]
BATHEASTON 1609-1812 [11,87]
BATHFORD 1608-62 1727-1810 [11,87]
BATHWICK C 1600 CMB 1615 CM 1668-1840 B
  1691-1840 [11,87,120,127]
BAWDRIP 1602-36 [87]
BECKINGTON Mf M 1754-1837 Mfc C 1559-1874 M
  1559-1837 B 1559-1900
BEDMINSTER 1599-1624 [87]
BEER CROCOMBE CB 1607-36 M 1542-1812
  [87,105,GCI]
BICKENHALL* M 1682-1812 [114] see also STAPLE
  FITZPAINE
BICKNOLLER 1617 [87]
BISHOPS HULL* M (1562-1812)-1837 [111,126]
BISHOPS LYDEARD 1595-1638 [88]

BLEADON (1608-23) CM 1710-1939 B 1710-1939 [17,87]
BOURTON 1615-30 [87]
BRADFORD CB 1594-1662 M 1558-1812 [87,108]
BRADLEY, WEST (1605-73) M 1813-37 [87]
BRATTON SEYMOUR M 1813-51
BRATTON 1608-63 [87]
BRENT, EAST M 1558-1611 B 1558-1622 [122]
BRENT KNOLL C 1622-1800 M 1679-1811 B 1678-1800
  [122]
BRENT, SOUTH see BRENT KNOLL
BREWHAM 1607/08 C 1868-1985 [87,127]
BRIDGWATER 1597-1669 [87]
BRIMPTON 1602-95 M 1813-37 [87]
BRISLINGTON C 1566-1812 M 1568-1808 B 1568-1812
  [122]
BROADWAY C 1598-1676 1700-1837 M 1599-1669
  1701-1836 B 1598-1675 1678-1837 [5,87,95]
BROCKLEY 1598-1640 [87]
BROMPTON RALPH 1603-42 [87]
BROMPTON REGIS 1638 [87]
BRUSHFORD 1622 [87]
BRUTON* 1554-1812 [29,30]
BUCKLAND DINHAM 1603-30 [87]
BUCKLAND ST MARY* CB 1599-1617 (M 1538-1812)
  [87,105,GCI]
BUCKLAND, WEST* CMB 1607-29 (M 1538-1812)
  [87,109]
BURNETT 1599-1639 [87]
BURNHAM ON SEA C 1630-1840 M 1630-1837 B
  1630-1811 [17]
BURRINGTON C 1598-1641 1662-3 1687-90 1695-1841
  M 1598-1640 1663 1687-1837 B 1598-1641 1662-3
  1687-91 1695-1838 [127]
BUTCOMBE 1605-1679 M 1605-1835 [87]
BUTLEIGH 1598-1637 Ext 1657-1748 [17,87]
CADBURY, NORTH 1558-1734 [4,87]
CADBURY, SOUTH 1607-79 M 1800-37 [87,117]
CAMEL, QUEEN CB 1607 [87]
CAMEL, WEST 1597-1629 [87]
CAMELEY 1605-1679 [87]
CAMERTON 1654-1812 [31]
CANNINGTON* 1607-1639 (M 1559-1812) [87,107];
  Rom Cath 1778-1838 [122]
CASTLE CARY CB 1564-1775 M 1564-1772 [8,87]
CATCOTT 1597-1640 [87]
CHAFFCOMBE 1623-38 M 1700-1837 [87,126]
CHARD C 1649-1729 M 1540-1544 1652-1729 B 1649-
  1711 [10]
CHARLECOMBE C 1712-1812 M 1719-1837 B 1710-
  1812 [14,87]
CHARLTON MB 1598 [87]
CHARLTON ADAM 1607-39 M 1707-1812 [87,102]
CHARLTON MACKERELL 1599-1663 M 1575-1812
  [87,102]
CHARLTON MUSGROVE 1615-79 [87]
CHARLYNCH* 1607-63 M 1607-1779 [87,107]
CHEDDAR 1608-75 [87]
CHEDDON FITZPAINE* 1607-37 M 1559-1812 [87,109]
CHEDZOY* 1597-1639 M 1558-1812 [87,113]
CHELLINGTON 1599-1681 [87]
CHELTON see MOORLINCH
CHELVEY 1599-1663 [87]
CHEW MAGNA 1605-23 CMB(I) 1562-1812 [28,87]
CHEWSTOKE 1605-23 [87] Mfc C 1666-1888 M 1666-
  1837 B 1666-1872
CHEWTON MENDIP 1623-39 [87]
CHILCOMPTON 1607-31 [87]

CHILTHORNE DORMER 1615-36 [87]
CHILTON CANTELOE 1607-66 [87]
CHILTON TRINITY 1661-85 [87]
CHILTON 1608-23 [87]
CHIPSTAPLE* 1607-23 1694-1837 [87,94/5]
CHISELBOROUGH 1558-1979 [32,117]
CHRISTON C 1559-1710 M 1550-1722 B 1549-1712
[118] CMB(l) 1548-1710
CHURCHILL 1609-1667 [87]
CLAPTON 1599-1663 [87]
CLAVERTON* 1582-1812 [33/4,87]
CLEVEDON 1607-66 [87]
CLOSWORTH 1598-1603 [87]
CLUTTON 1609-38 [87]
COKER, WEST 1608-39 [87]
COMBE, ENGLISH see ENGLISH COMBE
COMBE FLOREY 1566-1837 [2,87]
COMBE HAY (l) 1538-1777 [31,87]
COMBE ST NICHOLAS* 1636-39 M 1678-1812 [87,115]
COMPTON BISHOP 1606-21 [87]
COMPTON DANDO 1616-79 [87
COMPTON MARTIN 1559-1812 [31]
COMPTON PAUNCEFOOT 1590-1638 M 1813-37
[87,126]
CONGRESBURY 1605-23 [87]
CORFE* C 1567-1681 1683-1839 M 1556-1663 1687-
1840 B 1566-1839 [35/6,87,108]
CORSTON C 1567-1812 M 1586-1811 B 1569-1812 [12]
COSSINGTON 1606-40 [87]
COTHELSTONE* CB 1607-79 M 1607-1715 [87,108]
CRANMORE, EAST and WEST 1597-1663 [87]
CREECH ST MICHAEL* 1607-39 M 1665-1814 [87,108]
CREWKERNE* 1599 (M 1559-1812) [87,106,GCl]
CRICKET MALHERBIE 1604-37 M 1754-1837 [87,126]
CRICKET ST THOMAS 1599-1678 M 1813-51 [87]
CROSSCOMBE 1607-72 [87]
CROWCOMBE* 1594-1670 (M 1641-1812) [87,113]
CUDWORTH M 1813-36
CULBORNE M 1699-1808 1818-1951 [126]
CURLAND 1605 [87]
CURRY MALET 1597-1615 1682-1750 [87,127]
CURRY, NORTH* 1618-21 (M1539-1812) [87,103]
CURRY RIVEL* 1607-38 (M1642-1812) [87,104]
DINDER 1598-1640 [87]
DINNINGTON see SEAVINGTON
DITCHEAT 1605-23 [87]
DODINGTON* 1597-1679 (M1538-1805) [87,107]
DONYATT 1600-29 C 1712-1837 MB 1719-1837 [37,87]
DOULTING 1615-29 [87]
DOWLISH WAKE 1599-1619 [87]
DOWNHEAD 1615-30 [87]
DRAYTON* 1599-1639 (M1577-1812) [87,104]
DUNDRY Ext 1603-95 1800-12 [118]
DUNKERTON 1608-15 [87]
DURLEIGH 1599-1679 M 1683-1807 [87,107]
DURSTON 1606-1812 [86/7,95]
EASTON IN GORDANO Mfc C 1559-1898 M 1559-1837
B 1559-1919
EMBOROUGH 1569-1769 [87,117]
ENGLISH COMBE 1609-1673 C 1728-1812 M 1756-1812
B 1749-1812 [38,87]
ENMORE 1607-79 M 1653-1812 [87,107]
EVERCREECH 1629-39 Ext 1664-1739 [17,87]
FARLEIGH HUNGERFORD 1616 [87]
FARMBOROUGH CB 1559-1812 M 1562-1812 [39,40]
FIDDINGTON 1706-1922 [41,87,113]
FITZHEAD 1609-63 [87]

FIVEHEAD* 1598-1636 M (1656-1812)-37
[87,106,126,GCl]
FOXCOOT 1598-1639 [87]
FRESHFORD 1601-1688 C 1674-1763 1783-1812 M
1653-1812 B 1705-63 1783-1812 [42,87]
FROME (SELWOOD) CB 1558-1812 M 1558-1837 M(l)
1837-1898 [43-49,87,126]; Bapt Mf C 1834-1961
GLASTONBURY St Benedict 1607-63 Ext 1670-1805
[17,87]; St John 1597/8 Ext 1653-1796 [17,87]
GOATHURST* 1598-1679 (M 1539-1812) [87,113]
HALSE* CMB 1599 (M 1559-1812) [87,111]
HARDINGTON 1598-1649 [87]
HARPTREE, EAST 1597-1635 [87]
HARPTREE, WEST 1598-1680 [87]
HATCH BEAUCHAMP 1609-38 [87]
HATCH, WEST* C 1606-1812 (M 1604-1812) B 1604-
1812 [9,104]
HAWKRIDGE 1598-1623 [87] see also HATCH
BEAUCHAMP
HAZELBURY PLUNKETT C 1813-36 M 1754-1805 [127]
HEATHFIELD* M 1700-56 [109]
HIGH HAM* 1597-1670 (M 1569-1812) [87,102]
HILL FARRANCE* CB Ext 1594-1682 M (1701-1812)
[88,109,128]
HINTON BLEWETT 1623-29 [88]
HINTON CHARTERHOUSE 1546-1733 [39]
HINTON ST GEORGE* 1597-1669 (M 1632-1837)
[88,114]
HOLCOMBE 1604-39 [88]
HOLFORD* 1615-78 (M 1558-1812) [88,113]
HOLTON M 1813-37 [88]
HORNBLOTTEN M 1768-1849 [126]
HORSINGTON* (1558-1836) [50,88]
HUISH CHAMPFLOWER 1597-1638 [88]
HUISH EPISCOPI* 1615-23 (M 1698-1812) [88,102]
HUNTSPILL 1623 [88]
HUTTON 1621-68 M 1813-37 [88,126]
ILCHESTER* 1594-1666 [88,95]
ILMINSTER* 1660-1837 M (1662-1812) [51,114]
ILTON* 1616-35 1642-1837 M (1642-1811)
[52,88,105,GCl]
ISLE ABBOTS* 1593-1679 (M 1562-1837) [88,115]
ISLE BREWERS* 1598-1667 1705-1828 M (1705-1812)-
37 B 1705-1812 [52,88,105,GCl]
KEINTON MANDEVILLE 1629 M 1736-1851 [88,126]
KELSTON 1538-1812 [12]
KENN 1607-21 [88]
KEYNSHAM CB 1628-1807 M 1629-1812 [13]
KILMERSDON 1603-35 [88]
KILMINGTON* Ext 1655-87 (M 1582-1837) [115,128]
KILTON* 1621-64 (M 1683-1812) [88,113]
KILVE* 1618-38 (M 1632-1812) [88,113]
KINGSBURY EPISCOPI* C 1557-1850 (M 1557-1812)-
1850 B 1581-1869 [106,129,GCl]
KINGSDON* M 1540-1812 [102]
KINGSTON ST MARY 1677-1840 [74]
KINGSTON SEYMOUR 1622-39 [88]
KINGSTONE 1714-1837 [37]
KITTISFORD* 1621-78 (1694-1837 M 1695-1812)
[88,94,115]
LAMBROOKE, EAST C 1770-1860 [128]
LANGFORD BUDVILLE* M 1607-1812 [109]
LANGPORT* M 1728-1812 [102]
LANGRIDGE 1609-39 C 1763-1840 M 1813-1838 B 1763-
1840 [53/4,88]
LAVERTON 1609-39 [88]
LEIGH UPON MENDIP 1607-22 [88]

LEIGH 1639-40 [88]
LILSTOCK* 1607-79 (M 1661-1812) [88,113]
LIMINGTON* M 1695-1812 [103]
LOAD, LONG* M 1749-1808 [104]
LOPEN* 1609-39 (M 1723-1812) [88,114]
LUFTON 1598 [88]
LULLINGTON 1598-1639 1712-1840 [6,88]
LYDFORD, EAST 1615-28 [88]
LYDFORD, WEST 1623 [88]
LYMPSHAM CB 1737-1841 M 1754-1840 [55]
LYNCOMBE with WIDCOMBE 1813-40 [56]
LYNG M 1813-37 [126]
MAPERTON 1613-79 [88]
MARK Mfc C 1646-1748 M 1646-8 1654-1756 B 1568-74
    1583-1601 1646-1755
MARKSBURY 1563-1812 [14]
MARSTON BIGOTT 1607-39 [88]
MARSTON MAGNA (I) 1561-1735 [57,88]
MARTOCK* M 1559-1812 [104]
MEARE 1605-68 [88]
MELLS C 1826-40 B 1807-40 [119]
MERRIOTT M 1646-1812 [119]
MIDSOMER NORTON* 1616-1630 (M 1677-1837)
    [88,115]
MILBORNE PORT CB 1538-1813 M 1538-1754 [58]
MILTON CLEVEDON 1607-68 [88]
MILVERTON* CMB Ext 1541-1702 (M 1538-1812)
    [17,114]
MINEHEAD 1639 CM 1559-1840 B 1548-1840 [59-61,88]
MISTERTON 1613-39 Ext C 1744 1814-31 [17,88] Mfc
    CB 1558-1886 M 1558-1812 1814-1885
MONKTON COMBE 1559-1634 C 1561-1708 1771-1812
    M 1559-1639 1792-97 B 1561-1699 1771-1812
    [15,88]
MONKTON, WEST* 1599-1639 (M 1710-1812) [88,109]
MONTACUTE 1598-1695 [88]
MOORLINCH 1598-1623 [88] with CHELTON
MUCHELNEY* 1620-96 (M 1703-1812) [88,102]
NEMPNETT THRUBWELL Ext 1611-1812 [128]
NETTLECOMBE 1598-1673 [88]
NEWTON ST LOE 1538-1812 [12]
NORTHOVER* 1598-1810 M (1531-1812) 1816-50
    [95,102,126]
NORTHSTOKE C 1650-1812 M 1649-1810 B 1678-1812
    [14]
NORTON FITZWARREN* C 1556-1726 (M 1565-1812) B
    1566-1725 [9,109]
NORTON ST PHILIP CMB(I) 1584-1812 [62,88]
NORTON SUB HAMDON C 1558-1837 MB 1558-1850
    [63/4]
NUNNEY 1636-39 [88]
NYNEHEAD* 1605-69 (M 1670-1812) [88,109]
OAKE Ext CB 1594-1629 M 1594-1625
OARE 1599-1670 M 1813-51 [88] Mfc 1690-1826
ORCHARDLEIGH 1623-1839 [6,88]
ORCHARD PORTMAN* CB 1538-1840 M (1538-1812)-42
    [6,88,108]
OTHERY 1608 [93]
OTTERFORD* M (1588-1812)-37 [112,126]
OTTERHAMPTON* 1656-1749 [107]
OVERSTOWEY M 1558-1812 [107]
PAWLETT 1597-1623 [88]
PENDOMER 1609-23 M 1730-54 [88,126]
PENNARD, EAST* 1599-1679 M (1608-1812) [88,115]
PENNARD, WEST 1607-39 [88]
PENSELL WOOD 1597-1623 [88]
PERROTT, NORTH 1599-1637 [88]

PETHERTON, NORTH 1558-1837 (I) 1558-1837 [65,96-
    99,101]
PILTON 1616-69 [88]
PITCOMBE* 1567-1836 [94]
PITMINSTER CMB(I) 1542-1836 C 1544-1836 M 1813-36
    B 1542-1836 [3,66,88,108]
PITNEY* M 1623-1812 [103]
PODIMORE MILTON* M (1744-1812)-51 [103,118]
PORLOCK Mfc M 1837-1957
PORTBURY 1637 [88]
PRIDDY M 1813-36
PRISTON 1723-1812 [67]
PUCKINGTON M 1695-1812 [105,GCI]
PYLLE 1622-27 [88]
QUANTOXHEAD, EAST* 1608-98 (M 1654-1812)
    [88,113]
QUANTOXHEAD, WEST 1613 [88]
QUEEN CAMEL 1607 [87]
QUEEN CHARLTON CMB(I) 1594-1754 C 1568-1752 M
    1567-1742 B 1562-1738 [17,53]
RADDINGTON* 1814-36 [94/5]
RADSTOCK (I) 1719-1812 [57]
ROAD see RODE
RODE CB 1714-1840 M 1714-1837 [68/9,118]
RODNEY STOKE 1602-1744 [88] Mfc C 1654-1867 M
    1654-1901 B 1654-1906
RUISHTON* M 1679-1812 [109]
RUNNINGTON* M (1586-1812)-51 [112,126]
ST CATHERINE 1598-1630 [88]
ST MICHAEL CHURCH* 1695-1812 [70]
SALTFORD Ext 1599-1661 C 1709-1837 M 1713-1812
    1816-1837 B 1712-1837 [71,128]
SAMPFORD ARUNDEL M 1698-1812 [88,112]
SAMPFORD BRETT 1609-79 [88]
SEABOROUGH 1594-1623 M 1813-36 [88]
SEAVINGTON with DINNINGTON 1599-1674 [88]
SEAVINGTON ST MARY 1621-23 [88]
SHAPWICK 1605-40 [88]
SHEPTON BEAUCHAMP* M 1558-1812 [105,GCI]
SHEPTON MALLET 1566-1679 [88]
SHEPTON MONTAGUE 1617-30 [88]
SHIPHAM 1639 C 1674-1787 M 1560-1760 B 1606-1794
    [88,118]
SOMERTON* 1599-1699 (M 1697-1812) [88,103]
SOUTHSTOKE 1704-1812 [14]
SPAXTON* M 1558-1812 [107]
STANTON DREW 1599-1668 [88]
STANTON PRIOR 1571-1812 [14,17,88]
STAPLE FITZPAINE* 1623 [88]; with BICKENHALL (M
    1682-1812) [114]
STAWELL see MOORLINCH
STOCKLAND GAUNTS* M 1538-1807 [107]
STOCKLINCH MAGDALEN* 1712-55 [105,GCI] Mfc CB
    1712-24 1740-1812 M 1815-1927
STOCKLINCH OTTERSAY* 1609-62 (M 1558-1812)
    [88,105,GCI] Mfc C 1558-1660 1688-1900 M 1558-
    1660 1688-1751 1755-1812 1814-1900 B 1558-1660
    1688-1907
STOGUMBER 1559-1644 1653-1712 [72/3,88,128]
STOGURSEY* 1623 (M 1595-1812) [88,113]
STOKE GIFFARD see RODNEY STOKE
STOKE LANE see STOKE ST MICHAEL
STOKE, NORTH C 1559-1662 M 1605-1638 B 1603-1663
    CMB 1813-40 [54,88,128]
STOKE PERO 1613-30 [88]
STOKE ST MARY* 1635 (M 1679-1812) [88,108]
STOKE ST MICHAEL 1622 [88]

STOKE SUB HAMDON 1621-23 [88]
STOKE, UPPER 1598-1639 [88]
STONE EASTON 1594-1669 [88]
STOWELL 1613-36 [88]
STOWEY, NETHER* 1631-39 (M 1640-1812) [88,113]
STOWEY, OVER* 1568-1613 (M 1558-1812) [88,107]
STOWEY 1602-30 [88]
STRATTON ON THE FOSSE 1599-1666 (I) 1641-1782 [57,88]
STREET C 1600-1755 M 1599-1755 B 1599-1762 [1]
STRINGSTON* 1609-79 (M 1634-1812) [88,113]
SUTTON BINGHAM 1605-21 [88]
SUTTON, LONG* C 1560-1839 (M 1559-1812)-1840 B 1560-1840 [5,88,102,119]
SUTTON MALLETT see MOORLINCH
SWAINSWICK 1557-1840 [14,54]
SWELL* 1592-1630 (M 1559-1812) [88,105/6,GCI]
TAUNTON* St James M 1610-1837 [116]; St Mary Magd M 1558-1812 [110/1,GCI]
TEMPLE COMBE see COMBE ABBAS
THORNE COFFIN 1609-23 [88,126]
THORNE FALCON* M 1726-1812 [109]
THORNE ST MARGARET* 1623 (M 1721-1812) [88,112]
THURLBEAR* 1613-76 (M 1700-1812) [88,118]
THURLOXTON* 1558-1812 (M 1559-1812) [75,113]
TIMBERSCOMBE 1598-1678 [88]
TIMSBURY 1561-1812 [13,88]
TINTINHULL 1598-1623 [88]
TRENT 1598-1675 [88]
TRULL* 1598-1666 (M 1671-1812) [88,108]
TWERTON C 1682-1840 M 1587-1840 B 1538-1840 [12,76]
UBLEY 1609-23 [88]
UPHILL 1598-1623 [88]
UPTON 1623 [88]
WALCOT 1699 [88]
WALTON next STREET 1617-1663 [88]
WALTON IN GORDANO 1599-1662 [88]
WANSTROW 1605-78 [88]
WAYFORD 1613-39 C 1704-1896 M 1709-1837 [77,88]
WEARE 1598-1639 [88]
WEDMORE* C 1561-1812 M 1561-1839 B 1561-1860 [78-80]
WELLINGTON* 1616-1682 C 1683-1782 (M 1683-1812) B 1744-60 [81,88,112,128]
WELLOW 1599-1623 [88]
WELLS Cathedral C 1660/1-1982 M 1668-1754 1861-1981 B 1664/5-1980 [82]; St Cuthbert Ext M 1700-23 [17]
WESTBURY 1623-39 [88]
WESTON 1538-1840 [54,83]
WESTON BAMPFIELD 1623-83 M 1813-35 [88]
WESTON IN GORDANO 1593-1639 [88]
WESTON SUPER MARE* M 1668-1837 CMB(I) 1668-1850 [115,125]
WHEATHILL 1623 [88]
WHITE LACKINGTON* 1609-23 (M 1695-1837) [88,114] Mfc C 1678-1900 M 1678-1837 B 1678-1812 Banns 1755-1812 1825-1853
WHITESTAUNTON* M 1606-1812 [105,GCI]
WIDCOMBE M 1612-1754 [117]; with LYNCOMBE 1813-1840 [56]
WILTON 1558-1837 [84,88]
WINCANTON 1629-72 [88]
WINFORD 1609-39 [88]
WINSCOMBE 1598-1623 [88]
WINSFORD 1621-39 [88]

WITHAM FRIARY C 1695-1837 M 1696-1837 B 1684-1836 [85]
WITHIEL FLORY 1609-29 [88]
WIVELISCOMBE 1598-1637 [88]
WOOLLEY C 1563-1840 M 1564-1840 B 1560-1840 [11,54,88]
WOOTTON, NORTH 1608-39 [88]
WRAXALL* 1614-78 (M 1562-1812) [88,105,GCI]
WRINGTON 1806-7 [91]
YARLINGTON* 1599-1673 M 1700-1851 [88,126]
YATTON 1623-79 [88]
YEOVILTON* 1599-1623 M (1655-1802)-12 [88,103,126]

STAFFORDSHIRE

ACTON TRUSSELL and BEDNALL Mf M 1659-1744
ADBASTON* 1600-1839 [89] Mf 1600-1760 C 1813-1856
ALDRIDGE see BARR, GREAT
ALREWAS 1547-1795 [91/2]
ALSTONFIELD* 1538-1812 [93]
ARMITAGE* 1623-26 1673-1837 [6,89]
ASHLEY Mf 1551-1743
AUDLEY* 1538-1712 [94]
BAGNALL see BUCKNALL
BARLASTON* C 1573-1812 M 1598-1812 B 1551-1812 [7]
BARR, GREAT with ALDRIDGE 1654-1749 [90,131]
BARTON UNDER NEEDWOOD* 1571-1812 [8,9]
BEDNALL Mf C 1813-1875 see also ACTON TRUSSELL and BEDNALL
BERKSWICH* 1601-1812 [10]
BETLEY* 1538-1812 [11]
BIDDULPH 1558-1642 1653-1684 [135] Mf CB 1558-1640 1654-1754 M 1654-1812
BILSTON* C 1684-1746 M 1732-43 B 1727-1746 [12] Mf C 1684-1760 1801-1835 M 1747-1754 B 1727-1747
BLITHFIELD Mf C Ext 1693-1877
BLORE RAY Mf C 1813-1872
BLOXWICH* C 1721-91 B 1733-91 [13]
BLYMHILL* (1561-1812) 1813-37 [14,89]
BOBBINGTON Ext 1662-1721 [109] Mf C 1813-31
BRADELEY* C 1540-1779 MB 1538-1779 [129,131]
BRADLEY by STAFFORD Mf C 1636-1848 M 1636-1766
BRADLEY IN THE MOORS* 1674-1812 [26]
BRAMSHALL Mf C 1815-1877
BREWOOD* C 1561-1641 M 1562-1645 B 1562-1650 [15]
BRIERLEY HILL* (CB 1800-1812); Prim Meth C 1829-50 [94,118,131]
BROMWICH, WEST* All Saints C (1608-1658) 1660-1777 M (1608-1837) B (1608-1658) 1660-1678 [4,95-7,125,130,134,GCI]; Christchurch Mf CZ 1829-1635; Ebenezer Ind C 1803-1837; Mare's Green Ind C 1787-1837; Wes Meth C 1815-1837
BUCKNALL CUM BAGNALL* C 1758-1812 M 1765-1812 B 1763-1812 [16,131]
BURNTWOOD Mf 1826-1872
BURSLEM* 1578-1812 [17-19]
BURTON-ON-TRENT M 1790-1837 [119] Mf C 1663-1812
BUSHBURY* 1560-1812 [20]
BUTTERFIELD see MAYFIELD
BUTTERTON IN THE PEAK 1660-1708 1711-1751

CANNOCK CB 1744-64 M 1744-54 B 1811-12 [131] Mf 1660-1812
CASTLE CHURCH* 1568-1812 [21,122] Mf C 1813-1856
CAULDON C 1580-1869 M 1580-1837 B 1580-1856 [131]
CAVERSWALL Mf 1559-1812
CHALTON see MAYFIELD
CHAPEL CHORLTON Mf C 1802-35 1852-1876
CHEADLE Mf 1574-1682
CHEBSEY* (1660-1812) [22,131]
CHILLINGTON* Rom Cath 1720-1830 [88]
CHURCH EATON* 1538-1812 [94]
CODSALL* CB 1587-1812 M 1587-1843 [24]
COLWICH Mf C Ext 1659-1812
COPPENHALL* CM 1678-1837 [89]
COSELEY CB 1830-37; Coppice Part Bapt Z 1794-1837;
    Prov Bapt ZC 1809-1867; Darkhouse Bapt Z 1822-
    1837; Old Pres/Unit Meet Hse ZC 1779-1837 B
    1806-1837 [128]
CRESSWELL* Rom Cath C 1780-1819 [88]
CROXDEN* 1671-1812 [26]
DRAYCOTT IN THE MOORS CB 1676-1868 M 1671-
    1857
ECCLESHALL* 1573-1667 [27/8]
ELFORD Mf C 1663-1864 M 1663-1847 1871
ELLASTONE* 1538-1812 [29,30]
ELLENHALL* C 1599-1812 M 1563-1812 B 1539-1812
    [31] Mf C Ext 1813-1875
FAREWELL Mf C ExT 1711-1812
FORNTON Mf C 1813-1868
GNOSALL* CB 1572-1699 M 1572-1785 [32]
HAMSTALL RIDGWARE* 1598-1812 [33]
HANBURY Mf C 1574-1776 1780-1812 M 1574-1788
    Banns 1770-1803 B 1574-1812
HANLEY* St John Evang C 1789-1803 [98] Mfc C 1789-
    1806
HAUGHTON* 1570-1812 [34]
HIMLEY* 1665-1837 [35,89]
HINTS* 1558-1812 [36]
HORTON Mf C 1813-1870
IPSTONES* 1560-1715 [99]
KEELE* C 1540-1699 M 1543-1812 [37,131] Mf
    1540-1842
KINGSLEY* CB 1561-1795 M 1561-1754 [38]
KINGSWINFORD* CB (1603-1704)-(1724-1761) M (1603-
    1704)-(1724-1759) [98,117,121] Mf C 1813-1835
KINVER C 1560-1775 M 1560-1804 B 1560-1756 [100]
LANE END Mf C 1764-1809 1828-1868(gaps)
LAPLEY* 1538-1756 [39] Mf C Ext 1664-1877
LEEK 1634-94/5 [40] Mf CM 1695-1812 B 1678-1812
LEIGH Mf C Ext 1660-1854
LICHFIELD* Cathedral CB 1660-1744 M 1665-1754 [41]
    Mf C 1660-1875; St Chad Mf C 1659-1812(gaps); St
    Mary Mf C 1711-1812(gaps)
LONGTON Mf ZC 1834-39
MADELEY 1567-1812 [42,98]
MAER Mf C 1816-1878
MARCHINGTON 1609-70 1749-1812 [101/2] Mf ZC
    1813-1865
MAVESYN RIDWARE 1538-1812 [103]
MAYFIELD Mf C 1814-1868
MEERBROOK Mf C 1813-1863
MILWICH* 1573-1711 [43]
MUCKLESTONE* C 1555-1701 Z 1702-1747 C 1747-
    1812 MB 1555-1812 [44,126]; and WOORE* C
    1773-1782 1793-1808 [126] Mf C 1813-1869
NEWNBOROUGH Mf C Ext 1660-1809
NEWCASTLE UNDER LYME* (1563-1812) [45-47]

NEWCHAPEL Mf C Ext 1726-1809 1813-1856
NORBURY* CB 1538-1812 M 1538-1837 [133] Mf C Ext
    1673-1809 1813-1854 M(I) 1673-1852
NORTON CANES Mf C 1813-1859
NORTON IN THE MOORS* CB 1574-1751 M 1574-1837
    [48/9]
OAKAMOOR Mf C 1835-1855
OFFLEY, HIGH* 1659-1812 [98,131]
PATTINGHAM* 1559-1812 [50]
PELSALL* CB 1763-1812 [114]
PENKRIDGE* 1572-1735 [51]
PENN* C 1569-1748 M 1570-1753 B 1571-1754 [52]
PENNFIELDS Mf C Ext 1859-1877
PIPE RIDWARE* C 1571-1812 M 1565-1812 B 1561-1812
    [53]
QUARNFORD Mf C 1821-1854
QUARRY BANK Mf C 1845-1853
RANTON* 1655-1812 [54,132]
ROCESTER* 1566-1812 [55/6]
ROLLESTON Mf ZC 1813-1866
ROUNDOAK see BRIERLEY HILL
ROWLEY REGIS* 1539-1812 [57-59]
RUGELEY* CB (1569-1722)-1802 M (1569-1722)-1812
    [60,104]
RUSHALL* C 1660-85 (1686-1769) M 1660-1734 B 1660-
    1770 [114]
RUSHTON SPENCER Mf C Ext 1693-1812
SANDON Mf M 1661-1825
SEDGLEY* C (1558-1684)-1810 M (1558-1684)-(1781-
    1831) B (1558-1684)-1801 [61,105-109,123,128] Mf
    C 1831-1853
SEIGHFORD 1561-1812 [62,132]
SHARESHILL Mf ZC 1813-1836 1859-1868
STAFFORD St Chad (1636-1812); St Mary (1559-1671) M
    by lic 1770-1823 [63] see also BRADLEY by
    STAFFORD
STANDON* 1558-1812 [64]
STOKE UPON TRENT* 1629-1812 [65-68]
STONNALL Mf C 1823-1836
STOWE* 1574-1672 [69]
SWYNNERTON* 1558-1837 Mf C 1676-1868; Rom Cath
    C 1810-1842 M 1833-1841 D 1813-1819
    [98,115,132]
TAMWORTH* (1558-1614)-35 [70,111]
TATENHILL* 1563-1812 [71] Mf 1563-1812
TETTENHALL* C (1602-1741)-97 (M 1602-1839) B (1602-
    1732)-97 [1,72/3,124]
TIPTON* 1558-1836 [74]; Tipton Green Meth C 1809-
    1837; Bloomfield Wse Meth C 1823-1837; Wes
    Chap New Con, Dudley B 1830-1837; Ind,King
    St.,Dudley C Ext 1806-1825 [120]
TRENTHAM* 1558-1812 [75/6]
TUTBURY Ext M 1774-96 1813-31 [132] Mf 1673-1809
UTTOXETER Mf C Ext 1726-1770
WALSALL* C 1570-(1646-1675) M 1570-1649 (1662-
    1754) B 1570-1648; Rom Cath 1762-1766
    [77,88,112]
WALTON* see BERKSWICH
WATERFALL C 1602-1931 M 1602-1905 B 1602-1907
    [113]
WEDNESBURY Mfc C 1569-1812 B 1562-1812
WEDNESFIELD* CB 1751-1837 [79]
WEEFORD* 1562-1812 [80,132]
WESTON under LYZARD CM 1654-1837 B 1654-1812
    [81,89]
WESTON upon TRENT Mf C 1744-1809
WILLENHALL C 1642-1812 B 1727-1812 [5]

WOLSTANTON* 1624-1812 [82/3] Mf 1624-1768
WOLVERHAMPTON* C (1539-1660)-1733 1788-1839 M (1539-1776) B (1539-1660) 1784-1839; Rom Cath C 1788-1830 M 1810 B 1784-1828; various non-conf 1726-1837 [3,84,86-88,127]
WOORE see MUCKLESTONE
YOXALL* C 1644-1726 M 1682-1754 [2,132]

SUFFOLK

ACTON near Sudbury Ext M 1605-1802 [118]
AKENHAM Mfc C 1538-1811 1813-1903 M 1538-1809 1813-1901 B 1538-1689 1721-1811 1813-1905
ALDEBURGH* Ext M 1653-56 Mfc C 1558-1600 1607-8 1691-1907 M 1558-1601 1653-6 1691-1900 B 1558-1600 1608 1653-4 1691-1900
ALDERTON M 1674-1753 [267] Mfc CB 1674-1901 M 1674-1754 1783-1901
ALDHAM 1564-1812 [169]
ALPHAMSTONE Ext 1705-1811 [118]
ALPHETON M 1574-1837 [261]
AMPTON 1564-1812 [169]
ASHBOCKING Mf 1555-1900
ASHBY* M 1553-1837 [114] Mfc C 1553-1813 M 1553-1835 B 1558-1812
ASHFIELD MAGNA 1563-1812 [170]
ASHFIELD CUM THORPE C 1691-1812 MB 1698-1811 [258] Mfc C 1704-1812 M 1704-53 1777-1832 B 1705-41 1749-1807
ASPALL 1564-1812 [171]
ASSINGTON CM 1598-1812 [118]
ATHELINGTON M 1694-1753 [118] Mfc CB 1694-1900 M 1694-1753 1755-1811 1813-1900 Banns 1755-1822
BACTON 1539-1812 [4]
BADWELL ASH 1560-1811 [5]
BARDWELL C 1538-1713 M 1538-1837 B 1538-1713 [6,119]; Part Bapt Z 1817 1820-37 [257] Mf C 1651-1773
BARHAM CB 1562-1812 M 1563-1753 [7] Mfc C 1538-1577 1618-1812 M 1563-1812 Banns 1754-1825 B 1562-1821
BARNARDISTON C 1540-1809 M 1540-1837 B 1549-1809 [119]
BARNHAM 1563-1812 [172]
BARNINGHAM 1561-1812 [173]; Wes ZC Ext 1812-30 [257]
BARROW C 1542-1812 M 1544-1837 B 1544-1812 [166,167,168]
BARSHAM Mfc C 1558-1907 M 1561-1900 B 1558-1812
BARTON, LITTLE (I) 1663-1835 [8]
BARTON, MAGNA 1564-1812 [174]
BARTON MILLS 1663-1835 [9-11]
BAWDSEY M 1744-52 [261] Mfc C 1744-1901 M 1744-52 1755-1837 B 1744-1900
BAWDSEY Manor Chapel Mfc C 1894-1902
BAYLHAM Mf C 1661-1760 M 1661-1753 B 1661-1761
BEALINGS, GREAT CM 1813-40 C(I) 1538-1877 M(I) 1541-1840 B(I) 1541-1810 [259]
BEALINGS, LITTLE 1544-48 1558-1886 [13,14]
BECCLES M(I) 1586-1900 [260]
BEDFIELD Mfc C 1584-1702 1711-1882 1884-1901 M 1584-1694 1711-1900 B 1584-1702 1711-1901
BEDINGFIELD 1538-1935 [15]

BELSTEAD Mfc C 1539-1622 1653-99 1704-1899 M 1539-1640 1653-99 1704-1899 B 1539-1622 1653-99 1704-1986
BENHALL Mfc C 1560-1900 M 1561-1900 B 1560-1882
BENTLEY M 1538-1761 [118]
BERGHOLT EAST Mfc 1653-1900
BEYTON M 1552-1837 [261]
BILDESTON C 1563-1760 M 1559-1754 Ext [118]
BLAKENHAM, GREAT Mf C 1665-1794 M 1665-1753 B 1665-1793
BLYFORD Mfc C 1691-1811 1813-1901 M 1697-1761 1769-1810 1813-1900 B 1695-1782 1784-1812
BLYTHBURGH Mfc 1690-1870
BOULGE Mfc C 1621-59 1679-1986 M 1628-54 1679-1982 B 1621-58 1679-1985
BOXFORD (I) M 1557-1616 B 1557-1808 [261]
BOXTED M 1539-1850 [263]
BRADFIELD ST CLARE C 1538-1783 M 1541-1812 B 1540-1678 [120]
BRADFIELD ST GEORGE M 1555-1837 [257]
BRADFIELD COMBUST M 1538-1641 1660-1835 [257]
BRADLEY, MAGNA M 1703-1837 [270]
BRAISEWORTH 1565-1812 [175,258]
BRAMFIELD 1539-96 1693-1889 [16]
BRAMFORD Mfc 1553-1900
BRAMPTON Mfc C 1760-1900 M 1755-1899 B 1771-1812
BRANDESTON Mfc C 1560-1877 M 1559-1754 1813-1901 B 1559-1899
BRANDON 1565-1812 [176]
BRENT ELEIGH C 1589-1812 M 1590-1837 B 1590-1812 [120]
BRETTENHAM C 1584-1730 M 1584-1753 B 1584-1693 [17]
BRIGHTWELL with FOXHALL C 1653-1793 [88]
BROCKFORD see WETHERINGSETT cum BROCKFORD
BROCKLEY M 1560-1836 [257]
BROME C 1559-1812 M 1563-1812 B 1563-1812 [18,258]
BUCKLESHAM Mfc CM 1678-1899 B 1678-1901
BURES ST MARY C 1541-1812 M 1538-1837 B 1751-1812 [149/50]
BURGATE 1560-1806 [19,258]
BURGH 1547-1812 [29]
BURSTALL 1540-1887 [5]
BURY ST EDMUNDS St James C 1558-1800 M 1562-1837 B 1562-1800 [259,P]; St Mary C 1558-1814 M 1558-1837 B 1558-1812 [239-243]; Cong C 1656-1799 M 1684-90 D 1650-1730 [121]
BUTLEY Mfc C 1785-1900 M 1792-1899 B 1785-1901
BUXHALL 1558-1699 [21]
CAPEL ST MARY* M 1538-1837 [111,GCI]
CARLTON 1538-1886 [22]
CAVENDISH 1594-1837 [23/4,270]
CAVENHAM C 1539-1812 M 1540-1837 B 1540-1809 [116,121,151/2,261]
CHARLSFIELD Mfc C 1727-88 1790-1901 M 1727-50 1755-1836 1840-1901 B 1727-88 1790-1899
CHEDBURGH M 1542-1837 [257]
CHEDISTON 1653-1924 [18]
CHELLESWORTH Ext C 1559-1785 M 1559-1590 [118]
CHELMONDISTON Mfc C 1727-1896 MB 1727-1900
CHEVINGTON M 1813-37 [263]
CHILTON M Ext 1624-1753 B 1625-81 [118] Mf C 1626-49
CHILLESFORD CB 1740-1812 M 1742-3 [25]
CLARE CB 1558-1640 M 1558-1837 [26/7,267]; Bapt D 1822-37 [263]

CLAYDON M 1560-1754 [268] Mfc C 1560-1960 M 1560-1972 B 1559-1680 1711-1928
CLOPTON 1735-1812 [29,267]
COCKFIELD 1561-1812 [177,257]
CODDENHAM with CROWFIELD C 1539-1773 M 1543-1812 B 1538-1754 [30] Mf CB 1790-1812
COMBS* M 1568-1837 [111,GCI]
CONY WESTON 1563-1812 [178]
COOKLEY Mfc C 1538-1692 1715-1812 M 1538-1690 1716-1811 1813-1900 B 1538-1691 1715-1812
COPDOCK M 1701-1753 [267]
CORNARD, GREAT 1540-1837 [31]
CORNARD PARVA 1563-1812 [178]
COTTON 1564-1812 [179]
COWLINGE M 1558-1685 1706-1837 [268]
CREETING ALL SAINTS 1563-1812 [180]
CREETING ST PETER 1562-1812 [180]
CRETINGHAM Mfc C 1558-1900 M 1561-1900 B 1557-1680 1751-1901
CROWFIELD Mf CB 1790-1812; see also CODDENHAM
CULFORD* 1560-1778 [32]
CULPHO 1721-1886 [33]
DALHAM 1558-1837 [34,122]
DALLINGHOO M 1559-1752 [118]
DARSHAM Mfc 1538-1900
DEBACH Mfc C 1539-1901 M 1539-1641 1703-1812 1818-36 1838-1901 B 1539-1652 1655-1904
DEBENHAM C 1559-1803 M 1559-1805 B 1562-1803 [35/6]
DENHAM (Bury) St Mary 1539-1850 [P]
DENHAM (Eye) St John 1708-1812 [19]
DENNINGTON Mfc 1570-1864 M 1570-1944 B 1571-1975
DENSTON 1564-1812 [181]
DEPDEN CB 1564-1812 M 1564-1837 [182,261]
DRINKSTONE 1579-1812 [219]
DUNWICH ST PETER* M 1549-1658 [114] Mfc 1672-1837
EARL SOHAM Mfc C 1561-1900 M 1558-1651 1654-1899 B 1558-1888 1896
EARL STONHAM Mfc C 1654-1809 1813-1902 M 1654-1812 1814-1900 B 1654-1809 1813-1901
EASTON 1560-1950 [38]
EDWARDSTONE CB 1645-1812 M Ext 1646-1753 M 1754-1813 [118,270]
ELLOUGH C 1540-1812 M 1545-1754 B 1540-1812 [40]
ELMHAM, SOUTH C 1539-1812 M 1583-1812 B 1571-1812 [117] Mf CB 1761-1813
ELMSETT 1564-1812 [245]
ELMSWELL 1561-1812 [246]
ELVEDEN 1570-1812 [247]
ERISWELL 1567-1812 [220]
ERWARTON Mfc C 1558-1580 1584-1655 1661-1901 M 1560-80 1586-1668 1673-1752 1754-1899 B 1558-80 1585-1812
EUSTON 1561-1812 [247]
EXNING* C(M)B 1563-1812 [111,248,GCI]
EYE C 1538-1812 M 1538-1800 B 1538-1812 M(I) 1538-1800 [41/2,268]
FAKENHAM MAGNA 1563-1812 [249]
FALKENHAM Mfc C 1538-1900 M 1538-1697 1700-1901 B 1538-1812; Cong B 1813-1902
FARNHAM C 1559-1804 [268]
FELIXSTOWE CB 1653-1795 C(I) 1796-1813 M(I) 1654-1841 B(I) 1764-1812 [261,268,270]
FELSHAM 1568-1812 [249]
FINBOROUGH MAGNA 1563-1812 [250] Mfc C 1558-1883 M 1558-1700 1704-1850 B 1558-1900
FINBOROUGH PARVA 1596-1812 [250]
FINNINGHAM 1560-1812 [19]
FLEMPTON cum HENGRAVE M 1561-1837 [263] Mfc C 1561-1646 1668-96 1732-1812 1860-74 M 1561-1649 1668-96 1762-1842 B 1561-1649 1668-96 1732-1810
FORNHAM ALL SAINTS CB 1564-1812 M 1564-1837 [251,263]
FORNHAM ST GENEVIEVE 1564-1812 [252,263]
FORNHAM ST MARTIN CB 1564-1812 M 1564-1837 [252,263,266]
FOXHALL see BRIGHTWELL
FRAMSDEN C 1575-1810 M 1560-1812 B 1558-1812 [43]
FRECKENHAM C 1550-1773 M 1550-1837 B 1561-1773 [139]
FRESSINGFIELD* C 1687-1837 (M 1554-1837) B 1811-37 [44,114]
FRESTON M 1538-1884 [257]
FRISTON Mfc C 1561-1891 M 1543-1900 B 1541-1812
FRITTON Mfc C 1706-1904 M 1708-1837 Banns 1754-1906 B 1706-1812
FROSTENDEN CB 1538-1791 M 1538-1754 [46]
GAZELEY 1538-1812 [47]
GEDDING 1576-1812 [220]
GISLINGHAM CB 1558-1790 M 1558-1754 [258]
GLEMSFORD CB 1550-1782 M 1550-1837 [123-5]
GORLESTON & SOUTHTOWN Mf Ext C 1678-1811 M 1675-1799 B 1674-1812
GOSBECK CM 1561-1751 B 1561-1774 [28,268]
GROTON Ext C 1562-1784 M 1563-1753 [118]
GRUNDISBURGH* CB 1538-1851 Ext 1851-79 (M 1539-1837)-1851 B 1813-1851 [48,114,261]
GUNTON Mfc 1734-1754
HADLEIGH C 1631-1856 M Ext 1692-1792 [51,117/8]; Ind 1698-1742 [267]
HALESWORTH Mfc C 1653-1898 M 1653-1900 B 1653-1854
HARGRAVE 1564-1812 M 1710-1836 [221,263]
HARKSTEAD Mfc C 1660-1896 M 1654-1720 1723-1811 1813-99 B 1653-1901
HARLESTON 1567-1812 [221]
HARTEST 1563-1812 M 1559-1850 [222,261]
HASKETON 1540-1813 [5]
HAUGHLEY 1561-1812 [223]
HAVERHILL C 1660-1743 M 1677-1837 B 1677-1748 [126,266]
HAWKEDON C 1709-87 M 1710-1837 B 1710-84 [126,266]
HAWSTEAD 1558-1857 [52-6]
HELMINGHAM 1559-1812 [57]
HEMINGSTONE C 1553-99 M 1556-1753 [28]
HENGRAVE see FLEMPTON
HEPWORTH 1563-1669 [18]
HERRINGFLEET 1719-20 C 1747-48 Mfc CB 1706-1812 M 1709-1912
HERRINGSWELL 1563-1812 [224] M 1748-1837 [263]
HESSETT CB 1563-1812 M 1539-1837 [224,263,266]
HIGHAM ST MARY Ext C 1538-1783 M 1538-1774 [118]
HINDERCLAY 1563-1812 [225]
HITCHAM C 1575-1844 M 1600-1837 B 1607-1868 [143/4]
HOLBROOK Mfc CM 1559-1900 B 1559-1899
HOLLESLEY* CM 1623-1812 B 1637-1812 [141]
HOLTON 1538-1924 [58]
HONINGTON 1563-1812 [225]

HOO Mfc C 1653-1903 M 1653-1836 Banns 1756-1903 B 1653-1902
HOPTON 1561-1812 [226]
HORHAM M 1593-1753 [118]
HORRINGER* 1558-1850 [P]
HOXNE* CB 1548-1812 (M 1548-1837) [60,113,142]
HUNDON 1562-1812 [227]
HUNSTON 1561-1812 [232]
ICKLINGHAM All Saints 1563-1812; St. James 1563-1812 M 1559-1753 [228,268]
ICKWORTH* 1566-1890 [P] Mf 1566-1890
IKEN Mfc C 1669-92 1698-1810 1813-97 M 1669-1898 B 1669-1810 1813-1902
ILKETSHALL ST ANDREW Mf C 1581-1677 M 1559-1626 B 1541-1559
ILKETSHALL ST MARGARET Mf 1538-1757
INGHAM* C 1538-1804 M 1539-1787 B 1538-1811 [62]
IPSWICH St Clement (I) 1563-1686 [69] Mf CB 1710-1812 M 1710-1753; St Lawrence 1538-1812 [65]; St Margaret Mf M 1754-1781; St Mary Elms (I) 1557-1812 [70]; St Mary Key C 1562-1735 [5]; St Matthew 1558-1702 [63] Mf C 1703-74; St Nicholas CM 1539-1710 B 1551-1710 [64]; St Peter 1662-1790 [66/7]; St Stephen (I) 1586-1677 [68]
IXWORTH CB 1557-1812 M 1557-1837 [71,229,263]
IXWORTH THORPE 1561-1812 [230]
KEDINGTON Ext 1654-1812 [244]
KELSALE CB 1538-1812 M 1538-1886 [72]
KENTFORD M 1718-1835 [263]
KENTON 1538-1812 [57]
KERSEY M Ext 1541-1754 [118]
KESGRAVE C 1660-1705 1812-58 MB 1812-40 [257,268]
KESSINGLAND Mfc C 1561-1907 M 1561-1676 1698-1909 B 1568-1643 1658-1912
KETTLEBASTON 1564-1812 [230]
KETTLEBURGH Mfc C 1562-1652 1661-1881 M 1561-1651 1661-75 1680-1782 1785-1812 1814-1901 B 1561-1652 1661-1900
KIRKLEY C 1701-55 M 1751-53 B 1752-3 [96,257]
KIRTON Mfc C 1623-1885 MB 1623-1899
KNETTISHALL 1561-1812 [232]
KNODISHALL* 1566-1705 [73]
LACKFORD 1564-1812 [188]
LAKENHEATH 1563-1812 [183]
LANGHAM 1561-1812 [184]
LAVENHAM 1564-1812 [118,216-8] Ind C 1739-1823 [264]
LAWSHALL C 1563-1812 M 1559-1837 B 1558-1812 [128,189]
LAXFIELD Mfc 1579-1900
LAYHAM C 1538-1789 M 1544-1766 B 1563-1812 [118,190]
LEISTON WITH SIZEWELL Mfc 1538-1900
LETHERINGHAM 1588-1812 [74]
LEVINGTON 1562-1787 [68]
LIDGATE C 1553-1696 1701-1812 M 1548-1837 B 1547-1812 [129]
LINDSEY 1563-1812 [190]
LIVERMERE MAGNA 1564-1812 [191]
LIVERMERE PARVA 1563-1812 [191]
LOWESTOFT* (1561-1812)-1840 [75-9]; Ind C 1726-33 [SR/R21]
MARKET WESTON see WESTON, MARKET
MARTLESHAM* CB 1653-1840 (M 1653-1837) [80,81,111,117,GCI]
MELFORD, LONG CB 1563-1812 1877-1897 M 1563-1837 1877-1897 [130,192-4]; Ind C 1733-1825

B 1785-1836 [264]
MELLIS CB 1559-1812 M 1560-1807 [57]
MELTON House of Industry (for Loes and Wilford Hundreds) C(I) 1768-1826 B 1768-1825 [238,262]
MENDHAM* M 1678-1837 [113]
MENDLESHAM 1563-1812 [195]
METFIELD* C 1559-1881 M (1559-1837)-1920 B 1559-1888 [82/3,113]
METTINGHAM Mfc C 1653-1899 M 1653-1836 1838-99 Banns 1754-1852 B 1653-1900
MICKFIELD* M 1558-1837 [114]
MIDDLETON CUM FORDINGLEY Mfc 1653-1900
MILDEN C 1559-1757 M 1560-1837 B 1558-1757 [118,131]
MILDENHALL C 1559-1812 M 1559-1837 B 1559-1812 [153-7]; Wes Beck Row B 1830-37 [264]
MONEWDEN Mfc C 1705-1901 M 1705-1899 B 1705-1900
MONKS ELEIGH Ext C 1628-1775 M 1557-1772 B 1660-1743 [118,GCI]
MONKS SOHAM* 1712-1919 [84]
MOULTON M 1561-1836 [264]
MUTFORD Mfc CB 1681-1900 M 1681-1749 1753-1811 1813-1900 Banns 1755-1824 1833-1907
NACTON Ext CM 1562-1714 B 1562-1749 [85]
NAUGHTON CB 1563-1812 M 1563-1837 [196,264]
NAYLAND 1564-1812 [197]
NEDGING C 1559-1735 M 1560-1837 B 1560-1737 [131]
NEWMARKET All Saints CB 1633-1812M 1633-1837 [132,198]; St Mary CB 1567-1812 M 1567-1837 [133,199,200]
NEWTON near SUDBURY CM Ext 1558-1812 CM 1564-1812 [118,196]
NEWTON, OLD 1566-1812 [201]
NORTON CB 1539-1775 M 1539-1837 [86,131]
NOWTON C 1559-1783 M 1565-1837 B 1565-1783 [131]
OAKLEY CB 1539-1801 M 1539-1812 [18,43]
OCCOLD 1564-1812 [202]
ONEHOUSE 1565-1812; Stow House of Industry CB 1813-35 [202,257]
ORFORD C 1538-1728 B 1538-1630 [87/8]
OTLEY Mfc 1734-1900
OULTON Mfc C 1564-1666 1695-1900 M 1564-1663 1695-1703 1710-14 1716 1719 1724-1915 B 1564-1663 1695-1900
OUSDEN M 1675-1837 [262]
PAKENHAM 1568-1812 [203]
PALGRAVE 1564-1812 [204]
PEASENHALL Mfc C 1558-1680 1685-1856 MB 1559-1680 1685-1899
PLAYFORD M 1660-1729 [118]
POLSTEAD C 1558-1760 C Ext 1761-1837 M 1539-1760 M Ext 1761-1876 B 1538-1772 B Ext 1772-1876 [118,134]
POSLINGFORD C 1559-1922 M 1559-1840 B 1559-1840 [18,96]
PRESTON CB 1628-1785 M 1628-1843 [135]
RAMSHOLT M 1709-52 [267]
RATTLESDEN* 1558-1758 [89]
RAYDON M Ext 1562-1753 [118]
REDE M 1539-1835 [264]
REDGRAVE C 1538-1812 MB 1561-1812 [90]; with BOTESDALE Mfc C 1538-1646 1654-1900 M 1538-1646 1654-1899 B 1538-1646 1654-1892
REDISHAM Mfc C 1540-1902 M 1537-1709 1713-54 1756-1812 1840-1901 B 1540-1904
REDLINGFIELD 1565-1812 [205]

WESTERFIELD 1538-1838 [6] Mfc 1539-1812
WESTHORPE 1538-1812 [104]
WESTLETON Mfc 1545-1900
WESTLEY CB 1565-1812 M 1569-1837 [244,265]
WESTON, MARKET 1563-1811 [236]
WETHALL Mfc C 1559-1868 MB 1559-1899
WETHERDEN 1563-1812 [185]
WETHERINGSETT cum BROCKFORD 1564-1811 [186]
WEYBREAD* M 1687-1837 [114]
WHATFIELD 1564-1812 [187]
WHELNETHAM, GREAT* 1561-1850 [P]
WHELNETHAM, LITTLE* 1557-1850 [P]
WHEPSTEAD 1564-1812 [210]
WHERSTEAD 1590-1683 [105]
WHITTON CUM THURLESTON M 1600-1751 Mfc C
    1599-1812 M 1600-1810 B 1599-1698 1727-1873
WICKHAMBROOK 1567-1812 [211/2]; Ind 1727-71
    1830-35 [265]
WICKAM MARKET Mfc 1557-1900
WICKHAM SKEITH 1558-1812 [104]
WINGFIELD* 1538-1838 [107]
WINSTON Mfc C 1558-1844 MB 1558-1812
WISSETT 1559-1924 [115]
WISSINGTON C 1538-1812 M 1538-1754 B 1538-1660
    [118]
WISTON 1563-1812 [213]
WITHERSDALE* C 1653-1936 M 1657-(1660-1837)-1936
    B 1654-1935 [109,112]
WITHERSFIELD CB 1558-1776 M 1558-1837 [146]
WITNESHAM Mfc 1538-1900
WIXOE C 1675-1771 M 1676-1837 B 1675-1771 [265]
WOODBRIDGE* M 1545-1837 [112]
WOOLPIT C 1558-1734 M 1559-1837 B 1558-1734 [140]
WORDWELL* 1580-1850 [P]
WORLINGTON1563-1812 M 1719-1836 [213,265]
WORLINGWORTH Mfc C 1558-1895 M 1558-1899 Banns
    1823-1919 B 1558-1886
WORTHAM 1564-1812 [214]
WRATTING MAGNA 1569-1812 M 1598-1837 [237,265]
WRATTING PARVA CB 1564-1812 M 1676-1837
    [237,265]
WRENTHAM Ind C 1650-1700 [110]
WYVERSTON 1560-1812 [104]
YAXLEY 1564-1812 [215]
YOXFORD Mfc 1559-1900

SURREY

ABINGER* CB 1559-1840 M 1559-1812 [22,118] Mf C
    1813-1961
ADDINGTON* (1560-1812) C(I) 1813-1851 M(I) 1813-
    1837 [23,120]
ALBURY M 1734-1837 [98]; Irvingite ZC 1833-40 [21]
ALFORD CB 1658-1840 M 1659-1837 [99,135]
ASH 1548-1837 [3]
ASHTEAD CB 1662-1840 M 1663-1837 [96,120,134]
BAGSHOT Chapel C 1837-1840 B 1837-1841 [130]
BANSTEAD* (1547-1789) Ext 1547-1812 M 1754-1837
    [15,24,95] Mf C 1751-1876
BARNES 1538-1699 [8]
BATTERSEA M 1802-37 [97/8]
BEDDINGTON* (1538-1673)-1812 [13,25,122]
BERMONDSEY St James M 1830-37 [97]; St Mary Magd
    C 1548-1641 1674-1738 1740-63 M 1548-1641

1674-1700 B 1548-1641 1674-88 1725-38 [26/7,113-
    117]
BETCHWORTH 1558-1837 [28/9]; Brockham Bapt Z
    1781-1837 C 1781-1827 [21,28]
BISLEY C 1561-1841 M 1561-1753 1813-37 B 1561-1851
    [123,135]
BLETCHINGLEY1689 [104]
BOOKHAM, GREAT C 1632-1840 M 1695-1753 B
    1632-1840 [30,135]
BOOKHAM, LITTLE CB 1642-1840 M 1670-1812
    [103,136]
BRAMLEY C 1563-1840 M 1567-1744 1754-1812 B
    1676-1767 1772-1840 [121,136]
BRIXTON HILL Ind Union Z 1833-1837 CB 1834-1837;
    Wes Z 1824-1837 C 1825-1837 [21]
BUCKLAND 1560-1837 CB 1838-40 [14,130]
BURSTOW 1547-1942 [14/5,101]
BYFLEET C 1698-1840 M 1717-18 1729-1837 B
    1728-1812 [95,122,136]
CAMBERWELL St Giles C(I)1809-12 (I)1829-34 M(I)1803-
    08 B 1769-1799 [101,122] see also DULWICH
    COLLEGE
CAPEL 1653-1840 [101,136]
CARSHALTON M 1538-1837 [31]; Mf C 1800-1845; Rom
    Cath C 1798-99 [119,CRS25]
CATERHAM* 1543-1837 C 1838-1850 B 1838-51
    [32,130]
CHALDON 1564-1836 CB 1837-51 [18,130]
CHARLWOOD C 1595-1840 M 1596-1840 B 1598-1840
    [33]; Ind Z 1815-36 C 1818-37 B 1823-35 [21]
CHEAM CB 1538-1728 M 1538-1837 [31,100,128]; Rom
    Cath C 1755-88 M 1757-88 B 1755-80 [34,CRS2]
CHELSHAM* CB (1680-1812)-1840 M (1680-1812) 1814-
    1837 [23,96,137]
CHERTSEY C 1624-1756 M Ext 1607-1756 B 1607-1746
    [13,119] Mf C 1800-1852; Presb Z 1775-1837 C
    1758-1837 D 1811-37 B 1783-1837 [21]
CHESSINGTON CB 1656-1837 M 1656-1835 [100] Mf C
    1833-1850
CHILWORTH see ST MARTHA ON THE HILL
CHIPSTEAD* CB (1656-1812)-1840 M (1663-1812)-1837
    [35,96,137] Mf C 1813-1854
CHOBHAM M 1655-1837; Bapt Z 1810-36 DB 1824
    [21,95]
CLANDON, EAST C 1559-1840 M 1813-1838 B 1558-
    1840 [99,119]
CLANDON, WEST CB 1536-1775 M 1536-1775 1813-37
    [16,95]
CLAPHAM C 1552-1815 M 1551-1688 1792-1837 B
    1553-1840 1848-1854 [36,97,131,GCI]; Bapt Z 1781-
    1836; Ind CZ 1808-37; Ind Park Road (formerly Acre
    Lane) C 1819-37 [21,97]
COBHAM 1562-1812 [37]
COLDHARBOUR 1848-1940 [9]
COMPTON CB 1587 1639-1840 M 1723-1752 1800-1838
    [96,133,137]
COULSDON* C (1653-1812)-37 1858-80 MB (1653-
    1812)-37 [10,38]
CROYDON St James C 1829-1851 B 1829-1866 [119];
    St John C(I) 1877-1884 M 1800-1812 [119]; Shirley
    Chapel C 1836-40 B 1836-49 [101]; Ind George
    Street Z 1790-1836 C 1797-1836 B 1832; Wes
    North End Z 1818-37 C 1822-37 (I) B 1831-47
    [21,120]
DITTON, LONG C 1564-1840 M 1552-1837 B 1558-1858
    [13,127]
DORKING C 1538-1646 M 1539-1646 [39]; Ind West

Street Z 1736-1843 C 1718-1843 M 1729-1801 D 1736-1855 B 1730-1855 [21]; St Martin Stray Regs. C 1647-1812 M 1648-1800 B 1539-1776 [40]
DULWICH College Chapel CB 1616-1837 M 1634-1754 [41]
DUNSFOLD CB 1587 1628-1840 M 1628-1837 [118]
EFFINGHAM 1565-1837 [17]
EGHAM CB 1771-1812 [134]
ELSTEAD 1538-1609 1628-1758 C 1759-1840 B 1759-1812 [12,137]; Ind ZC 1834-37 [21]
EPSOM St Martin C 1695-1894 M 1695-1899 B 1695-1913 [106/7]; Ind Church Street Z 1819-36 C 1826-37 B 1829-36; Ind Little Chapel ZC 1779-1811 B 1807 [21]
ESHER M(I) 1688-1812 [105]
EWELL M 1723-1812 [119]
EWHURST M 1614-1838 [99] see also GUMSHALL
FARLEY* CB (1679-1812)-1840 M (1680-1812) 1814-32 [42,96,137] Mf C 1813-1866
FARNHAM C 1539-1840 M 1539-1837 B 1539-1713 [1,43-46,111/2]; Bible Christ Z 1786-1836 C 1786-1837; Ebenezer ZC 1794-1837 DB 1827-36 [21]
FELDAY see GUMSHALL
FETCHAM C 1559-1651 1683-1840 M 1754-1805 1813-37 B 1562-1657 1684-1840 [96,128]
FRENSHAM C 1559-11840 M 1649-1792 B 1562-1840 [18,47,128]
FRIMLEY C 1590-1812 MB 1606-1837 [48]
GATTON* (CB 1599-1812) CB(I) 1813-41 M (1599-1812)-1836 [49,96,130] Mf C 1813-1865
GODALMING C 1582-1688 M 1583-1688 B 1583-1686 [22]; Ind Harts Lane Z 1786-1836 C 1786-1837 B 1786-1828 [21,104]
GOMSHALL, FELDAY & EWHURST Ind ZC 1723-37
GUILDFORD Holy Trinity C 1813-1840 M 1813-1837 B 1813-1840 [98]; St Mary C 1540-1724 1813-40 B 1540-1653 1698-1724 1813-40 [18,102]; St Nicholas 1562-1681 CB 1813-1840 M(I) 1562-1812 [102]; Ind C 1707-33 M 1770-73 D 1708-72 [21]; Ind New Chapel Z 1801-37 C 1803-38; Wes ZC 1828-40 [21]
GUMSHALL with FELDAY & EWHURST Ind ZC 1823-37 [21]
HAMBLEDON C 1587 1617-1840 M 1586-87 1617-1837 B 1587 1617-1915 [96,123,137]
HASCOMBE CB 1693 M 1658-1754 [99,104]
HASLEMERE* (C 1594-1842 M 1573-1837 B 1573-1842) [50,123]; Ind Z 1783-1834 C 1789-1800 1803-36 D 1808-24 B 1824 [21];
HEADLEY M 1663-1837 [31]
HOLMWOOD CB 1838-40 [137]
HORLEY C 1578-1847 M 1578-1847 B 1578-1847 [51,101,123]
HORNE C 1614-1694 1711-1840 M 1783-1805 B 1614-1840 [120,130]
HORSELL C 1653-1770 M 1654-1754 B 1653-1765 1813-40 [104,120]
HORSLEY, EAST CB 1666-1840 [118]
HORSLEY, WEST CB 1600-1840 [129]
HORSLEYDOWN see St John Horsleydown, SOUTHWARK; Cong (Goat Yard Passage) M 1660-1700 [98]
KEW C 1714-91 1800-20 1822-40 M 1714-83 1800-37 B 1714-85 1800-1822 [120,127]
KINGSTON UPON THAMES C 1542-1882 M 1542-1870 B 1542-1840 [52-64,GCI]; Bapt Z 1781-1837 D 1799-1836 B 1799-1837; Ind Z 1795-1802 C 1785-1803; Ind Heather Street ZC 1776-1856 D 1835-36 1839-

55 B 1802-36 1839-55 [21]
KINGSWOOD C 1836-80 [137]
LEATHERHEAD 1656-1840 [103/4]; Ind Z 1827-37 B 1832-37 [21]
LEIGH CB 1579-1838 M 1581-1838 [18]
LINGFIELD 1663-1780 [66]
MALDEN M 1676-1754 [120]
MERROW CB 1536-1812 M 1536-1812 1814-36 [6,95]
MERSTHAM* (1538-1812) CB 1813-1840 [67,134]
MITCHAM CB 1563-1778 M 1563-1753 [68-70]
MOLESEY, EAST C 1668-1840 B 1681-1840 [134]
MOLESEY, WEST CB 1729-1840 M 1813-37 [100,137]
MORDEN* (1634-1812) CB 1813-1840 [25,71,137]
MORTLAKE (1599-1678) [72]; Diss Ministers C 1719-52 B 1752 [21]
NEWDIGATE C 1560-1840 B 1599-1840 [128]
NORMANDY see WORPLESDON
NORWOOD, LOWER Ind Z 1818-37 C 1821-37 DB 1821-37 [21]
NORWOOD, WEST M 1825-37 [98]
NUTFIELD M 1813-37 [99]
OAKWOOD* (C 1700-1814)-1840 M 1697-1751 (B 1696-1812)-1840 [22,118]
OCKHAM 1568-1840 [7]
OCKLEY CB 1539-1840 M 1539-1599 [129]
OXTED CB 1689 M 1655-1837 [98,104]; Ind with LIMPSFIELD ZC 1812-36; Pains Hill Chapel Z 1822-35 C 1824-36 [21]
PEPERHAROW C 1588 1692-1840 (gaps) 1926-86 M 1689-93 1699-1833 1838-1986 B 1587 1689-1986 [99,118,133]
PERRY HILL see WORPLESDON
PIRBRIGHT CB(I) 1574-1733 CB 1733-1840 M 1574-1837 [95,104,133]
PUTNEY* (CB 1620-1812 M 1620-1870) [74-76]; Ind Z 1816-18 1827-34 C 1817-19 1827-34 [21]
PUTTENHAM C 1562-1840 M 1562-1837 B 1562-1885 [19,100]
PYRFORD CB 1665-1840 M 1667-1837 [95,104]
REIGATE Ind ZC 1835-37 [21]
RICHMOND C 1583-1812 MB 1583-1780 [77-9]; Rom Cath C 1794-1839 [CRS7]; Ind Vine Yard Z 1812-36 C 1831-36 [21]
RIPLEY see SEND
ROTHERHITHE Ext 1556-1804 [GCI]
ST MARTHA ON THE HILL C 1778-1900 M 1794-1835 B 1780-1900 [95,130]
SANDERSTEAD* (1565-1812) CB 1813-1840 [80,138]
SEALE CB 1743-1837 M 1755-1837 [120]
SEND and RIPLEY C 1653-1839 M 1654-1936 B 1653-1877 [96,126]
SHACKLEFORD C 1866-1987 M 1866-1986 B 1865-1986 [133]
SHALFORD C 1567-1840 M 1581-1651 1657-1837 B 1783-1837 [125,138,P]
SHERE CM 1547-1691 B 1546-1691 [125]
SHIRLEY C 1836-1927 M 1849-1932 B 1836-1933 [109/10] see also CROYDON
SOUTHWARK Christchurch C 1819-33 M 1807-12 1831-33 B 1825 1831-32 [81,124]; St George the Martyr M 1602-27 [104]; St John Horsleydown C(I) 1813-22 M(I) 1733-98 [105,121]; St Olave C 1583-1608 1583-1597 [83]; Cathedral/St Saviour M 1605-25; St Thomas Apostle M(I) 1614-1753 [105]; Rom Cath St George London Road M 1788-1809 M 1823-37 [82]; Christchurch Bapt Mf C 1772-1827; Colliers Ind Cong Mf C 1751-1836

STOKE D'ABERNON* C (1619-1812)-37 MB (1619-1812)-37 [10,84,104]
STREATHAM M 1538-1754 (I)1785-1812 [85,97,104,GCI]
SUTTON* (1636-1837) C 1838-1851 B 1838-1852 [86,118]
TANDRIDGE M 1695-1837 [96]
TATSFIELD* (1679-1812) C 1813-1840 M 1814-1837 B 1813-1865 [42,96,138]
THAMES DITTON 1693-94 [104,GCI]; Ind Weston Green Z 1787-1836 C 1816-36 [21]
TITSEY* (1579-1812) CB 1813-16 1818-35 1837-44 M 1815-1836 [35,96,130]
TOOTING Ind Z 1786-1836 C 1786-1837 B 1786-1834 [21]
WALTON ON THAMES M 1639-1777 [GCI]
WALTON ON THE HILL C 1581-1840 M 1631-1837 B 1631-1840 [31,120,127]
WANBOROUGH* C 1561-1675 1764-74 M 1561-1658 1668 B 1591-1664 [42]
WANDSWORTH C 1603-1787 M 1603-1837 B 1603-1678 1727-1787 [87,124]; Bapt Bridge Field Z 1816-37 B 1825-36; Ind ZC 1811-37 D 1814-37 B 1815-37 [21]
WARLINGHAM* CB (1653-1812)-1840 M (1653-1812)-36 [23,96,138]
WEYBRIDGE C 1625-1779 M 1625-1770 1813-36 B 1625-93 [18,99]; Rom Cath see WOBURN LODGE
WIMBLEDON* 1538-1812 [88]
WINDLESHAM C 1677-1899 M 1677-1783 B 1677-1865 [89,138]
WISLEY C 1667-1901 M 1666-1833 1837-1901 B 1669-1901 [95,139]
WITLEY 1653-1900 [90,91]
WOBURN LODGE* Rom Cath 1750-1874 [92,118]
WOKING, OLD C 1813-37 M 1653-1837 B 1813-40 [98,104,124]; Ind Z 1778-1835 C 1778-1836 [21]
WOLDINGHAM* (1765-1812) C 1813-40 B 1813-65 [42,139]
WONERSH CB 1539-1812 M 1539-1774 [93/4]
WOODMANSTERNE 1566-1837 [31,104/5]
WORPLESDON C 1538-1840 M 1570-1837 B 1570-1718 1726-1840 [99,125,132]; Ind Perry Hill and Normandy Chapel Z 1823-36 C 1823-37 [21]
WOTTON* (1596-1812) CB 1813-1840 [22,139]

SUSSEX

Sussex Military M 1750-1812 [188]

ALBOURNE M 1813-37 B 1813-93 [164/5]
ALCISTON C 1808-1812 M 1755-1840 B 1808-1892 [27,154,165]
ALDINGBOURNE CB 1558-1777 M 1558-1758 1813-41 [5,19,164]
ALDMODINGTON see EARNLEY cum ALDMODINGTON
ALFRISTON M 1754-1836 [164]; Ebenezer Ind ZC 1801-1837 [22]
AMBERLEY M 1560-1840 B 1813-1875 [20,28,189]
ANGMERING* (1562-1687) B 1678-1812 [19,20,183,P]
APPLEDRAM CB 1594-1812 M 1599-1842 [29,164]
APULDRAM see APPLEDRAM
ARDINGLEY 1558-1812 M 1813-1836 [20,164]; Ind (Cong) see LINDFIELD

ARLINGTON CB(I) 1606-98 M 1755-1837 B 1813-98 [27,189]
ARUNDEL C Ext 1569-1811 M 1560-1804 B Ext 1566-1840 [20,168/9]; Cong C 1796-1837 [22]; Rom Cath Arundel Castle: Domestic Chapel C 1748-1863 Ext 1849-1863 B 1748-1785 [CRS27]; Fitzalan Chapel B 1415-1925 [CRS27]
ASHBURNHAM M 1607-1837 B 1708-1785 [153,189]
ASHINGTON cum BUNCTON C 1571-1840 M 1583-1840 B 1571-1840 [13,19,20,117,198]
ASHURST Ext C 1634-1814 M 1634-1803 B 1639-1809 1813-1911 [20,165]
BALCOMBE CB 1539-1812 M 1539-1837 [20,187]
BARCOMBE M 1580-1837 [27]
BARLAVINGTON Ext C 1572-1622 1634-1666 M 1572-1618 1633-1733 B 1572-1622 1633-1809 [19,20]
BARNHAM Ext 1590-1680 C 1676-1812 M 1677-1774 B 1675-1812 [5,13,19,20]
BATTLE C 1653-64 M 1654-1754 B 1654-1785 CM 1813-37 [30]; Eng Presb Z 1769-1836 [23]; Mount St Unit Chapel D 1792-1861 [195]
BECKLEY Ext C 1598-1803 M 1603-1837 B 1602-1800 [20,195]
BEDDINGHAM CB 1593-1840 Z 1689-1711 M 1593-1837 [27]
BEEDING see SELE
BEPTON 1613 1630-1812 M 1814-1845 [10] Ext 1592-1622 C 1686-1762 M 1664-1754 B 1667-1784 [19,20]
BERWICK B 1800-97 [187]
BERSTED, SOUTH Ext C 1681-1798 M 1694-1801 B 1691-1837 [20]
BEXHILL-ON-SEA CB 1558-1837 M 1559-1837 [31/2,154]
BIGNOR C 1630-1790 M 1678-1772 B 1640-1788 [19,20]
BILLINGSHURST Ext 1558-1812 M 1813-1841 [8,164]; Gen Bapt/Free Christ Ch.(Unit) D 1755-1980 [175]; Calv Ind see WISBOROUGH GREEN
BINDERTON 1584-1641 [19,154] see also DEAN, WEST (Chichester)
BINSTED C 1639-1838 M 1638-1837 B 1638-1851 [19,20]
BISHOPSTONE 1633-1727 B 1813-93 [27,165,189]
BLATCHINGTON, EAST C 1563-1804 M 1563-1837 B 1563-1894 [27,33,165]
BLATCHINGTON, WEST 1636-1640 [158]
BODIAM CB 1557-1837 M 1570-1837 C(I) 1557-1967 [34,189,GCI]
BOGNOR Ind Hanover Chap C 1827-1837 [22] see also BERSTED, SOUTH; Wes see CHICHESTER
BOLNEY* 1541-1812 [P,GCI]
BOSHAM C 1557-1968 M 1557-1988 B 1557-1965; Cong C 1823-36 [22,35/6,154,184,189,198] Mf C 1557-1895 M 1557-1902 B 1577-1886
BOXGROVE 1561-1812 [17,20]
BRAMBER C Ext 1606-1709 M 1584-1650 1711-1812 B Ext 1612-1803 [164,187]
BREDE CM 1559-1812 [37,158]
BRIGHTLING M 1606-1837 [153]
BRIGHTON St Nicholas C 1558-1761 1813-37 M 1559-1837 B 1587-1761 1826-1831 [20,39-44,196]; College Chap C 1903-65 M 1941-65 [38]; Bible Christian ZC 1824-37 [22]; Calv Ind, West Street Z 1812-38 C 1835-38 [22]; Ebenezer Calv Meth, Union Street C 1825-37; Salem Part Bapt, Bond Street Z 1775-1837 B 1783-1834 [23]; Presb, Union Street

BRIGHTON (continued) ZC 1812-37 [22]; Wes Meth, Dorset Gardens C 1808-37 [22]; Chapel Royal Ext C 1820-21 [20]; Ind, Ship Street C 1700-1811 B 1800-22 [23]; Hanover Presb C 1826-38 [22]; Lady Hunt Conn, London Road C 1830-36 [22]; Lady Hunt Conn, North Street C 1781-1837 B 1813-14 [22]; Middle Street Synagogue M 1837-1913 [199]

BROADWATER C 1558-1839 M 1571-1842 B 1558-1831 [45/6]

BUNCTON see ASHINGTON

BURPHAM Ext C 1693 1703-4 M 1690 B 1703-4 1712 CMB(I) 1571-1754 [20,185]

BURTON Ext C 1583-1761 M 1750 B 1582-1780 [20]; Rom Cath (Burton House Chapel) C 1721-1865 M 1720-1823 B 1813-1858 [CRS22]

BURTON cum COATES B 1789-1812; Ext M 1880 B 1813-1854 [20]

BURWASH CB 1558-1698 M 1558-1827 B Ext 1560-1722 [47/8]; Ind Calv Cong ZC 1764-1835 [22]

BURY Ext C 1617-1676 M 1616-1788 B 1603-1761 CMB(I) 1700-1837 [20,185]

CATSFIELD C 1606-1852 M 1606-1838 B 1606-1837 [49]

CHAILEY C 1538-1842 M 1539-1837 B 1538-1822 [50]

CHALVINGTON C 1539-1812 M 1540-1834 B 1813-93 [37,158,165,187]

CHAPLE, NORTH see NORTHCHAPEL

CHICHESTER All Saints in the Palant CB 1563-1812 M 1564-1840 [18,187]; Mf C 1563-1812; Bishop's Palace Chapel C 1700-1722 M 1699-1754 [51]; St Andrew CB 1563-1812 M 1568-1840 [19,52-4]; St Bartholomew C 1571-1812 M 1573-1750 1832-40 B 1572-1812 [2,19,53]; Mf C 1571-1812; Cathedral C 1664-1747 M 1665-1747 B 1665-1751 [55]; St Martin C 1561-1813 M 1561-1840 B 1569-1812 [52/3,184,187]; St Olave CB 1569-1812 M 1569-1840 [19,52/3]; Mf C 1642-1812; St Pancras C 1559-1812 M 1559-1840 B 1558-1812 [16,19,53]; St Peter the Great, alias Sub-deanery C 1558-1756 M 1558-1754 1813-40 B 1558-1766 [18,53,55,184]; St Peter the Less CB 1587-1812 M 1587-1838 [19,52,187] (I) 1679-1812 [187]; Mf C 1679-1812; Bapt Chapel Eastgate C 1729-1808 [7];
Lady Hunt Conn, West Street C 1783-1837 [22]; Presb or Unit C 1730-1837 [22/3]; Wes Meth Circuit C 1831-37 [22/3]; Garrison Barracks C 1856-1984 [178]

CHIDDINGLEY CB 1605-1812 M 1605-1837 [37,164]

CHIDHAM CB 1625-1812 M 1625-1838 [56,164] Ext 1591-1725 [19,20]

CHILTINGTON, EAST M 1601-1812 [37]

CHILTINGTON, WEST Ext C 1733-59 M 1596 B 1626-1793 [20]

CHITHURST Ext C 1663-1775 M 1662-1733 B 1638-1780 [20]

CLAPHAM C 1571-1837 M 1572-1836 B 1572-1837 [20,57]

CLAYTON CB 1601-1840 M 1601-1837 [57]

CLIFFE (Lewes) 1606-58 M 1755-1837 [92,158]

CLIMPIMG Ext C 1632-1809 M 1635-1790 B 1635-1807 [20]

COCKING* CB 1558-1837 (M 1558-1837) [14/5,19,20,58,187]

COLD WALTHAM Ext C 1598-1798 M 1567-1828 B 1625-1773 [20]

COMPTON B 1813-1839 [189]

COOMBES M 1542-1812 [164]

COPTHORNE see HOATHLEY, WEST

COWDRAY Rom Cath (Cowdray House Chapel) C 1745-1837 M 1745-1822 B 1745-1830 [59,CRS1]

COWFOLD* CB (1558-1812) M (1558-1812)-40 [P,164]

CRAWLEY 1611-1839 Ext C 1653-1800 M 1688-1750 B 1676-1812 [11,177]

CROWHURST CB 1558-1757 M 1558-1752 1813-37 [60,154]

CUCKFIELD* (1598-1699) C 1700-1812 M 1813-37; Ext C 1659-1811 M 1606-1759 B 1671-1786 [P,20,158,189]; Ebenezer Chapel C 1833-96 M 1851-72 B 1834-85 [154]; Ind C 1821-37 [23]

DALLINGTON M 1813-42 [154]

DEAN, EAST (Chichester) 1571-1840 [61]

DEAN, EAST (Eastbourne) C 1559-1841 M 1558-1844 B 1559-1891 [20,62,162,165]

DEAN, WEST (Chichester) C 1559-1812 M 1559-1840 B 1554-1812 [1,19,20,164]

DEAN, WEST (Eastbourne) M Ext 1681-1752 B 1813-1894 [165,179]

DENTON C 1813-37 M 1754-1812 B 1813-94 [154,164/5]

DIDLING CB 1663-1730 M 1663-1745 [63] see also TREYFORD cum DIDLING

DITCHLING C 1557-1837 Z 1653-62 M 1556-1837 B 1556-1837 [60]; Gen Bapt C 1812-33 B 1821-1901 [64/5]

DUNCTON Ext C 1552-1696 M 1601-79 1754-1837 B 1551-1679 [19,187]

DURRINGTON 1753-1812 [13,19] Ext C 1609 1618 1627-1752 M 1627-1749 B 1626-1752 [19,P]

EARNLEY cum ALMODINGTON C 1562-1725 M 1562-1620 B 1562-1781 CMB(I) 1562-1812 [6,19,189]

EARTHAM M 1754-1840 [20,164]

EASEBOURNE CB 1770-80; Ext C 1634-1790 M 1633-1796 B 1641-1811 [20,66]; Rom Cath see COWDRAY

EASTBOURNE 1558-1837; Wes Meth C 1808-25 [20,23,67,164]

EASTERGATE Ext C 1742-1808 M 1670-1812 B 1699-1802 [20]

EDBURTON CB 1558-1812 M 1562-1812 [68/9]

EGDEAN Ext C 1634 1646-1861 M 1665-1753 B 1630 1670-1812 [20]

ELSTED Ext C 1630-93 M 1635-1805 B 1639-1786 [20]

ETCHINGHAM C 1561-1812 M 1561-1837 B 1561-1752 [14,153/4,162,176]

EWHURST CB 1754-1805 M 1632-40 1664-1837 [154,195]

FAIRLIGHT M 1651-1830 [195]

FALMER 1606-1840 [70]

FELPHAM C 1554-1812 M 1557-1838 B 1557-1812 [13,19,20,71,158,164] Mf C 1554-1875

FERNHURST C 1932-55 M 1932-64 [201]

FERRING CM 1559-1840 B 1558-1840 [20,72]

FINDON Ext C 1706-1763 M 1745-1768 B 1718-1772 [20]

FIRLE, WEST C 1606-1812 M 1607-1812 B 1606-1812 1813-94 [70,165]

FISHBOURNE, NEW CB 1589-1812 M 1589-1837 [19,164]

FITTLEWORTH Ext C 1564-1848 M 1585-1840 B 1561-1854 [20]

FLETCHING C 1653-1690 M 1551-1812 B 1653-1678 [70,178,189]

FOLKINGTON CB 1754-1882 M(I) 1754-1878 M Ext 1776-1973 [154,164]

FORD CB 1572-1900 M 1590-1898 [13,19,20,73,159,189]

FRAMFIELD CB 1687-1812 M 1687-1797 B Ext 1714-1866 [159,189]

FRANT C 1545-1812 M 1544-1812 B 1543-1812 [74/5]

FRISTON C 1547-1845 M 1547-1843 B 1547-1891 [163]

FUNTINGTON Ext C 1590-1641 1705-21 M 1590-1641 1667 1705-54 B 1590-1641 1667 1705-21 [76,178,180]

GLYNDE CB (1558-1812)-1840 M (1558-1812)-1836 C Ext 1839-1875 B Ext 1823-1888 [77,159]

GORING-BY-SEA 1560-1840 [9,19,20,199]

GRAFFHAM Ext C 1630-1794 M 1634-1811 B 1630-1809 [20,78]

GREATHAM see WIGGONHOLT cum GREATHAM

GRINSTEAD, EAST* CB (1558-1661)-1812 M (1558-1661)-1840 [P,79,80,163/4]; Lady Hunt Conn C 1812-37 [23]

GRINSTEAD, WEST Ext C 1710-1792 M 1708-1791 B 1708-1808 [20]

GUESTLING CB 1686-1812 M 1686-1837 [153,190]

GULDEFORD, EAST M 1606-1837 [163,195]

HAILSHAM CB 1558-1812 M 1558-1838 Z 1696-1702 [77,81/2,159,164]; Bapt C 1795-1837 [23]

HAMSEY 1583-1812 [77,159,190]

HANGLETON 1727-1851 M Ext 1615-1712 [179,190]

HARDHAM C 1642-1812 M 1688-1752 B 1662-1812 [83]; Ext CM 1592-1622 C 1682-1693 M 1724-1809 B 1592-1608 1737-1798 [19,20]

HARTFIELD CB 1696-1812 M 1696-1837 [155,164,190]

HARTING C 1567-90 CMB(I) 1567-1812 [84] Mf CB 1590-1812 M 1790-1753; Ind C 1827-37 [23]

HASTINGS All Saints CMB 1559-1749 C Ext 1559-1603 1692-1801 M 1559-1607 1636 1655-8 1683-4 1700-1801 Ext 1750-1801 B 1559-1590 Ext 1559-1602 1715-1798; St Andrew C(I) 1877-1970 M(I) 1871-1969; St Clement M 1677-1772; St Mary-in-the-Castle M 1828-37; Croft Chapel (Cong or Ind) C 1818-1854; Wes Meth C 1819-37 [23,85,159,190/1,195]

HEATHFIELD M 1581-1837 [77,155]

HEIGHTON, SOUTH M 1557-1749 [77]

HELLINGLY CB 1753-1808 M 1753-1812; Ind Burlow C 1835-37; Bapt ZC 1801-37; Ind Calv ZC 1830-37 [23,191]

HENFIELD M 1751-56 1800-10 [7]; Ind C 1832-37 [23,164]

HERSTMONCEUX M 1813-37 B 1813-93; Cong C 1812-37; Ind C 1812-37 [22,164/5]

HEYSHOTT Ext C 1650-1804 M 1605-1773 B 1663-1807 [20]

HOATHLY, EAST C 1813-37 M 1753-1812 B 1813-82 [164/5,191]

HOATHLY, WEST CB 1606-1752 M 1606-1812 [12,164,191]; Lady Hunt Conn ZC 1828-1837 [23]

HOLLINGTON C 1728-1812 M 1606-1813 B 1729-1812 [153,191]

HORSHAM* (1541-1635) [P,19] Mf Ind C 1776-1800; Bapt C 1628-1832 BD 1720-1837; Gen Bapt Z 1628-1836; Ind Z 1812-37 C 1776-1836 B 1827-36; Wes Meth C 1832-36 [22/3]

HORSTED KEYNES 1638-1837 [88/9]

HOUGHTON CB 1560-1837 M 1560-1839 [20,178]

HOVE* 1538-1812 [13,90]

HUNSTON CB 1583-1875 M 1583-1902 [183]

HURST GREEN Wes see ROBERTSBRIDGE

ICKLESHAM M 1670-1812 Ext C 1711-1809 M 1664-1798 B 1664-1834 [20,195]

IDEN M 1606-1837 [155,195]

IFIELD C 1568-1726 M 1568-1754 B 1569-1730 [14,191]

IFORD CM 1557-1836 B 1557-1883 [91,165]

IPING Ext C 1630-1810 M 1662-1810 B 1633-1812 [20] see also CHITHURST and ROGATE

ISFIELD CB 1570-1693 M 1571-1693 1754-1837 [155,159]

ITCHENOR Wes see CHICHESTER

ITCHINGFIELD M 1584-1837 Ext C 1700-1864 B 1700-1876 [19,192]

KEYMER 1601-1812 [160,192]

KINGSTON (Lewes) 1557-1654 CM(I) 1560-1778 B 1813-83 (I) 1560-1778 [91,187] KINGSTON BY SEA 1592-1838 [155]

KINGSTON (Ferring) C 1570-1660 M 1571-1658 B 1570-1672 [92]

KIRDFORD Ext C 1630-1779 M 1662-1736 B 1635-1783 [20]

LANCING Ext C 1632-1798 M 1639-1786 B 1611-1806 [20]

LAUGHTON C 1558-1838 M 1557-1838 B 1558-1891 [20,93,165]

LAVANT, EAST CB 1653-1812 M 1653-1733 Ext 1610-1618 C 1680-1792 M 1684-1753 B 1680-1808 [19,20,94]

LEWES All Saints M 1754-1837 Ext 1561-1694 C 1738-1809 M 1702-1758 B 1573-1778 [6,20,92,160]; St Anne 1679-1812 [95]; St John sub Castro 1602-1812 [97]; St Mary Westout see St Michael; St Michael C 1575-1812 M 1606-1642 1653-1812 B 1653-1812 [96,188]; St Peter Westout see St Anne; St Thomas see Cliffe ; Bethesda Chapel ZC 1817-1842 [92,188]; Westgate United Free Christian ZC 1742-1834 [92,188]; Bapt C 1779-1836 [23]; Lady Hunt Conn C 1808-37 [23]; Ind Tabernacle ZC 1817-39 [92,188]; Ind Calv C 1812-15 [23]; Ind Calv Refuge Z 1795-1815 C 1812-1815 [23]; Part Bapt Z 1775-1836 [23]; Wes Meth C 1808-37 [23];

LINCH C 1693 1701-1812 M 1706-1837 B 1706-1840 [20,98]

LINCHMERE 1558-1727 1742-1812 Ext C 1634-1640 1800-01 M 1787 [20,183]

LINDFIELD C 1558-1812 MB 1559-1812 [19,99]; Ind (Cong) Z 1799-1837 C 1815-1837 [23]

LITLINGTON C 1728-1812 M 1731-1835 B 1732-1894 [92,165]

LITTLEHAMPTON 1591-1753 Ext C 1688-1839 M 1735-1810 B 1688-1847 [19,20,100]; Wes see CHICHESTER

LODSWORTH C 1557-1866 M 1557-1897 B 1557-1902 [19,20,101/2,179,194]

LULLINGTON M 1813-1836 [164] see also ALFRISTON

LURGASHALL 1559-1840 [20,103/4,179]

LYMINSTER Ext C 1636-1800 M 1640-1780 B 1636-1775 [20]

LYNCH see LINCH

LYNCHMERE see LINCHMERE

MADEHURST 1572-1837 [20,179,192]

MALLING, SOUTH CB 1629-1812 M 1630-1755 [192]

MARDEN UP see UPMARDEN

MARDEN, NORTH CB 1590-1840 M 1594-1840 [105]

MARDEN, EAST CB 1571-1839 M 1584-1838 [105]

MARESFIELD CB 1806-12 M 1538-1758 [92,192]

MAYFIELD CB 1666-95 1739 M 1570-1837 [106,155]

MERSTON C 1587-1812 M 1587-1811 B 1593-1812 [155,179]

MIDDLETON Ext C 1636-1800 M 1640-1780 B 1636-1775 [20]

MIDHURST C 1565-1780 M 1565-1812 B 1565-1778
[4,20,156,179]; Ind Z 1783-1834 C 1789-1800 1803-
36 D 1808-24; Rom Cath see COWDRAY
MILLAND see TROTTON with TUXLITH
MOUNTFIELD M 1649-1837 [153]
MUNDHAM, NORTH CB 1558-1812 M 1559-1811
[107,156,160]
NEWHAVEN M 1553-1837 [157,188]; Lady Hunt Conn Z
1785-1827 C 1798-1832 [23]
NEWTIMBER 1558-1840 [21,160]
NORTHCHAPEL 1716-1837 [108,189]
NORTHIAM CB 1738-1812 M 1813-37 C(I) 1588-1812
[192,GCI]
NUTHURST CB 1559-1840 M 1562-1840 [11,106,173]
ORE M 1659-1837 [153]
OVING 1561-1670 Ext C 1754 M 1759-1796 B 1756-1811
[19,21,192]
OVINGDEAN 1704-1841 [160]
PAGHAM 1662-89 [110] Ext 1610 1618 C 1708-1783 M
1706-1841 B 1706-1840 [19,21]
PARHAM CB 1538-1840 M 1540-1834 [193]
PATCHAM 1558-1840 [111]
PATCHING Ext C 1645 M 1577-1783 B 1637-1684 [21]
PEASMARSH M 1608-1837 [153]
PENSHURST M 1577-1834 [153]
PETT M 1607-1837 [153]
PETWORTH 1559-1700 [112]; Ind (Cong) Z 1785-1837 C
1827-1837 [23]
PEVENSEY CM 1569-1837 B 1569-1891 [113,165]
PIDDINGHOE C 1540-1840 M 1555-1837 B 1592-1884
[114,166]
PLAYDEN C 1638-1837 M 1606-1837 B 1651-1837
[115,195] see also GULDEFORD, EAST
PLUMPTON CM 1558-1840 M 1814-1906 B 1558-1893
[106,116,166,193]
POLING 1665-42 [19,117] Ext C 1605-1805 M 1605-1760
B 1605-1808 [19,21]
PORTSLADE Ext C 1773-1799 M 1608-1839 B 1616-
1874 [179,181]
POYNINGS C 1559-1837 M 1559-1836 B 1559-1894
[193,195]
PRESTON C 1787-1840 M 1754-1840 B 1786-1840; Ext
1606-1812 [13,90,106] see also HOVE
PRESTON, EAST C 1573-1840 MB 1573-1837
[19,21,118,161]
PULBOROUGH 1595-1617 [12,193]
RACTON MB Ext 1684-5 [180]
RINGMERE M 1605-1837 [119]
RIPE B 1813-93 [166]
ROBERTSBRIDGE Wes C 1832-37 [157,195]
RODMELL M 1610-1812 B 1813-93 [106,166]
ROGATE Ext C 1685-1782 M 1641-1802 B 1633-1803
[21]
ROTHERFIELD C 1813-50 M 1539-1812 [120/1]; Bapt Z
1748-1836 [23]
ROTTINGDEAN C 1558-1841 M 1558-1838 B 1558-1840
[122,195]
RUDGWICK 1538-1812 [161]; Calv Ind see also
WISBOROUGH GREEN
RUMBOLDSWYKE 1613 1630-1812 [123]
RUSPER 1560-1812 [12,121]
RUSTINGTON C 1586-1840 M 1569-1837 B 1568-1837
Ext C 1856-89 [21,99]
RYE CM 1538-1635 B 1538-65 [124]; Bapt Z 1789-1836
[23]; Ind later Cong ZC 1819-1838 [22]; Part Bapt Z
1769-89 [23]; Wes Meth C 1795-1837 [22]
SALEHURST C 1575-1812 MB 1575-1837 Ext ZCB 1837-

1953 [125/6,188]
SEAFORD C 1559-1693 M 1559-1699 1813-37 B 1559-
1693 1813-92 [121,127,157,163,166]
SEDLESCOMBE C 1803-1812 M 1607-1838 B 1678-1725
1803-1812 [153,157,193]
SELE (or BEEDING) ExT C 1568-1840 M 1561-1827 B
1554-1891 [20]
SELHAM C 1565-1840 M 1566-1839 B 1566-1840
[21,128]
SELMESTON C 1813-40 M 1756-1840 B 1813-93
[121,166] C Ext 1817-1851 [161]
SELSEY CM 1584-1796 B 1584-1862 [19,129,166]
SHIPLEY M 1754-1812 [121] Ext C 1609-1742 M 1613-
1753 B 1639-1770 [21]
SHOREHAM, NEW C 1564-1837 M 1565-1837 B 1567-
1837 [21,179,199]; Lady Hunt Conn (later Ind) Z
1798-1837 C 1802-1837 [23]
SHOREHAM, OLD C 1566-1837 M 1565-1837 B 1566-
1663 1671-1837 [21,163,197]
SIDLESHAM CB 1566-1812 M 1567-1812 [19,130,157]
Mf C 1566-1812; Wes see CHICHESTER
SINGLETON CM 1558-1840 B 1559-1840 [14,131,179]
SLAUGHAM Ext 1654-1780 [12] Mf C 1654-1876 M
1654-1875 B 1654-1880
SLINDON Ext C 1686-1761 M 1749 1768 B 1715-1812
[21]; Rom Cath (Slindon House Chapel & St
Richard's) C 1698-1868 M 1739-1855 B 1753-1874
[CRS7]
SLINFOLD 1556-1714 Ext 1558-1812; Hayes Ind C 1813-
27 [11,23]
SOUTHEASE B 1813-93 [166]
SOUTHOVER M 1559-1812 [121]
SOUTHWICK M 1725-1741 Ext C 1654-1869 M 1681-
1888 B 1659-1891 [21]
STANMER 1663-1754 C 1813-1900 [193]
STAPLECROSS in EWHURST Wes ZC 1832-37 [157]
STEDHAM Ext C 1637-1755 M 1727-1748 B 1668-1778
[21]
STEYNING 1565-1925 [21,132-4]
STOKE, NORTH C 1565-1812 MB 1566-1812 [21,135]
STOKE, SOUTH CB 1553-1812 M 1553-1839
[21,135,164]
STOKE, WEST C 1560-1812 M 1564-1841 B 1554-1812
[19,164,180] Mf C 1560-1812
STOPHAM C 1544-1803 M 1544-1765 B 1545-1802
[19,21,136-8]
STORRINGTON 1549-1837 [21,171/2]
STOUGHTON Ext 1592-1611 1625-71 [19,117,180]
STREAT B 1813-1908 [166]
SULLINGTON M 1555-1700 [1878]
SUTTON CM 1813-1837 B 1813-1871 [193] Ext 1592-
1622 1633 C 1635-1805 M 1637-1807 B 1639-1795
[19,21]
TANGMERE CB 1538-1812 M 1539-1837 [19,139,164]
TARRING, WEST 1540-1743 [141]
TARRING NEVILLE M 1571-1812 B 1813-94 [140,166]
TELSCOMBE C 1684-1840 M 1701-1840 B 1697-1840
[161]
TERWICK C 1813-1837 B 1813-1883 [193]
THAKEHAM Ext C 1630-1771 M 1611-1809 B 1630-1807
[21]
TICEHURST C 1559-1837 M 1559-1840 B 1559-1843
[140,142-4,195]
TILLINGTON Ext C 1572-1810 M 1572-1841 B 1572-
1857 [14,21]
TORTINGTON Ext C 1576-1711 M 1614-1780 B 1570-
1809 [21]

TREYFORD cum DIDLING C 1573 1632-1725 M 1573 1687-1745 B 1573 1632-1740 [19,21,145]
TROTTON with TUXLITH Ext C 1614-1790 M 1664-1799 B 1592-1803 [21]
TURNER'S HILL (Worth) see HOATHLY, WEST
TUXLITH see TROTTON
TWINEHAM 1606-1840 [170,GCI]
UCKFIELD Rockhall Bapt Z 1783-1836 [23]
UDIMORE C 1560-1840 M 1560-1837 B 1559-1893 [140,153,161,166,GCI]
UPMARDEN Ext 1594-1618 [19]
UP WALTHAM 1601-18 C 1750-1800 M 1640-1812 B 1698-1805 Ext 1554-1790 [19,21,148]
WADHURST Part Bapt Z 1812-1836 B 1832-1836 [23]
WALBERTON C 1556-1850 M 1558-1849 B 1558-1850 [3,19,21,146/7,GCI]
WALDRON CM 1564-1851 B 1564-1857 [200]
WARBLINGTON cum EMSWORTH M 1644-1930 [123]
WARMINGHURST 1716-54 [13] Ext C 1637-1790 M 1633-1796 B 1630-1787 [21]
WARNHAM CM 1558-1812 B 1558-1870 [14,149,164]
WARNING CAMP M Ext 1633-1640 [179]
WARTLING B 1813-94 [166]
WASHINGTON Ext C 1566-1812 M 1565-1803 B 1567-1808 [21]
WEPHAM see BURPHAM
WESTBOURNE Ext C 1634-1801 M 1637-1796 B 1634-1800[21]
WESTFIELD M 1552-1837 [153]
WESTHAM 1571-1812 B 1813-79 [166,174]
WESTHAMPNETT CB(I) 1584-1881 M(I) 1604-1880 [198]
WESTMESTON B 1813-94 1908 [166]
WHATLINGTON M 1640-1837 [153]
WIGGONHOLT cum GREATHAM CM 1583-1840 B 1583-1883 [21,186,178,193,198]
WILLINGDON 1560-1840 B 1840-94 [140,150,188]
WILMINGTON C 1616-1890 M 1599-1836 B 1616-1885 [161,167,193]
WINCHELSEA M 1606-1837 [12,21,153]
WISBOROUGH GREEN Ext 1560-1812 [12,21]; Bapt Ext 1826-1836; Ind C 1822-1825; Calv Ind C 1826-36 [22/3,65]
WITHYHAM M 1606-1754 [164]
WITTERING, EAST 1590-91 C 1625-1812 M 1625-1840 B 1625-1908 [7,117,164,166]; Ext 1571-1614 [19]
WITTERING, WEST Ext 1538-1618 [19]; C 1621-1812 M 1621-1840 B 1621-1909 [7,19,164,166]
WIVELSFIELD C 1559-1659 M 1559-1666 B 1559-1660; Bapt C 1771-1836 B 1785-92; Lady Hunt Conn ZC 1789-1831 C 1830-1836; Part Bapt Z 1771-1836 [22,65,140]
WOODMANCOTE* 1582-1812 [151]
WOOLAVINGTON Ext M 1665-1779 B 1639-1801 [21]
WOOLBEDING Ext 1592-1622 C 1667 1680-1747 M 1684-1811 B 1670-1808 [21]
WORTH C 1558-1840 MB 1559-1840 [11,105,152]
WORTHING Ind Chapel Street ZC 1808-1837 [23]
YAPTON Ext C 1611-1810 M 1611-1801 B 1611-1807 [21]

WARWICKSHIRE

ALDESTREY see AUSTREY
ALLESLEY C 1569-1845 Z 1701-12 M 1562-1863 B 1561-1863 [5,6,51]
ALNE, GREAT CB 1704-11 1748-50 M 1704-11 1748-53 [3] Mf 1616-1700
ALVESTON Mf CB 1539-1812 M 1539-1814
ANST(E)Y M(I) 1591-1812 M 1813-1837 [4,38,GCI] Mf C 1589-1880 M 1589-1837 B 1589-1930
ARLEY Mf C 1557-1641 1663-1767
ASTON Birmingham C 1544-1741 1829-31 1840-42 M 1544-1744 B 1544-1741 [7,8,50]
ATHERSTONE ON STOUR M(I) 1611-1813 M 1813-37 [4,37/8,GCI]
AUSTREY C 1558-1760 M 1558-1753 B 1558-1768 [9] Mf 1672-1809
AVON DASSETT Mf 1559-1799
BAGINTON M 1813-37 [4]
BALSALL C 1828-33
BARCHESTON Mf Banns 1823-1884
BARFORD Mf CB 1538-1799 M 1538-1812
BARMINGTON M 1585-1812 [3]
BARTON ON THE HEATH* M 1577-1810 [40] Mf C 1575-1812 M 1577-1836 B 1580-1809
BAXTERLEY MB 1662-74
BEARLEY Mf Banns 1823-80 M 1839-1879
BEAUDESERT 1607-1837 [WA/L5] Mf ZC 1774-1793
BIDFORD ON AVON M 1813-37 [4] Mf 1612-1876
BILTON, NEW Mf M 1868-1910
BINLEY Coventry M 1800-37 [4] Mf C 1873-1920 M 1874-1946 B 1873-1934
BINTON Mf C 1540-1903 M 1540-1892 B 1608-1700 1802-1812
BIR(DING)BURY M 1813-36 [4] Mf C 1559-1977 M 1559-1836 B 1559-1812
BIRDINGTON see MARTON and BIRDINGTON
BIRMINGHAM St Martin C 1554-1708 M 1554-1706 B 1554-1704 [10,42] Mf C 1708-1839 M 1708-1839 B 1708-1837; St Philip M 1715-1800 [11] Mfc M 1715-1800; Rom Cath St Peter C 1657-1824 M 1658-1804 B 1657-1792 [39,40]; St Stephen Mf C 1844-1876; St Mary's Chapel,Whittal Street CB 1774-1779; Old Cannon Street Cong M 1837-1858 [51]
BISHOPS TACHBROOKE* M 1538-1812 [40] Mf C 1538-1812 M 1538-1806 B 1538-1802
BISHOPTON Mf 1609-1700
BOURTON ON DUNSMORE with FRANKTON Mf CM 1560-1812 B 1560-1796
BOURTON ON DUNSMORE M(I) 1560-1812 [37/8,GCI]
BRAILES Mf Banns 1823-76
BRINKLOW M 1750-99 [4] Mf C 1558-1812
BROWNSOVER Mf CB 1593-1812 M 1596-1837
BUBBENHALL Mf C 1559-1598 1662-1914 M 1738-1836 B 1738-1812
BULKINGTON Mf CMB 1660-1809 C 1775-1861 M 1754-1876 B 1775-1812
BURMINGTON Mf C 1711-1812 M 1583-1680 1816-34
BURTON HASTINGS Mf C 1574-1938 M 1574-1834 B 1574-1812
BURTON DASSETT Mf CMB 1668-1805 C 1813-1876 M 1754-1837 B 1813-1871
BUTLERS MARSTON M & M(I) 1538-1812 [37/8,GCI]
CALDECOTE Mf C 1876-1961 M 1839-1954 B 1813-1961
CHADSHUNT Mf Banns 1881-1922 also see GAYDON

CHARLECOTE* M 1543-1812 [40,GCI] Mf C 1874-1910
    M 1837-1978 B 1813-1978
CHERINGTON Mf C 1561-1894 M 1561-1837 1886-1978
    B 1561-1979
CHESTERTON CB 1538-1812 M 1538-1837
CHILVERS COTON Mf C 1654-1878 M 1654-1876 B
    1654-1878
CHURCHOVER Mf C 1658-1670 1721-1756 M 1849-59
CLIFFORD CHAMBERS CB 1538-1837 M 1816-1836
    [3,4]
CLIFTON-ON-DUNSMORE CB 1594-1855 M 1594-1837
    [54] Mf C 1594-1876 M 1594-1837 B 1594-1882
COLESHILL Mf 1538-1704
COMBROKE Mf C 1803-1881 M 1832-37
COMPTON WYNATES Mf M 1856-1935
COMPTON VERNEY Mf B 1880-1923
COMPTON, LONG M(I) 1608-1812 [37/8,GCI]; Private
    chapel of Sir Wm Sheldon of WESTON C 1763-1784
COMPTON, LITTLE C 1588-1985 M 1589-1643 1656
    1698 1773-1984 B 1588-1984 [45]
CORLEY MB 1662-1674 [51] Mf CMB 1653-1686 C 1876-
    1942 M 1838-1948 B 1888-1932
COUGHTON Mf CB 1673-1736 M 1673-1768
COVENTRY St Michael 1640-1742 [12,43,49,91]; Holy
    Trinity 1561-1653 [44,48] Mf C 1561-1904 MB 1561-
    1848; St Thomas Mf C 1898-1913
CUBBINGTON C 1606-1840 M 1590-1840 B 1559-1840
    [13] Mf C 1875-1914 M 1876-1926 B 1875-1903
CURDWORTH Mf M 1875-1936
DUNCHURCH Mf CMB 1538-1748 CM 1748-1876 B
    1748-1812
EDGBASTON 1636-1812 M 1813-1837 [P,53,55]
ELMDON 1742-1846 [14]
ETTINGTON M(I) 1623-1812 [37/8,GCI]
EXHALL SAINT GILES Coventry M 1803-37 [4]
EXHALL and WIXFORD Mf 1540-1812
FARNBOROUGH Mf C 1558-1883 M 1558-1841 B 1558-
    1812
FENNY COMPTON M(I) 1627-1812 [37/8,GCI] Mf C
    1627-1876 M 1627-1846 B 1702-45 1809-1882
FILLONGLEY Mf 1813-1846
FOLESHILL Mf C 1554-1876 MB 1565-1877
FOXCOTE Rom Cath C 1765-1801 [15,50]
FRANKTON Mf C 1813-1949 MB 1813-59 Banns 1824-
    1963 see also BOURTON ON DUNSMORE
GAYDON Mf 1873-1930; GAYDON and CHADSHUNT M
    1754-1837
GRANDBOROUGH Mf CB 1581-1982 M 1581-1837
    Banns 1824-1959
GREAT PACKINGTON see PACKINGTON, GREAT
GRENDON Mf CMB 1567-1666 C 1766-1918 M 1754-
    1940 B 1567-1899
HALFORD* M 1552-1812 [40,GCI] Mf C 1874-1912 M
    1813-35
HAMPTON LUCY Mf 1559-1812
HAMPTON IN ARDEN C 1590-1732 MB 1599-1732 [2]
    Mf C 1813-48
HARBOROUGH MAGNA Mf 1540-1838
HASELEY 1588-1633 [1] Mf CM 1743-1876 B 1743-1879
HATTON* CB 1538-1663 M 1538-(1558-1812) [1,40]
HENLEY IN ARDEN 1546-1700 [36]
HILLMORTON Mf 1813-1873
HOCKLEY (Birmingham) CB 1823-37 M 1830-37 [20]
HONEYBOURNE C 1614-1639 M 1611-1639 B 1625-6
    [3]
HONILEY Mf C 1745-1812 1814-1835 M 1745-1835 B
    1814-1835

HONINGTON M(I) 1571-1812 [37/8,GCI]
HUNNINGHAM Mf C 1717-1878 MB 1717-1812
IDLICOTE M(I) 1557-1812 [37/8,GCI]
ILMINGTON Mf M 1813-1837
KENILWORTH Mf C 1630-1876 M 1630-53 1754-1880 B
    1630-84 1715-1878
KINETON Mf C 1546-1876 M 1546-1877 B 1546-1886
KINWARTON 1566-1723 [17] Mf 1639-1700
KNOWLE 1682-1812 (I) 1682-1912 [18]
LADBROKE Mf C 1559-1879 M 1560-1837 Banns 1823-
    1877
LEA MARSTON MB 1662-74
LEAMINGTON PRIORS M(I) 1704-1812 [37/8,GCI] Mf C
    1618-1901 M 1618-1842 B 1618-1842
LEAMINGTON HASTINGS Mf C 1559-1877 M 1559-1837
    B 1559-1811 1813 -1886
LIGHTHORNE Mf C 1538-1885 M 1538-1837 B 1538-
    1812
LILLINGTON C 1540-70 1643-1645 M 1541-70 1643
    1647 1658 B 1539-1570 1644 [51] Mf C 1539-1885
    M 1539-1877 B 1539-1878
LITTLE PACKINGTON see PACKINGTON, LITTLE
LONG COMPTON see COMPTON, LONG
LOWER SHUCKBURGH see SHUCKBURGH, LOWER
LOXLEY Mf C 1540-1803 M 1540-1837 B 1540-1812
MARTON and BIRDINGTON Mf M 1660-1812 B 1559-
    1812
MARTON M 1813-35 [4] Mf C 1813-1876
MEREVALE M 1813-1837 [4]
MERIDEN Mf 1687-1876
MIDDLETON Mf C 1677-1899 M 1681-1899 B 1675-1894
MILVERTON Mf 1742-1812
MONKS KIRBY Mf 1649-1877 M 1653-1876 B 1653-1877
MORETON MORRELL M 1692-1750 1772-1837 B 1678-
    1813 [51] Mf C 1678-1877 M 1678-1836 B 1678-
    1812
MORTON BAGOT Mf C 1664-1812 M 1678-1857 B 1664-
    1786
NAPTON M 1813-33 [4]
NAPTON-ON-THE-HILL Mf 1813-1846
NETHER WHITACRE Mf 1813-1845 C 1869-1922
NEW BILTON see BILTON,NEW
NEWBOLD PACEY Mf C 1554-1877 M 1554-1883 B
    1554-1812
NEWBOLD ON AVON Mf CM 1559-1876 B 1559-1882
NEWBOLD ON STOUR C 1838-1900 M 1839-1920 B
    1836-1899 [51]
NEWTON REGIS Mf C 1591-1875 M 1591-1836 B 1591-
    1812
NORTON LINDSEY Mf CB 1742-1812 M 1742-1837
OSCOTT Rom Cath C 1760-66 [CRS13]
OVER WHITACRE Mf CMB 1568-1624 (fragments) C
    1653-1910 M 1653-1787 1815-1836 Banns 1824-
    1916 B 1653-1953
OXHILL Mf C 1572-1881 M 1572-1837 B 1572-1812
PACKINGTON, LITTLE Mf C 1629-1964 M 1629-1937 B
    1629-1967
PACKINGTON, GREAT Mf C 1528-1948 M 1538-1933
    Banns 1824-1959 B 1538-1846
PILLERTON PRIORS Mf 1613-1667
PILLERTON HERSEY Mf C 1611-1700 1873-1914 M
    1611-1700 Banns 1824-1879 B 1611-1700
POLESWORTH Mf C 1631-1905 M 1631-1902 B 1631-
    1947
PRESTON BAGOT Mf CMB 1612-1700 C 1612-1973 M
    1612-1836 1839-1959 B 1612-1797 1813-1971
PRIORS HARDWICK M(I) 1662-1812 [37/8,GCI]

RADWAY 1605-1701 [3] Mf C 1813-1877 M 1813-1837
Banns 1823-76 B 1813-1879
RATLEY Mf 1701-1812
ROWINGTON 1612-1812 [19]
RUGBY St Andrew CB 1755-1815 M 1754-1837 [4,52] Mf
M 1754-1876
RYTON ON DUNSMORE Mf C 1539-1864 M 1539-1837
B 1539-1879
SHELDON C 1558-1839 M 1558-1858 B 1558-1841 [20]
SHERBOURN with FULBROOK Mf C 1587-1810 1813-
1879 M 1587-1785 B 1567-1810
SHERBOURN Mf C 1621-1876 MB 1621-1812
SHILTON Mf C 1695-1871 M 1695-1837 Banns 1754-
1928 B 1695-1879
SHOTTESWELL Mf C 1564-1880 MB 1564-1846
SHUCKBURGH, LOWER Mf C 1800-1846 M 1800-1846
B 1813-1846
SHUSTOKE Mf 1813-1843
SHUTTINGTON CB 1557-1812 M 1557-1837 [22] Mf
1557-1838
SNITTERFIELD* M 1561-1812 [40] Mf Banns 1864-78
SOLIHULL 1538-1668 [23]
SOUTHAM C 1539-1809 M 1539-1812 B 1539-1808
[2,24/5,52]
SPERNALL Mf C 1562-1812 M 1562-1836
STIVICHALL Mf 1813-1844
STOCKINGFORD Mf 1824-1844
STOCKTON Mf C 1871-1875
STOKE Mf 1809-63
STONELEIGH Mf C 1634-1876 M 1634-1879 B 1634-
1877
STRATFORD UPON AVON C 1558-1652 M 1558-1812
[26,27,28] Mf M 1558-1812
STRETTON-ON-DUNSMORE Mf CB 1681-1783 M 1681-
1730 1742-1753
SUTTON UNDER BRAILES M 1578-1837 [GL/R66,91] Mf
C 1605-1812 M 1605-1837 B 1715-1812
SUTTON COLDFIELD C 1565/6-99 M 1565/6-98 B 1565-
99 [52]
TACHBROOK Mf C 1847-1877 M 1837-1876
TANWORTH IN ARDEN 1558-1924 [29]
TEMPLE GRAFTON M(I) 1612-1812 [37/8,GCI] Mf C
1759-1804 1875-1879 M 1754-1812 1873-1827
Banns 1876-1939 B 1759-1804 1875-1931
TREDINGTON Mf C 1781-1838
TYSOE 1575-1837 [30]
UFTON 1660-1709 [3]
ULLENHALL 1546-1700 [36]
WALSGRAVE ON SOWE Mf C 1558-1876 M 1558-1749
1754-1876 B 1558-1797 1813-1877
WAPPENBURY Mf CB 1753-1812 M 1754-1837
WARMINGTON Mf Banns 1824-1829
WARWICK All Saints Mf C 1872-1876; St Mary 1611-39
[3]; St Nicholas Mf C 1695-1861 M 1695-1802 (gap)
B 1652-1811
WASPERTON 1538-1837 [20] Mf Banns 1826-1877
WEDDINGTON 1663-1812 [32] Mf C 1663-1876 M 1663-
1864 B 1663-1705
WEETHLEY Mf CB 1813-1979 M 1847-1976
WELLESBOURNE Mf C 1560-1897 M 1560-1878 Banns
1820-1938 B 1560-1931
WESTON UNDER WETHERLEY Mf C 1780-1982 M
1754-1984 B 1780-1984
WESTON ON AVON Mf CB 1686-1813 M 1686-1941
WESTWOOD Mf C 1895-1947 M 1875-1940 B 1873-1933
WHATCOTE Mf CB 1572-1810 C 1813-1978 M 1572-
1837 B 1813-1980

WHITACRE, NETHER see NETHER WHITACRE
WHITACRE, OVER see OVER WHITACRE
WHITCHURCH M(I) 1562-1812 [37/8,GCI]
WHITNASH Mf C 1813-1871
WILLEY Mf CM 1661-1844 B 1661-1766 1813-1844
WILLOUGHBY CB 1625-1793 M 1625-1753 [52] Mf C
1794-1877 M 1754-1862 B 1794-1878
WISHAW Mf 1815-1832
WITHYBROOK Mf C 1653-1879 M 1653-1836 B 1653-
1782 1809-1832
WIXFORD see EXHALL
WOLFHAMPCOTE 1558-1768 [34,46]
WOLFORD Mf C 1656-1877 M 1656-1837 B 1656-1878
WOLSTON Mf CM 1665-1876 B 1665-1855
WOLVEY Mf C 1653-1907 M 1653-1943 Banns 1816-
1948 B 1653-1937
WOOTTON WAWEN (1546-1700) [36]: Rom Cath C
1765-1819 M 1786-1809 [35,CRS2]
WORMLEIGHTON Mf C 1586-1875 M 1586-1837 B 1642-
1812
WROXALL Mf CB 1587-1643 1664-1812 M 1587-1643
1664-1730 1756-1898
WYKEN Mf 1662-1809 B 1813-1911

WESTMORLAND

APPLEBY M 1665-1690 [P]; Grammar School Irregular M
1729-1790 [P]
APPLETHWAITE B 1857-1934 [31]
ASBY C(I) 1657-1798 M(I) 1657-1776 B(I) 1657-1784 [1]
ASKHAM* 1566-1812 [2]
BAMPTON* C 1650-1812 MB 1637-1812 [3]
BARTON* CM 1666-1830 B 1666-1830 [4] Mf CM 1666-
1812 B 1666-1830
BOLTON* C 1647-1812 M 1665-1812 B 1663-1812 [5]
Mf C 1813-1879
BROUGH under STAINMORE* C 1559-1812 M 1560-
1812 B 1556-1812 [6,30]
BROUGHAM* 1645-1812 [7] Mf C 1813-1877
BURTON CB 1653-1726 M 1654-1725 [8]
CLIBURN* 1565-1812 [9]
CROSBY GARRETT* C 1569-1812 MB 1559-1812 [10]
CROSBY RAVENSWORTH* CB 1568-1812 M 1569-1812
[11]
CROSTHWAITE cum LYTH* C 1569-1812 M 1570-1812
B 1568-1812 [12] Mf C 1813-1871
DUFTON 1571-1837 [13] Mf 1571-1837
GRASMERE M 1813-1818 [P]
KENDAL* (C 1558-1631 M 1557-1631 B 1555-1631)
[14,15] Mf C 1558-1631 M 1557-1631 B 1555-1631;
Rom Cath C 1762-1840 [CRS32]; Inghamite C 1756-
1837 B 1779-1855 [YK/R196]; Presb Market Place
Chapel ZC 1687-1843 B 1756-1855 [L4]; Unit Bapt
Z 1801-1839 [L4]; see also CROSTHWAITE cum
LYTH
KENTMERE M 1700-1812 [P]
LOWTHER* CB 1540-1812 M 1539-1812 [16]
LYTH see CROSTHWAITE cum LYTH
MALLERSTANG C 1714-1839 B 1813-1839 [17]
MARTINDALE* C 1633-1853 M 1636-1871 B 1683-1904
[18]
MARTON, LONG CB 1586-1837 M 1588-1837 [19]
MIDDLETON in LONSDALE* C 1670-1812 M 1677-1812
B 1671-1812 [20]

MILBURN* CB 1678-1812 M 1679-1812 [21]
MORLAND* CB 1538-1743 M 1538-1742 [22]
NEWBIGGEN* 1571-1812 [23]
ORMSIDE Mf ZC 1762-1864
PATTERDALE Mf ZC 1746-1872
PRESTON PATRICK CM 1704-1714 B 1703-15 [8] Mf
1704-1800 see also BURTON
RAVENSTONEDALE CB 1571-1812 M 1577-1812 [25-
27]; Cong C 1811-1837 B 1817-1833 [27]; Diss ZC
1735-1809 [27]; Presb C 1775-1809 B 1776-1813
[27]; SFrs Z 1655-1821 M 1656-1834 B 1659-18396
[27]
SELSIDE Chapel 1753-1812 [31] see also KENDAL
SHAP* 1559-1830 [28]
TEMPLE SOWERBY M 1700-1755 [P] Mf ZC 1774-1776
1813-1875
WARCOP* 1597-1744 [29]
WINSTER Ext 1720-1881 [31]

WILTSHIRE

ALDBOURNE CB 1637-1836 M 1608-15 1608-1837
[89,90,96]
ALDERBURY M 1800-1837 [96]
ALDERTON* M (1606-1812)-1837 [69,87,96]
ALLCANNINGS* (1578-1812) M 1813-37 [9,59]
ALLINGTON* M 1623-1837 [71,87]
ALTON BARNES* C 1592-1782 M (1597-1812)-38 B
1602-1782 [10,74,87]
ALTON PRIORS CB 1664-1812 M 1605-78 1702-1838 (I)
1605-1838 [11,87,96]
ALVEDISTON M 1594-1837 [59,87]
AMESBURY C 1624-39 1813-76 M 1599-1837 B 1610-39
[1,59,96]
ANSTY M 1655-1838 [87]
ASHLEY* M 1607-32 (1658-1812)-37 [59,71,96]
ASHTON KEYNES CB 1582-1840 M 1583-1840 [12];
Leigh Chapelry M 1605-1753 [65]
ATWORTH M 1585-1637 1800-37 [96]
AVEBURY M 1612-1837 (I) 1607-1837 [59,96]; Diss
1696-1702 [101]
BARFORD ST MARTIN M 1623-37 [96]
BAVERSTOCK* M (1559-1812)-34 [59,73]
BAYDON M 1578-1696 1754-1837 [59,96]
BEDWIN, GREAT M 1585-1837 [59]
BEDWYN, LITTLE M 1610-1726 1754-1837 [96,106]
BEECHINGSTOKE* C 1566-1837 M (1590-1812)-37
[76,87,96,116]
BEMERTON M 1631-1837 [100]
BERWICK BASSETT CB 1674-99 M 1580-1627
1674-1837 (I) [59,84,96] Mf ZC 1775-1875
BERWICK ST LEONARD M 1626-36 1724-1839 [96,106]
BERWICK ST JAMES M 1609-1837 [96]
BERWICK ST JOHN M (I) 1559-1837 [3,59]
BIDDESTONE 1605-80 M (I) 1688-1837 [84,96]
BISHOPS CANNINGS 1591-1812 M 1813-1837
[59,96,118]
BISHOPSTONE (Salisbury) M 1606-1842 [60,96]
BISHOPSTONE (Swindon) M 1573-1837 [60]
BISHOPSTROW C 1686-1890 M 1611-1837 B 1686-1812
[8,60,96,113]
BLACKLAND M 1594-1740 [96]
BLUNSDON ST ANDREW C 1650-1840 M 1655-1840 B
1656-1840 [84]

BLUNSDON BROAD CB 1585-1677 M 1585-1672 [84]
BOSCOMBE* M (1625-1812)-40 [71,87]
BOWERCHALKE M 1701-1837 (I) 1608-1837 [60]
BOX M 1538-1837 [96]
BOYTON* CB 1561-1810 (M 1560-1837) [80,100,101]
BRADFORD ON AVON M 1566-77 1579-1799 1800-37
[60,87,113]; see also WINSLEY
BRADLEY, NORTH C Ext 1603-1638 C 1667-1837
[109,111]
BRAMSHAW M 1597-1836 [60]
BRATTON* C 1542-50 (M 1542-1837) [3,80,100]
BREMHILL M 1597-1837 [60]
BREMHILLHAM M 1813-35 [60]
BRINKWORTH* M 1605-(1653-1812)-1837 [61,73]
BRITFORD* C 1587-1842 M (1573-1812)-1837 B
1572-1842 [15,61,71]
BRIXTON DEVERILL M 1655-1798 1800-38 [61,71]
BROAD BLUNSDON C 1679-1840 M 1585-1840 (I)
1585-1684 [14,100]
BROAD CHALKE 1538-1780 M 1781-1837 [16,61]
BROAD HINTON M 1800-37 [61]
BROKENBOROUGH M (I) 1609-1745 [96]
BROMHAM M 1560-1837 [61]
BROUGHTON GIFFORD M 1622-37 1800-37 (I)
1667-1837 [61,96]
BULFORD* M (1608-1812)-1837 [71,87]
BURBAGE M 1561-1837 [87]
BURCOMBE C 1662-1713 M 1611-1837 (I) 1612-1837
[3,61,96]
BUTTERMERE M 1786-1804 1813-42 [87,96]
CALSTONE WELLINGTON M 1760-1837 (I) 1605-1837
[62]
CASTLE EATON* C 1549-1840 M (1549-1812)-40 [74,84]
CHALFIELD, GREAT M 1813-48 [96]
CHARLTON (Malmesbury) M 1607-09 1620-35 1661-
1812 1828-1837 [108]
CHARLTON (Pewsey)* C 1611-1837 M (1696-1812)-
1838 [62,75,116]
CHERHILL M 1690-1837 [62,96]
CHERINGTON see CHIRTON
CHEVERELL, GREAT C 1622-1837 M 1622-1637 1653-
1837 B 1622-37 1653-1812 [93,100,116]
CHEVERELL, LITTLE C 1623-37 1647 1649 1653-1812 M
1623-26 1654-1837 B 1622-35 1654-1812
[62,93,100]
CHICKLADE M 1722-1837 [96,108]
CHILMARK M 1611-1837 [62]
CHILTON FOLIAT M 1706-1837 [62,108]
CHIPPENHAM M 1578-1611 1619-1632 1653-1687 1800-
1837 [62,100,108]
CHIRTON* M (1588-1812)-1837 [62,74]
CHISLEDON/CHISELDON* C 1605-1842 M (1641-1812)-
1837 B 1606-1837 [62,76,111,116]
CHITTERNE ALL STS CB 1653-1862 M 1654-1862
[62,92]
CHITTERNE ST MARY CB 1653-1862 M 1654-1862 (I)
1608-1838 [62,92]
CHITTOE ZC Mf 1846-75
CHOLDERTON* M (1608-1812) 1814-39 [62,75]
CHRISTIAN MALFORD* M (1653-1812)-1837 (I) 1605-35
1653-1837 [62,78]
CHUTE M 1582-1837 [62]
CLEVERTON see LEA
CLYFFE PYPARD* M 1576-1837 [78,96]
CODFORD ST MARY M 1800-1837 [62]
CODFORD ST PETER C 1621-1900 M 1620-1837 B
1597-1840 [17,106]

COLERNE* M (1560-1575)-1639 (1640-1652)-1660 (1661-1812)-1837 [62,72,73]
COLLINGBOURNE DUCIS * M 1654-1837 [80,100]
COLLINGBOURNE KINGSTON M 1606-1837 [63,108]
COMPTON BASSETT M 1559-1753 1800-1837 [63,97]
COMPTON CHAMBERLAIN M 1800-1837 [63]
COOMBE BISSETT 1636-1840 [7]
CORSHAM M 1748-1766 1775-1837 [63,108]
CORSLEY, GREAT CB 1608-1803 M 1608-1816 (I) 1800-1837 [3,8,63,87,108]
COULSTON, EAST M 1714-51 1800-1837 [63]
CRICKLADE ST MARY C 1684-1840 M 1686-1837 B 1683-1840 [7]
CRICKLADE ST SAMPSON C 1672-1840 M 1695-1839 B 1695-1840 [7]
CRUDWELL* M (1662-1812)-1837 (I) 1605-1837 [71,63]
DAUNTSEY C 1672-1702 M 1665-1837 (I) 1605-1837 B 1776-1812 [63,101]
DEVIZES* St John (M 1559-1837) [79,100]; St Mary M 1740-47 1800-1837 [63,100]
DILTON C 1652 1718-19 M 1585-1647 1654 1662-1755 B 1670-74 1687-88 [103]; Chapel M 1754-1837 [108]
DINTON M (I) 1754-1838 [63,97]
DITTERIDGE C 1584-1840 M 1589-1838 B 1587-1840 [7,18]
DONHEAD ST ANDREW M 1622-1837 [97]
DONHEAD ST MARY 1622-1841 [63,83]
DOWNTON M 1800-1837 B 1813-39 [63,101]
DRAYCOT CERNE M 1607-1679 1692-1837 [63,108] Mf ZC 1813-75
DURNFORD CB 1574-1812 M 1574-1836 (I) 1574-1837 [2,19-21,63]
DURRINGTON* M (1591-1812)-1837 [63,70]
EASTON C 1580-1812 M 1582-1835 B 1583-1812 [22]
EASTON GREY M 1725-1838 [64,97]
EASTON ROYAL M 1582-1757 1800-1837 [64,87]
EBBESBOURNE WAKE M 1654-1841 (I) 1622-1841 [64]
EDINGTON C 1695-1840 M 1597-1695 1800-23 B 1678-1854 [64,103]
EISEY* C 1574-1837 (M 1575-1837) B Ext 1628-75 [7,78,97,111]
ENFORD M 1800-12 [64]
ERLESTOKE 1689-1850 [23,64,111,116]
ETCHILHAMPTON* (CB 1630-1812 M 1630-1812)-1837 [9,64]
EVERLEIGH CB 1660-1757 M 1605-1659 1661-1837 [64,87,103]
FARLEY see PITTON
FIFIELD BAVANT M 1793-1837 [64]
FIGHELDEAN M 1654-1836 (I) 1654-1837 [64]
FISHERTON ANGER M 1754-1837 [97]
FISHERTON DE LA MARE M 1800-1837 [64]
FITTLETON M 1609 [97]
FONTHILL BISHOP C 1813-1949 M 1624-1690 1800-1837 [87,97,116]
FONTHILL GIFFORD C 1664-1800 M 1622-1837 B 1661-1800 [87,101]
FORD see LAVERSTOCK
FOVANT M 1541-1760 1800-1837 [64]
FOXLEY M 1605-1837 [64]
FROXFIELD M 1565-1838 [87,105]
FUGGESLSTON* with BEMERTON M 1608-1837 [80,100]
FYFIELD (Marlborough) M 1605-1837 [100]
GARSDON M 1605-1837 [64]
GRIMSTEAD, WEST C 1717-1982 M 1717-48 1755-57 1769-1982 B 1717-1983 [109]

GRITTLETON* C 1576-1837 M (1573-1812)-1837 [64,69,116]
HAM M 1605-1841 [64]
HANKERTON* M 1607-1679 (1700-1837) [78,97]
HANNINGTON 1571-1840 [24]
HARDENHUISH C 1736-48 1813-1837 M 1747-1837 B 1781-91 1810-1812 [109]
HARNHAM, WEST C 1567-1770 M 1568-1759 B 1567-1754 [4]
HEDDINGTON M 1539-1836 [88,97]
HEYTESBURY* M 1582-(1654-1837) [78,97,106]
HIGHWAY M 1609-1753 1813-1837 [97]
HIGHWORTH 1538-1840 [25,26]
HILL DEVERILL M 1685-1837 (I) 1587-1837 [64]
HILPERTON M 1622-1837 [64,106]
HINTON, LITTLE M 1648-1840 [106]
HOLT M 1568-1837 [108]
HOMINGTON CB 1675-1840 M 1621-70 1675-1840 [7,97,100]
HORNINGSHAM M 1654-79 1713-22 1739-78 [88]
HUiSH* M (1684-1812)-1837 [64,75]
HULLAVINGTON M 1694-1754 [64]
IFORD see WESTWOOD
IDMISTON with PORTON* CB 1577-1702 (M 1577-1812)-1837 [4,65,76,97]; see also PORTON
IMBER C 1623-96 1709-1942 M 1623-96 1709-1943 B 1623-96 1709-1976 [65,102]
KEMBLE* M 1605-(1679-1812)-1837 [65,74]
KENNETT, EAST M 1609-23 1655-1836 [65]
KINGSTON DEVERILL* M 1608-(1706-1812)-37 [65,69,97]
KINGTON ST MICHAEL* M (1563-1837) [80,100] CB C.I. 1563-1812
KNOOK* M 1591-92 1616-37 (1695-1837) [78,97,106]
KNOYLE, EAST* M (1538-1812)-1837 [65,71]
KNOYLE, WEST* M 1608-(1719-1837) [78,97,106]
LACOCK CM 1559-1842 B 1559-1840 [27,85]; Lacock Abbey Rom Cath C 1792-1809 [85]
LAKE see WILSFORD
LANDFORD M Ext 1608-1670 M 1671-1837 [98] Mf ZC 1789-1876
LANGFORD, LITTLE M 1699-1835 [105]
LARKHILL St Alban Garrison Church C 1921-50 M 1933-60 [102]
LATTON* C 1576-1837 (M 1578-1837) B Ext 1578-1805 [7,80,100,110] Mfc C 1797-1920 M 1837-1925 B 1797-1812
LAVERSTOCK with FORD* (M 1726-1812)-1837 [65,78]
LAVINGTON, WEST* CB 1597-1803 M 1597-1837 [94,117]
LEA & CLEVERTON M 1605-1837 Ext 1605-1753 [5,65]
LEIGH M 1605-1753 [65]
LEIGH DELAMERE* M (1735-1812)-51 [69,97,100]
LIDDINGTON M 1611-36 1675 1693-1837 [65,106]
LIMPLEY STOKE M Ext 1611-1837 [65,106]
LITTLETON DREW M 1620-1837 [106]
LONGBRIDGE DEVERILL CM 1682-1837 [97,110]
LUCKINGTON* M 1574-1837 [79,98]
LUDGERSHALL M 1600-1837 [88,106]
LYDIARD MILLICENT* C 1578-1840 M (1580-1837)-40 B 1580-1840 [28,76]
LYDIARD TREGOZ C 1666-1951 M 1607 1619-1967 B 1666-1871 1891-98 [7,29,30,106]
LYNEHAM M 1813-1837 [88]
MADDINGTON M 1754-1836 [100]
MALMESBURY M 1591-1837 [98]

MANNINGFORD ABBAS C 1539-1837 M 1707-1837 [100,117]

MANNINGFORD BRUCE C 1605-1837 M 1606-85 1703-37 [105,117]

MARDEN* C 1622-1837 M (1693-1812)-1837 [65,74,117]

MARKET LAVINGTON* C 1622-1837 M (1673-1812)-1837 [65,76,98,117]

MARLBOROUGH* St Mary the Virgin M (1602-1812)-1837 (I) 1511-85 [65,70,GCI]; Ss Peter and Paul M (1611-1812)-1837 (I) 1607 1611-1837 [65,70,98,GCI]; Providence Chapel ZC 1805-1837 [31]

MARSTON MEYSEY C 1742-1974 M 1742-1840 B 1744-1840 [85]

MARSTON, SOUTH 1539-1840 [32]

MARTIN M 1813-1837 [98]

MELKSHAM CB 1568-1734 M 1568-77 (I) 1754-1837 [33,66]

MERE* M (1561-1812)-1837 [66,69]

MILDENHALL M 1560-1839 [98]

MILSTON* CB 1540-1696 (M 1540-1812)-1837 [1,66,71]

MILTON LILBOURNE 1686-1812 M 1686-1837 [34,88]

MINETY* C 1606-1852 M 1605/6 (1607-1812)-1837 B 1605-1881 with gaps [35,76]

MONKTON DEVERILL* M 1608-(1749-1812)-33 [69,88,106]

NETHERAVON C 1579-1837 M 1680-1837 [117]

NETHERHAMPTON 1622-1701 [51]

NEWNTON, LONG* M 1606-32(1653-1812)-1837 (I) 1606-1837 [66,71,88]

NEWNTON, NORTH M 1767-69 1800-39 [88]

NEWTON, SOUTH C 1695-1841 M 1695-1837 B 1695-1845 [110]

NEWTON TONY* M (1591-1812)-1837 [66,71]

NORTON BAVANT* M 1663-1812 [73]

NORTON COLEPARLE M 1813-1837 (I) 1606-1837 [66]

NUNTON & BODENHAM M 1623-71 1674-1837 [106]

ODSTOCK C 1541-1812 M 1561-1839 B 1543-1812 [109]

OGBOURNE ST GEORGE M 1603-1837

ORCHESTON ST GEORGE C 1647-1812 M 1609-1638 1647-1812 B 1656-1812 [111] Mf ZC 1813-75

ORCHESTON ST MARY M 1608-1837 [106]

OVERTON 1682-1717 M(I) 1605-1837 [5,98]

PATNEY* M (1594-1812)-1837 [74,100]

PEWSEY 1568-1840 [36]

PITTON with FARLEY M 1669-1837 [36]

PLAITFORD M 1764-1837 [98]

PORTON M 1754-1837 [67,76] see also IDMISTON

POTTERNE M 1575-1837 [98]

POULTON CB 1695-1979 M 1703-1977 [37]

PRESHUTE* M (1606-1812)-1837 [67,72,GCI]

PURTON* C 1564-1840 M (1558-1812)-1840 B 1558-1840 [38,75]

RAMSBURY CB 1678-1812 M 1660-1837 [39,40,98]

RODBOURNE CHENEY M 1605-07 1621-26 1655-1837 [98]

ROLLESTONE* CB 1653-1812 (I) 1813-1837 M 1608-38 (1654-1812)-1829 (I) 1654-1837 [3,74,88]

SALISBURY* Cathedral (M 1564-1812) [75,86,105]; St Edmund (M 1559-1837) [81,82,86]; St Martin (1559-1812) [77,86]; St Thomas (M 1570-1812) [73,86]

SEAGRY M 1611-1753 [98,100]

SEDGEHILL M 1607 1622-38 1669 1710-1837 [88]

SEEND M 1813-1837 [98]

SEMINGTON C 1586-1837 [117]

SEMLEY M 1798-1837 [98]

SEVENHAMPTON C 1649-62 1813-40 M 1649-66 [102]

SHALBOURNE M 1587-1673 1694-1837 [99]

SHERRINGTON* CB 1608-1841 M 1608-(1677-1837) [80,102]

SHERSTON MAGNA* M Ext 1603-1632 M (1653-1812)-1837 [67,69]

SHORNCOTE M 1708-1837 (I) 1619-1837 [67,77]

SHREWTON 1562-1700 [4]

SOMERFORD KEYNES M 1560-1721 1726-1809 (I) 1561-1837 [67,88]

SOMERFORD, GREAT* M 1605-1812 [74,100]

SOMERFORD, LITTLE* M (1606-1812)-1837 [67,74]

SOPWORTH* M (1698-1812)-1837 [67,69]

SOUTHBROOM* M 1572-1837 [74,100] Mf C 1572-1770

STANTON FITZWARREN 1542-1840 [41]

STANTON ST BERNARD C 1568-1812 M 1568-1836 B 1568-1809 [42,100]

STANTON ST QUINTON C 1679-1843 M 1679-1837 B 1679-1812 [105,109]

STAPLEFORD M 1637-1837

STAVERTON M 1687-1808 1815-1822 [88,99]

STEEPLE ASHTON M 1654-1798 1800-1837 (I) 1558-1837 [67,99]

STERT* C 1579-1837 M (1579-1812)-38 [67,72,111]

STOCKTON* M (1590-1812)-1837 [67,71]

STOURTON CB 1570-1800 M 1570-1836 [43,67]

STRATFORD TONY 1562-1776 CB 1778-1812 M 1780-1837 [1,109]

STRATFORD SUB CASTLE* M (1654-1837) (I) 1610-1837 [82,100]

STRATTON ST MARGARET 1608-1840 [44]

SUTTON BENGER M 1654-1838 [105]

SUTTON VENY CB 1565-1812 M 1599-1637 1654-1837 [3,67,105]

SWALLOWCLIFFE CB 1737-1837 M Ext 1585-1692 M 1748-1836 [45,99] Mf ZC 1813-77

SWINDON 1589-91 1606-09 1619-1840 [46,110]

TILSHEAD C 1603-1837 [117]

TOCKENHAM M 1620-23 1632 1655-1836 [99]

TEFFONT MAGNA M 1800-1837 [68]

TILSHEAD 1603-1745 [4]

TISBURY Ext C 1563-1600 M 1563-1659 B 1563-1630 [102]

TOCKENHAM M 1620-23 1632 1635-1836 [99]

TOLLARD ROYAL 1688-1840 [47]

TROWBRIDGE M 1538-1839 [6,68]

UPAVON M 1813-1837 (I) 1625-1837 [68,88,99]

UPTON SCUDMORE M 1608-1837 [105]

UPTON LOVELL C 1611-1812 M 1625-1837 B 1625-1812 [85]

URCHFONT* M (1538-1812)-1837 [68,72]

WANBOROUGH CB 1582-1653 M 1582-1651 1830-1837 M(I) 1582-1812 [88,99]

WARDOUR Rom Cath M 1749-1837 [99]

WARMINSTER Ext 1556-1677 M 1587-1837 [48]

WELLOW CB 1570-1880 M 1572-1837 [49,100]

WESTBURY M 1791-1837 [88]; and WHORWELLSDOWN Workhouse Deaths 1836-40 [102]

WESTPORT M 1605-1751 1802-1837 [105]

WESTWOOD CB 1666-1727 M 1671-1753 1826-1837 [4,88]

WHITEPARISH* M 1560-1837 [79,99]

WHORWELLSDOWN see WESTBURY

WILCOT M 1754-1837 [88,99]

WILSFORD with LAKE C 1672-1812 M 1696-1810 B 1610-1812 [50]

WILSFORD (Pewsey) M 1750-1768 [68]

WILTON C 1626-42 1663-1713 M 1615-1649 1663-1837

B 1663-1713 [51,106]
WINSLEY* C 1724-1843 M 1623-1694 1701-22, (1724-1846) B 1724-1861 Ext [52,88]
WINTERBOURNE BASSETT M Ext 1607-1838 [99]
WINTERBOURNE DAUNTSEY C Ext 1709-98 M 1561-1832 [102]
WINTERBOURNE EARLS M 1559-1837 [100]
WINTERBOURNE GUNNER M 1560-1619 [88]
WINTERBOURNE STOKE M(I) 1608-1836 [99]
WINTERSLOW* M 1598-1812 [74,100]
WISHFORD, GREAT M 1558-1838 [88,99]
WOODBOROUGH* M 1567-1837 [76,100]
WOODFORD C 1538-1837 M 1567-1837 B 1655-1783 [53-56,100]
WOOTTON BASSETT M 1584-1675 1701 1722-1837 [68,105]
WRAXALL, NORTH M 1677-1900 [8,57,106]
WROUGHTON M 1609 1615-25 1654-1837 [68]
WYLYE* 1581-1837 [58,100]
YATESBURY C 1606-1892 M 1706-1750 B 1706-1812 [109,117]
YATTON KEYNELL* M (1653-1812)-1837 [68,70]

WORCESTERSHIRE

ALDERMINSTER* M 1613-1812 [54]
ALNE, GREAT see WARWICKSHIRE
ALSTONE* M 1550-1805 [54]
ARELEY 1564-1812 [36]
ASTLEY Mf M 1950-1976
ASTON WHITE LADIES 1558-1840 [4]
BADSEY Ext 1537-1733 Mf C 1538-1812
BAYTON Mf 1638-1877
BELBROUGHTON Mf 1615-1700
BENGEWORTH Mf 1611-1700 ZC 1838-1837
BEOLEY Mf 1538-1720 CB 1813-1970 M 1754-1964
BERROW Mf 1611-1700
BIRTSMORTON* M 1539-1812 [55] Mf 1609-1700
BISHAMPTON C 1599-1949 M 1603-1949 B 1600-1949 [67] Mf 1616-1700
BOCKLETON C 1574-1718 1789-1837 M 1575-1718 1754-1812 B 1574-1837 [8]
BRADLEY GREEN 1562-1812 [9]
BRADLEY* M 1630-1812 [54]
BRANSFORD Chapelry Mf C 1813-1944 M 1813-1838 see also LEIGH with BRANSFORD
BRETFORTON 1538-1837 [10] Mf C 1838-1875
BRICKLEHAMPTON Mf C 1718-1784 M 1723-1749 B 1722-1784
BROADWAY C 1562-1750 M 1539-1812 B 1539-1797 [11]
BROMSGROVE CB 1590-1712 M Ext 1590-1712 [67]; Wes C 1815-1837; Ind & Bap 1788-1836; Ind C 1739-1837 B 1775-1837; Catshill Bapt C 1830-1837; SFrs Ext 1635-1797
BUSHLEY 1538-1837 [12,55] Mf 1538-1812
CASTLEMORTON M 1609-41 [13]
CHADDESLEY CORBET M 1601-25 [4]; Rom Cath C 1752-1823 M 1804 1807-1817 D 1763-1804 1807-1819 [CRS17]
CHURCH LENCH* M 1702-1812 [54]
CHURCHILL (in Oswaldslow)* CB 1564-1794 M 1564-1839 [14,55] Mf 1564-1794
CLEEVE PRIOR M 1599-1837 [55]

CLENT Mf 1562-1626 CB 1637-1812 M 1637-1805
CLIFTON UPON TEME 1598-1837 [15]
COMBERTON, GREAT Mf 1540-1705 1721-1964
COMBERTON, LITTLE* M 1540-1812 [55] Mf 1543-1964
CRADLEY Cradley Chapel, now St Peter's CB 1785-1839 M 1802-1839 B 1785-1844 [15]; Bapt 1783-1837 [15]; Presb C 1736-1837 [16]
CROPTHORNE 1557-1717 [17]
DODDENHAM with KNIGHTWICK 1538-1812 [28]
DORMSTONE C 1615-1739 M 1612-1736 B 1633-1735 [18,GCI] Mf 1612-1700
DOVERDALE Mf C 1704-1875
DRAKES BROUGHTON Mf M 1905-1969
DROITWICH C 1544-1840 M 1544-1837 B 1544-1838 [60]
DUDLEY St Edmund 1540-1611; Old Meeting House C 1743-1837 [19,20]; Ind C 1806-1825; Wes B 1830-1837
EARLS CROOME Mf CB 1644-1812 M 1644-1836
EASTHAM 1571-1837 [21,55] Mf 1572-1812
ELMBRIDGE* M 1570-1812 [54]
ELMLEY CASTLE M 1705-40 [6] Mf C 1813-1881 M 1813-1836 Banns 1823-1846 B 1813-1937
FLYFORD FLAVELL Mf C 1676-1966 MB 1676-1965
FRANKLEY* 1598-1748 M 1798-1812 B 1813-1900 [55,56]
HADRESFIELD Mf CB 1742-1812 M 1742-1836
HAGLEY (I) 1538-1899 [1]
HALESOWEN CB 1559-1643 1717-1761 M 1559-1643 1717-1754 [22/3,62]
HALL GREEN CB 1704-1840 M 1704-46 [53]
HALLOW Mf M 1962-1970 Banns 1936-1962
HANBURY* 1577-1837 [24,53,59]
HANLEY CHILD M 1754-1837 [21,55] see also EASTHAM
HANLEY WILLIAM* (M 1586-1837) Ext 1586-1800 [21,55] see also EASTHAM
HARTLEBURY 1540-1711 1744-1812
HARVINGTON Mf C 1573-1972 M 1572-1837 Banns 1824-1972 B 1570-1972
HIMBLETON* M 1711-(1713-1812) [5,55]
HUDDINGTON* CB 1695-1812 (M 1695-1835) [5,55]
INKBERROW CB 1613-1778 M 1613-1754 [2]
IPSLEY Mf Banns 1932-1974
KEMPSEY* M 1690-1812 [54] Mf M 1967-1975 B 1874-1950
KIDDERMINSTER 1539-1636 [6,25] see also STONE (Kidderminster)
KINGS NORTON CB 1546-1844 M 1546-1837 [26,27] Mf 1613-1700
KINGTON* C 1587-1812 (M 1588-1836) B 1654-1809 [18,54,GCI] Mf 1600-1700
KNIGHTWICK see DODDENHAM
KYRE, GREAT Mf C 1740-1875
LEIGH with BRANSFORD Mf C 1538-1856 M 1538-1906 B 1538-1838
LEIGH SINDON Lady Hunt Conn ZC 1821-1837 [HR/R13]
LENCHWICK see NORTON and LENCHWICK
LITTLETON, NORTH & MIDDLE M 1662-1812 [55]
LITTLETON, SOUTH M 1539-1812 [55]
LONGDON Mf C 1737-1929 M 1737-1837 B 1737-1882
MALVERN, GREAT 1556-1837 [29] Mf 1556-1618 C 1801-1868 M 1754-1864 B 1801-1837
MALVERN LINK Mf C 1846-1882 MB 1846-1855
MALVERN, LITTLE 1691-1837 [30]; Rom Cath C 1783-1864 B 1826-75 [15]

MALVERN, WEST Mf C 1844-1946 M 1844-1965 B 1845-
1951
MARTLEY C 1626-1838 MB 1626-1837 [69] Mf C 1625-
1926 M 1625-1923 B 1625-1953
MATHON Mf C 1631-1943 M 1631-1964 B 1631-1893
MITTON, LOWER see STOURPORT
MOSELY SAINT MARY C 1761-1841 B 1762-1850 [32]
MYTTON 1693-1731 [6]
NETHERTON Bapt C 1654-1798 [33]
NORTHFIELD C 1560-1841 M 1560-1837 B 1560-1850
[34]
NORTON and LENCHWICK Mf C 1538-1868 M 1538-
1837 B 1538-1839
OFFENHAM M 1543-1812 [54]
OLDBURY CB 1714-1812 [35]
OLDSWINFORD C 1719-1819 MB 1719-1813 [40-
43,64/5]
ORLETON M 1571-1837 [21,55] Mf CB 1660-1851 M
1660-1840 see also EASTHAM
OSWALDSLOW see CHURCHILL (in Oswaldslow)
PEDMORE (I) 1539-1886 [3]
PENDOCK Mf C 1584-1928 M 1584-1836 Banns 1823-
1948 B 1584-1813
PENSAX 1563-1812 [37] Mf CB 1791-1963 M 1813-1961
PERSHORE see PINVIN
PIDDLE, NORTH C 1565-1812 M 1571-1812 B 1571-1812
[5,55] Mf 1612-1700
PINVIN Mf C 1559-1800 1813-1968 M 1559-1796 1823-
1968 B 1602-1779 1848-1968
PIRTON Mf 1612-1700
POWICK 1611-1731 [38] Mf 1611-1700
QUEENHILL Mf 1581-1731 CB 1789-1812 M 1754-1837
REDDITCH M 1808-12 [54]; St David Mf C 1955-1966; St
Stephen Mf C 1946-1972 M 1949-1973 Banns 1946-
1980
REDMARLEY D'ABITOT Mf C 1539-1965 M 1539-1969 B
1539-1905
ROMSLEY C 1736-1841 M 1736-1753
ROUS LENCH M 1539-1812 [54]
ROWLEY REGIS Mf 1606-1700
RUSHOCK M 1667-1837 [55] Mf 1608-1700
SALFORD PRIORS Mf 1614-1700
SALWARPE Mf 1613-1968
SAPEY, LOWER Mf 1661-1849
SEDGEBERROW Mf C 1566-1972 M 1566-1751 1785-
1972 B 1566-1970
SEVERN STOKE 1538-1600 [53] Mf C 1897-1982
SHELSLEY WALSH Mf C 1729-1965 M Ext 1729-1947 B
1730-1947
SHIPSTON ON STOUR M 1572-1812 [54]
SHRAWLEY Mf C 1719-1940 M 1719-1867 B 1719-1894
SPETCHLEY 1539-1840 [4,39] Mf C 1539-1962 M 1539-
1963 B 1539-1966
STONE (Kidderminster) 1601-1812 [66] Mf C 1601-
1929 M 1601-1960 B 1601-1966
STOURBRIDGE Wes C 1809-1837; Ind C 1776-1837 [63]
STOURPORT Lower Mitton 1693-1840 [31]
STRENSHAM Mf C 1569-1908 M 1569-1837 B 1569-
1812
SUCKLEY Lady Hunt Conn ZC 1821-18378 [HR/R13]
TARDEBIGGE Mf C 1566-1857 M 1566-1908 B 1579-
1867
THROCKMORTON Mf C 1717-1812 M 1545-1754
TIDMINGTON M 1693-1812 [54]
TREDINGTON C 1541-1838 M 1560-1837 B 1560-1861
UPTON ON SEVERN Mf C 1694-1812 M 1951-1972
UPTON SNODSBURY 1577-1837 [44/5,55] Mf 1577-

1837
WARNDON Mf CB 1561-1962 M 1561-1951
WASHBOURNE, LITTLE Mf C 1813-1981
WELLAND 1608-1812 [46] Mf 1608-1700 C 1813-1875
WELLESBOURNE Mf 1611-1700
WHATCOTE Mf 1611-1700
WHICHFORD Mf 1610-1700
WHITCHURCH Mf 1610-1700
WHITTINGTON Mf C 1663-1895 M 1653-1837 B 1658-
1811
WICHENFORD Mf 1599-1700
WICK Mf C 1608-1932 M 1608-1871 B 1608-1724 1863-
1971
WICKHAMFORD Mf C 1538-1967 M 1556-1954 B 1538-
1966
WITLEY, GREAT C 1538-1874 M 1538-1835 B 1538-1849
[58] Mf C 1538-1874 M 1538-1835 B 1538-1908
WOLVERLEY C 1539-1860 M 1539-1643 1657-1860 B
1539-1646 1654-1860 [56,68]
WORCESTER Cathedral CB 1693-1811 (M 1693-1754)
[45] Mf 1693-1811; St Alban 1630-1812 [48]; St
Andrew Mf C 1770-1936 B 1770-1812; St Barnabas
Mf C 1883-1926 M 1885-1926 B 1895-1920; St
Helen CM 1538-1812 B 1556-1812 [50/1]; St John
Bedwardine Mf C 1558-1870 M 1559-1837 B 1558-
1842; St Martin Mf C 1788-1841 M 1762-1825 B
1788-1831; St Michael Bedwardine Mf C 1546-1902
M 1546-1837 B 1546-1812; St Nicholas Mf C 1564-
1966 M 1563-1958 B 1564-1904; St Peter Mf C
1686-1836 M 1686-1837 B 1686-1856; St Swithin Mf
C 1538-1927 M 1538-1917 B 1538-1953; St George
Rom Cath 1685-1837 [49]
WRIBBENHALL C 1723-1814 [52]
WYRE PIDDLE Mf C 1716-1971 M 1716-1837
WYTHALL Mf C 1760-1967 M 1854-1937
YARDLEY see HALL GREEN

YORKSHIRE

ABERFORD 1540-1812 [11]
ACKLAM Mf 1626-40 1661-73 1687-1861
ACKWORTH Mf 1558-1812 M(I) 1538-1600
ACOMB Mf 1634-39 1661-71 1686-1875
ADDINGHAM* 1612-1812 [13]
ADEL 1606-1812 [14]
ADLINGFLEET C 1694-1761 M 1752 B 1694-1820 [287]
ADWICK LE STREET (I) 1680-1907 [279] Mf C
1547-1867 M 1547-1837 B 1547-1812
ALDBOROUGH* 1538-1611 [15]
ALLERSTON Mf 1604-17 1661-1868
ALLERTHORPE Mf 1600-15 1661-2 1673 1681 1704-
1848 see also THORNTON on SPALDING MOOR
ALLERTON MAULEVERER* CM 1564-1812 B 1557-1812
[16]
ALMONDBURY* 1557-1703 [17-19,280] M(I) 1754-1781
[175]
ALNE Mf 1600 1634-1649 1680-1838
AMOTHERBY see APPLETON LE STREET
AMPLEFORTH Mf Ext 1601-1870
ANSTON Mf 1598-1605 1622 1631-40 1661-1890
APPLETON LE STREET Mf 1600-42 1661-1853
ARDSLEY, EAST Mf 1598-1812
ARDSLEY, WEST see WOODKIRK
ARKENDALE Mf C 1813-1848

ARKENGARTHDALE 1727-1812 [176/7,287]
ARMLEY C 1665-1711 M 1665-1697 B 1704-11 1717 Mf
    C 1664-1812; see also LEEDS Chapelries
ARNCLIFFE* 1663-1812 [178]
ARRAM see ATWICK; also LECONFIELD
ASKHAM BRYAN* 1604-1837 [20]
ASKHAM RICHARD* 1579-1837 [16,20]
ASKRIGG Mf 1674-1701
ATWICK 1538-1708 CM(I) 1813-40 [21,283] Mf
    1711-1812
AUGHTON* 1610-1812 [22]
AUSTERFIELD* (1559-1812) M(I) 1813-37 [23,67]
AYSGARTH 1709-1840 [10]
AYTON, GREAT* 1600-1812 [24]
BADSWORTH Mf C 1635-1843 M 1610-55 1684-1839 B
    1583-1879
BAGBY Mf 1556-1639 C 1653-1894 M 1653-1839 B
    1653-1812
BAILDON Mf 1621-1812
BARDSEY Mf CB 1538-1812 Mf M 1538-1754
BARLBY Mf 1781-1860(gaps) see also
    HEMINGBOROUGH Chapelry
BARLEN Mf 1781-1860
BARMLEY MOOR Mf 1600-28 1660-1852
BARNINGHAM Mf M 1732-1844
BARNOLDSWICK 1587-1837 [179]; Bapt Bridge Chapel
    Z 1785-1837 B 1785-1817; Diss 1717-1776 [180]
BARNSLEY Mf CB 1568-1790 M 1568-1808
BARTON LE STREET Ext 1600-37 [266] Mf 1600-
    1699(gaps) 1705-1840
BARWICK IN ELMET* 1600-1812 [181]
BAWTRY Mfc 1653-1900
BEDERN Mf 1768-73 1821-28 1854-1856
BEESTON CB 1720-1812 M 1720-1753; see also Leeds
    Chapelries
BENTHAM* C 1673-1812 M 1668-1812 B 1666-1812 [25]
BILTON IN AINSTY CB 1803-1842 [269] Mf 1571-1864
BINGLEY* 1577-1686 [26]
BIRDFORTH Chapelry Mf 1632-37 1664-1872; see also
    COXWOLD
BIRDSALL Mf 1603-1835
BIRKIN Mf 1631-42 1661-1862
BIRSTALL* 1558-1687 [27,273]
BISHOPSTHORPE* 1631-1837 [268] Mf 1631-40 1663-
    1835
BISHOP WILTON Mf 1601-1662(gaps) 1694-1856
BLACKTOFT* 1700-1812 [23]
BOLTBY Chapelry Mf 1600-13 1631-40 1857-61; see
    also FELIXKIRK
BOLTON ABBEY 1689-1812 [182] Mf Ext 1634-1688
BOLTON BY BOWLAND* 1558-1812 [29,30]
BOLTON CASTLE cum REDMIRE Mf C 1753-1848
BOLTON IN CRAVEN 1667-90 [287]
BOLTON ON DEANE 1561-1673 [9]
BOLTON PERCY Mf 1604-10 1633-40 1666-1854
BOSSALL Mf 1601-05 1631-39 1661-79 1711-1863; see
    also BUTTERCRAMBE, FLAXTON and SAND
    HUTTON
BOWES CM 1615-1837 B 1670-1699 1701-1837 [31,183-
    5]
BOYNTON* 1813-1840 [283] Mf C 1573-1812 M
    1588-1812 B 1563-1812
BRACEWELL 1600-1639 [269]
BRADFIELD* (1559-1722) M 1723-1840 [186,270] Mfc C
    1559-1914 M 1559-1904 B 1559-1899
BRADFORD C 1598-1602 M 1596-1708 B(I) 1820-32
    [187,399,GCI]; Mfc CB 1599-1633 1655-1735 M

1599-1735; see also THORNTON
BRAITHWELL* 1559-1837 [32/3]
BRAMHAM CB 1678-1737 M 1586-1620 [188,266]
BRAMLEY CB 1717-1812 M 1724-1753; see also LEEDS
    Chapelries
BRANDSBURTON* 1558-1837 [34]
BRANDSBY Mf 1631-42 1663-1888;BRANDSBY HALL
    Rom Cath C 1820-40 [283]
BRANTINGHAM* 1653-1841 [35,283]
BRAYTON Mf 1617-1761(gaps) 1793-1836; see also
    SELBY with BRAYTON
BRETTON, WEST Mf C 1753-1784
BRIDLINGTON Priory C 1613-37
BRODSWORTH* 1538-1813 [36]
BROMPTON Mf C 1788-1903 M 1788-1915 B 1788-1951
BROOMFLEET Mf CB 1861-1871
BUBWITH CB 1600-1767 M 1600-1753 [37] Mf 1600-
    1640(gaps) 1662-1865
BUGTHORPE Mf 1631-2 1661-1856
BULMER Mf 1596-1604 1633-40 1660-1865
BURGHWALLIS* CM 1596-1814 B 1596-1809 [38]
BURNBY Mf 1601-06 1628-40 1720-1842
BURNSALL in CRAVEN CM 1567-1812 B 1559-1812
    [189-191,274] Mf 1901-29
BURTON AGNES Mf CMB Ext 1600-1716 CMB 1718-
    1839 CB 1840-42
BURTON FLEMING* (1538-1812) CB 1813-1840 M 1813-
    1837 [39,283]
BURTON LEONARD Mf 1672-1755 1811-12
BURYTHORPE Mf 1633 1661-1857
BUTTERCRAMBE Chapelry Mf 1631-40 1663-81; see
    also BOSSALL
BYLAND, OLD Mf C 1777-1875
CALVERLEY 1574-1720 [192-4]
CANTLEY* 1539-1812 [40]
CARLTON (Snaith) 1598-1812 [41]
CATTON Mf 1600-41 1662-1867; see also STAMFORD
    BRIDGE
CAVE, NORTH Mf 1629-39 1661-81 1691-36
CAVE, SOUTH Mf CB 1558-1724 M 1558-1783
CAWOOD Mf 1636-41 1663-1839
CAYTON 1684-1800 CB 1801-1840 [195,GCI]
CHAPEL ALLERTON CB 1723-1812 M 1725-1754; see
    also LEEDS Chapelries
CHERRY BURTON* (1561-1740)-1841 [42,279]
CLAPHAM* 1595-1683 [43] Mf 1595-1812; Inghamite CB
    1754-72 [196]
CLAYTON see FRICKLEY
CLOUGHTON Chapelry see SCALBY ST LAWRENCE
COATHAM B(I) 1855-1976 [284]
COLEY see NORTHOWRAM
COLLINGHAM* 1579-1837 [44]
CONISTONE see BURNSALL
COPGROVE 1584-1790 [197]
COPMANTHORPE Chapelry Mf 1759-1874; see also
    YORK St Mary
COVERHAM with HORSEHOUSE Mf M 1805-1845
COWLAM Mf Ext 1600-1812
COWTHORPE* 1568-1797 [23]
COXWOLD* 1583-1666 [45] Mf 1601-10 1631-40 1660-
    1848; see also BIRDFORTH
CRAMBE Mf 1601 1633-41 1661-1835
CRAYKE, M(I) 1700-1812 [284] Mf 1558-1812
CROFTON* 1617-1812 [46]
CROPTON Chapelry see MIDDLETON
CUMBERWORTH Banns 1754-87; Chapelry 1708-44
    1777-79 [287]

CUNDALL* with NORTON LE CLAY 1582-1780 [193]
DALBY CB 1656-1812 M 1656-1836 [199,GCl] Mf 1632 1663-1881
DANBY IN CLEVELAND* 1585-1812 [47]
DANBY, WEST WITTON & LEYBURN Rom Cath C 1742-1840 [CRS13]
DARFIELD Mf C 1598-1854 M 1598-1850 B 1598-1847
DARRINGTON* 1567-1812 [48] Mf C 1813-1849
DARTON Mf CB 1647-1812 M 1609-1753
DEANHEAD see SCAMMONDEN
DENT* C 1611-1713 1771-1800 M 1611-1669 1771-1800 B 1611-1669 [266] Mf 1611-1812
DEWSBURY* 1538-1653 [200]
DONCASTER* (M 1557-1837) Ext 1719-1843 [201,262/3]
DOWNHOLME Mf ZC 1813-1848
DRAX Mf 1632-41 1666-1892
DRIFFIELD, GREAT Mf Ext CB 1600-1875 M 1600-1837
DRIFFIELD, LITTLE Mf Ext 1600-1740
DRYPOOL* CB 1572-1812 M 1572-1807 [49] Mf C 1572-1812
DUNNINGTON Mf 1628-37 1661-1847
EARBY Bapt Z 1802-1837 [180]
EASBY Mf ZC 1801-1848
EASINGWOLD* 1599-1837 [50/1]
ECCLESFIELD 1558-1619 M 1622-1840 [202,270] Mfc C 1599-1904 M 1558-1912 B 1558-1909
EGTON Mf CB 1656-1812 M 1656-1797
EGTON BRIDGE Rom Cath C 1835-40 M 1837-40 [269]
ELLAND* 1559-1714 [203-5]
ELLERKER see BRANTINGHAM
ELVINGTON Mf 1600-39 1661-1873
EMLEY* 1600-1836 [52/3] Mf 1600-1794 CB 1794-1812
ERYHOLME C 1575-1789 M 1575-1754 B 1575-1789 [206]
ESCRICK Mf 1608 1622 1631-38 1661-1886
ESTON* 1590-1812 [54] Mf C 1813-1878
ETTON Mf 1600-40 1661-1887
EVERINGHAM Mf 1600-40 1660-1883
EVERINGHAM PARK* (St Mary's Domestic Chapel) Rom Cath CMD 1771-1884 [CRS7]
FANGFOSS M 1813-1836 [283] Mf Ext 1601-1875
FARLINGTON Chapelry Mf 1632-39 1663-1837; see also SHERIFF HUTTON
FARNHAM* 1569-1812 [55]
FARNLEY Mf C 1724-1812; see also LEEDS Chapelries
FEATHERSTONE Mf 1558-1812
FELIXKIRK Mf 1598-1617 1632-41 1661-1866; see also BOLTBY
FELKIRK 1701-1812 [207]
FERRIBY, NORTH Mf 1600-10 1626-39 1662-1852
FEWSTON* 1593-1812 [208/9]
FILEY C 1573-1640 1683-1730 1789-1840 M 1571-1640 1695-1731 1754-1840 B 1571-1605 1690-1739 1789-1840 [6,210,286]
FLAXTON Chaplery Mf 1606-79 CB 1867-1870; see also BOSSALL
FLOCKTON 1713-1812 [147-9]
FOSTON Mf 1622 1631-40 1661-1835
FOSTON ON THE WOLDS Mf 1599 1602-1639 1661-1872
FRICKLEY* with CLAYTON 1577-1812 [56]
FULFORD Mf 1603 1632-40 1661-1865
FULL SUTTON see SUTTON, FULL
FULNECK United Brethren Mf C 1742-1959 B 1749-1958
GANTON Mf Ext CMB 1601-1750 CMB 1790-1837 CB 1838-67

GARFORTH 1631-1812 [57]
GARGRAVE 1558-1812 [58]
GARSDALE Mf M 1805-1843
GARTON ON THE WOLDS Ext CMB 1600-1720 CMB 1722-1837 CB 1838-87
GATE HELMSLEY M 1754-1837 [283] Mf CB 1689-1812 M 1689-1753
GIGGLESWICK* 1558-1769 [59,271]
GILLING, EAST 1573-1812 [60]
GILLING (Helmsley) Mf C(l) 1813-1877
GISBURNE* 1558-1812 [61/2] Mf C 1745-1838 M 1745-1837 B 1746-1837
GIVENDALE Mf 1606-22 1640 1696-1860
GOATHLAND C 1669-1736 M 1670-1731 B 1669-1729 [213,284]
GOLDSBOROUGH Mf CB 1707-1812 M 1707-60 1784-1802 1804-12
GOODMANHAM Mf 1600-16 1629-39 1661-1874
GRIMSTON, NORTH Mf 1606 1626-36 1662-1673 1684-1862
GRINDLETON (Chapelry) Mfc B 1813-1924
GRINTON in SWALEDALE* CB 1640-1807 M 1640-1802 [63] Mf C 1824-1847
GRISTHORP see FILEY
GUISBOROUGH 1600-1615 [294]; see also NEWTON by GUISBOROUGH
GUISELEY* 1584-1812 [214,277,289]
HACKNESS* (1557-1783)-1840 [64,215,GCl]; Harwood Dale Chapel C 1778-1840 M 1757-1839 B 1779-1840 [215]
HALIFAX* 1538-1593 [65/6,216] Mf 1538-1543; see also NORTHOWRAM/COLEY
HALTONGILL see ARNCLIFFE
HAMPSTHWAITE* CB 1603-1794 M 1603-1807 [67]
HAREWOOD* CB 1614-1812 M 1621-1812 [68] Mf B 1614-1812
HARPHAM Mf Ext 1600-1698 CMB 1700-24 1726-1838 CB 1839-42
HARROGATE* 1748-1812 [265]
HARSWELL Mf 1600 1625-38 1665-81 1695-1852
HARTSHEAD* 1600-02 1608-09 (1612-1812) [69,269]
HARTWITH Mf C 1751-1812 M 1752-54 B 1751-1802
HARWOOD DALE see HACKNESS
HASLERTON, EAST see HASLERTON, WEST
HASLERTON, WEST Mf 1626-39 1661-1865
HATFIELD M 1556-1838 [217]
HAWNBY C 1654-88 M 1695-1722 B 1653-1722 [218]
HAWORTH* C 1654-1688 M 1695-1722 B 1653-1722 [218] Mf 1645-1727 Mfc C 1645-1911 M 1645-1901 B 1645-1885
HAXBY Mf 1605-09 1631-40 1661-74 1686-1867
HAYTON Mf 1601-89(gaps) 1695-1760 1771-1867
HEDON in HOLDERNESS Rom Cath see NUT HILL & HEDON
HEADINGLEY 1634-1837 [219]; see also LEEDS Chapelries
HEALAUGH Mf 1633-41 1661-1869
HELMSLEY, UPPER M 1754-1837 [283] Mf 1631-1857
HELPERTHORPE Mf 1631-39 1661-76 1693-1870
HEMINGBROUGH Mf 1661-2 1673 1689-1867; see also BARLBY
HEMSWORTH* 1654-1812 [70]
HEPTONSTALL* 1593-1660 [71]
HESLERTON, EAST Mf CB 1561-1840 M 1561-1837
HESLERTON, WEST Mf C 1561-72 B 1705-39
HESLINGTON Ext 1639-40 1653-1837 [72]; Mf 1639 1683-1870

HESSLE Mf 1600-10 1628-39 1661-1836
HICKLETON* 1626-1812 [73]
HINDERWELL 1601-1812 [281/2] Mf C 1765-1872
HINDERSKELFE Mf C 1813-1842
HIPSWELL Mf C 1770-1875
HOLBECK CB 1764-1812; see also LEEDS Chapelries
HOLME Mf 1559-1650
HOLME ON SPALDING MOOR* Rom Cath CM 1744-1840 [CRS4]
HOLMPTON M 1739-1837 [269]
HOLTBY Mf CB 1679-1812 M 1679-1753
HOOK Mf C 1695-1812 M 1683 1695-1723 1755-82 B 1678-1878
HOOTON PAGNELL* 1538-1812 [74]
HORBURY* 1598-1812 [75]
HORNBY 1558-1813 [3,220] Mf 1681-1824
HORESEHOUSE see COVERHAM with HORSEHOUSE
HORTON IN RIBBLESDALE Mf 1556-1812
HOVINGHAM Chapelry Mf 1598-1612 1626-38 1663-79 1689-1856
HOWDEN* 1543-1770 [76-79] Mf C 1775-1812 M 1770-1812 B 1775-1804; Ighamite C 1792-1837 D 1822-1830
HUBBERHOLME see ARNCLIFFE
HUDDERSFIELD Mf CB 1562-1812 M 1580-1801
HUDSWELL Mf M 1736-1840
HUGGATE* 1539-1812 [221]
HULL Holy Trinity M 1538-1600; God's House Hospital M 1695-1714 [286]
HUNSINGORE Mf CB 1626-1801 M 1626-1812
HUNSLET* 1686-1812; see also LEEDS Chapelries
HUNTINGTON Mf 1598-1604 1632 1638 1665-1853
HURSTWAITE Mf 1660-1877
HUTTON BUSCEL 1572-1837 [222] Mf 1600-09 1625-39 1661-1864
HUTTON WANDESLEY (or LONG MARSTON) Mf 1645-60 C 1694-1865 M 1694-1837 B 1694-1885
HUTTONS AMBO Mf 1632-37 1661-1839
IDLE (Bradford) Upper Chapel B 1810-1837 [284]
ILKLEY* 1597-1812 [80]
INGLEBY GREENHOW 1539-1800 [224]
INGLETON* CB (1607-1813) M 1607-1813 M(l)grooms 1813-1837 [286]
KEIGHLEY* 1562-1736 [81-83]
KEYINGHAM see HOLDERNESS
KILBURN* 1600-1812 [84]
KILDWICK* C 1575-1789 M 1575-1754 B 1575-1771 [85-88]; see also SILSDEN (Chapelry)
KILHAM Mf Ext 1622-1662 CMB 1693-1751 1753-1837 CB 1838-76
KILNWICK 1754-1841 [279] Mf 1558-1756
KILNWICK PERCY Mf 1661-66 1693-1877
KINGSTON upon HULL see SCULCOATES
KIPPAX* 1539-1812 [89]
KIPPING IN THORNTON Bradford Ind C 1756-1807 B 1786-1803 [P]
KIRBY GRINDALYTHE Mf 1605 1626-40 CB 1661-1866 M 1661-1836
KIRBY HILL* 1576-1812 [90]
KIRBY UNDERDALE Mf 1636-39 1661-1840
KIRK DEIGHTON Mf CB 1600-1786 M 1600-1754
KIRK ELLA Mf CMB Ext 1600-1713 CMB 1715-1840 CB 1742-57 1864-77
KIRK FENTON C 1630-70 1681-1693 M 1681-93 B 1627-93 CMB 1771-74 [4]
KIRKBURN Mf CMB Ext 1601-1689 CMB 1691-1837 CB 1838-75

KIRKBURTON 1541-1711 [225/6] Mf (I)1653-1710
KIRKBY FLEETHAM Mf 1591-1812 C 1813-1848
KIRKBY MALHAM* 1597-1690 [91] Mf 1600-07 1632-1846
KIRKBY OVERBLOW Mf 1647-1812
KIRKBY RAVENSWORTH Mf C 1737-183 M 1737-1884
KIRKBY WHARFE Mf 1602-05 1666-1868
KIRKELLA 1558-1841 [227]
KIRKHAMMERTON Mf C 1714-51 M 1755-1812 B 1714-1812
KIRKHEATON Mf CB 1600-1812 M 1600-1754 1796-1812
KIRKLEATHAM* (CM 1559-1812) M 1813-1920 B (1559-1812)-1975 [92,284,294]
KIRKLINGTON* 1568-1812 [93]
KIRKTHORPE see WARMFIELD
KNAPTON Chaplery Mf CM 1805-1878; see also WINTRINGHAM
KNARESBOROUGH Ext 1560-1753 [265] Rom Cath C 1765-1840 M 1825-1840 B 1765-1789 [CRS22]
LANGTOFT Mf 1601 1626-28 1663-73 1684-1854
LANGTON C 1653-1713 M 1655-62 B 1654-1724 [228] Mf C 1600-01 1628-38 1661-1845 CB 1869-1871
LASTINGHAM Ext 1559-1858
LAWKLAND Mf 1816-1861; Rom Cath Mf C 1816-1861
LEAKE Mf C 1810-1875
LECONFIELD 1551-1631 1740-1812 [5,283] Mf 1601-11 1626-39 1660-1861
LEDSHAM* 1539-1812 [94]
LEEDS C 1571-1776 M 1571-1769 C 1571-1832 [95-101,294,GC!]; Chapelries 1724-1812 [102-4]; George St Indep ZC 1807-37 [266,294]
LEYBURN see DANBY, WEST WITTON & LEYBURN
LINTON IN CRAVEN* 1562-1812 [105/6]
LINTON UPON OUSE (Newton upon Ouse) Rom Cath C 1771-1840 M 1795-1837 [CRS17]
LOCKINGTON Mf 1599-1609 1626-39 1661-1874
LONDESBOROUGH Mf 1600-10 1626-39 1661-1865
LOWTHORPE Mf Ext 1600-1704 CMB 1706-1813 CB 1814-89
LUND Mf C 1602-80 M 1587-1687 B 1586-1653
LYTHE* 1634-1837 [107/8]
MALTBY* 1597-1812 [109]
MALTON, NEW St Micheal Mf 1600-08 1625-41 1644-1856; St Leonard Mf 1601-20 1630-39 1662-1843
MALTON, OLD C 1606-1863 M 1606-1840 B 1606-1843 [229]
MANFIELD* 1594-1812 [230]
MARKET WEIGHTON Mf 1600-05 1621-39 1661-1881; see also SHIPTONTHORPE
MARSKE (Richmond) M 1570-1984 B(I) 1569-1984 [264,284] Mf C 1738-1848; Rom Cath Ext C 1789-1830 [269]
MARSKE (Cleveland)* CB (1569-1812) M (1569-1812)-1984 [110,284]
MARSTON, LONG Mf C 1624-1865; see also HUTTON WANDESLEY
MARTON C 1572-1865 MB 1572-1866 [272]
MARTON in the FOREST Mf 1601 1638-9 1671-1837
MASHAM Mf M 1754-1812
METHLEY* 1560-1812 [111]
MIDDLESBROUGH Wes Meth 1860-1886 [284]
MIDDLETON (Pickering) (I)1671-1840 [284]
MILLINGTON Mf Ext 1601-1860
MIRFIELD* (CB 1559-1776 M 1559-1754) [112/3] Mf 1755-1812; Moravian Mf CZ 1743-1910 M 1860-1923 B 1794-1916

MONK FRYSTON CB (1538-1678)-1756 M (1538-1678)-1812 M(I) 1542-1680 [9,231,GCI]

MOOR MONKTON Mf 1628-40 1660-1870

MORLEY* Non Conf Old Chapel C 1742-1840 B 1737-1888 [250]; Ind New Chapel C 1804-18 1828-1836 [284]

MUKER 1638-1670 1700-1842 [8]

MUSTON Mf Ext 1600-1719 1729-52 1754-1811 1813-36

MYTON UPON SWALE 1654-1812 [51,114] Mf 1598-1610 1628-39 1660-1856

NABURN Mf 1662-1706 1722-1849

NAFFERTON Mf Ext 1600-1685 CMB 1689-1704 1706-1836 CB 1837-98

NETHERTON 1881-1905 [266]

NEWTON by GUISBOROUGH Mf C 1725-1812

NEWTON on OUSE Mf 1631-9 1661-1878

NIDD HALL Rom Cath C 1780-1823 [CRS3]

NORMANBY C 1699-1769 B 1719-1812 [GCI]

NORMANTON Mf CB 1538-1812 M 1538-1754

NORTHOWRAM/COLEY Old Chapel 1644-1752 [232]

NORTON Mf 1605-39 1661-1879

NORTON LE CLAY see CUNDALL

NUNBURNHOLME M 1814-1837 [283] Mf 1605-6 1627-40 1661-1855

NUNKEELING Mf CM 1598-1812 B 1559-1812

NUT HILL with HEDON in HOLDERNESS Rom Cath C 1774-1849 M 1788-1793 1797-1844 B 1797-1846 [CRS35]

ORMESBY 1599-1899 CMB(I) 1599-1703

OSBALDWICK Mf 1632-41 1660-1875

OSMOTHERLEY Rom Cath C 1771-1839 [284]

OSWALDKIRK* 1538-1837 [115] Mf 1538-1656

OTLEY* C 1562-1753 M 1562-1750 B 1562-1751 [116/7] Mf CB 1745-83 C 1791-97 M 1747-54 B 1790-97; Pool Chapel Mf CB 1790-1797

OTTERINGTON, SOUTH Mf 1601 1631-33 1666-85 1701-1855

OUSEBURN, GREAT* Mf C 1658-1737 1813-1822 M 1658-1737 1754-1812 B 1658-1737 1813-1820

OUSEBURN, LITTLE* Mf 1565-1812 CB 1666-87 1700-1846 M 1666-87 1700-1837

OVER SILTON Mf 1601 1632-1638 C 1661-1877 MB 1661-1861

OVERTON Mf 1601-41 1661-1812 CB 1813-1848

PANNALL Mf CB 1558-1775 M 1558-1754

PATELEY BRIDGE Mf 1551-1715

PATRICK BROMPTON Mf C 1727-1848

PATRINGTON 1570-1731 [118]

PENISTONE Mf C 1643-1844 M 1643-1785 B 1643-1840

PICKHILL* with ROXBY C 1571-1812 M 1567-1812 B 1576-1812 [119]

POCKLINGTON Mf 1601-12 1661-73 1694-1856; see also YAPHAM

POOL Chapelry see OTLEY

PONTEFRACT* C (1585-1641) 1647-72 MB (1585-1641) 1647-53 [120,269]

POPPLETON, NETHER Mf 1634 1661-1878

POPPLETON, UPPER Chapelry Mf 1846-1873; see also YORK St Mary

RASKELF* 1747-1812 [21] Mf Ext 1600-1751

RAWMARSH C 1558-1812 M 1558-1753 B 1560-1812 [7]

REDCAR B(I) 1832-96 [269]; see also WILTON Cleveland; Prim Meth Station Rd M 1931-59 [284]; West Trinity Meth M 1907-80 [284]

REDMIRE see BOLTON CASTLE cum REDMIRE

REIGHTON CMB Ext 1600-1836

RICCALL* CB 1669-1813 M 1669-1753 [122]

RICHMOND 1556-1632 [233]; see also MARSKE (Richmond)

RICHMONDSHIRE* M 1653-60 [123]

RILLINGTON* CB 1638-1812 M 1638-1803 [124] Mf 1626-39 1661-1845; see also SCAMPSTON

RIPLEY Mf CB 1560-1812 M 1564-1801

RIPON* 1574-1628 [125]

RIPPONDEN Mfc C 1684-1817 M 1687-1702 1750-54 B 1684-1700 1750-1817

ROBIN HOOD'S BAY C 1812 [286]

ROKEBY* 1598-1837 [126]

ROMALDKIRK 1655-88 1697-1812 CB(I) 1578-1655 [234,286]

ROOS 1571-1679 [235]

ROSEDALE Mf C 1783-1876

ROTHERHAM C 1541-1563 M 1540-1837 B 1542-1563 [260/1,287]; Meth C 1811-37 [266]

ROTHWELL* 1538-1812 [127-9]

ROUNTON, EAST* 1595-1837 [130]

ROUNTON, WEST Mf C 1727-1917 M 1725-1914 B 1725-1917

ROUTH M 1750-1837 [269]

ROWLEY Mf 1605 1607 1620-40 1663-1861

ROXBY CB 1758-1835 [294]; see also PICKHILL

ROYSTON Mf CM 1558-1633 B 1557-1633

RUDSTON* C 1813-1842 M 1813-1839 B 1813-1840 [287] Mf CMB Ext 1599-1692 CMB 1694-1703 1706-1836

RUFFORTH Mf 1582-1600 1633-37 1660-1852

RUSTON, LITTLE Mf CMB Ext 1600-1708 CMB 1710-1836 CB 1837-89

RUTHER Mf 1603-15 1631-40 1661-1888

RYLSTONE* CB 1559-1812 [236/7]

RYTHER Mf 1550-1812

SADDLEWORTH 1613-1800 [238/9] Mfc M(I) 1800-1837; Ind CZ 1836 [266]

SALTBURN Meth (Regent Circus later Albion Terrace) M 1911-1969 [284]

SALTERFORTH Inghamite C 1753-1837 B 1756-1837 [196]; Mfc Bapt C 1753-1837 B 1756-1837

SALTON 1573-1813 [GCI]

SANCTON Mf 1599-1640 1661-1864

SAND HUTTON Chapelry Mf 1634-40 1661-1681; see also BOSSALL

SANDAL MAGNA 1598-1630 [240] Mf 1651-1812 M 1813-1832

SAXTON IN ELMET* 1539-1812 [131]

SCALBY St Lawrence (I) 1556-1840 [285]

SCAMMONDEN with DEANHEAD CB 1746-1812 [241]

SCAMPSTON Chapelry Mf 1866-67; see also RILLINGTON

SCARBOROUGH Mf Ext 1602-82

SCHOLES United Free Church B 1898-1965 [284]

SCORBOROUGH 1653-1791 [28]

SCRAYINGHAM Mf 1626-34 1664-1865

SCRUTON 1572-1837 [298]

SCULCOATES* (1538-1772) C 1813-20 M 1816-24 [132] Mfc M(I) 1813-21; Christ Church Chapelry Mf CM 1822-1841; Rom Cath C 1798-1808 [286]

SEAMER Northallerton 1559-1838 [1/2,GCI]

SEATON ROSS Mf 1600-13 1626-39 C 1660-1920 M 1660-1887 B 1660-1887

SEDBERGH* C 1606-1800 MB 1594-1800 [242-4]

SELBY Mf C 1579-1627 1689-1886 M 1583-1637 1653-1867 B 1581-1642 1689-1886; with BRAYTON 1746 1760 1780-1803

SESSAY* 1600-1812 [133] Mf 1600-05 1628-40 1662-1837

SETTRINGTON* (CB 1559-1812) M (1559-1715)-(1729-1812) [134,269] Mf 1559-1856

SHEFFIELD C 1560-1752 M 1560-1736 B 1560-1719 [135-140,284,288];

SHERBURN IN ELMET Mf 1603-4 1622-41 1653-1866

SHERBURN IN HARFORD LYTHE Mf 1604 1626-40 1661-1889

SHERRIFF HUTTON Mf 1628-37 1663-1856; see also FARLINGTON

SHIPTONTHORPE Chapelry Mf 1600-05 1620-25 1661-86 1701-1870; see also MARKET WEIGHTON

SILKSTONE Mf 1558-1784 C 1813-1830 M 1784-1825

SILSDEN Chapelry Mf 1740 1769-1843(gaps); see also KILDWICK

SILTON, OVER see OVER SILTON

SKELTON Mf 1600-01 1628-37 1662 1673-1872

SKERNE Mf 1600 1610 1626-36 1660-1872

SKIDBY Mf 1600 1626-39 1661-73 1688-1835

SKIPSEA M 1750-1837 [269]

SKIPTON IN CRAVEN C 1592-1837 MB 1592-1812 [245-7,266]

SKIPWITH Mf CB 1670-1779 M 1710-54

SKIRLINGTON see ATWICK

SKIRPENBECK Mf 1631-36 1661-1876

SLAIDBURN Mf C 1688-1812 M 1630-40 B 1630-1694 1735-1796

SLEDMERE Mf 1626-39 1663-1866

SLINGSBY Mf 1600 1625-39 1661-1854

SNAITH* C 1558-1656 MB 1537-1656 [141/2] Mf CB 1656-1727 M 1662-1727

SPOFFORTH Mf C 1598-1732 M 1617-1727 B 1599-1727

STAINLEY, SOUTH Mf CB 1658-1812 M 1658-1754

STAINTON in CLEVELAND Mf M 1754-1837

SNAINTON (Pickering) (I) 1713-1812 [284]

STAMFORD BRIDGE Chapelry Mf 1604 1630-33; see also CATTON

STARFORTH* 1665-1700 [248]

STILLINGFLEET Mf 1599 1632-40 1662-1883

STILLINGTON Ext 1654-1731 [286]

STOCKTON ON THE FOREST Mf 1600-15 1635-36 1661-74 1687-1864

STOKESLEY* 1571-1750 [143]

STRENSALL Mf 1600-04 1633-38 1663-1882

SUTTON, FULL Mf 1597-1610 1629-39 1661-1864

SUTTON ON THE FOREST Mf 1603-04 1631-39 1663-1856

SUTTON UPON DERWENT Mf 1628-40 1661-73 1685-1883

SWILLINGTON* C 1543-1812 M 1540-1812 B 1539-1812 [144]

TADCASTER Mf 1598 1632-41 1666-1859

TANKERSLEY 1598-1840 [264] Mf C 1588-1838 M 1595-1797 B 1687-1812

TERRINGTON* 1600-1812 [145] Mf 1598-1604 1631-41 1661-1863

THIRSK* 1556-1721 [146]

THORGANBY Mf 1610 1626-39 1661-1874

THORMANBY Mf 1605-10 1626-40 1660-1835

THORNABY ON TEES Mf C 1844-76

THORNE M 1565-1697

THORNER Mf 1606-07 1632-39 1661-1842

THORNHILL* 1580-1812 [147-9]

THORNTON Chapelry Mf CB 1682-87 1716-1837; see also BRADFORD

THORNTON ON SPALDING MOOR Mf 1602-11 1611-1848; see also ALLERTHORPE

THORNTON WATLASS Mf C 1746-1848

THORP ARCH Mf 1603 1631-39 1633-1860

THORPE BASSETT CB 1604-1642/3 1657-1837 M 1631-1642/3 1656/7-1835 [295] Mf 1604-06 1627-42 1656-1874

THORPE SALVIN* 1592-1726 [150]

THUSCROSS Mf 1715-31

TICKHILL C 1542-1812 [249]

TINSLEY C 1711-1854 M 1713-1851 B 1711-1851 [283]; Non Conf B 1676-1739 [250]

TOCKWITH Mf CB 1866-91

TOPCLIFFE and MORLEY Non Conf 1654-1739 [250]

UPLEATHAM B 1654-1812 [283]

WADDINGTON* 1599-1812 [151]

WADWORTH C 1574-1920 MB 1575-1920 [251]

WAKEFIELD All Saints Mf 1600-1812; St John Mf CM 1795-1812 B 1796-1812

WALTON IN AINSTY* 1619-1837 [152] Mf 1619-1837

WARMFIELD C 1590-1609 M 1595-98 1602-06 [266]

WARTER Mf 1598-1602 1620-39 1661-1887

WATH UPON DEARNE* 1598-1779 [153]

WATTON Mf 1626-41 1661-1865

WEAVERTHORPE Mf 1631-39 1661-1852

WELBURY Mf Ext 1604-1681

WELWICK M 1754-1840

WENSLEY* 1538-1837 [154/5] Mf C 1750-1847

WESTON 1639-1812 [130]

WESTOW Mf 1626-40 1661-1873

WHARRAM LE STREET Mf 1631-36 1663-73 1686-1836

WHARRAM PERCY Mf 1628-39 1661-1848

WHELDRAKE Mf 1631-40 1661-98 1708-1781

WHENBY C 1724-1981 M 1724-1982 B 1724-1863 [286] Mf 1600 1631-42 1660-1863

WHITBY* (1600-76) C 1660-1768 M 1676-1774 B 1676-1768 [156,278,290-3]; St Mary C 1768-1782 M 1768-1781 B 1775-1782 [296]; Rom Cath C 1792-1840 M 1819-35 B 1817-1830 [269,284]

WHITGIFT Mf 1562-1812

WHITKIRK* 1603-1700 [118] Mf 1701-1837

WHIXLEY Mf CB 1568-1812 M 1568-1754

WIGGINGTON Mf 1598-1601 1631-39 1662 1689-96 1709-1876

WIGHILL Mf 1600-09 1631-41 1666-1861

WILBERFOSS Mf 1600-04 1626-41 1660-1875

WILTON Cleveland St Cuthbert B 1601-1983 [269,284] Mf C 1719-1866; see also REDCAR

WINESTEAD* 1578-1812 [157]

WINTRINGHAM* 1558-1812 [158] Mf C 1563-1914 MB 1558-1914; see also KNAPTON

WISTOW Mf 1635-41 1663-1839

WITTON, EAST Mf M 1751-1836;

WITTON, WEST Rom Cath see DANBY, WEST WITTON & LEYBURN

WOLD NEWTON C 1813-40 M 1786-1834 B 1811-16 [286] Mf C 1722-1812 M 1725-1785 B 1708-85

WOODKIRK or WEST ARDSLEY Mf C 1652-1812 M 1654-1832 B 1654-1812

WOOLLEY Mf C 1600-1898 M 1600-1936 B 1600-1885

WORTLEY Leeds Cong CZ 1802-37 [266]

WRAGBY* 1538-1812 [159]

WRESSLE Mf 1600 1626-40 1662-1866

WYCLIFFE Rom Cath C 1763-1809 [286]

WYKEHAM Mf 1601-10 1628-41 1661-1851

YAPHAM Chapelry Mf 1623 1696-1700 1712-1856; see also POCKLINGTON

YARM 1649-1837 [252/3]

YEDINGHAM Mf 1626-39 1663-1878

YORK* All Parishes Mfc M(I); All Saints Pavement (1554-1738) [160/1] Mfc M(I) 1701-1750 1801-1837; All Saints North Street Mf 1626-41 1661-1865; Holy Trinity Micklegate 1586-1777 [256] Mf CB 1777-1837 M 1754-1837; Holy Trinity Goodramgate (1573-1837) [162,254] Mf 1601 1627-39 1666-1865; Holy Trinity Kings Court 1716-1837 [163,284]; Minster C 1686-1799 M 1681-1762 B 1634-1836 [257,P] Mf B 1814-1836; St Barnabus Mf M 1940-52 B 1935-75; St Crux 1539-1714 (C 1716-1837 MB 1678-1837) [164,267,283] Mf 1626-42 1661-1872; St Cuthbert Mf C 1581-1944 M 1581-1975 B 1581-1895; St Denys Mf CB 1558-1812 M 1558-1750; St Edward Mf C 1849-1866; St Giles Copmanthorpe CB 1759-1837 [254]; St Gregory see St MARTIN cum St Gregory; St Helen Mf 1601 1626-40 1662-91 1703-1892; St John Ouse Bridge Mf 1570-1874; St Laurence 1606-1812 [165]; St Margaret Mf 1600-09 1628-41 1660-1866; St Martin 1557-1837 [166,254]; St Martin cum Gregory 1539-1734 [258] Mf 1600-1679(gaps) 1700-1869; St Mary Bishophill Junior 1602-1837 [167,254] Mf 1626-39 1666-1865; St Mary Bishophill Senior Mf 1600-1698 1702-1812 1844-1871(gaps); St Mary Castlegate 1604-1837 [168/9]; St Maurice M 1648-1812 [259]; St Michael le Belfry 1565-1778 [170/1] Mf C 1565-1963 M 1565-1975 B 1565-1854; St Michael Spurriergate Mf 1598-1691; St Nicholas Mf 1600-01 1604; St Nicholas without Walmgate Bar 1600 1601 1604 [287]; St Olave 1538-1644 [172]; St Sampson Mf 1626-40 1663-1851; St Saviour Mf 1626-39 1661-1869; Little Blake Street Chapel/St Wilfred Rom Cath C 1771-1838 [CRS35]; York Bar Convent Chapel Rom Cath C 1771-1826 [CRS4]; see also COPMANTHORPE and POPPLETON, UPPER

CHANNEL ISLANDS

ALL ISLANDS 1567-1722

GUERNSEY, TORTEVAL Mf C 1841-1875

GUERNSEY Mfc Civil Registration ZD 1840-1907 M 1840-1901; Z(I) A-S 1840-1966 M(I) 1841-1966 D(I) 1840-1963

JERSEY, ST HELIER Zion Chapel C 1827-1841

SARK C 1570-1576 1588-1605 M 1570-1600

ISLE OF MAN

ANDREAS B 1800-1849 [1] Mf ZC 1666-1883

ARBORY B 1729-45 1747 1770-86 1788-1848 1872-1929 [2] Mf ZC 1652-1883

BALLAUGH Ext B 1598-1697 1699-1764

CASTLETOWN St Mary Mf M(I) 1850-1883

DOUGLAS St George Mf C 1781-1883 M(I) 1786-1895

KIRK BRADDAN B 1700-1800 [1] Mf ZC 1626-1883 M 1683-1883

KIRK GERMAN Mf M(I) 1673-1883

KIRK MICHAEL B 1900-1981 [1]

KIRK PATRICK B 1849-1874 [1] Mf M(I) 1714-1837

KIRK RUSHEN Mf C 1709-1883

KIRK SANTAN B 1656-1985 [1]

LEZAYRE B 1696-1861 [1]

LONAN Mf CB 1718-1849 M 1718-1883

MALEW B 1645-1849 [1]

MAROWN B 1908-1961 [1]

MAUGHOLD B 1849-61 1883-1950 [1]

ST MARKS Mf C 1772-1883

IRELAND

Covering the province of Northern Ireland and the Republic of Ireland, unless otherwise stated, these records are Church of Ireland.

ANTRIM

AGHALLEE Ext 1811-45 [31]
BELFAST St Anne, Shankhill (now Cathedral) M(I) 1745-99; Ext CM 1825-44 [28]; St George CM 1817-1870 [27]; Trinity C 1844-77 [28]; First Presb C 1757-1790 B 1712-1736 [29]
BLARIS Ext 1714-23
BUSHMILLS Presb C 1824-36 [31]
DERVOCK Presb C 1827-31 [13]
MAGHERAGALL Ext C 1825-35 [31]
SHANKILL see BELFAST St Anne's Cathedral
MALONE (I) C 1842-87 M 1842-44 [30]

CORK

BALLYMODAN Ext C 1695-1863 M 1695-1845 B 1695-1878 [31]
KILBROGAN C 1752-1872 M 1753-1863 B 1707-1877 [31]

DOWN

LOUGHINISLAND C 1760-1806 1816-37 M 1760-1800 1825-94 B 1760-91 1816-37 [31]
EWRY Presb C 1779-96 1809-1822 M 1781-97 1820-29
KILKEEL C 1816-1842 MB 1816-1827 [28]

DUBLIN

CLOGHRAN C 1782-1864 M 1738-1839 B 1732-1864 [10,31]
CRUMLIN C 1740-1863 M 1764-1827 1832-1863 B 1740-1862 [11]
DALKY see MONKSTOWN UNION
DONNYBROOK* M 1712-1800 [20]
DUBLIN* Christ Church Cathedral B Ext (I) to 1878 [G128]; St Andrew CB Ext (I) 1672-1822 (M 1672-1800) [14,G126]; St Anne (M 1719-1800) M Ext (I) from 1800 [14,G126]; St Audoen M 1672-1800 B(I) 1672-92 [14]; St Bride C 1633-1713 (M 1632-1800) [14]; St Catherine 1679-1715 Ext 1636-1687 M (1715-1800) [15,16]; St James Ext 1636-1687 [15]; St John the Evangelist 1619-99 (M 1700-1798) Ext (I) CB from 1700 M from 1799 [17,20,G126]; St Luke (M 1716-1800) [16]; St Marie (M 1697-1800) [16]; St Mary Ext C 1698-1836 M 1813-28 B 1699-1823; St Michael (M 1656-1800) [20]; St Michan CB 1636-1700 M 1636-1800 Ext C 1701-96 B (I) from 1700 [18,19,20,G125,G128]; St Nicholas Within (M 1671-1800 B 1671-1863) [20]; St Nicholas Without (C 1694-1739 M 1699-1738 B 1697-1720) [21]; St Patrick's Cathedral (1677-1800) [22]; St Paul Ext (I) from 1700 (B 1702-18) [G126]; St Peter & St Kevin (1669-1761) [23]; St Werburgh (M 1704-1800) Ext (I) CB from 1627 M from 1800 [16,G126]; Trinity College, Provost Winter (Ind) (CMB 1650-60) [7]; French Conformed Church of St Patrick & St Mary

C 1668-1818 M 1680-1788 B 1680-1830; Merrion Row Hug B 1719-1731 [M26]
FINGLAS* B 1664-1729 [20]
KILGARVEN ZC 1811-50 M 1812-1947 B 1819-50 1878-1960
KILLINEY see MONKSTOWN UNION
KILMACUD to 1764 see MONKSTOWN UNION
MONKSTOWN UNION* 1669-1800 [26]
TILLORGAN Ext (I) 1782-1869 [G126]
ULLY see MONKSTOWN UNION

FERMANAGH

ENNISKILLEN Ext CB 1673-1772
LISKNASKEA (I) 1804-15 [30]

KERRY

BLENNERVILLE M 1830-33 [31]
CASTLEMAINE Lodden Presb M 1853-1859 [31]
KILGOBBIN M 1713-51 [31]
TRALEE M 1796-1817 [31]

KILDARE

NAAS Ext 1679-1852 [G126]

KING'S

BALLYBOY Ext C 1709-48 1797-1868 M 1709-48 1806-1868

LONDONDERRY

AGHADOWEY C 1845-86 M 1845-90
DERRY see LONDONDERRY
DRUMACHOSE Ext C 1857-68 B 1855-74 [31]
LONDONDERRY St Columb's Cathedral 1642-1703 [12]
TEMPLEMORE, see Londonderry

LIMERICK

LIMERICK COUNTY British Armed Forces M(I) 1698-1842 [25]
ABINGTON M(I) 1813-45 [25]
ADARE M(I) 1826-45 [25]
ANEY (I) 1759-1802 M(I) 1761-2 1785 [25]
ARDCANNY M(I) 1802-45 [25]
BALLINGARY Ext CB 1698-1735 M(I) 1698-1715 1730-34 1785-1845 [25]
DOON M(I) 1812-45 [25]
KILFERGUS M(I) 1815-45
KILFINANE M(I) 1804-24 1831-45 [25]
KILKEEDY M(I) 1803-45 [25]
KILMEEDY M(I) 1805-45 [25]
KILSCANNEL M(I) 1825-45 [25]
LIMERICK St Johns M(I) 1697-1845 [25]; St Michael M(I) 1799-1845 [25]; St Munchin M(I) 1734-68 1797-1845 [25]; St Mary Cathedral M(I) 1726-54 1759-1845 [25]; St Patrick M(I) 1700-1704 [25]
NANTINAN Ext M 1784-1821 B 1783-1820
RATHKEALE M(I) 1744-1845 [25]

LOUTH

DARVER see DROMISKIN with DARVER
DROMISKIN C 1799-1840 M 1805-42 B 1802-1907 [L58]
(includes DARVER to 1831)
KILSARAN C 1818-40 MB 1818-1908 [L58]
MANFIELDSTOWN C 1825-84 M 1824-45 B 1838-84
[L58]
STABANNON C 1688-1847 M 1703-1907 B 1699-1907
[L58]

MAYO

ADERGOOLE see CROSSMOLINA
BALLINA see KILMOREMOY
CROSSMOLINA C 1768-1817 M 1768-1815 B 1768-
1821 [10,31]
KILFIAN see CROSSMOLINA
KILLALA C 1757-69 M 1757-67 B 1757-72 [10,31]
KILMOREMOY C 1768-1820 MB 1768-1823 [10,31]
MOYNAUNAGH see CROSSMOLINA

QUEEN'S

PORTARLINGTON French Colony C 1694-1810 M 1694-
1808 B 1695-1816 [HS19]

SLIGO

CASTLE CONNOR CB 1867-72 [10,31]

TIPPERARY

CASHEL* Liberties 1654-57 [7]

TYRONE

ARBOE C 1775-1871 M 1773-1845 B 1776-1900 [28]
BALLYCLOG Ext 1826-89 [31]
CASTLECAULFIELD C 1746-1870 M 1741-1882 B 1741-
1870 [8,9]
CLONOE C 1825-59 M 1819-42 B 1826-63
DONAGHENRY Ext B 1733-59 [31]
DONAGNMORE St Michael see CASTLECAULFIELD
DRUMGLASS Ext 1677-1849 [31]
KILLYMAN Ext 1747-1860 [31]
KILSKEERY C 1767-1835 Ext 1837-44 M 1778-1841 B
1796-1841 [30]
TULLANISKEN Ext 1804-73 [31]

WATERFORD

CROOKE see DUNMORE EAST
DUNMORE EAST (UNION) 1730-1864 [30]
FAITHLEGG see DUNMORE EAST
KILL ST NICHOLAS see DUNMORE EAST
LISMORE Cathedral M 1692-1869
RATHMOYLAN see DUNMORE EAST
WATERFORD Cathedral 1655-1707; Presb C 1770-1813
M 1761-1802 [30]

WESTMEATH

KILLUCAN 1700-75 [24,G125]
RATHCONNELL Ext (I) 1797-1861 [G126]

WEXFORD

KILBEGGAN Ext 1715-1736
KILLURIN see WHITECHURCH
WHITECHURCH Ext 1715-1736

SCOTLAND

OLD PAROCHIAL REGISTERS - ALL SCOTLAND Mfc
Surname Index to CM to 1855
Civil Registration ALL Scotland Mf ZMD(I) 1855-1920
SFrs ALL Scotland Z 1647-1874 M 1656-1875 D 1667-
1878 [20]

Entries are CHURCH of SCOTLAND unless otherwise
indicated.

ABERDEENSHIRE

ABERDEEN St Nicholas & Old Machar Mfc(I) CM to
1854; St John Episc C 1778-1855 M 1818-1855
[33]; St Machar Episc C 1730-1752 [33]; St Pauls
Episc C 1720-1827 M 1720-47 1767-1841 [26-30]
Military C 1753-90 M 1753-57; Trinity Episcopal CM
1753-1803 [21,22]
CHAPEL HALL and TILLYDESK see MACTERRY
CRUDEN St James the Less (Episc) C 1807-1861 M
1807-1869 B 1807-1870 [19]
CUMINESTOWN Episc C 1848-1883 M 1848-1879 B
1848-1880 [38]; see also TURRIFF
DEER, OLD (Episc) C 1681-1834 M 1687-1732
[17,31/2,39,40]
ELLON St Mary on the Rock (Episc) CB 1803-1871 M
1807-1870 [14] (United congregations of UDNEY,
BAIRNIE, KINHARRACHIE and TILLYDESK); Old
Meldrum congregation CB 1804-07 [14]
FOLLA-RULE C 1717-1859 MD 1820-1859 [18]
FOVERAN B 1753-1854 [15]
FRASERBURGH Episc 1766-1884 [25]
KINHARRACHIE Episc see ELLON
LONGSIDE St John Episc C 1727-1860 M 1743-44 1812-
30 1851-1889 B 1817-1885 [37]
LONMAY Episc C 1727-68 1803-1928 M 1727-32 1827-
1926 DB 1826-1929 [16]
MACTERRY C 1772-1790 [14]
MELDRUM, OLD see ELLON
STRACHAN B Ext 1831-42 [M39]
TILLYDESK C 1775-1801 [SRS30]; see also BAIRNIE,
Episc ELLON, MACTERRY
TURRIFF St Congan Episc C 1776-1894 M 1799-1895 B
1813-1893 [38] see also CUMINESTOWN
UDNEY Episc C 1763-1801 [14]; see also ELLON

Scotland

ANGUS

AIRLIE Mf Z 1682-1854 M 1682-1861 D 1706-1824
ARBROATH Mf B 1825-54
CLOVA see CORTACHY & CLOVA
CORTACHY and CLOVA Mf ZM 1662-1854 B 1697-1854
DUNDEE All parishes Mfc (I) CM to 1854; St Peter B
    1837-1866; Rom Cath Cathedral, St Andrew C
    1795-1838 M 1806-1827 B 1804-1816 [2] Mf C
    1795-1838 M 1806-27
GLAMIS Mf C 1677-1867 MB 1699-1715 1834-1854
GLENISLA Mf ZM 1719-1854 D 1748-1793
GUTHRIE Mf Z 1664-1854 M 1693-1854 D 1716-1794
KINGOLDRUM Mf Z 1700-1854 M 1743-1854 D 1747-
    1854
KINNELL Mf ZM 1657-1854 D 1657-1663 1814-1854
KIRRIEMUIR Mf C 1716-1854 M 1821-54 B 1788-91
    1830-54
LINTRATHEN Mf ZM 1717-1854 D 1717-93 1820-1854
OATHLAW Mf ZM 1717-1854 D 1720-46 1783-1790
RESCOBIE Mf Z 1685-1854 M 1783-1854 B 1784-1794
RUTHVEN Mf ZM 1744-1854 D 1744-1798
ST VIGEANS Mf Z 1820-1854 M 1790-1854 B 1836-1854
TANNADICE Mf Z 1694-1854 M 1717-1768 B 1722-1773

ARGYLLSHIRE

CAMPBELTOWN Mf Z 1659-1854 M 1681-1854 B 1773-
    1854
CRAIGNISH Mf ZM 1755-1854 D 1755-1820
DUNOON and KILMUN Mf ZM 1742-1854 D 1742-1781
KILMUN see DUNOON and KILMUN

AYRSHIRE

ARDROSSAN Mf ZM 1734-1854 C(I) 1843-1854
AYR Mf Z 1664-1854 M 1687-1854 D 1766-1854
BEITH Mf ZM 1659-1854 D 1659-1819
COLMONELL Mf Z 1759-1854 M 1820-1854
CUMNOCK, NEW Mf Z 1706-1854
CUMNOCK, OLD Mf Z 1704-1854 M 1737-1854 B 1783-
    92
DREGHORN Mf ZM 1749-1854
DUNDONALD Mf Z 1673-1854 MD 1676-1854
GIRVAN Mf Z 1733-1854 M 1769-1854 D 1769-1819
IRVINE Mf Z 1687-1854 MD 1721-1819
KILMARNOCK Mf Z 1640-1854 M 1687-1854 D 1728-
    1819
KILMAURS Mf ZM 1688-1854 D 1688-1820
KILWINNING Mf C 1669-1854 M 1678-1854
LOUDON Mf ZM 1673-1854 B 1811-1857
MAUCHLINE Mf ZMD 1670-1854
MUIRKIRK Mf Z 1718-1854 M 1739-1854 B 1773-1900
STEVENSTON Mf ZM 1700-1854 D 1700-1849

BANFFSHIRE

BANFF St Andrew Episc CM 1723-1752 [24] (includes
    some Presb C)
PORTSOY St John the Baptist Episc 1799-1911 [23]

BERWICKSHIRE

BUNKLE and PRESTON CM 1684-90 [1]

COLDINGHAM Mf Z 1694-1854 M 1690-1854 B 1694-
    1744
COLDSTREAM Mf ZM 1690-1854 D 1695-1854
DUNS Mf Z 1615-1854 M 1797-1867 D 1797-1854
EARLSTON Mf ZM 1694-1854 D 1694-1820
ECCLES Mf ZM 1697-1854 D 1754-1854
EYEMOUTH Mf ZM 1710-1854 D 1710-1792
FOGO Mf ZM 1660-1854 D 1820-1854
GREENLAW Mf Z 1699-1854 MD 1648-1854
HUTTON Mf ZMD 1700-1854
LADYKIRK Mf 1697-1854 D 1697-1822
LAMBERTON TOLL Mf Irreg M 1833-1848; see also
    MORDINGTON
LANGTON Mf ZM 1728-1854 D 1728-1822
MORDINGTON M Ext 1737-1854 Mf ZMD 1721-1854;
    see also LAMBERTON TOLL
NENTHORN Mf Z 1702-1854
POLWARTH Mf ZM 1652-1854 D 1652-1843
PRESTON see BUNKLE and PRESTON

BUTESHIRE

BUTE, NORTH Mf ZM 1844-54
KILBRIDE Mf ZM 1723-1854
KILMORY Mf ZM 1701-1854
KINGARTH Mf Z 1727-1854 M 1820-1854 D 1727-1819
LOCHRANZA Mf Z 1732-1846 M 1819-1840
ROTHESAY Mf ZM 1691-1854
SHISKIN Mf Z 1732-1852 M 1785-1861

CAITHNESS

CANISBAY CM 1652-66 [SRS48] Mf ZM 1652-1721 1747-
    1854

DUMFRIESSHIRE

ANNAN Ext M 1797-1854; Mf Z 1703-1854 M 1764-1854;
    see also WIGTON <CUL>
APPLEGARTH and SIBBALDIE Mf ZMB 1749-1854
BRYDEKIRK Mf ZM 1836-1854
CANONBIE Mf Z 1693-1854 M 1768-1854 B 1768-1805
DUMFRIES Mf Z 1605-1854 M 1616-1854 D 1617-1854
GRETNA Mf ZM 1730-1854
GRETNA HALL Irreg M 1829-55 [SRS80]
HALFMORTON Mf Z 1787-1854 MD 1820-1854
HODDAM Mf Z 1748-1854 M 1746-1819
KIRTLE Mf Z 1838-1844
LANGHOLM Mf ZM 1668-1854 B 1675-1854
LOCHMABEN Mf Z 1741-1854 M 1765-1854 B 1766-
    1819
MAXTON Mf ZMD 1689-1854
MIDDLEBIE Mf ZM 1744-1854
MOFFAT Mf Z 1723-1854 M 1709-1854 D 1709-81 1819-
    1854
MORTON Mf ZM 1692-1854
MOUSEWALD Mf Z 1751-1854 M 1784-1854 B 1783-
    1854
PENPONT Mf Z 1728-1854 M 1845-1854
RUTHWELL Mf Z 1723-1854 M 1807 1844-1854 B 1773-
    1775
SANQUHAR Mf ZM 1693-1854 D 1820-1854
SIBBALDIE see APPLEGARTH and SIBBALDIE
ST MUNGO Mf ZM 1700-1854
TINWALD Mf Z 1789-1854

TORTHORWALD Mf ZMD 1696-1854
TUNDERGARTH Mf ZMD 1791-1854
TYNRON Mf ZMD 1742-1854

DUNBARTONSHIRE

DUMBARTON Mf C 1666-1854 M 1682-1854 D 1642-1795

EDINBURGHSHIRE see MIDLOTHIAN

EAST LOTHIAN

DUNBAR Mf Z 1672-1854 M 1651-1854 D 1737-1854
HADDINGTON Mf ZM 1619-1854 D 1619-1785
HOLYROOD HOUSE see EDINBURGH
WATTINGHAME Mf ZM 1627-1854
YESTER Mf ZM 1654-1854

FIFE

ABDIE Mf Z 1620-1854 M 1691-1854 D 1784-5
ABERDOUR Mf Z 1663-1854 M 1650-1854 D 1658-9 1790-1854
AUCHTERMUCHTY Mf ZMD 1649-1854
COLLESSIE Mf CM 1696-1854 B 1723-1854
CRAIL MF ZM 1655-1854 D 1655-1819
CREICH Mf Z 1695-1854 M 1694-1854 D 1785-1854
CUMBRAES Mf ZM 1730-1854
CUPAR Mf ZMD 1654-1854
DUNFERMLINE CM 1561-1685 [SRS44]
FALKLAND Mf Z 1669-74 1702-1855 M 1661-1856 B 1670-1706 1737-1853
KIRKCALDY Mf Z 1614-1854 M 1615-88 1732-1867 B 1732-1743
MONIMAIL Mf ZM 1656-1854 D 1697-1854
MOONZIE Mf Z 1713-1854 M 1741-1855 D 1821-54
NEWBURGH Mf ZM 1654-1855
ST ANDREWS Episc CM 1722-87 [SRS49]; Mf Z 1627-1854 M 1638-1854 B 1732-1854
ST LEONARDS Mf Z 1667-1854 M 1668-1854
STRATHMIGLO Mf C 1719-1854 M 1702-1854 B 1714-1854

FORFARSHIRE see ANGUS

HADDINGTONSHIRE see EAST LOTHIAN

INVERNESS

ABERNETHY and KINCARDINE Mf C 1730-1854 M 1730-1819 1822-1854
ALVIE Mf C 1713-1854 M 1713-1789 1826-1854
BENBECULA Mf Z 1848-54 M 1848-51
HARRIS Mf ZC 1823-1854 M 1838-1854
KILMUIR Mf Z 1823-1854 M 1839-1854 see also STENSCHOLL
KINCARDINE see ABERNETHY
PORTREE Mf ZM 1800-1854
SLEAT Mf Z 1813-1853 M 1813-1852
SNIZORT Mf Z 1823-1854 M 1823-1856
ST KILDA Mf Z 1830-1851 M 1830-1849 D 1830-1846

STENSCHOLL Mf Z 1838-1839 M 1838-1843 see also KILMUIR
STRATH Mf Z 1820-1854 M 1823-1854
UIST, NORTH Mf ZM 1821-1854
UIST, SOUTH Mf M 1839-1848

KINCARDINESHIRE

MUCHALLS St Ternan Episc C 1727-1952 M 1738-1949 B 1813-1954 [2,3,36]
STONEHAVEN Scotch Episc C 1793-1878 [34]; St James the Great Episc C 1758-1815 M 1770-1880 B 1828-1864 [35]

KIRKCUDBRIGHTSHIRE

BALMAGHIE Mf Z 1768-1854 M 1805-1854
BORGUE Mf Z 1742-1854 M 1741-1854 B 1764-1854
BUITTLE Mf Z 1736-1854 M 1737-1854 B 1789-1852
CARPHAIRN Mf Z 1758-1854
COLVEND Mf ZMB 1715-1787 Z 1781-1854 M 1840-1854 B 1838-1854
CROSSMICHAEL Mf ZM 1751-1854 D 1820-54
DALRY Mf ZM 1691-1854 D 1820-54
GIRTHON Mf ZMD 1699-1854
KIRKBEAN Mf Z 1714-1820 M 1714-1790 B 1714 1824-1854
KIRKCUDBRIGHT Mf Z 1706-08 1743-1854 M 1743-1805 1820-1854 B 1826-1853
KIRKGUNZEON Mf Z 1702-1854 M 1812-1854
KIRKMABRECK Mf Z 1703-1854 M 1820-1854 B 1820-1840
KIRKPATRICK DURHAM Mf Z 1769-1854
LOCHRUTTON Mf Z 1698-1854 M 1697-1854 B 1766-90 1820-1854
MINNIGAFF Mf ZM 1694-1854
TWYNHOLM Mf Z 1694-1722 1762-1854 M 1694-1719 1763-1854 D 1762-68 1835-1854
URR Mf Z 1760-1854 M 1770-1854

LANARKSHIRE

BARONY see GLASGOW
BIGGAR Mf ZM 1730-1854
BLANTYRE Mf ZM 1677-1854 D 1677-1843
BOTHWELL Mf Z 1671-1854 M 1692-1702 1761-90 1827-54 B 1754-1854
CALTON Mf Z 1846-53
COVINGTON and THANKERTON Mf ZMD 1772-1854
CRAWFORD and LEADHILLS Mf Z 1698-1854
CRAWFORDJOHN Mf Z 1694-1854 MD 1693-1854
CULTER Mf ZMD 1700-1854
DALSERF Mf ZMD 1738-1854
DALZIEL Mf ZM 1648-1854 D 1648-1819
DOLPHINGTON Mf ZM 1717-1854
DOUGLAS Mf Z 1691-1854 MD 1698-1854
GLASGOW all parishes (in Royalty, Barony, Govan & Gorbals) Mfc(I) CM to 1854; High Church Mfc (I) to 1854; Barony Mf ZM 1672-1854 D 1778-1835; see also CALTON and PORT GLASGOW
HAMILTON Mf ZM 1645-1854 D 1647-1714
LEADHILLS see CRAWFORD & LEADHILLS
MONKLAND, OLD Mf Z 1695-1854 M 1790-1854
MOTHERWELL see DALZIEL
THANKERTON see COVINGTON and THANKERTON

LINLITHGOWSHIRE see WEST LOTHIAN

MIDLOTHIAN

BAIRNIE C 1763-1775 [SRS30]; see also TILLYDESK and
ELLON (Episc)
CANONGATE see EDINBURGH
EDINBURGH M 1595-1800 [SRS27/32/53]; Greyfriars
Burying Ground B 1658-1700 [SRS26]; Canongate
Kirk CMB 1564-67 [SRS90] see also Holyrood
House; Holyrood House, Chapel Royal (or Abbey) M
1564-1800 B 1706-1900 [SRS25/46]
GREYFRIARS see EDINBURGH
LASSWADE Mfc C 1650-1733 M 1642-1759 B 1689-95
LEITH Episc 1733-75 M 17368-758 [SRS81]
LEITH, SOUTH Irreg M 1697-1818 [SRS95]
RESTALRIG B 1728-1854 [SRS32]
WHITTINGHAME see WATTINGHAME

PEEBLESHIRE

TWEEDSMUIR Mf ZMD 1644-97 1720-1854

PERTHSHIRE

ABERNETHY Mf C 1690-1733 1749-1854 M 1690-1727
1783-94
ALYTH Mf Z 1623-1854 M 1623-1754 1786-1854 D 1624-
51 1688-1736
BLAIRGOWRIE Mf ZMD 1647-1854
CALLANDER Mf ZMD 1710-1854
CAPUTH Mf Z 1677-1854 M 1671-1854 B 1722-1795
1833-1838
DOWALLY Mf ZM 1705-1854 B 1750-1847
DUNBLANE Mf ZM 1653-1854 D 1828-1854
DUNKELD Mf Z 1672-1854 M 1707-1861 D 1806-7
DUNKELD, LITTLE Mf ZM 1759-1854
KIRKMICHAEL Mf Z 1720-1854 M 1770-1855 B 1784-
1789
LOGIERAIT Mf Z 1650-1854 M 1650-1754 1760-1854 D
1760-1815
MADDERTY Mf C 1701-1854 M 1702-1847 B 1758-99
1837-53
MEIGLE Mf C 1727-1854 M 1732-1854 B 1728-65
MENTEITH see PORT OF MENTEITH
METHVEN Mf ZM 1667-1854 D 1783-87 1822-3
MUTHILL C 1697-1846 C(I) 1847-1886 [10]
PERTH Mf ZMD 1561-81 Z 1614-1854 M 1756-1854 D
1820-1830
PORT OF MONTEITH Mf ZM 1697-1854

RENFREWSHIRE

ABBEY see PAISLEY
GREENOCK East Kirk Mf Z 1809-1854 M 1809-1855;
Middle (New) Kirk Mf ZM 1741-1854 B 1741-1752;
West (Old) Kirk Mf Z 1698-1854 M 1698-1855 B
1698-1747
KILBARCHAN CM 1649-1772 [SRS41]
PAISLEY Abbey Mf Z 1676-1854 M 1670-1854 B 1759-
1864; Low Kirk or Burgh Z 1738-1854 M 1739-1854;
Middle Kirk Mf 1788-1854; High Kirk Mf ZM
1788-1854
PORT GLASGOW Mf Z 1696-1854 M 1769-1854

RENFREW Mf ZM 1673-1854 D 1732-1828

ROSS & CROMARTY

KILMUIR-EASTER Mf C 1738-1854 M 1783-1854 B 1783-
89 1820-54
TAIN Mf Z 1719-26 1767-1854 M 1808-1854; United Free
C 1843-1855 [2]
TARBAT Mf Z 1801-1854 M 1809-1854

ROXBURGHSHIRE

ECKFORD Mf ZM 1694-1854 D 1694-1820
EDNAM Mf ZMD 1666-1854
HAWICK Mf Z 1634-1854 M 1699-1800 1821-1854 D
1758-1854
KELSO Mf Z 1598-1854 MD 1597-1854
LINTON Mf ZM 1732-1854
MAKERSTON Mf ZMD 1692-1854
MELROSE C 1642-1820 M 1645-1822 B 1760-1819
[SRS45]
MINTO Mf ZMD 1703-1854
MOREBATTLE Mf ZMD 1726-1854
OXNAM Mf ZMD 1700-1854
ROXBURGH Mf ZMD 1624-1854
WILTON Mf Z 1694-1854 MD 1707-1854

SELKIRKSHIRE

ETTERICK Mf ZMD 1693-1854
GALASHIELS Mf ZMD 1714-1854
KIRKHOPE Mf ZM 1851-1854
ROBERTTON Mf Z(I) 1679-1854 CM 1679-1854 B 1744-
1801
SELKIRK Mf Z(I) 1697-1854 CM 1697-1854 B 1741-1854
YARROW Mf ZM 1691-1854 B 1731-1854

STIRLINGSHIRE

CAMPSIE Mf C 1646-1855 M 1646-1860 B 1646-1854
DENNY Mf Z 1679-1854 M 1680-1854 B 1783-1788
FALKIRK Mf Z 1594-1854 M 1599-1854 B 1817-1861
FINTRY Mf Z 1659-1854 M 1667-1854 B 1818-19
KILSYTH Mf ZM 1619-1854 D 1841-1853
POLMONT Mf Z 1729-1854 MD 1731-1854
STIRLING Z 1587-91 C 1587-94 1671-86 [2,12] Mf ZM
1585-94 Z 1671-1854 C 1820-1854 M 1723-1854 D
1727-1854

SUTHERLAND

DURNESS 1764-1814 [SRS38]
LAIRG Mf Z 1768-1854 M 1784-1854 D 1804-1844
LOTH Mf Z 1795-1854 M 1809-1854
ROGART Mf Z 1768-1854 M 1769-76 1838-1854
TONGUE Mf Z 1791-1854 M 1792-1854

WIGTOWNSHIRE

LESWALT see PORTPATRICK
PENNINGHAME Mf ZM 1695-1854
PORTPATRICK Irreg M 1759-1826; Mf ZM 1720-1854 D

1720-1819
STONYKIRK see PORTPATRICK
STRANRAER Mf Z 1695-1854 M 1712-1853 B 1847
1850; see also PORTPATRICK
WHITHORN Mf Z 1763-1854 M 1796-1854
WIGTOWN Mf Z 1736-1855 M 1731-82 1832

WEST LOTHIAN

BATHGATE Mf CM 1672-1854 B 1698-1853
LINLITHGOW Mf Z 1687-1854 Z(I) 1613-1688 M 1652-
1854 D 1652-1825
TORPICHEN 1673-1714 [SRS40]

SHETLAND

DUNROSSNESS Wes Meth C 1848-1868 M 1851-1854
[3]
LERWICK Wes ZC 1831-74
NORTHMAVINE Wes Mf C 1830-1874 M 1844-1879
ROOE, NORTH Wes Mf C 1874-1879 M 1844-1874
TINGWALL M 1696-99
UNST M 1797-1863 [SRS78] Mf C 1776-1855 M 1797-
1854 B 1833-1854; Free Church Mf Z 1842-1849

WALES

ANGLESEY

BEAUMARIS C 1723-81 M 1724-53 B 1724-1781 [66]
HOLYHEAD St Cybi 1682-1840 [16]
LLANFAETHLU 1678-1840 [20,36]
LLANFAIR YN NEUBWLL CB 1677-1841 M 1677-1837
[21,36]
LLANFIHANGEL YN NHYWYN C 1679-1838 M 1692-
1835 B 1685-1838 [36]
LLANFWROG CB 1672-1840 M 1677-1839 [22]
RHOSCOLYN (I) 1732-60 1780-1801 [70]

BRECKNOCKSHIRE

CRICKADARN Mf CB 1734-56 1775-82 M 1734-1970 B
1813-1983
DEVYNNOCK Ind C 1775-1837 Calv Meth ZC 1790-1837
[66]
FAENOR Mf C 1813-1923 M 1755-1847 B 1813-1905
1923-50
GLASBURY 1660-1836 [13]
LAMBEDDER see LLANDILOPORTHOLE
LLANBEDR Mf 1704-1849
LLANDEFEILOG FACH Mf 1712-1837
LLANDEFEILOG TREGRAIG Mf 1710-1839
LLANDILORFAN see LLYMEL
LLANFIHANGEL CWM DU Mf C 1688-1799
LLANILEU see LLANDILOPORTHOLE
LLYWEL Welsh Calv Meth ZC 1813-37 [68]; Ind C 1822-
1837 B 1830-1837 [68]; Zoar Calv Meth ZC 1728-
1836 [68]; Zoar Chapel,Pentrefelin B 1824-1837;
Llandilorfan Calv Meth ZC 1822-1834 [68]
MAESYBERLLAN Part Bapt Z 1803-1837 [68]
PATRISHSHW see LLANDILOPORTHOLE

TALACHDDW 1600-1679 [L3]
TRECASTLE see LLYWEL

CAERNARVONSHIRE

ABERERCH* Ext C 1652-1774 M 1684-1762 B
1664-1725
CONWAY* 1541-1793 [10]
CRICCIETH* Ext C 1675-1798 M 1715-67 B 1696-1807
[M3]
DYNEIO Ext C 1749-88 B 1765-1837 [M3]
LLANARMON Calv Meth ZC 1812-36
LLANBEDROG Ext C 1691-1812 M 1691-1802 B 1692-
1868
LLANDYGWNNING Mf CB 1780-1812 M 1779-1812
LLANFAIRFECHAN C 1660-1810 MB 1635-1812 [3]
LLANFIHANGEL BACHELLAETH Ext C 1693-1804 M
1723-97 [M3]
LLANGIAN* Ext C 1709-57 M 1710-50 B 1709-1864 [M3]
LLANGYBI Ext C 1701-1812 M 1708-49 B 1702-1874
[M3]
LLANNOR C 1757-1811 B 1760-1803 [M3]
LLANYSTUMDWY Ext C 1658-1845 M 1664-1793 B
1662-1902

CARDIGANSHIRE

ABERARTH Calv Meth C 1816-1836 [80]
ABERPORTH M 1813-1837 [45,46]
BANGOR TEIFI M 1813-1837 [45,46]
BETWS BLEDRWS M 1813-37 [45,46]
BETWS IFAN M 1813-37 [45,46]
BETWS LEUCU M 1813-37 [45,46]
BLAENPENNAL M 1813-37 [45,46]
BLAENPORTH 1716-1812 M 1813-1837 [35,45,46]
BRONGWYN with TROEDYRAUR and PEN BRYN Ind C
1785-1816 M 1813-37 [66]; Nonconf Chapel C 1814-
1837 [71]
CAPEL CYNON M 1813-37 [45,46]
CARDIGAN M 1813-37 [45,46]
CELLAN M 1813-37 [45,46]
CILCENNIN M 1813-37 [45,46]
CILIAU AERON M 1813-37 [45,46]
DIHEWYD M 1813-37 [45,46]
EGLWYS FACH M 1754-1837 [45,46,93]
EGLWYS NEWYDD M 1811-18378 [45,46] Mf 1811-1888
FERWIG M 1813-37 [46]
FFOSFIN Calv Meth C 1807-35 [67]
GARTHELI M 1813-37 [45,46]
GLYNARTHEN see BRONGWYN and TREWEN
GWNNWS M 1813-37 [45,46]
HAWEN see BRONGWYN and TREWEN
HENFYNYW M 1813-37 [45,46]; Ind Neuaddlwyd C
1831-37 [67]
HENLLAN M 1813-37 [45,46]
LAMPETER M 1813-37 [45,46]
LLANAFAN M 1813-37 [45,46]
LLANARTH M 1813-37 [45,46]
LLANBADARN ODWYN M 1813-37 [45,46]
LLANBADARN TREFEGLWYS M 1813-37 [45,46]
LLANBADARNFAWR Calv C 1812-37 M 1695-1736 1754-
1837 [45/6,93]; Calv Ponterwyd 1813-37 [67]
LLANDDEINOL M 1813-37 [45,46]
LLANDDEWI ABERARTH M 1813-37 [45,46]
LLANDDEWI BREFI M 1813-37 [45,46]
LLANDYFRIOG CB 1725-1812 M 1725-1837 [67]

LLANDYGWYDD C 1677/8-1802 M 1677/8-1752 1813-37 B 1677/8-1740 [35,45,46]
LLANDYSUL M 1813-37 [45,46]
LLANERCH AERON M 1813-37 [45,46]
LLANFAIR CLYDOGAU M 1813-37 [45,46]
LLANFAIRORLLWYN M 1813-37 [45,46]
LLANFAIRTREFHELYGEN see LLANDYFRIOG
LLANFIHANGEL-Y-CREUDDYN M 1813-37 [45,46]; Calv Meth C 1822-1837 [67]
LLANFIHANGEL GENAU'GLYN M 1735-1837 [45,46,93]
LLANFIHANGEL YSTRAD M 1813-37 [45,46]
LLANFYNYDD M 1813-37 [49,50]
LLANGEITHO M 1813-37 [45,46]
LLANGOEDMOR M 1813-37 [45,46]
LLANGRANNOG M 1813-37 [45,46]
LLANGWYRYFON M 1813-37 [45,46]
LLANGYBI M 1813-37 [45,46]
LLANGYNFELIN M 1754-1837 [45,46,93]
LLANGYNLLO M 1813-37 [45,46] see also TROEDYRAUR
LLANILAR M 1813-37 [45,46]
LLANINA M 1813-37 [45,46]
LLANLLWCHAEARN M 1813-37 [45,46]
LLANRHYSTUD M 1813-37 [45,46]
LLANSANTFFRAID M 1813-37 [45,46]
LLANWENOG M 1813-37 [45,46]
LLANWNNEN M 1813-37 [45,46]
LLANYCHAEARN M 1813-37 [45.46]
LLECHRYD M 1813-37 [45,46]
LLEDROD M 1813-37 [45,46]
MWNT M 1813-37 [45,46]
NANTCWNLLE M 1813-37 [45,46]
PENBRYN C 1726-1838 M 1736-1837 B 1736-94 [35,45,46] see also BRONGWYN
PENMORFA Calv ZC 1813-37 [70]
RHOSTIE M 1813-37 [45,46]
SILIAN M 1813-37 [45,46]
STRATA FLORIDA M 1813-37 [45,46]
TREFGARON M 1813-37 [45,46]
TREFILAN M 1813-37 [45,46]
TREMAIN M 1813-37 [45,46]
TREWEN Ind Z 1819-37 C 1814-37 see also BRONGWYN
TROEDYRAUR CB 1655-1803 M 1655-1753 1813-37; Calv Twrgwyn C 1808-37 [71[see also BRONGWYN [45,46]
YSBYTY CYNFYN M 1762-1837 [45,46,93]
YSBYTY YSTWYTH M 1813-37 [45,46]
YSTRAD MEURIG M 1813-37 [45,46]

CARMARTHENSHIRE

CARMARTHENSHIRE M 1813-37 [49] M(I) 1813-37 [50]

ABERGWILI CB 1813-75 M 1661-1875 [5,49/50] Mf CMB 1661-1721 CB 1723-1902 M 1723-1934
ABERGORLECH C(I) 1883-1988 M(I) 1901-69 B(I) 1813-75 [89]
ABERNANT (I) CB 1813-75 M 1754-1875 [38,49/50]
BETWS M 1813-37 [49/50]
BRECHFA M 1813-37 [49/50] C(I) 1813-1886 M(I) 1806-1970 B(I) 1813-1915 [89]
CARMARTHEN* 1671-1799 M 1813-37 [49,50,P]
CENARTH M 1813-37 [49,50] Mf C 1701-68 1775-1909 M 1701-1837 B 1701-68 1775-1844
CILYCWM M 1813-37 [49,50]

CILYMAENLLWYD M 1813-37 [49,50]
CYFFIG M 1813-37 [49,50]
CYNWYL ELFED CB 1813-75 M 1743-1837 [38,49 50]
CYNWYL GAEO M 1813-37 [49,50] Mf C 1698-1979 M 1697-1754 1783-1970 B 1698-1970
EGLWYS BACH Bryndinion Calv Meth ZC 1825-1837; Pwllterfyn Calv Meth ZC 1813-37 M 1813-37
EGLWYS CYMUN M 1813-37 [49,50]; Mf 1690-1869
EGLWYSFAIR A CHURIG M 1813-1875 [49,50]
EGREMONT M 1813-37 [49,50]
HENLLAN AMGOED M 1813-37 [49,50]
HEOL ANST Meeting House M(I) 1913-87 [89]
KIDWELLY M 1627-1809 1813-37 Ext CB 1765-1809 [3,4,49,50]
LAUGHARNE C 1651-1812 M 1639-40,1645-1799 1813-37 B 1645-1812 [3,4,49,50,54]
LLAN-NON M 1813-37 [49,50]
LLANARTHNEY CB (I) 1813-75 M (grooms) 1720-1875 M 1813-37 [38,49,50]
LLANBOIDY C(I) 1813-75 M 1813-37 [49,50] CMB 1798 1802 1804 1806-9 [49/50,53,67]
LLANDAWKE M 1813-37 [49,50]
LLANDDAROG CB(I) 1813-75 M(grooms) 1736-1875 M 1813-37 [38]
LLANDDEILO ABERCYWYN M 1813-37 [49,50]
LLANDDEUSANT M 1813-1837 [49,50]; see also LLANTHOYSAINT
LLANDDOWROR CB 1813-75 M 1720-1875 (grooms) 1813-37 [39,49,50]
LLANDEILO M 1813-37 [49,50]
LLANDEILO FAWR C 1679-1776 M 1683-1769 1813-37 B 1679-1779 [49,50,80]
LLANDINGAD M 1813-37 [49,50] Mf C 1733-1909 M 1733-1904 1937-65 B 1733-1911
LLANDYBIE M 1813-37 [49,50]
LLANDYFAELOG M 1813-37 [49,50]
LLANDYFEISANT M 1813-37 [49,50]
LLANEDI M 1813-37 [49,50]
LLANEGWAD C(I) 1813-1901 M 1813-37 M(I) 1701-1913 B(I) 1813-1905 [49/50,89]
LLANELLI C 1688-1800 M 1687-1837 B 1693-1886 [49/50,WS/L37]
LLANFAIR-AR-Y-BRYN M 1813-37 [49,50]
LLANFALLTEG M 1813-37 [49,50]
LLANFIHANGEL ABERBYTHYCH 1675-1766 C 1875-1922 M 1698-1875 B 1813-1875 [1,49,50,90]
LLANFIHANGEL ABERCONWIN CB(I) 1813-1875 [67]
LLANFIHANGEL AR-ARTH C 1813-75 M 1756-1875 B 1813-75 [49/50,90]
LLANFIHANGEL CILFARGEN C 1813-1934 M 1755-1838 Banns 1785-1875 [49/50,90]
LLANFIHANGEL RHOS Y CORN C 1813-1986 M 1754-1966 B 1813-1985 [49/50,90]
LLANFYNYDD C 1813-1989 M 1698-1875 B 1813-1989 [91]
LLANGADOG M 1813-37 [49,50]
LLANGAIN CB(I) 1813-75 M(I) 1772-1875 M 1813-37 [39,49,50]
LLANGAN M 1813-37 [49,50]
LLANGATHEN C 1813-1972 M 1747-1970 B 1813-1965 [49/50,91]
LLANGELER M 1813-37 [49,50] Mf C 1704-1877 M 1704-1804 1813-1921 B 1704-1804 1813-1900
LLANGENDEIRNE M 1671-1754 Ext C 1665-1811 B 1668-1807 [1]
LLANGENNECH M 1813-37 [49,50]
LLANGLYDWEN M 1813-37 [49,50]

LLANGUNNOR M 1675-1754 CB Ext 1678-1786 CB(I)
1813-75 M (grooms) 1678-1875 M 1813-37
[1,39,49,50]
LLANGYNDEYRN M 1813-37 [49,50]
LLANGYNIN CB 1813-75 M(I) 1756-1875 M 1813-37
[39,49,50]
LLANGYNOG CB(I) 1813-1875 M 1813-37 [49,50,68]
LLANLLAWDDOG CB 1813-75 M 1695-1875 [5,49,50]
LLANLLWCH CB(I) 1813-1875 M(grooms) 1754-1875 M
1813-37 [39,49,50]
LLANLLWNI M 1813-37 [49,50] Mf C 1739-58 1787-1923
M 1739-58 1813-1971 B 1739-53 1787-1910
LLANPUMPSAINT CB 1813-75 M 1695-1875 [5,49,50]
LLANSADURNEN C 1663-1812 M 1667-1812 B
1665-1812 [53]
LLANSADWRN M 1813-37 [49,50]
LLANSADWRNEN M 1813-37 [49,50]
LLANSAWEL M 1813-37 [49,50]
LLANSTEPHAN C Ext 1677-1753 M 1697-1739 1813-37
B 1714-58 [3,4,49,50]
LLANTHOYSAINT Calv Meth ZC 1816-37 [68]
LLANWINIO CB(I) 1813-75 M(grooms) 1754-1875 M
1813-37 [49,50]
LLANWRDA M 1813-37 [49,50]
LLANYBYDDER M 1813-37 [49,50]
LLANYCRWYS M 1813-37 [49,50]
MARROS M 1813-37 [49.50]
MEIDRIM CB(I) 1813-75 M(grooms) 1654-1875 1813-37
[42,49,50]
MERTHYR CB(I) 1813-75 M(grooms) 1686-1875 M 1813-
37 [40,49,50]
MYDDFAI M 1813-37 [49,50]
NEWCHURCH (I) 1813-75 M(grooms) 1742-1875 M
1813-37 [40,49,50]
PEMBREY M 1813-37 [49,50]
PENBOYR M 1813-37 [49,50] Mf C1752-1901 M 1752-
1970 B 1752-1947; St Barnabas M 1907-64
PENCARREG M 1813-37 [49,50]
PENDINE M 1813-37 [49,50]
ST CLEARS (I) CB 1813-75 M(grooms) 1682-1875 M
1813-37 [40,49,50] Mf 1672-1854
ST ISHMAEL M 1561-1641 1678-1753 1813-37 [4,49,50]
TALLEY M 1813-37 [49,50]
TRELECH A'R BETTWS (I) CB 1813-75 M(grooms) 1663-
1875 M 1813-37 [40,49,50]
WHITLAND M 1813-37 [49,50]

DENBIGHSHIRE

ABERCHWILER Calv Meth ZC 1812-1837 [78]
ABERGELE Betws Abergele Calv Meth ZC 1811-1837
[76]; Brynllwyni Calv Meth ZC 1830-1837 [76];
Ebenezer & St George Ind ZC 1832-1837 [76];
Mount Sion Calv Meth ZC 1810-1837 [76]
BRYN EGLWYS Calv Meth ZC 1820-1837 [76]
CEFN MERIADOG Calv Meth ZC 1810-1835 [76]
CERRIGYDRUDION Calv Meth ZC 1811-1837 [76];
Hermon Indep ZC 1799-1837 [76]
CHIRK C 1705-58 M 1719-54 B 1708-57 [23,75]
COLWYN BAY see ABERGELE
CORWEN see CERRIGYDRUDION
CYFFYLLIOG Calv Meth ZC 1812-37 [77]
DENBIGH 1684-1837 [36]; Wes ZC 1814-1837 [78];
Middle Calv Meth ZC 1810-37 [78]; Indep C 1763-
1837 [79]
DERWEN Calv Meth ZC 1818-1837 [76]

EFENECHTYD C 1693-1812 M 1693-1811 B 1694-1812
[2]; Calv ZC 1826-1837 [77]
EGLWYSBACH Pwllterfyn Calv Meth ZC 1813-1837;
Bryndionyn Calv Meth ZC 1825-1836 [76]
EVENECHTYD see EFENECHTYD
GLYNDYFRDWY Calv Meth ZC 1835 [76]
GLYNTRAEAN Erwallo Calv Meth ZC 1830-36 [77]
GRESFORD CB 1660-1810 M 1660-1812 [59]
GWYTHERIN Calv Meth ZC 1814-1837 [76]
HENLLAN Capel Mawr Calv Meth ZC 1810-37 [78];
Henllan Green Calv Meth ZC 1824-37 [78]; Groes
Calv Meth ZC 1834-37 [78]
HOLT CB 1740-1812
ISYCOED C 1749-1816 M 1750-1837 B 1750-1813
LLANARMON DYFFRYN CEIRIOG Calv Meth ZC 1812-
1836 [77]
LLANBEDR DYFFRYN CLWYD Ext C 1656-1891 M 1690-
1868 B 1652-1883 [80]
LLANDYRNOG Calv Meth ZC 1811-1837 [78]
LLANELIAN Calv Meth ZC 1825-37 [76]
LLANELIDAN C 1686-1812 M 1696-1812 B 1694-1811
[2,80]; Calv Meth ZC 1810-1837 [77]
LLANFAIR DYFFRYN CB 1732-1812 M 1755-1812 [65];
Calv Meth ZC 1823-1837 [77]
LLANFAIR TALHAEARN Calv Meth ZC 1822-37 [76]
LLANFWROG CB 1638-1755 1760-1840 M 1638-1840
[80]; Bapt ZC 1790-1837 [37,77]
LLANGERNYW Calv Meth Pandt Tudur ZC 1811-1837
[76]; Calv Meth Cefn Coch and Pandy ZC 1810-
1837 [76]
LLANGOLLEN C 1670-1780 M 1699-1786 B 1670-1790
[80]; Calv Meth Pontcysyllte ZC 1805-1937 [77];
Cong ZC 1811-37 [77]; Wes ZC 1812-37 [77]
LLANGWM Ind ZC 1799-1837 [76]
LLANGWYFAN Ind ZC 1834-37 [78]
LLANGYNHAFAL CB 1706-1779 M 1706-1747 [2]; Calv
Meth ZC 1814-37 [78]
LLANNEFYDD M 1754-1812; Bapt Z 1805-37 [78]; Calv
Meth ZC 1810-37 [78]
LLANRHAEADR-YNG-NGHINMEMCH Calv Meth Pentre
ZC 1812-37; Prion ZC 1825-37; Saron ZC 1834-37
[78]
LLANSANNAN 1667-1812 [24]; Bapt Z 1814-30; Calv
Meth ZC 1811-37; Tanyfron Calv Meth ZC 1812-
1837 [78]
LLANSANTFFRAID GLANCONWAY Calv Meth ZC 1813-
37 [76]
LLANSILIN Cong ZC 1813-37 [77]
LLANTYSILIO Z 1759-1812 C 1671-1717 1721-1755
1759-1812 M 1671-1717 1721-1812 B 1671-1717
1721-55 1758-1812; Pentredwr Calv Meth ZC 1829-
1836 [77]; Horeb Calv Meth ZC 1821-1836 [77]
LLANVERRES C 1611-1845 M 1612-1834 B 1611-1897
[80]
LLANYCHAN C 1677-1874 M 1677-1833 B 1676-1832
[37,80]
LLANYNYS C 1626-1880 M 1626-1837 B 1626-1837
[27,80]
LLYSFAEN Calv Meth ZC 1834-37 [76]
NANT GLYN CB 1720-79 M 1720-45 [80]; Calv Meth ZC
1811-37 [80]
PENTREFOELAS Calv Meth ZC 1833-36 [76]
RUABON C 1559-1812 M 1559-1812 B 1559-1812 [85/6]
RUTHIN C 1609-85 M 1608-47 B 1614-1720 [80]; Mill
Wes ZC 1813-37 [77]; Pendref Ind ZC 1824-37 [77];
Rhos Calv Meth ZC 1813-37 [77]
WREXHAM C 1618-1756 M 1632-1754 B 1620-1756

[22,55-6,60]
YSBYTY IFAN Bethel Ind ZC 1806-37; Capel Mawr Calv
Meth ZC 1812-37 [76]

FLINTSHIRE

BANGOR-ON-DEE C 1797-1812 M 1754-1812
CAERWYS 1673-1812
CILCAIN CB 1576-1812 M 1576-1843 [73]
GWAENYSGOR 1538-1812
HALKYN C 1595-1706 1719-1803 M 1595-1698 B 1594-
1698 1764-1803
HANMER M 1749-1787 Ext CMB 1563-1850 [4,67]
HOLYWELL C 1728-37 B 1714-23 [66]; Rom Cath
Secular Mission C 1730-1802 Jesuit Mission C
1779-1829 [CRS3]
HOPE C 1668-1731 1781-1812 M 1668-1731 1754-1812
B 1668-1731
MELIDEN 1602-1718
MOLD C 1612-1772 1798-1812 M 1604-44 1653-1812 B
1611-47 1652-1722
NERCWYS (NERQUIS) CB 1732-1812 M 1755-1812
NORTHOP 1656-1812
RHUDDLAN 1681-1742 [2]
TREMEIRCHION C 1604-1812 M 1604-1812 B 1604-1812
[2,80]
WHITFORD CM 1643-1812 B 1662-1812

GLAMORGAN

CARDIFF SS John & Mary C 1813-40 Late C 1841-68 M
1813-40 B 1813-41 [6,7]; Bethany Babt Z 1804-37
Deaths 1807-37; Ind C 1818-1837 [8]; Wes C 1798-
1837 [8]
CHAPEL HILL St Mary CB 1813-1900 M 1837-1900 [98]
COYCHURCH C 1760-1850
FLEMINGSTONE Mf 1576-1725
LLANEDRYN 1700-1837 [29,36]
LLANGYFELACH Mf 1676-1794
LLANSAMLET CB 1807-12 [75]
LLANTRISANT Ind C(I) 1819-1844 B(I) 1813-1817 [53]
LLANTRITHYD C 1597-1810 M 1571-1751 B 1571-1810
[68]
LOUGHOR M 1754-1837 [4]
MARGAM ABBEY C 1672-1843 (I) 1843-94 M 1666-1837
(I) 1813-1887 B 1672-1840 (I) 1840-1953
[28,33,34,69]
OYSTERMOUTH CM 1714-1840 B 1719-1840 [29]
PENARTH C 1835-63 M 1831-79 B 1832-86
PENDEULWYM Mf CM 1569-1632 B 1569-1633
PETERSTON SUPER ELY CB 1749-1812 M 1754-1812
[30]
PORT TALBOT see MARGAM ABBEY
ST ATHAN Mf C 1679-95 1750-1812 M 1683-95 1720-
1812 B 1663-95 1719-50 1760-67 1771-1812

MERIONETHSHIRE

LLANDDERFEL Ext 1602-1721 1757 [4]
LLANGAR CB 1614-1806 M 1615-1708 1724-1811 [80]

MONTGOMERYSHIRE

MONTGOMERYSHIRE Mf 1663-1853; Catholic Records
see Mf Westminster Cathedral Archives

BETTWS Calv Meth (I) C 1826-1836 [66]
BUTTINGTON* Mf 1660-1848
FORDEN Ind C 1827-36 [67,92]
HYSSINGTON Mf 1660-1870
KERRY 1602-1812 [17,18]
LLANSANTFFRAID YM MECHAIN C 1813-1911 M 1789-
1837 B 1759-67 [68]
LLANYMYNECH 1666-1812 [SH/R47]
MONTGOMERY Rom Cath CM 1747-1752 [CRS14]

MONMOUTHSHIRE

Non conformist Registers see Herefordshire Parish
Records

ABERGAVENNY Rom Cath C 1740-1838 M 1741-1776 D
1743-1817 [CRS27]; Rom Cath in CofE Register
CMB Ext 1653-1779 [CRS27]
BEDWAS C 1635-1715 M 1715-39 B 1656-1730 [4]
BEDWELLTY M 1815-1817 [36]
BETTWS NEWYDD CB 1813-1974 M 1796-1836 [66]
BISHTON C 1793-1899 M 1800-13 1838-1900 B 1806-11
1814-1900 [72]
CAERLEON C 1695-1878 M 1695-1924 B 1695-1893 [43]
CAERWENT C Ext 1660-1712 C 1752-1900 M 1706-13
1753-1834 1839-1900 B 1568-1646 1661-1711 1752-
1811 1813-1900 [19,72]
CHEPSTOW Ext 1558-1837 [9] Ext 1595-1924 [42]
COURTFIELD Rom Cath 1773-1834 [CRS4]
CWMCARVAN CMB 1660-1705 C 1728-1900 MB 1743-
1900 [74]
CWMYOY see LLANDIOPORTHOLE
DINGESTON C 1742-1900 M 1755-75 1779-1811 1814-
1900 B 1755-1900 [74]
DIXTON C 1661-1869 M 1661-1837 B 1661-1852 [66] Mf
C 1661-1870 M 1661-1837 B 1661-1852
GOLDCLIFF B 1813-1981 [67]; Chapel C 1871-1911 [87]
GOYTRE CB 1695-1844 M 1695-1869 [14]
GROSMONT 1589-1672 1678-1900 [15,87]
ITTON CB 1813-1900 M 1838-1898 [98] Mf C 1725-1868
KEMEYS COMMANDER C 1813-1973 M 1813-1970 [67]
KEMEYS INFERIOR C 1701-1840 M 1701-1837 B 1701-
1838 [67]
KILGWRWG CB 1813-1900 [98]
LANGUA Mf CB 1714-1810 M 1714-1843
LLANARTH* Rom Cath C 1781-1838 B 1781-94 [CRS3]
LLANBADOG* 1582-1709 [19]
LLANDDEWI FACH C 1741-1798 1813-61 M 1741-54
1813-36 B 1741-1845 [53]
LLANDDEWI RHYDDERDH 1670-1783 [19]
LLANDEGFEDD C 1746-1859 M 1747-1832 B 1747-1850
[53]
LLANDILOES C 1711-1719 M 1711-1718 [75]
LLANDILOPORTHOLE Meth Calv C 1811-37 [67]
LLANDOGO CB 1813-1900 M 1755-1900 [98]
LLANDYRNOG Calv Meth ZC 1811-1837
LLANFAIR DISCOED* C (1568-1812)-1900 M (1568-
1812)-1836 B (1568-1812)-1900 [19,72]
LLANFAIR KILGEDIN C 1833-1844 M 1733-1837 B 1733-
1839 [35]
LLANGATTOCK LINGOED C 1696-1900 M 1696-1753
1755-1837 1840-1900 B 1696-1900 [87]
LLANFIHANGEL PONTYMOEL C 1739-1869 MB 1739-
1855 [75]

LLANFIHANGEL YSTERN LLEWERN* 1685-1812 [19]
LLANGOVAN C 1680-1900 M 1680-1749 1755-1900 B
1680-1900 [53,67]
LLANGYBI C 1679-1838 M 1679-1839 B 1678-1840 [74]
LLANOVER C 1661-1852 M 1661-1837 B 1661-1896 [35]
LLANTHEWY SKIRRID CB 1549-1729 1813-1900 M
1549-1729 1815-1900 [88]
LLANTILIO CROSSENNY* 1577-1644 [25]
LLANTILIO PERTHOLEY C 1591-1899 M 1591-1893 B
1591-1900 [82]; Rom Cath in C of E Register CMB
Ext 1693-1804 [CRS27]
LLANTRISSENT C 1813-43 B 1813-40 [68]
LLANVIHANGEL CRUCORNEY 1629-1802 [26]
LANVIHANGEL GOBION C 1813-1977 M 1813-36 1844-
1968 B 1813-1975 [68]
LLANWENARTH see LLANDILOPORTHOLE
LLANWERN C 1750-1811 1814-1900 M 1820-1900 B
1755-1786 1815-1900 [88]
MALPAS C 1813-1930 M 1759-1932 B 1813-1925 [69]
MAMHILAD 1682-1837 [75]
MATHERN CB 1565-1739 1742-1792 1813-1900 M 1565-
1739 1754-1835 1837-1900 [72]
MONMOUTH St Mary - Rom Cath in C of E Register ZB
Ext 1601-1831 [CRS27]; Monmouth Mission Rom
Cath cm 1791-1830 [CRS27]
MOUNTON C 1813-1900 M 1845-1900 B 1790-1811
1813-1898 [98]
NASH C 1813-1943 M 1758-1970
NEWCHURCH C 1710-1942 M 1710-1970 B 1710-1897
[41]
NEWPORT St Woolos Cathedral C 1702-1742 1769-1905
M 1702-1749 1754-1900 B 1692-1742 1769-1825
1829-1871 [61-64]; Ind C 1770+ [P]; Wes Meth
Circuit C 1877-1900; Wes Meth, Price Street C
1880-1900; Wes Meth, Maindee C 1896-1900 [88]
ORCOP Mf CB 1661-1852 M 1661-1840
PANTEG C 1598-1838 MB 1598-1837 [37,70]
PENALLT CB 1779-1900 M 1765-1900 [70,98]
PENRHOS* 1577-1644 [25]
PENYCLAWDD CB 1727-1900 M 1727-1811 1815-1900
[70]
PERTHIR* Rom Cath C 1751-1818 M 1777-78 B 1776-78
[CRS1]
REDWICK CB 1785-1900 M 1754-1811 1813-1900 [99]
ROCKFIELD Rom Cath in C of E Register ZB Ext 1696-
1812 [CRS9]
ST ARVANS CB 1802-1900 M 1792-1900 [99]
ST BRIDES NETHERWENT 1813-1900 [99]
ST MAUGHANS Rom Cath in C of E Register ZB Ext
1739-1793 [CRS9]
ST PYR (ST PIERRE) 1813-1900 [99]
SKENFRITH CMB 1639-1900 [88]
TINTERN CB 1813-1900 M 1756-1811 1814-1900 [99]
TREDYNOG C 1695-1874 M 1695-1764 1813-37 B 1695-
1848 [74]
TREGARE C 1751-1812 M 1751-1900 B 1751-1900 [75]
TREVETHIN C 1652-1709 1714-1837 M 1652-1709 1714-
1837 B 1652-1709 1806-1834 [32,35,37]
TROSTREY C 1723-1801 1805-1975 M 1761-1802 1804-
12 1816-36 B 1731-1802 1805-1975 [71]
UNDY C 1813-91 M 1754-1812 1838-1900 B 1813-1900
[99]
WELSH BICKNOR* Rom Cath (Courtfield Domestic
Chapel) C 1773-1832 M 1808-31 B 1808-32 [CRS3]
WHITSON C 1744-1986 M 1729-1970 B 1728-1815 [71]

PEMBROKESHIRE

M(I) 1813-37 [48]

AMBLESTON M 1813-1837 [47/8]
AMROTH M 1813-1837 [47/8]
ANGLE M 1813-1837 [47/8]
BAYFIL M 1813-1837 [47/8]
BEGELLY C 1757-1800 M 1771-99 1813-37 B 1757-82
[47/8,51]
BLETHERSTON M 1813-37 [47/8]
BOSHERSTON M 1813-37 [47/8]
BOULSTON C 1799-1878 1937-9 M 1754-1809 1813-37
B 1813-83 1890-91 [47/8]
BRAWDY M 1813-37 [47/8]
BRIDELL M 1813-37 [47/8]
BURTON M 1754-1837 [47/8,66]
CAMROSE M 1813-37 [47/8]
CAPEL COLMAN M 1813-37 [47/8]
CAREW C 1780-1819 M 1779-1837 B 1778-1812
[47/8,51]
CASTLEBYTHE M 1813-37 [47/8]
CASTLEMARTIN M 1813-37 [47/8]
CILGERRAN M 1813-37 [47/8]
CILRHEDYN M 1813-37 [47/8]
CLARBESTON M 1813-37 [47/8]
CLYDAU M 1813-37 [47/8]
COSHESTON C 1723-40 1752-1825 M 1723-53 1761-
1837 B 1723-40 1752-1812 [47/8,51]
CRINOW M 1813-37 [47/8]
CRUNWEAR M 1813-37 [47/8]
DALE M 1813-37 [47/8]
DINAS* M 1813-37 [47/8] Mf CMB 1675-1703 1799-1879
EGLWYSWRW M 1813-37 [47/8]
FISHGUARD M 1813-37 [47/8]
FREYSTOP M 1813-37 [47/8]
GRANSTON M 1813-37 [47/8]
GUMFRESTON 1799-1806 M 1813-37 [47/8,51]
HAROLDSTON ST ISSELS M 1813-37 [47.48]
HAROLDSTON WEST M 1813-37 [47/8]
HASGUARD M 1813-37 [47/8]
HAVERFORDWEST St Martin C 1722-1812 M 1729-1884
B 1721-1839; St Mary C 1642-43 1678-1850 M
1594-1637 1699-1704 1728-1837 B 1614-1620 1683-
1706 1728-1839 St Thomas C 1716-1907 M 1713-
1852 B 1712-1879 [44,47/8]
HAYSCASTLE M 1813-37 [47/8]
HENRY'S MOAT M 1813-37 [47/8]
HERBRANDSTON M 1813-37 [47/8]
HODGESTON M 1813-37 [47/8]
HUBBERSTON M 1813-37 [47/8]
JEFFRESTON C 1730-1837 M 1761-1775 1801-37 B
1748-1837 [47/8,51]
JOHNSTON M 1813-37 [47/8]
JORDANSTON M 1813-37 [47/8]
LAMBSTON M 1813-37 [47/8]
LAMPETER VELFREY M 1813-37 [47/8]
LAMPHEY 1813-37 [47/8]
LAWRENNY C 1716-93 1801-03 1819-36 M 1717-54
1780-99 1813-37 B 1717-61 [47/8,52]
LETTERSTON M 1813-37 [47/8]
LITTLE NEWCASTLE M 1813-37 [47/8]
LLANDDEWI VELFREY M 1813-37 [47/8]
LLANDEILO M 1813-37 [47/8]
LLANDELOY M 1813-37 [47/8]
LLANDYSILIO M 1813-37 [47/8]

LLANFAIR NANT-GWYN M 1813-37 [47/8]
LLANFAIR NANT-Y-GOF M 1813-37 [47/8]
LLANFIHANGEL PENBEDW M 1813-37 [47/8]
LLANFYRNACH M 1813-37 [47/8]
LLANGOLMAN M 1813-37 [47/8]
LLANGWM M 1813-37 [47/8]
LLANHOWEL M 1813-37 [47/8]
LLANLLAWER M 1813-37 [47/8]
LLANRHEITHAN M 1813-37 [47/8]
LLANRHIAN M 1813-37 [47/8]
LLANSTADWELL M 1813-37 [47/8]
LLANSTINAN M 1813-37 [47/8]
LLANWNDA M 1813-37 [47/8]
LLANYCEFN M 1813-37 [47/8]
LLANYCHAER M 1813-37 [47/8]
LLANYCHLWYDOG M 1813-37 B 1783-1812 [47/8,52]
LLAWHADEN M 1754-1837 [47/8]
LLYS Y FRAN M 1813-37 [47/8]
LOVESTON 1799-1837 [80]
LUDCHURCH C 1779-1839 M 1783-1837 B 1779-1790
    [47/8,52]
MAENCLOCHOG 1813-37 [47/8]
MANORBIER M 1813-37 [47/8]
MANORDEIFI/DIVY CB 1724-70 M 1724-47 1735-53
    1813-37 [47/8,69]
MANOROWEN M 1813-37 [47/8]
MARLOES M 1813-37 [47/8]
MARTLETWY C 1757-85 1827-37 M 1757-80 1813-37 B
    1757-85 1809-11 1813-37 [47/8,52]
MATHRY M 1813-37 [47/8]
MELINE M 1813-37 [47/8]
MINWEAR C 1753-81 M 1757-98 1813-37 B 1753-1808
    [47/8,52]
MONINGTON M 1813-37 [47/8]
MONKTON M 1813-37 [47/8]
MORFIL M 1813-37 [47/8]
MOYLGROVE M 1813-37 [47/8]
MYNACHLOGDDU M 1813-37 [47/8]
NARBERTH 1813-37 [47/8]
NASH see UPTON
NEVERN M 1813-37 [47/8] Mf C 1663-1909 M 1663-
    1754 1759-82 1913-37 B 1663-1869
NEW MOAT M 1813-37 [47/8]
NEWPORT M 1813-37 [47/8]
NEWTON NORTH 1813-37 [47/8]
NOLTON M 1813-37 [47/8]
PEMBROKE ST MARY M 1813-37 [47/8]
PEMBROKE ST MICHAEL M 1813-37 [47-48]
PENALLY M 1813-37 [47/8]
PENRHYDD M 1813-37 [47/8]
PONTFAEN M 1813-37 [47/8]
PRENDERGAST C 1702-44 1760 1767-90 M 1813-37
    [47/8,52]
PUNCHESTON M 1813-37 [47/8]
PWLLCROCHAN M 1813-37 [47/8]
REDBERTH CB 1802-1809 M 1813-37 [47/8,52]
REYNALTON M 1813-37 [47/8]
REYNOLDSTON 1786-1802 [52]
RHOSCROWTHER M 1813-37 [47/8]
ROBESTON WATHEN M 1813-37 [47/8]
ROBESTON WEST M 1813-37 [47/8]
ROCH M 1813-37 [47/8]
ROSEMARKET M 1813-37 [47/8]
RUDBAXTON M 1813-37 [47/8] Mf 1799-1886
SLEBECH 1799-1820 M 1813-37 [47/8,52]
SPITTAL M 1813-37 [47/8]
ST BRIDES 1799-1877 [47/8] Mf M 1813-37

ST DAVIDS M 1813-37 [47/8]
ST DOGMAELS M 1813-37 [47/8]
ST DOGWELLS M 1813-37 [47/8]
ST EDRENS M 1813-37 [47/8]
ST ELVIS M 1813-37 [47/8]
ST FLORENCE 1799-1805 M 1813-37 [47/8,52]
ST ISHMAELS M 1813-37 [47/8]
ST ISSELLS C 1656 1685 1799-1837 M 1656 1775 1801-
    37 B 1656 1685 1800-37 [47/8,71]
ST LAWRENCE M 1813-37 [47/8]
ST NICHOLAS M 1813-37 [47/8]
ST PETROX M 1813-37 [47/8]
ST TWYNELLS M 1813-37 [47/8]
STACKPOLE ELIDOR M 1813-37 [47/8]
STEYNTON M 1813-37 [47/8]
TALBENNY M 1813-37 [47.48]
TENBY M 1813-37 [47/8]
TREFGARN M 1813-37 [47/8]
TREGARN M 1813-37 [47/8]
UPTON & NASH C 1800-26 M 1800-37 B 1800-06 1809-
    20 [47/8,52]
UZMASTON M 1813-37 [47/8]
WALTON EAST M 1813-37 [47/8]
WALTON WEST M 1813-37 [47/8]
WALWYN'S CASTLE M 1813-37 [47/8]
WARREN M 1813-37 [47/8]
WHITCHURCH M 1813-37 [47/8]
WHITECHURCH M 1813-37 [47/8]
WISTON M 1813-37 [47/8]
YERBESTON 1801-35 M 1813-37 [47/8,52]

RADNORSHIRE

ABEREDW CMB Ext 1687-1722 C 1740-1900
    Illegitimate 1822-46 M 1741-1971 B 1740-1901 [92]
DISCOED* Mf CB 1680-1805 M 1680-1933
DISSERTH 1734-1812 [11]
LLANANNO Bapt Z 1792-1837 [37]
LLANBEDR PAINSCASTLE* Mf 1687-1850
LLANBISTER* Mf 1702-1840
LLANFIHANGEL RHYDITHON Mf C 1732-1944 M 1732-
    1837 B 1732-1812
LLANGYNLLO Mf C 1744-1986 M 1744-1970 B 1744-
    1925
MAESYRHELEM (Llananno) Bapt Z 1792-1837
MICHAELCHURCH ON ARROW 1662-1837 [83]
PRESTEIGNE Mf C 1561-1912 M 1561-1922 B 1561-
    1904
RADNOR, NEW CB 1644-1708 M 1655-1708 [31]
RADNOR, OLD Mf C 1736-1870 M 1736-54 1804-70 B
    1736-1870

OVERSEAS

ANTIGUA

St George (Fitches Creek) Ext C 1734-1828 M 1734-1879 B 1734-1827 [WI/R1]; St John C 1689-1860 M 1690-1850 B 1689-1837 [WI/R1]; St Mary (Old Road) Ext B 1733-1860; St Paul (Falmouth) Ext C 1725-1853 M 1725-1839 B 1726-1840 [WI/R1]; St Peter (Parham) Ext C 1726-1864 M 1773-1885 B 1726-1829 [WI/R1]; St Philip Ext C 1767-1835 M 1686-1797 B 1686-1855 [WI/R1]

ARGENTINA

Buenos Aires (Hurlingham Ch Hall) CM 1909-46

ASCENSION ISLAND see ST HELENA

AUSTRALIA

New South Wales
M 1788-1800 Mfc (I) CB to 1856 Z 1856-1899 M to 1899 D 1856-99
48th Foot (Northants Regt) C 1817-1824
Burragorang Rom Cath B 1855-1947
Cox's River Rom Cath B 1873-1938
Sydney M 1815-1817; First Fleet (St Philip) C 1787

Northern Territory
Mfc Alien Z(I) 1888-1922 Alien D(I) 1875-1922
Anthony Lagoon (Police Station Mortuary) D(I) 1890-1949
Darwin Alien Z 1888-1922 D 1875-1922
Katherine (Mortuary) D(I) 1887-1941
New Castle Waters (Police Station Mortuary) D(I) 1893-1932

Queensland
Mfc (I) CB 1829-1856 M 1839-1899 D 1856-1899 B 1829-1856
Brisbane M 1868-72 [1] Mfc M(I) 1856-1899 D(I) 1856-1894
Moreton Bay ZMD(I) 1846-1860 [2]

South Australia
Mfc (I) ZM 1842-1906 D 1842-1905
Adelaide (St Paul) C 1860-1870; Hospital D 1840-1842
Morialta (St John) C 1873-1920 M 1873-1915

Tasmania
Hobart Bapt B 1835-1886
Oatlands B 1827-1836
Sidmouth (Auld Kirk Presb Cemetery) B 1840-1982 [P]

Victoria
Mfc (I) ZD 1837-1895 M 1837-1913 Mfc C(I) 1896-1913
Barry's Reef (Private Register) D 1894-1902
Castlemaine (Presb) M 1853-1859

Western Australia
Mfc (I) Z 1841-1895 MD 1841-1896

Bunbury (Pioneer Park) B 1839-52

BANGLADESH
see INDIA

BARBADOS

Christ Church M 1643-1800; St James M 1693-1800; St John M 1657-1794; St Joseph M 1718-1800; St Lucy M 1750-1798; St Micheal's Cathedral (Bridgetown) M 1648-1800; St Peter M 1779-1800; St Philip M 1672-1800; St Thomas M 1723-1800 [ALL in WI/L12]

BENCOOLEN
see INDONESIA

BERMUDA
1784-1914 [WI/R6-7]

BRAZIL

Recife (Pernambuco British Cemetery) B 1822-1916

BURMA
European B 1826-1980

CANADA

British Columbia
Mount View B 1892-1895
Osoyoos Cemetery B 1937-1971

New Brunswick
St John (City and County) M to 1839 [4]

Nova Scotia
Z(I) 1864-1877 [G6]
Halifax (St Paul) 1749-1768 [1] 1931 [L8]

Ontario
Rev Robert McDowall Register Presb M 1800-1836
Adolphustown Presb C 1782-1839
Ameliasburgh Presb C 1801-1839
Amherst Isle Presb C 1834-1840
Brantford Bapt Ext CD 1833-1884
Camden Presb C 1800-1839
Cramhe Presb C 1799-1820
Ernestown CM 1787-1814 [3]; Presb C 1800-1820
Fredericksburgh Presb C 1800-1840
Fort Hunter (Indian) 1735-1745
Hallowell M 1803-1823; Presb C 1779-1820
Halton see Palermo
Hamilton Presb C 1787-1803; see also Palermo
Kingston (St George) 1785-1811 [1]; Presb (St Andrew) C 1802-1869 M 1822-68 [2]
Loughboro Presb C 1791-1837
Markham Circuit Prim Meth C 1851-1866
Marysburgh Presb C 1799-1837
Milton see Palermo
Murray Presb C 1798-1820
Palermo Circuit Meth 1901-1956
Pittsburgh Presb C 1800-1809
Portland Presb C 1791-1807
Quinte Bay M 1836-1838
Rawdon Presb C 1803

115

Richmond Presb C 1811-1832
Sheffield Presb C 1831-1839
Sidney Presb C 1800-1820
Sophiasburgh Presb C 1800-1828
Thurlow Presb C 1802-1839
Toronto (St James Cathedral) Mfc C 1807-1908
Tyendinaga Presb C 1826-1837

Quebec
Bapt Mf 1860-1882; Cong Mf 1862-1881; Prot Mfc
1790-1875
Dalesville Bapt 1837-1843
Levis County Prot M 1820-1948 [3]
Montreal 1766-1787; (St Sulpice) 1706-1980 [1];
Rom Cath Irish M 1851-1899
Quebec Garrison Church (CofE) Mf 1797-1815
Riviere du Loup en Bas (CofE) Mf 1841-1875
St Charles aux Mines C(I) 1717-1723
St Joseph (CofE) 1835-1950 [2,10]

Saskatchewan
Mistawasis (Indian Mission) Presb M(I) 1905-1922
Pleasantville Presb M(I) 1903-1905

CYPRUS

Nicosia (SS Paul & Barnabas) C 1939-52

DENMARK

Copenhagen (British Legation) 1835-1899; (St
Albans) 1887-1899 [1]

EGYPT

Alexandria (British Army Camp) 1801 [MAL/R1-2]

FALKLAND ISLANDS

Port Stanley (Christ Church Cathedral) C 1840-1949
M 1844-1949 B 1838-1949 [1-3]
South Georgia ZMD 1910-1948

FRANCE

Bordeaux (Guyenne) civil M : Saint Andre 1704-
1792; Saint Christoly 1737-1792; Sainte Colombe
1611-1789; Sainte Croix 1641-1790; Saint Eloi
1668-1790; Sainte Eulalie 1618-1790; Saint Mexant
1619-1790; Saint Michel 1654-1791; Saint Nicolas
de Graves 1640-1789; Saint Pierre 1635-1790; Saint
Projet 1659-1791; Puy-Paulin 1662-1790; Saint Remi
1678-1788; Saint Seurin 1669-1792; Saint Simeon
1667-1791 [all in L1]
Caen (Normandy) Prot 1560-1572 [1]
Loudon (Poitou) Prot C 1566-1577 M 1566-1582 [2]
St Germain-en-Laye (Seine) Jacobite Ext 1689-1720
[3-4]
Verdun-sur-Meuse (Lorraine) English Prisoners Ext
C 1804-1814 MB 1806-1814 [5]

FRENCH WEST INDIES

Guadaloupe (British Garrison) 1813-1816

GEORGIA, SOUTH see FALKLAND IS.

GERMANY

Nuremburg (Bavaria) St Sebald B 1517-1572 [1]

GREECE

Athens (St Paul CofE) C 1834-1891 M 1840-1945 B
1840-1941 [1]
Corfu Is. C 1865-1974 M 1866-1946

GUYANA

Demarara (Orphan Chamber) Ext B 1812-1821

HOLLAND see NETHERLANDS

INDIA

Amritsar (St Paul) C 1878-1946 M 1853-1944 [8,9]
Benares (St Mary) C 1810-1854 M 1810-1840 B
1810-1855 [24]
Calcutta (St John) C Ext 1732-1848 M Ext 1723-
1859 B Ext 1757-1813 [L33]; (Out Station) M 1759-
1779 [2]; (Lall-Bazar) Bapt C Ext 1800-1908 [L19]
Canwar (Sudasherghur) M Ext 1863-1917 [16]
Cochin (Dutch Reform) M Ext 1751-1801 [L12]
Coorg (Christchurch, Polibetta) B 1892-1962
Dalhousie (St John) C 1862-1935 M 1865-1942 B
1860-1932 [8,9]
Delhi (St Mary Rom Cath) Ext C 1900 M 1861-1922
B 1860-1932 [8,9]; (St Andrew Ch of Scotland) Ext
C 1876-1929 B 1887-1913 [10]
Fatehgarh Camp MD 1777-1857 [2,4]
Fort St George see Madras
Gulmarg CM 1896-1941 [1]
Gurdaspur Z 1902-41 C 1870-1930 M Ext 1871-1945
B Ext 1868-1944 [8,9]
Jhansi (St Martin) Ext C 1841-1862 M 1888-1928 [7]
Jutogh (near Simla) B 1888-1945 [8,9]
Kalka C 1901-1943 M 1921-1942 B 1883-1943 [9]
Kasauli Ext C 1845-1919 M 1857-1919 B 1843-1945
[9]
Madras (St Mary) M 1680-1800 B 1680-1900
[14,15]; (Ch of Scotland Christian College) C 1842-
1929
Meerut (St John) B Ext 1857
Ootacamund M 1831-1866 [16]
Sanawar (near Kussowlee) M 1849-1948 [10,17]
Simla (Christ Church) Ext C 1838-1914 M 1838-
1944 B 1838-1945 [7-10]; Rom Cath Cathedral Ext
C 1867-1923 M 1881-1942 B 1863-1943 [7]
Srinagar C 1863-1941 M 1876-1941 B 1849-1941
[18-20]
Tranquebar (Danish Zion) M 1767-1845 [21]

There are also a number of abstracts of vital events
in India from various sources, please consult the
card catalogue in the Library.

INDONESIA

Bencoolen (Sumatra) Macao Prot Cemetery B 1777-
1858 [ASI/R2]

IRAN

Teheran (Akbarabad Prot Cemetery) British B 1811-1969

ITALY

Rome (St Paul-within-the-Walls) C 1867-1944 M 1870-1939 B 1868-1941 [1]

JAMAICA

St Andrew M 1666-1679; St Catherine M 1669-1679

KUWAIT

Kuwait (Old Cemetery) B 1909-1935

MALAYSIA

Sarawak Chaplaincy C 1848-1951 M 1844-1953 Z 1910-1949 [ASI/M1]

MALTA

British Garrison Ext 1801-1818 [1-2]; Pieta ta Braxia B 1857-1899 [M1]

MEXICO

Real del Monte (English Cemetery) B 1861-1949

MONACO

Monaco (SPG Chapel) C 1892-1950 M 1925-1951 B 1893-1950 [1]

MONTSERRAT

St Anthony C 1722-1729 M 1723-1729; St George CM 1721-1729 B 1721-1728; St Patrick C 1727-1729 M 1721-1729 B 1728; St Peter C 1721-1729 M 1722-1729 B 1721-1728

NETHERLANDS

Rotterdam (British) M 1576-1811 [3]

NETHERLAND ANTILLES

Curacao (Portugese Jewish Females) ZM 1743-1831

NEW ZEALAND

Mfc ZM 1840-1920 D 1848-1920 War D 1914-1918 Wellington D 1840-1847

PAKISTAN see INDIA

PAPUA and NEW GUINEA

British New Guinea D 1888-1906

PITCAIRN IS. 1790-1854

PORTUGAL

Lisbon (English Church) M 1721-1863; English Cong 1781-1807 [1]

ST HELENA

Ascension Island CD 1839-1861 M 1840-1859

ST KITTS-NEVIS

Christ Church (Nichola Town) C 1721-1823 M 1730-1821 B 1722-1820 [WI/R4]; Holy Trinity (Palmetto Point) C 1732-1831 M 1732-1828 B 1733-1829 [WI/G6]; St Ann (Sandy Point) C 1719-1763 B 1719-1752 [WI/R4]; SS George and Peter (Basterre) CB 1743-1800 M 1748-1820 [WI/R2]; St George (Nevis) 1716-1743; St James (Nevis) CB 1740-1745; St John (Capisterre) CB 1721-1729 1756-1805 [WI/R4]; St John (Figtree) C 1729-1800 MB 1729-1799; St John (Nevis) CB 1733-4; St Mary (Cayon) C 1721-1809 M 1758-1801 B 1721-1821; St Paul (Nevis) Ext CB 1726-7; St Peter CM 1733-4; St Thomas (Middle Island) C 1729-1814 M 1729-1832 B 1729-1802 [WI/R3]; St Thomas (Nevis) CB 1733-4

SARAWAK see MALAYSIA

SINGAPORE

Singapore (St Andrew Cathedral) C 1823-1870 M 1826-1870 B 1820-1875 [ASI/R1]

SOUTH AFRICA

Cape of Good Hope Ext C 1810-1821 M 1806-21 D 1795-1815 [1]; Dutch Reform Church M Ext 1813-26

Melmoth (Zululand) C 1896-1982 [2]
Port Elizabeth Holy Trinity 1858-98

SWEDEN

SODRA VING Mf Fodde & Dode 1704-1852 Vigde 1704-49 1755-90 1792-1852

SWITZERLAND

Chateau d'Oex (Vaud) British B 1871 1889-1946

SYRIA

Aleppo Z Ext 1717-1790 CMB 1756-1800 B 1653-1906 D Ext 1655-1918

TRINIDAD & TOBAGO

Tobago English Prot 1781-1817 [WI/R5]

TURKEY

Smyrna (British Chapel) 1800-1832

UGANDA

Masindi and Hoima CM 1921-1963

UNITED STATES

Alabama
Lawrence County M 1820-1835

California
Anaheim (Holy Cross Cemetery) B 1911-1918; (St Boniface) B 1880-1918; (Yorba Cemetery) B 1911-1918
Butte County M 1851-1860
Capistrano (Old San Juan Mission) C 1780-1854 M 1842-1924 D 1831- 1928
Colusa County M 1853-1860
El Dorado County M 1844-1860
Mendocino County M 1859-1860
Napa County M 1850-1877 D 1873-1905
Nevada County M 1854-1861
Orange County Z 1889-1912 M 1890-1898 D 1889-1906
Placer County M 1851-1860
Plumas County M 1854-1859
Sacramento County M 1850-1860
Santa Ana (Trinity United) Presb C 1881-1905
Santa Barbara County M(I) 1878-1884 M 1885-1914
Shasta County M 1852-1860
Siskiyou County M 1852-1860
Solano County M 1850-1858
Sonoma County M 1844-1860
Sonora (Burden Funeral Home) B 1862-1891; (Springfield Burial Ground) B 1852-1857
Sutter County M 1850-1860
Tehama County M 1854-1860
Trinity County M 1857-1860
Tuolumne County Z 1858-1888 M 1852-1879 D 1894-1915
Yolo County M 1850-1860
Yuba County M 1850-1860

Colorado M 1866-1881
Baca County M 1889-1899
Boulder County M 1863-1884
Conejus (Our Lady of Guadalupe) Rom Cath M 1860-1881
Denver (Trinity Meth) C 1861-1903 M 1861-1885; (Calvary Cemetery) B Ext 1870-1908
Douglas County M 1909-1917
Jefferson County M 1868-1881
Kit Carson County M 1890-1929
Littleton (Cemetery) B 1864-1907
Prowers County M 1889-1894
Weld County M 1881-2

Connecticut M to 1699
Ashford Ext M 1750-1850 D to 1850; (Westford)
Cong CMD 1768-1937
Avon D to 1850; Cong CMD 1798-1921
Barkhamstead D to 1850
Berlin D to 1850
Bethlehem D to 1850
Bolton D to 1850
Bozram D to 1850
Branford D to 1850
Bristol D to 1850
Brookfield D to 1850
Brooklyn D to 1850
Clinton D 1809-1878
Farmington see Avon

Groton M(I) 1749-1785
Haven, North Cong C 1760-1789
London, New M Ext to 1850
Middletown Z 1730-1850
Pomfret B Ext 1780-1839
Stonington Z to 1730
Stratford Z Ext to 1730
Westford see Ashford
Wethersfield Z to 1850

Delaware M to 1699
New Castle County Z 1810-1853

District of Columbia
Washington (Christ Church Prot Episc) ZD 1791-1806

Georgia
Milledgeville M(I) 1806-1842

Indiana
Wayne County M 1811-1830

Kentucky
Campbell County M 1808-1810
Florence (Hopeful Luth) C(I) 1811-1842 M(I) 1835-1842
Scott County (Rev Marshall) M(I) 1793-1831
Shelby County M 1792-1800

Louisiana
Arcadia M Ext 1896-1912
Avoyelles see Hessmer
Baton Rouge (St John the Baptist, Brusly) M Ext 1841-1879
Brusly see Baton Rouge
Cornerview (St Theresa) see New River
Destrehan (Little Red Church) C Ext 1741-1755 D Ext 1739-1755
Hessmer (St Alphonse, Avoyelles) B 1922-1948
Iberville (St Gabriel) M 1788-1820
Jackson M Ext 1880-1910
Lakeland (Immaculate Conception) C 1873-84 M 1873-91 B 1883-99
Morganza (St Anne) M 1786-1842
New Orleans (Christ Church Episc Cathedral) CMD Ext 1849-1900; (Parish Church) C 1729-30 B 1726 1729-34; (St Louis of France Cathedral) C 1744-1776 1841-45 M 1731-33 1764-1837 B 1724-5 1772-1820 1833-4 Ext 1841-43 B 1843-48; Irish M 1806-40 1849-59; (St Patrick) M(I) 1833-1907; (Holy Trinity) C(I) 1869-73; (St John the Baptist) M(I) 1845-1865; (St Mary) C(I) 1838-55 M(I) 1848-52
New River (Sacred Heart of Jesus) (I) C 1863-1882 M 1864-1894 B 1863-1908
Opelousas (St Landry) M 1807-1815
Paincourtville (St Elizabeth) (I) C 1844-9 M 1839-1848
Plattenville (Assumption) M(I) 1817-1880
St Charles M 1883-1889
St James C 1757-1787 M 1770-1781 B 1773-1783
St Martinville (Zion Prot Episcopal) C 1870-1902
Tensas M 1861-1866
Trebonne M(I) Ext 1814-1899
Vacherie (Our Lady of Peace) (I) C 1856-63 M 1856-1885
Violet (Our Lady of Lourdes) CM(I) Ext 1801-1864 C

1873-76 B(l) 1854-59

Maine M to 1699

Maryland M to 1777
Baltimore County Black M 1778-1846
Frederick County (All Saints) C 1728-1781 M 1743-1775
Thurmont (Apple's Church) Luth & Ref C 1773-1848

Massachusetts M to 1699
Bradford ZMD to 1849
Cambridge (First Church of Christ) C 1658-1830 M 1701-1831 D 1783-1830
Danvers ZMD to 1849
Dedham D 1637-1720 Mf C 1635-1845
Groton ZMD to 1849
Ipswich ZMD to 1849
Lancaster Mf 1643-1850
Marshfield ZMD to 1850
Plymouth (First Church) C 1724-1787 D 1760-1798
Plymouth Colony M to 1650

Michigan
Bloomfield, West (Pine Lake Cemetery) D 1897-1952 B 1831-1988
Cass County M 1850-1873
Detroit (St Mary German Cathedral) CM 1835-1847; (St Paul Cathedral) B 1880-1890
Oakland County D 1867-1875
Pontiac (Oakhill Cemetery) B 1869-1906
Rose Township BD c1837-c1986
Washtewaw County D Ext 1867-1874
Wayne County D 1868-1871

Mississippi
Biloxi (Old Fort) D 1720-1723
Natchez M 1788-1798

Missouri
Jackson County D 1883-4
Kansas City D 1874-5 1879-80

New Hampshire M to 1699

New Jersey M to 1699
Basking Ridge C 1795-1817
Belleville (Second River, Dutch Reform) C 1727-1794
Bergen (Dutch Reform) CM 1789-1877 B 1789-1810
Boundbrook (Presb) C 1810-1815
Burlington (St Mary) CM 1703-1836 B 1767-1836
Burlington County Z 1753-1773 M 1782-1794
Cape May (Bapt) M 1808-1822
Cape May County M 1807-1817
Cheesequakes (Bapt) M 1798-1835
Cranbury (First Presb) C 1745-1759 1790-1833 M 1790-1819
Daretown (Pittsgrove Bapt) M 1772-1793
Delaware (St James Episc) C 1769-1823
Dumont (North Schraatenburgh, Dutch Reform) D 1783-1824
East Jersey M 1666-1688
Elizabeth (St John Episc) C 1750-1775 1792-1826 M 1751-1787
Essex County M 1795-1816
Fairfield (Gansegat, Dutch Reform) C Ext 1741-48

Freehold and Middletown (Dutch Cong) C 1709-1818 1835-1851 M Ext 1736-1838
Gloucester County M to 1880
Greenwich (St James/Straw Church Luth) C 1770-1836
Haddonfield (SFrs) M 1712-1808
Hamilton Square (Bapt) M 1837-1854
Hunterdon County M 1778-1780; (Bapt) M 1831-1868
Kingston (Presb) C 1792-1849 M 1793-1850
Marlboro see Freehold and Middletown
Mendham (Hilltop Presb) C 1805-1832
Mercer County M 1838-1848
Metuchen (First Presb) C 1816-1827 M 1794-1822
Middletown M 1684-1699; (Bapt) C 1721-1787 D 1786-1811; (Dutch Cong) see also Freehold and Middletown
Monmouth County M 1794-1849
Montgomery (Harlingen, Dutch Reform) C 1727-1802 M 1799-1802
Morris County M 1795-1835
Morristown (Hanover Presb) C 1746-1834 M 1746-1844
New Egypt (Meth) M 1837-38
New Providence (Presb) C 1764-1797 M 1763-1796
Newark M 1795-1807 B 1795-1806
Newton M 1684-1705
Oldwick (Zion Luth) M 1770-1843
Piscataway ZMD 1668-1805 Ext B 1789-1932
Plainfield see Rahway
Pompton Plains (Dutch Reform) M 1736-1809
Rahway and Plainfield (SFrs) D 1705-1767 1811-1892
Salem County M 1795-1809
Shrewsbury M 1691-1696; (Christ Church) C 1733-1824 MB 1734-1824; (SFrs) Z 1670-1883 M 1674-1853 DB 1707-1896
Spotswood (St Peter Episc) C 1788-1850 B 1790-1850
Stillwater (Presb) C 1806-1850
Sussex County M 1777-1810
Washington (Presb) C 1817-1827 M 1817-1849
Walltown (Meth) C 1812-1815 M 1807-1827 B 1806-1827
West (Moravian Mission) C 1742-1762
Westfield (Presb) C 1766-68 M 1759-1765 1773-1803
Woodbridge ZMD 1668-1781

New York M to 1699
Amenia (Jabez Flint) M 1797-1803
Athens see Loonenburg
Ballston Meth (St John, East Line) C 1877-1941 M 1878-1941 B 1880-1944
Castleton Z Slaves 1800-1822
Catskill (Dutch Reform) C 1732-1800 M 1732-1833
Claverack C 1727-1800 M 1727-1929
Courtlandtown (Dutch Reform) C 1740-1830
Coxsackie (Dutch Reform) C 1738-1800 M 1797-1875
Douglaston (Zion Church of Little Neck) 1830-1880
Fishkill (Dutch Reform) M 1731-1834
Flushing (St George Episc) C 1788-1853 M 1782-1885 B 1790-1896
Goshen Presb C 1773-1851 M 1776-1885 D 1805-1850
Helderberg (Dutch Reform) M 1794-1829

Hopewell (Dutch Reform) M 1766-1829
Jamaica (Low Dutch Reform) C 1702-1873 M 1813-1876 D 1835-1898
Jerusalem (Dutch Reform) M 1794-1829
Kakiat see Tappan
Kings County Z(slaves) 1800-1821
Kingston (Old Dutch) C 1706-1737 B Ext 1739-1795 B 1805-1816
Loonenburg (Zion Luth) C 1725-1800 M 1705-1783 D 1710-1729
Narragansett (French Church) C 1686-90 M 1687-89 B 1687-91
New Salem (Dutch Reform) M 1794-1829
New Utrecht (Dutch Reform) C 1718-1799
New York (St Mark in the Bowery) C 1799-1842; (St Peter) Ext C 1787-1800; (Trinity Church) C 1784-1809 M 1748-1861; (City) D 1795; (Coroner's Reports) D 1795-1819 1823-1842; Z(slaves) 1799-1814; (Dutch) C 1639-1800 M 1639-1866 B 1804-1813 [1/2]; Episc (St Jude Free or British Immigrant Church) 1843-1853; Luth (Swamp Church) M 1752-1776; Luth C 1725-1783 M 1776-1791 B 1704-1785; (Mayor Gideon Lee Civil Register) M 1833-34; Presb (Fifth Ave) C 1808-1859 M 1868-1892; (Rev Edward Mitchell) M 1804-1834; Brooklyn Bapt (Rev H.M. Gallagher) M 1866-1887; Harlem (Dutch Reform) C 1806-1836 M 1813-4 B(accounts) 1818-1827; Staten Island (Dutch Reform) C 1739-1790
Oyster Bay see Wolver Hollow
Poughkeepsie (Dutch Reform) M 1746-1835 see also Rumbout
Princetown (Dutch Reform) M 1794-1850
Redhook (St Paul Luth) see Rhinebeck Flats
Rotterdam (First/Woesting Ref) C 1800-1838
Rhinebeck Flats (Dutch Reform) C 1730-1800
Rumbout and Poughkeepsie Presb M 1825-1846
Saugerties (Katsbaan Dutch) C 1802-1815 M 1735-1829 1848-1872
Schenectady (Dutch Reform) M 1694-1768
Shawangunk (Dutch Reform) M 1789-1816
Tappan (Dutch Reform) M 1699-1831; (Irregular Dutch Reform) C 1767-1778 M 1768-1777
Western (Judge Rudd) M 1805-1826
Wolver Hollow (Dutch Reform) C 1741-1834
Yonkers (St John Episc) CD 1820-26 M 1820-40

North Carolina M to 1699
Durham County M 1881-1906
Flat Rock (St John-in-the-Wilderness) C 1840-1893 M 1855-1892 B 1847-1923

Ohio
Cincinnati (First Presb - Covenant First) C 1811-1840

Pennsylvania
Abington (Presb) M 1716-1821
Albany (Jerusalem Luth and Ref) C 1768-1784 1796-1863
Bensalem (Dutch Reform) C 1710-1738
Bethlehem (Moravian) M 1742-1800
Bern (Dutch Ref Cong) C 1738-1835
Buckingham (SFrs) M 1730-1810
Carlisle (1st Presb) M 1785-1812
Chester (St Paul Episc) M 1704-1733
Churchville (Presb) M 1738-1810
Emaus (Moravian) M 1758-1800

Flakner Swamp (Reformed) M 1748-1800
Falls (SFrs) M 1700-1800
Heidelberg (St John Ref Hain's/Höhn's) C 1745-1805
Litiz (Moravian) M 1743-1800
Loretto (St Michael) Rom Cath CM 1799-1840 D 1793-1899
Middletown (SFrs) M 1685-1810
Mifflin (Zeigler's Luth) M 1824-26
Nazareth (Moravian) M 1742-1800
Neshaminy (Presb) M 1785-1804
Hew Hanover (Luth) M 1745-1809
Newtown (Edward Hunter) M 1798-1809
Paxtang & Derry M 1741-1810
Perkiomen (St James Episc) M 1788-1810
Philadelphia (1st Presb) M 1702-45 1760-1803; (2nd Presb) M 1763-1812; (3rd Presb) M 1785-1799; (SFrs) M 1382-1756; (St Michael's & Zion) M 1745-1800; (St Paul) M 1759-1806; (Moravian) M 1743-1800; (Christ Church) M 1709-1806; (Swedes' Church) M 1750-1810; (German Reformed) M 1748-1802; (1st Baptist) M 1761-1803
Quakertown (SFrs) M 1752-1810
Weisenburg (Rev Johannes Helffrich) M 1790-1810 B 1790-1795

Rhode Island M to 1699

South Carolina M to 1699
Georgetown (Meth) CM 1811-1837 D 1816-1856

Tennessee
Rutherford County M Ext 1824-1871

Texas
Cherokee County Z(l) 1872-1875
Clay County M(l) 1876-1891
San Augustine M 1837-1846

Utah
Salt Lake City (Cemetery) B 1848-1856

Vermont
Bennington M Ext 1809-1828

Virginia M to 1699; SFrs Ext Z 1668-1717 M 1682-1728 DB 1674-1723
Alexandria (St Paul Episc) Ext 1809-1861
Bristol Z 1720-1792
Campbell County M 1800-1810
Farnham Ext C 1672-1781
Fredericksburg M Ext 1782-1860
Gretna (Winston Dalton) ZMD 1730-1844
Loudon County M 1757-1853
Madison (Hebron Luth) Z 1750-1825
Monongalia County M 1795-1812
Orange County M 1772-1810
Rockingham (Upper Peaked Mountain Church) C 1791-1817 1827-1832
St Paul's C Ext 1725-1773 M Ext 1716-1793
Surry County M Ext 1679-1791

West Virginia
Aurora (Salem Evangelical Luth) C 1792-1812

Wisconsin
St Croix County M 1852-1867